The U.S. Army
and the Texas Frontier Economy

1845–1900

MILITARY HISTORY SERIES ☆ TEXAS A&M UNIVERSITY

65

The U.S. Army and the
1845–1900

TEXAS A&M UNIVERSITY PRESS

Texas Frontier Economy

by Thomas T. Smith

COLLEGE STATION

The views expressed herein are those of the author and do not purport to reflect
the positions of the Department of the Army or the Department of Defense.

The paper used in this book meets the minimum requirements
of the American National Standard for Permanence
of Paper for Printed Library Materials, Z39.48-1984.
Binding materials have been chosen for durability.

Library of Congress Cataloging-in-Publication Data

Smith, Thomas T., 1950–

    The U.S. Army and the Texas frontier economy, 1845–1900 / Thomas
T. Smith.

      p. cm. — (Texas A&M University military history series ; no. 65)

    Includes bibliographical references and index.

    ISBN 0-89096-882-9 (cloth)

    1. Public contracts—Texas—History—19th century. 2. United
States. Army—Procurement—History—19th century. 3. Texas—
Economic conditions. 4. Texas—History—1846-1950. I. Title.
II. Series : Texas A&M University military history series ; 65.

    HD3861.U62T47 1999

    330.9764'05—dc21   99-11376

                                              CIP

2d Lt. Walter W. Hudson
Company G, First Infantry Regiment

The first regular officer killed in the Texas Indian Wars

Walter W. Hudson, born in Kentucky, rose in the ranks from private to first sergeant during the Mexican War. Commissioned as a brevet second lieutenant in June, 1848, Hudson led a mounted detachment of Company G, First Infantry, out of Fort McIntosh at Laredo against Indian raiders. On February 24, 1850, he pursued and attacked a Tonkawa war party that had raided the post stables, recovering a Mexican boy being held captive. The following day, Hudson and his detachment attacked a camp of Tonkawas who had committed a murder near the post. On April 6, 1850, near the Nueces River, Hudson and his men fought a group of Indians who had stolen horses at Laredo. The Indians fled and his detachment recovered thirty of the animals. The next morning, Hudson continued his pursuit and again attacked the raiders. One soldier died in the skirmish, and five, including Hudson, were wounded. Second Lieutenant Hudson died of his wounds at Fort McIntosh twelve days later (April 19, 1850). In June, 1857, the army named a post on the Devil's River Camp Hudson in his honor.

Contents

Illustrations

Following page 102

MAPS

Tables

Acknowledgments

I wish to thank the following people for their efforts in support of this work: My mentor and comrade, Prof. Joseph G. "Chip" Dawson III of Texas A&M University for his constant encouragement and demanding standard of scholarship; Prof. Robert Wooster of Texas A&M University–Corpus Christi, and Prof. Jerry D. Thompson, dean of the College of Arts and Humanities at Texas A&M International at Laredo, for their many helpful comments and suggestions for improvements to this work; Texas historian Ben Pingenot of Fort Clark at Brackettville for reading the draft and for his valuable suggestions and insights into Texas borderlands military history; Prof. Richard V. Francaviglia of the University of Texas at Arlington, and Andrew Hall of Galveston for sharing their knowledge of Texas maritime history; Chris Floerke at the Institute of Texan Cultures for her endless patience with this impatient researcher; Mr. James W. Kenney of San Antonio for offering his knowledge of Texas military cemeteries; Dr. Kurt H. Hackemer of the University of South Dakota for sharing his research on the origins of the military-industrial complex; Karl C. Gebert of San Antonio, who generously provided information and articles regarding matters of the mail and postal affairs; my wife Holly and children Miles and Dustin for their encouragement and support, and for patiently following the regiment these many years; and—lastly and most importantly—to the three thousand contributors to *The New Handbook of Texas,* without whom the details of the nooks and crannies of Texas history would have remained a void in this study.

The U.S. Army
and the Texas Frontier Economy

1845–1900

CHAPTER I

The Army Dollar in Texas

H. H. McConnell, a former Sixth Cavalry first sergeant and the mayor of Jacksboro, Texas, estimated that between 1868 and 1873 nearby Fort Richardson put a half million dollars a year into local citizens' pockets. In 1891, the San Antonio *Express* stated that the army poured a hundred thousand dollars per month or over a million dollars a year into the city's economy. According to nineteenth-century army pay and quartermaster records, both assessments are overestimates by half but demonstrate amply that municipal leadership was acutely aware of the impact of the army dollar on local economies. Jacksboro and San Antonio had a fort–satellite village relationship with the army that was characteristic of other Texas towns such as Uvalde, Brackettville, Del Rio, San Angelo, El Paso, Fort Stockton, Fort Davis, Brownsville, Rio Grande City, Eagle Pass, Corpus Christi and Laredo.[1]

Texas historian Joe B. Frantz captured the essence of the fort-town relationship when he declared:

> *The fort in effect issued invitations for the restless and the questing to move into a region. Equally it issued invitations for those already present to remain. Forts then were protectors, and forts were colonizers. . . . The government, usually federal, poured money into underdeveloped regions, somewhat as it does today, to pay and supply troops. . . . How fast the West and Texas would have been built up without this continuous influx of federal money cannot be determined, but simple logic recognizes how much more swiftly the process went because Washington was forever pumping dollars of all the taxpayers to build the new area. . . . Texas, then, as part of the total American experience, felt the force of forts in its life. No story of the Texas heritage can be complete without telling the role its forts played in making that heritage possible.[2]*

One goal of this study is to determine a solid estimate of the bottom line, the dollar amounts poured into the lifeblood of the Texas economy, and to analyze the economic relationships involved in the process. But money itself is not the central focus of this work. It is about innovative and energetic Texans, struggling communities in a raw environment, exhausted and frustrated army quartermasters, soldiers surviving on a shoestring budget, mismanaged fiscal appropriations, failures and successes in planning and organization, ingenious adaptation, and, at times, about nature's victory over the best of man's intentions and vitality. Money was simply the vehicle; the real story involves human beings trying to make the best of extraordinarily difficult circumstances.

In many respects the U.S. Army, mid-nineteenth-century America's largest corporate body, and the State of Texas, its largest geopolitical organization, shared a symbiotic relationship. For three decades of the last half of the nineteenth century the Department of Texas was the army's most extensive and most expensive theater of war. The bold winged eagle emblazoned on regimental colors and stamped on brass uniform buttons symbolized national combat power applied to the Texas frontier conflict. The army tried to provide security for both Anglo and Tejano citizens, maintain a controlled international border between often-hostile neighbors, and protect peaceful Indians against their Texan and Indian foes. Less visible was a second eagle at work in Texas, one that represented the cadre of army logisticians trying to feed, shelter, equip, and move the legion of combat soldiers.

Overall, the army's economic impact in Texas was most significant in two historic periods. The first was in the post-Republic years 1845 through 1860, just after the Mexican War, when an immature and cash-poor Texas frontier economy lacked a viable network of communities, communications, and transportation. As a result of the California gold strike, Congress in March, 1849, authorized the largest U.S. regular-issue coin—the "Double Eagle" twenty-dollar gold piece. The weight of the coin was double that of the previous most valuable legal specie, the ten-dollar "Eagle." Army disbursement for pay or services in this antebellum period was almost entirely by hard coin. The second period of important army effect on Texas' economy was in the post–Civil War decade spanning the period 1866 to 1876, when the scarcity of basic material goods, currency, and security—as well as the fallout from massive wartime inflation—all but wrecked the state.

The army's economic influence in Texas also had a regional significance, being more important to the southwestern coastal tract and that frontier area west of the 97th meridian—the army's primary operational zone—than to the original settlement belt of the eastern Texas woodlands. Finally, the army's impact on the Texas economy was not one of boom and bust, but rather a pattern of initial fits and starts followed by a steady and reasonably dependable input into a developing marginal economic network.

The role of the soldier as scout and skirmisher has long captured the public imagination and the interest of the historical community. However, the role of the soldier as nation-builder and colonizer, while perhaps more significant, is far more pedestrian and thus generally overlooked by scholars.

The best and earliest book-length study of the soldier's importance as the advance guard of civilization is Francis Paul Prucha's *Broadax and Bayonet* (1953). Prucha traces the army's contributions to the antebellum Anglo development of the upper Mississippi River valley and argues that soldier labor on military roads and bridges, along with forts as the nucleus of civil growth and stability, were more crucial to the region than the army's Indian-fighting combat power. In 1956, Robert G. Athearn, in *William Tecumseh Sherman and the Settlement of the West,* focused on the grim Civil War warrior as the commander of the Division of the Missouri and as the architect of western development through his championship of railroad construction and emigrant trails. Historian Michael Tate's 1980 essay, "The Multi-Purpose Army on the Frontier," outlined the diverse nature of the army's mission in the West and issued a call for further research on the army dollar and frontier economics.[3]

Tate's call was initially answered by two complementary studies of army logistics in Arizona and New Mexico. Robert W. Frazer's *Forts and Supplies: The Role of the Army in the Economy of the Southwest, 1848–1861* (1983), and Darlis A. Miller's *Soldiers and Settlers: Military Supply in the Southwest, 1861–1885* (1989) offer the most significant and complete scholarship on the general subject. Frazer's work on antebellum New Mexico and Miller's study of the post–Civil War era generally conclude that the army was the largest employer in the region, and that army quartermaster operations—and the federal dollar supporting military logistics—were the most significant ingredient in the internal and economic expansion of New Mexico in the nineteenth century. While both studies offer a wealth of detailed information on contracts, prices, merchants, and local financial interrelationships, neither work presents a broad analysis of market trends, economic patterns, nor an overall estimate of total dollar input across the wide spectrum of military economic activity.[4]

When compared to Texas in the last half of the nineteenth century, New Mexico had less than 15 percent of the Lone Star State's population, 4 percent of the corn crop, 10 percent of the livestock value, and 4 percent of the cattle. In general, New Mexico had fewer agricultural resources, a more arid climate, and less economic potential than its colossal neighbor to the southeast. Because of New Mexico's relatively meager development, the army dollar represented a higher ratio of influence than it did in Texas' more mature economy and culture.[5]

The few studies on the general economic evolution of nineteenth-century Texas all but ignore or undervalue the military's contribution. As a historical problem, the army dollar's impact on the development of the Texas frontier has attracted little attention from scholars. The one partial exception to this trend is Leroy P. Graf's "The Economic History of the Lower Rio Grande Valley, 1820–1875."[6] In Graf's view, the commercial and logistical activities associated with the military operations of the Mexican War were the most significant factor in the early economic growth of the lower Rio Grande Valley. In addition to the development of towns and of steam navigation on the Rio Grande, the influx of traders brought North American dominance of business on both sides of the river. The attendant publicity of potential profits in Mexican trade lured postwar commercial enterprises into the lower valley, and the region remained the gateway to trade and shipping for northeastern Mexico until eclipsed by Monterrey in 1882, with the opening of the railroad connecting central Texas, Laredo, and Monterrey. However, Graf's broad study focuses on the lower valley's strategic commercial position, particularly in terms of Mexican trade, rather than analyzing the valley's internal economic growth. Therefore, Graf offers the reader a broad look at the military-economic results of the Mexican War, but no examination of the relationship between the army and the river towns in succeeding decades.[7]

The published histories of federal military activities in Texas are plentiful and often contain anecdotes about soldier or army spending but lack a cogent analysis of the overall army input to local economies. There are a few exceptions to this trend. Joe B. Frantz's "The Significance of Frontier Forts to Texas" has already been cited. Robert Wooster's classic study of Texas frontier garrison life, *Soldiers, Sutlers, and Settlers* (1987), has a chapter devoted to the economic concerns of fort families, and his *History of Fort Davis, Texas* (1990), the best published history of a Texas fort, captures the full range of military-commercial association at a frontier post. In "The Merchants and the Military," W. H. Timmons explores the importance of the economic relationship and interdependence between the army and early El Paso founders such as James W. Magoffin, Simeon Hart, and Benjamin Franklin Coons. Roy Swift and Leavitt Corning Jr. in *Three Roads To Chihuahua* (1988), and Ben E. Pingenot in "The Great Wagon Train Expedition of 1850," address the army's contribution to the military routes to El Paso, which became the cornerstone of economic development in the Trans-Pecos region. In *Indianola* (1977), Brownson Malsch demonstrates not only the army's role in the growth of a Texas port but in turn that port's part as a gateway to Texas' frontier economy. Although primarily a study of blue-water and coastal activities, Richard V. Francaviglia's *From Steam To Sail: Four Centuries of Texas Maritime History* (1998) credits the army quartermasters with playing the crucial role in developing steamship navigation on the Rio Grande and views federal military spending as an important stimulus to Texas coastal and port development. Earle B. Young, in *Galveston and the Great West* (1997), records the cooperation between local boosters, the federal and state governments, and the army Corps of Engineers in creating Texas' premier deepwater port. Finally, my 1992 article titled "Fort Inge and the Texas Frontier Economy," analyzes the impact of a single fort on the economic growth of a local community.[8]

The fact that the body of historical scholarship on local and regional economies of the nineteenth-century Texas frontier is both scant and sketchy is not surprising. Such historical work requires documentation as a foundation for appraisal, and the written record is insufficient at best. The civil administrators of frontier communities did an adequate job of capturing the important records of land transactions and other legal proceedings, but their offices were not sufficiently staffed to snare the data required to assess the evolution of commerce and economy. Each decade the central government financed a significant local effort to exact personal, fiscal, agricultural, and commercial statistics for enumeration in the federal census. The census offers useful milestones at ten-year intervals but, as will be apparent in this study, a historian struggling with the interim is often forced to induce or deduce, to infer, to presume, to estimate, to imply, or simply to offer an educated guess. A dramatic antithesis to poor records in local communities is the voluminous collection of evidence from the federal military record in nineteenth-century Texas. Congress demanded a written account for nearly every penny spent. The army faithfully complied. Authentic comparative analysis requires sufficient data from two spheres, which is not feasible when comparing the comprehensive published fiscal documentation kept by the army with that of the occasional financial illumination scratched in a leather-bound volume in a county courthouse or yellowed Texas newspaper. The army record simply overwhelms those available in the civilian community. However, the alternatives to a complete comparative analysis in this case are to be content with a blank page of history or to cut the Gordian knot.

The vast majority of the army's dollar input in Texas stemmed from the logistical activities of four War Department bureaus; the Paymaster's Department, the Bureau of Engineers, the Commissary of Subsistence Department, and the Quartermaster's Department. The mid-nineteenth-century U.S. Army did not have a centralized staff system. Each of the separate War Department bureaus—and the brigadier general at its head—answered directly to the politically appointed secretary of war rather than to the senior general of the field army.

The paymaster general usually had four or five Paymaster's Department officers in Texas. They were responsible for riding a lengthy circuit to pay soldiers. Until 1870, nearly all disbursements were made in specie, a boon of gold or silver coin for cash-poor Texas communities. Texas army paymasters disbursed over $38 million in the state between 1849 and 1900. As this study will later demonstrate, not all soldier pay went directly into the pockets of barkeepers; it was also used to support merchants, commercial investments, business ventures, and local real estate markets.

The Corps of Engineers supervised fort construction, surveyed and mapped many Texas waterways, and spent prodigious energy and $13 million on river and harbor improvements within the state, virtually transforming Galveston, in 1898, into a deepwater port. The adventuring "Topogs" of the Corps of Topographical Engineers were responsible for exploring, surveying, and mapping the military routes that would eventually form frontier Texas' transportation and communication network. These practical routes advanced by the topographical engineers played a key role in the army development of lines of communications such as wagon roads, mails, and a frontier telegraph system built between 1875 and 1879. These lines of communication, although fiscally inexpensive, served as the foundation for the commercial infrastructure of north, central, and western Texas. They had an exponential value far greater than the federal dollars expended as commercial wagon freight expanded and the use of the mails for monetary transactions and business coordination became more common.

The officers of the Commissary of Subsistence, often called the Subsistence Department, were responsible for feeding soldiers and citizen employees entitled to army rations. These officers, and their temporary acting assistants at each post, arranged for beef contracts, as well as purchase of the

ration, with portions of its components such as beans and flour being purchased locally in Texas when available. The dollar impact of the Subsistence
Department in Texas was not locally consequential because the majority of
rations were contract-purchased from large trading hubs in the East and
Midwest. However, the requirement to transport the thousands of barrels of
these rations would affect the financial fortunes of Texas wagon freighters,
steamboat captains, and railroad companies. The Subsistence Department's
purchase of fresh beef in Texas was likewise modest when measured against
the grand scale of the Texas cattle industry, but the army provided a significant
contribution by escorting cattle drives and by recovering stolen cattle.

Of all army bureaus, the Quartermaster's Department had the widest
fiscal scope and most extensive impact on the various facets of commercial
activity in Texas. Formally established in 1818, the Quartermaster's Department was responsible for logistics. This responsibility included providing all
troop transportation and material both on land and water; furnishing horses
for the cavalry and artillery, and horses and mules for wagons; supplying the
army with wagons, ambulances, and harnesses; purchasing animal forage;
purchasing and distributing clothing, equipment, lumber, and hardware;
building barracks, storehouses and hospitals; and repairing roads, bridges,
and railroads. Additionally, because Texas—unlike other parts of the West—
retained control of the public domain when it became a state and the federal
government thus did not own land there, quartermasters were responsible
for negotiating leases and paying for the use of military sites. Besides these
requirements internal to their department, quartermasters had to provide
transportation services for other army agencies. This included moving rations for the Commissary General of Subsistence, transporting hospital stores
for the surgeon general, hauling all arms and ammunition for the Ordnance
Bureau, or outfitting all exploration and survey parties for the chief of engineers.[9]

In the course of fulfilling its extensive variety of requirements the
Quartermaster's Department spent $32 million to support operations in Texas
in the last half of the nineteenth century. While each of these areas is examined more closely in subsequent topical chapters, a brief summation of army
quartermasters' contributions to economic development in the state would
include such purchases as $1 million worth of horses and mules and $9 million for the forage to feed them. The department spent $5 million leasing,
buying, or constructing forts to house soldiers, horses, and mules, as well as
$1.5 million on wood and charcoal fuel for the posts. An additional $6.8
million was spent on moving, supplying, and equipping the troops and ani-

mals in Texas forts. In the process of meeting these logistical demands in Texas, the Quartermaster's Department also became a major source of capital for the state's burgeoning long-haul wagon-freight industry. It also played a significant role in the rise of Texas ports such as Indianola and Corpus Christi, developed steamboat navigation on the Rio Grande, and helped make San Antonio the commercial hub of the Texas frontier.

A quartermaster's responsibilities were complex and challenging, in spite of Texas department commander Brig. Gen. David E. Twiggs's wry complaint that the duty of the quartermaster was to "Make himself comfortable," and to "make every one else as uncomfortable as possible." The Quartermaster's Department at no time had enough commissioned officers to meet the administrative or management demands of the job. It was authorized only thirty-seven officers in the antebellum period, and fifty-seven in the decade after the Civil War. As a consequence, regular officers of the line had to be temporarily appointed to assume that duty—usually at the smaller posts and within the regiments. Such an augmentee was Lt. Ulysses S. Grant. An infantry officer, he vigorously protested his assignment as a regimental quartermaster in the Fourth Infantry on the Rio Grande during the Mexican War. Grant's experience gave him a keen appreciation for logistics that would serve him well in the Civil War. The one hundred additional line officers serving as quartermasters in 1853, for example, or the 150 officers with similar duties in 1870, usually lacked expertise and thus exacerbated the complications of supply on the Texas frontier. Having no enlisted authorization, the quartermasters had to pull troops from line units to serve as teamsters, laborers, and mechanics—a requirement that had a detrimental impact on an army that was already overstretched on the nineteenth-century frontier.[10]

Besides their lack of formal training, regimental officers assigned to quartermaster duty had an additional burden in that accountability and supply discipline within the army was far from ideal. A Second Cavalry lieutenant serving in Texas as the temporary regimental quartermaster in the late 1850s observed that he was "held individually, personally, and officially responsible for [public property] . . . but where many of the officers and all the men are new and without experience, they seem to imagine that public property belongs to anyone who can get possession of it. I had to be constantly on the alert. . . ."[11]

Tables 1 and 2 present an outline of the sums expended by the army in Texas in the last half of the nineteenth century. In simple economic terms, the figures in Tables 1 and 2 can be best understood when viewed in relative proportion to the overall Texas economy of the period. The $70 million army

TABLE I.

SUMMARY OF ARMY EXPENDITURES IN TEXAS, 1849–1900
(IN MILLIONS OF DOLLARS)

Category	Period 1849–1860	1869–1879	1880–1889	1890–1900	Total
Total Texas operations costs					
(quartermaster expenditures + soldier pay)	11.3	27.9	17.8	13.7	70.7
Army quartermaster expenditures in Texas	3.6	16.7	7.6	4.3	32.2
Army pay in Texas	7.7	11.2	10.2	9.4	38.5
Total army expenditures, all states	182.0	484.8	409.0	852.0	1,972.8
Texas spending as a percent					
of total army expenditures, all states	6.2%	5.8%	4.4%	1.6%	3.6%

Source: Texas expenditures are calculated from each year's "Report of the Quartermaster General of the Army," and "Report of the Paymaster General," in the annual *Report of the Secretary of War,* 1849–1900. Total army expenditures are from Charles L. Shrader, *U.S. Military Logistics: A Research Guide, 1607–1991,* Appendix B.

TABLE 2.
AVERAGE ANNUAL ARMY EXPENDITURES FOR TEXAS OPERATIONS, 1849–1900

Category	Period 1849–1860	1869–1879	1880–1889	1890–1900	Total Av.
Average annual Texas operations costs (soldier pay + quartermaster expenditures)	$966,046	$2,539,541	$1,775,239	$1,243,620	$1,474,843
Average annual army quartermaster expenditures in Texas	$306,600	$1,520,096	$759,522	$389,040	$672,391
Average annual army pay in Texas	$659,446	$1,019,445	$1,015,717	$854,580	$802,452
Average annual Texas quartermaster spending as a percent of total army quartermaster expenditures	5.3%	11%	6.7%	4.1%	6.7%
Average annual army quartermaster expenditures, all states	$5,784,905	$13,819,054	$11,336,149	$9,488,780	$10,035,686

Source: Calculated from each year's "Report of the Quartermaster General of the Army," and "Report of the Paymaster General," in the annual *Report of the Secretary of War,* 1849–1900.

operational dollars dispersed in the state between 1849 and 1900 was equal to twice the $34 million total valuation in real and personal property assessed when Texas joined the United States. In 1844, prior to the Mexican War, Texas had only $500,000 worth of exports and about the same in imports. By the start of the war, Texas exports had increased to $820,000 and imports to $1.2 million—a $380,000 trade deficit that was piled onto a public debt of almost $10 million. Texas' total valuation of real and personal property in 1849 was $46 million, of which 30 percent was in slaves. That figure increased to $294 million by 1860, of which 36 percent was in slaves, representing a growth of $248 million over the decade. The total army dollars dispersed in Texas operations for the same period was $10 million, or about 4 percent of the state's value growth. Because of the Civil War, inflation, devaluation, and the end of slave holding, Texas lost about $144 million in valuation between 1860 and 1869. The first real upswing came with an increase in valuation of $5 million in 1868–69, a year in which the army dispersed $2 million in Texas. In the 1870s, Texas property valuation increased $134 million. The army disbursed $27 million in operational funds in the state during that time, equivalent to 20 percent of the valuation increase. Army operational expenditures in Texas during the 1880s equaled 4 percent of the total valuation increase in state property. From 1849 to 1889 Texas' real and personal property valuation grew from $46 million to $729 million. The army disbursed $58 million in Texas during the same period, equivalent to 8 percent of the valuation growth.[12]

Texas, either as a republic or a state, lacked the economic clout to expend the funds necessary to secure its borders or to conduct large-scale operations on its frontier. The army spent 6 percent of its budget, $3.6 million, in Texas from 1852 to 1855. During this same period the state government appropriated $2.1 million, with a meager $95,000, or 5 percent, earmarked for frontier defense—defensive appropriations that the state was quick to demand the federal government repay. The army spent $5.7 million in Texas on the escalating frontier conflict from 1856 to 1861. The state appropriated $375,000 for defense during that same period, nearly 24 percent of the entire state budget. That money was repaid to the state by the federal government in 1906. In the 1870s the army spent about $2.5 million per year in Texas—nearly 6 percent of its total budget, and about equivalent to the operating budget of New York City's police force during the period. From 1870 to 1873, Texas appropriated $4.7 million, of which 12 percent (about $607,000) was spent on defense in the form of state police, minutemen militia, and two companies of rangers. From 1874 to 1877, just over $803,000 in state funds, or 25 percent of the total state budget of $3.1 million, went to defense. Altogether, the army spent nearly $28 million in the 1870s on Texas' security. The state in turn expended $1.5 million for its own defense, of which more than $1 million was reimbursed to it by the federal government in 1888 and 1891.[13]

Although second to the $38 million in army pay in quantities expended in Texas, the $32 million worth of fiscal operations of the Quartermaster's Department represent the widest diversity of activity (see Table 3). There were four distinct phases of Quartermaster logistical operations in Texas, each with its own unique characteristics and varying degrees of impact on the state's differing economic activities. During the Mexican War (1846 to

TABLE 3.

ARMY QUARTERMASTER EXPENDITURES IN TEXAS

BY ECONOMIC ACTIVITY, 1849–1900

Category	Period				
	1849–1860	1869–1879	1880–1889	1890–1900	Total
QM expenditures in Texas	$3,679,200	$16,721,000	$7,595,200	$4,279,400	$32,274,800
	(100%)	(100%)	(100%)	(100%)	(100%)
Animal forage—corn, oats, hay	$1,196,000	$4,614,000	$2,500,000	$742,000	$9,052,000
	(32.5%)	(27.5%)	(33%)	(17.3%)	(28%)
Transportation	$812,000	$2,918,800	$1,989,000	$1,147,000	$6,866,800
	(22%)	(17.4%)	(26%)	(26.8%)	(21.2%)
Building repair & construction	$191,900	$2,484,100	$727,100	$965,500	$4,368,600
	(5.2%)	(14.8%)	(9.5%)	(22.5%)	(13.5%)
QM civilian employees	$1,020,800	$1,100,000	$608,200	$481,700	$3,210,700
	(27.7%)	(6.5%)	(8%)	(11.2%)	(9.9%)
Horse & mule purchases	$140,100	$825,400	$157,700	$120,700	$1,243,900
	(3.8%)	(4.9%)	(2%)	(2.8%)	(3.8%)
Rents & leases	$149,200	$125,900	$57,400	$34,500 0	$367,000
	(4%)	(0.7%)	(0.7%)	(0.7%)	(1.1%)
Misc. expenses	$169,200	$4,652,800	$1,555,800	$788,000	$7,165,800
	(4.8%)	(28.2%)	(20.8%)	(18.7%)	(22.5%)

Note: Percentages reflect the percent of total QM expenditures in Texas in each listed category for the decade.

Source: Calculated from each year's "Report of the Quartermaster General of the Army," in the annual *Report of the Secretary of War*, 1849–1900.

1848), logistical activities were generally confined to the coast and that portion of the lower Rio Grande navigable by river steamer, with the majority of supply and transportation services being contracted outside the state. In the post–Mexican War deployment phase (1848 to 1854), the army attempted to rely on government wagons, soldier labor, and small, piecemeal local purchases. The heyday of the big Texas contracts and large-scale operators lasted from 1855 to the end of the 1870s. Finally, in the 1880s, Texas' growing rail system tied into the national rail network, making relatively inexpensive and reliable long-distance transportation available to army logisticians, again causing them to seek long-haul contractors outside the state.

CHAPTER 2

The Army Logistical System in Texas

In the mid-nineteenth century, the staffs of the Quartermaster's Department and the Commissary of Subsistence, rather than commanders, were responsible for supplying the army in the field. The Mexican War of 1846 to 1848 was the first real test of the capabilities of American logisticians to sustain a large-scale expeditionary operation on foreign soil. Texas and northern Mexico were immature theaters with little in the way of resident infrastructure such as improved roads, industry, a skilled labor pool, or adequate harbor facilities. The cartridge fired by a soldier, the ration that kept him in the fight, the pan that cooked the bacon, the ax that fueled the cooking fire, and the mule-drawn wagon that hauled that bullet, bacon, frying pan, and blade all had to be transported by capricious sea into the theater. The same was true for the corn that fed the mule that drew the wagon. Of course, if some harried quartermaster loading a ship in Philadelphia or New York or New Orleans forgot to include the leather harness that hitched the mule to the wagon, neither the wagon nor the soldier was going to move. It was, quite simply, a "bring your own" war.

The fundamental cause of the conflict was a boundary dispute between the Republic of Mexico and the new state of Texas—backed by its new protector, the United States. Established folkways, old Spanish maps, political memory, and the Mexican government all considered the traditional border of Mexico's Department of Tejas as being the Nueces River. Texans, however, claimed all land touching the east bank of the Rio Grande—or Rio Bravo del Norte as it was sometimes called by Mexican citizens. In April, 1844, Pres. John Tyler ordered Bvt. Brig. Gen. Zachary Taylor to form and command an observation force on the Louisiana border to await events brewing in Texas. In late June of 1845, Pres. James K. Polk ordered Taylor and his so-called

Army of Occupation to the Texas coast as a show of force. Taylor sent his mounted troops overland and loaded his infantry on steamboats in New Orleans. On July 26, 1845, the steamer *Alabama* carried the Third Infantry to St. Joseph's Island. A few days later, on July 31, an advance party of two companies landed near the mouth of the Nueces River at the tiny trading hamlet of Corpus Christi. An army with a voracious appetite for material backed by a legion of gold and silver soon followed. While dragoon sabers and infantry bayonets ultimately carved a permanent Texas border with Mexico, paymasters' strongboxes and quartermaster contracts helped shape the state north of that boundary.[1]

At the beginning of the Mexican War, the Quartermaster's Department was authorized only thirty-seven officers, which Congress would increase by only an additional fourteen during the war. The pinchpenny Congress was also responsible for the shortage of materiel needed in a crisis. Events and operations moved at a faster pace than the system of congressional appropriation, quartermaster contracting, and American manufacturing. Congress did not appropriate the first dollar to supply the campaign until the Battle of Palo Alto—ten months after Taylor's army arrived on the beach at Corpus Christi.[2]

The man responsible for supplying the army in the field was the quartermaster general, Bvt. Maj. Gen. Thomas S. Jesup, a Virginian and veteran of the War of 1812. In all, Jesup served forty-two years—from 1818 to 1860—as the able, intelligent, and intensely active chief of army logistics. For the Mexican War, Jesup established a theater logistical headquarters at New Orleans run by his deputy quartermaster, Lt. Col. Thomas F. Hunt, a thirty-year veteran. Hunt supervised all logistical operations forward of the Mississippi River. Jesup sent Col. Trueman Cross to serve as Taylor's chief quartermaster. Colonel Henry Whiting replaced Cross after Cross was killed in Texas in April, 1846. Later, in October of 1846, when Maj. Gen. Winfield Scott's campaign from Veracruz to Mexico City was in the planning phase, Jesup moved to Texas to personally supervise Scott's logistics operation staging out of Brazos Santiago.[3]

When Brigadier General Taylor's army arrived on the beach at Corpus Christi in the summer of 1845, his men found about forty souls and a ranch and trading post founded by Henry L. Kinney in 1839. Kinney, a Pennsylvanian, had visited Texas in 1832 and returned in 1839 as a trader and smuggler, establishing his base of operations on the west bank of the Nueces River on Corpus Christi Bay.[4]

The army's arrival attracted humanity of the worst sort like a plague of

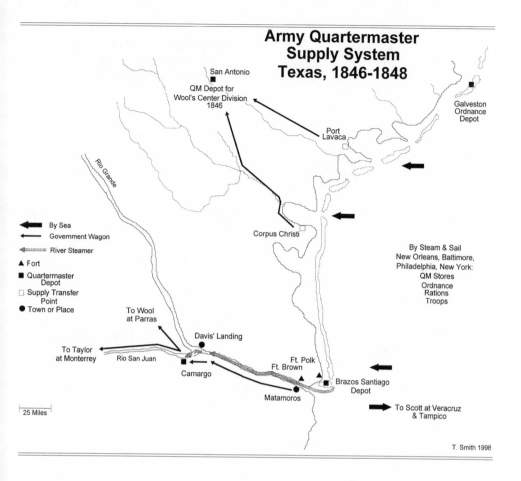

Army Quartermaster Supply System Texas, 1846-1848

San Antonio

QM Depot for Wool's Center Division 1846

Galveston Ordnance Depot

Port Lavaca

Rio Grande

By Sea
Government Wagon
River Steamer
▲ Fort
■ Quartermaster Depot
□ Supply Transfer Point
● Town or Place

Corpus Christi

By Steam & Sail
New Orleans, Baltimore,
Philadelphia, New York:
QM Stores
Ordnance
Rations
Troops

To Wool at Parras

Davis' Landing

To Taylor at Monterrey   Rio San Juan

Camargo

Ft. Polk
Ft. Brown

Matamoros

Brazos Santiago Depot

To Scott at Veracruz & Tampico

25 Miles

T. Smith 1998

flies. One officer at Corpus Christi noted at the time: "Every fresh arrival of troops was followed by some portion of vast herds of liquor selling harpies. . . . In a short time hundreds of temporary structures were erected . . . and in them, all the cut-throat thieves and murderers of the United States and Texas seemed to have congregated."[5]

For six months Taylor camped his army of 3,900 soldiers—a third of the regular army—on the beach at Corpus Christi, where they used the time to prepare for the coming conflict. Meanwhile, his logisticians struggled to supply the regiments. Lacking a deepwater port, they unloaded seagoing vessels at nearby St. Joseph's Island, where the Quartermaster's Department had established a depot. Several government-owned, shallow-draft steamers carried cargo from St. Joseph's Island across the bay to Corpus Christi. As commander of the small army, Taylor paid scant attention to his logistical problems, generally failing to plan for the future. More importantly, he rarely

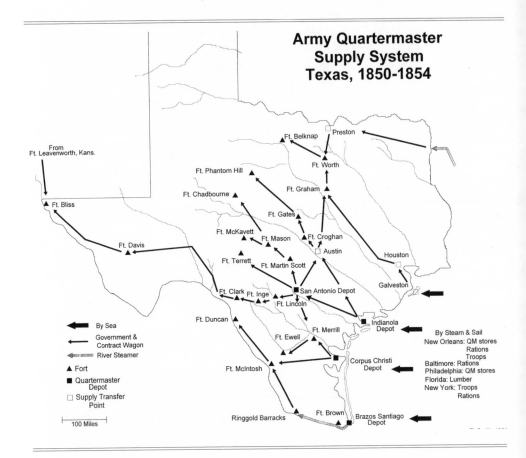

Army Quartermaster Supply System Texas, 1850-1854

From Ft. Leavenworth, Kans.

Ft. Belknap
Preston
Ft. Worth
Ft. Phantom Hill
Ft. Chadbourne
Ft. Graham
Ft. Bliss
Ft. Gates
Ft. McKavett
Ft. Mason
Ft. Croghan
Austin
Ft. Davis
Ft. Terrett
Houston
Ft. Martin Scott
Galveston
Ft. Clark
Ft. Inge
San Antonio Depot
Ft. Lincoln
Ft. Duncan
Indianola Depot
Ft. Merrill
Ft. Ewell
Corpus Christi Depot
Ft. McIntosh
Ft. Brown
Ringgold Barracks
Brazos Santiago Depot

By Sea

Government & Contract Wagon

River Steamer

▲ Fort

■ Quartermaster Depot

□ Supply Transfer Point

100 Miles

By Steam & Sail
New Orleans: QM stores
Rations
Troops
Baltimore: Rations
Philadelphia: QM stores
Florida: Lumber
New York: Troops
Rations

gave Quartermaster General Jesup at the War Department any hint of his anticipated needs for future operations, leaving the logisticians to, as Jesup put it, "guess what might be wanted" of the requirements to support the army. It took a prompting by the Quartermaster's Department to get Taylor to send his engineers to discover if the Rio Grande was navigable by steamship. One of Taylor's West Point–trained engineers, although fond of the general, considered him "ignorant of the use to which the staff department can be put. . . ."[6]

For his own part, in September, 1846, Taylor complained to the secretary of war about the Quartermaster's Department's lack of "proper foresight and energy." Similar complaints against the logistical system were frequent throughout the war. One young regular officer wrote home from Texas, "Everything is done here in the loosest way and the government is losing millions by the imbecility or corruption of the Quartermaster Department."[7]

In spite of intraservice bickering, the logistical system built up Taylor's army at Corpus Christi until the general had sufficient combat power to move forward into the disputed territory. Taylor executed his orders in March, 1846, marching the army toward Matamoros. During the six months Corpus Christi played host to Taylor's army, the village ballooned from a few dozen inhabitants to a town of two thousand citizens—nearly all of them in some way connected to servicing the needs of the soldiers. With the soldiers' departure, the town became, in the eyes of one remaining Third Infantry officer, "a scene of desolation. . . . Oh! Corpus Christi, thou child of the army, how thou hast fallen." He noted that many of the "Corpus Christians, the worst set of Christians under the sun," had taken up their belongings and walked toward the Rio Grande to regain the army, and thus continued "to prey upon us."[8]

When the army moved west from Corpus Christi, a combat train of 307 wagons and carts, carrying twenty days of rations, moved overland with it. Taylor's main supply tail, under the command of Maj. John Munroe, a War

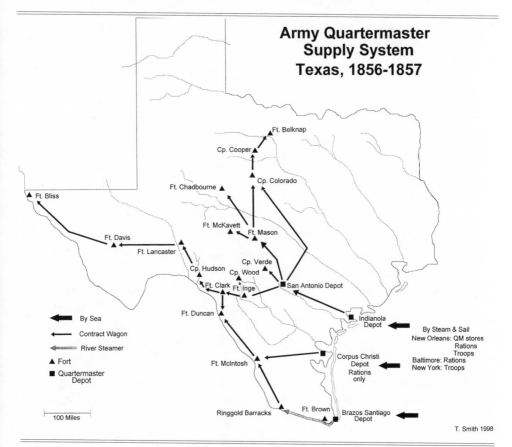

ARMY LOGISTICAL SYSTEM

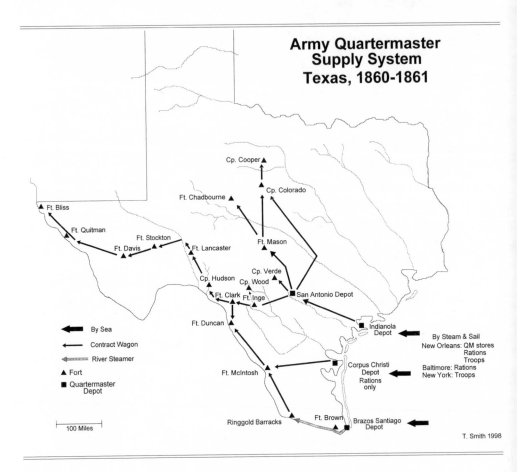

**Army Quartermaster
Supply System
Texas, 1860-1861**

Cp. Cooper ▲

Cp. Colorado ▲

Ft. Chadbourne ▲

Ft. Bliss ▲

Ft. Quitman ▲

Ft. Stockton ▲
Ft. Davis ▲

Ft. Lancaster ▲

Ft. Mason ▲

Cp. Verde ▲
Cp. Hudson ▲   Cp. Wood ▲

Ft. Clark ▲ Ft. Inge ▲   ■ San Antonio Depot

Ft. Duncan ▲

■ Indianola
Depot

By Sea
Contract Wagon
River Steamer
▲ Fort
■ Quartermaster
Depot

Corpus Christi
Depot
Rations
only

By Steam & Sail
New Orleans: QM stores
Rations
Troops
Baltimore: Rations
New York: Troops

Ft. McIntosh ▲

100 Miles

Ringgold Barracks

Ft. Brown ▲

Brazos Santiago
Depot

T. Smith 1998

of 1812 veteran, moved by sea on three ships from Corpus Christi, down the
coast along Padre Island, then through a shallow inlet called Brazos de Santiago
to the Laguna Madre. Munroe got his command ashore on March 24, immediately putting the entire party of sutlers, laborers, and sailors to work on
a field fortification to be called Fort Polk, at Point Isabel, near the former
Mexican village of El Frontón de Santa Isabel. Taylor arrived within a few
days, made contact with the supporting depot, and continued his army's
march toward the Rio Grande opposite Matamoros.[9]

In the coming months Point Isabel and nearby Clark Island or Brazos
Island became the key forward logistical center for the entire war as Taylor
fought the battles of Palo Alto and Resaca de la Palma, captured Matamoros,
and launched his campaign into northeastern Mexico. Called by one young
officer a "perfect purgatory" of heat and sand, Brazos Santiago and Point
Isabel did not form an ideal port complex, but it was the closest one avail-

able to the field army. Because of the bay's shallow eight-foot depth at the south end of the Laguna Madre and the sandbar across the gap between Brazos and Padre Islands, deep-draft sea vessels had to anchor offshore outside "The Arms," and lighter cargo by shallow-draft vessel onto the beach at Brazos Island. Cargo was then transferred three miles across the bay to Point Isabel for the overland haul to Matamoros, or sent by mule and wagon from Brazos Santiago down the beach to the mouth of the Rio Grande to be transshipped onto light steamers for the trip upriver. Supplies began to pour into Brazos Santiago by sea: uniforms, boots, and tents from Schuylkill Arsenal at Philadelphia, and knapsacks, canteens, and cooking gear from Pittsburgh and Cincinnati. The trip by sea-steamer to Brazos Santiago required a five- or six-day trip from New Orleans and a fourteen-to-twenty-day trip from upper eastern seaboard ports such as New York or Boston.[10]

Although it was the site of extensive quartermaster, clothing, subsistence, and ordnance depots throughout Taylor's campaign in northeastern

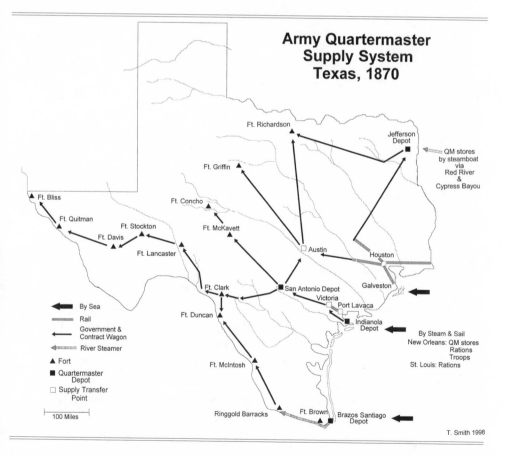

ARMY LOGISTICAL SYSTEM

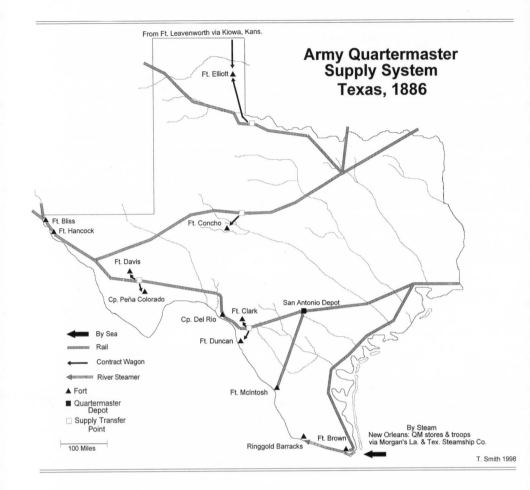

Army Quartermaster Supply System Texas, 1886

From Ft. Leavenworth via Kiowa, Kans.

Ft. Elliott

Ft. Bliss
Ft. Hancock
Ft. Concho
Ft. Davis
Cp. Peña Colorado
Ft. Clark
San Antonio Depot
Cp. Del Rio
Ft. Duncan
Ft. McIntosh
Ft. Brown
Ringgold Barracks

By Sea
Rail
Contract Wagon
River Steamer
▲ Fort
■ Quartermaster Depot
□ Supply Transfer Point

100 Miles

By Steam
New Orleans: QM stores & troops
via Morgan's La. & Tex. Steamship Co.

T. Smith 1998

Mexico, Brazos Santiago remained something of a slapdash operation with little real system, order, security, or protection of supplies. Quartermaster General Jesup finally sent a young friend, former Kentucky businessman and newly commissioned quartermaster Maj. Thomas B. Eastland, to put the place in order to support Winfield Scott's campaign to Mexico City. Eastland arrived on March 21, 1847, and found ten vessels offshore waiting to be lightered. It took a week to unload them as the seven steam lighters were "in a deplorable state." Eastland found mountains of unguarded supplies exposed to theft and ruin from the weather, a drunken workforce, liquor smuggling across the beach at night, unauthorized grog shops, and a general lack of discipline.[11]

To remedy the situation, Eastland weighed in with a heavy fist and prodigious energy. During his first ten days on the job he coordinated the repair of crucial steam lighters; organized a strong guard to slow down pilfering and smuggling; sent to New Orleans for lumber to build warehouses and a hospital; sent crews out to cut palmetto logs for constructing a six-vessel wharf; sent to General Taylor for permission to clean out the grog shops and unemployed camp followers; sent 270 horses, 300 mules, one hundred wagons, and sixty teamsters to Taylor's army; and shipped another hundred wagons and 600,000 rations to Scott at Veracruz.[12]

Eastland's 150,000 feet of lumber arrived on May 1, and within three weeks he had completed six wharves, a warehouse, and nearly finished a hospital at Point Isabel. When he forcibly evicted the harpies, layabouts, and grog shops, Eastland suddenly found himself indicted by the Fourth District Court of Texas for "Sundry acts of tyranny and oppression."

"I shall not deny," he explained to the judge, "that I have been obliged to exercise authority in a somewhat summary manner . . . indispensably

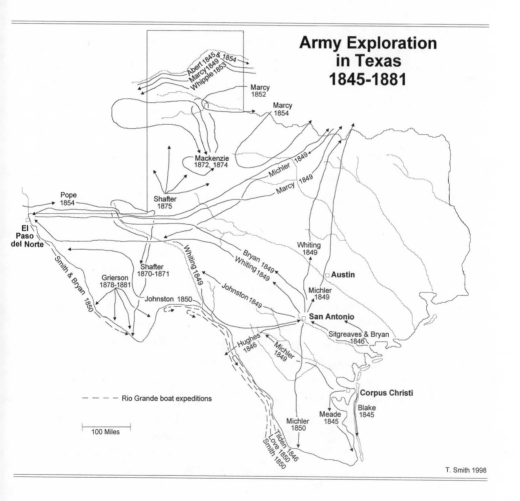

Army Exploration in Texas 1845-1881

necessary to protect the public interests."[13] At one time the site of empty dunes and a few crude huts, the port complex of Brazos Santiago–Port Isabel became the major forward depot for Taylor's move to Saltillo. Under Eastland's guidance it also became the major forward depot and transshipping point for supplies needed to support Scott's move from Veracruz to Mexico City. In the post–Mexican War years, until about 1874, it would supply Texas' Rio Grande forts and help shape the economic destiny of the Rio Grande Valley.[14]

As Taylor's army moved first to Matamoros and then onward to Monterrey and Saltillo, the supply line extended from Brazos Santiago to Camargo and then to Monterrey. Logisticians toiled to lighter supplies across the bay to Point Isabel to meet the Matamoros road. However, they moved most of the cargo by pack mule or wagon from Brazos Santiago nine miles down the beach across the Boca Chica to the mouth of the Rio Grande, and then upriver by shallow-draft steamer. The transfer depot, located two miles up from the river's mouth, became a considerable operation itself. The depth of the sandbar at the river's mouth was three to five feet, and in June, 1847, the quartermasters and Mexican labor force constructed a sizable wharf to eliminate the need for lightering.[15]

Moving upriver, the next important logistical link for Taylor's army was Fort Brown—or Fort Texas as it was named when it was established opposite Matamoros on March 27, 1846, by the Seventh Infantry. Fort Brown and the postwar village of Brownsville would become a transportation hub for trade with northeastern Mexico, and the center of Rio Grande navigation.[16]

While Brazos Santiago remained the crucial logistical link with the sea, Taylor's quartermasters pushed the lines of communication 140 miles upriver from Fort Brown and established a forward supply depot at the Mexican town of Camargo. In September, 1846—when Taylor left the river and began his westward march into the northern Mexico interior—Camargo served as the river terminal for his line to the sea. Camargo's two thousand inhabitants were favorably disposed toward the regulars who took over the town on July 14, 1846. However, after the arrival of the volunteers, a number of robberies and murders turned the population hostile.[17]

Captain George H. Crosman, a clever, industrious quartermaster officer, controlled Camargo. Like Eastland at Brazos Santiago, Crosman instilled discipline, threw out layabouts, fired drunkards, and clamped down on the gambling and grog shops that seemed to spring up overnight. The logistical strain at Camargo was additionally eased in August, 1846, when Taylor sent the bevy of women camp followers back to New Orleans.[18]

By July, 1846, a dozen river steamers were working the Rio Grande. Steamers came upriver opposite Davis' Landing, the future site of Rio Grande City and Ringgold Barracks, turned west into the San Juan River, and traveled four miles more to Camargo. The major depot was on the river's north bank across from town. Cargo was shuttled across on the *Troy,* a ninety-two-ton, stern-wheeled steam ferry. In the seven-month period from August, 1846, to February, 1847, fifteen different steamers made forty-one of the four-to-ten-day voyages up the Rio Grande to move supplies or troops to and from Camargo and the mouth of the great river. During the same period, eighteen major pack-mule and wagon trains departed Camargo for the eight-day trip to Taylor's supply point at Monterrey. These typically consisted of groups of sixty to 150 wagons, and at least four of the pack trains included more than a thousand mules.[19]

The lack of a serious threat from the Mexican navy helped insure the security of Taylor's seaborne logistical chain, and the speed of communications improved week by week. The fastest recorded trip from the eastern seaboard was made by Lt. Lewis A. Armistead, who carried military dispatches from Washington, D.C., to Camargo by ship in fourteen days. Newspapers such as the New Orleans *Picayune* were usually only two weeks old when they arrived at Camargo.[20]

The difficulties of contending with an underdeveloped theater, an arid environment, Mexican guerrilla raids and a hostile population were exacerbated in the summer of 1846 when Comanche Indians launched a series of raids in the Camargo area. In October Comanches wounded a Kentucky mounted volunteer while he was out hunting. In January, 1847, the volunteer forces regained some support from the population by deploying a hundred soldiers from the Second Ohio Infantry to nearby ranches in an effort to protect local citizens from Indian attacks. Taylor's Camargo–Monterrey supply line was also vulnerable. Mexican cavalry temporarily closed operations on February 22, 1847, when Brig. Gen. José Urrea captured a train of 110 wagons and three hundred pack mules, killing fifty teamsters in the process. On March 7, a second train lost forty wagons. Taylor responded by providing additional forces to guard his lines of communication. Although Urrea withdrew by the end of March, Taylor's supply line remained vulnerable to occasional raids by irregulars.[21]

The Rio Grande river-borne supply operation also led to the development of an important postwar military station in the river valley. Located on the Rio Grande opposite Camargo was a critical steamboat wood-fuel site known as Davis' Landing. It was owned and operated by Henry Clay Davis, a Kentuckian who moved to Texas in 1833 and married into an important Tejano family. Davis' Landing eventually spawned Fort Ringgold and Rio Grande City.[22]

In September, 1846, when Taylor advanced from Camargo, other collateral military events in Texas would help shape the postwar economic fortunes of Texas communities—all connected with the expedition of Brig. Gen. John E. Wool's Division of the Center forming at San Antonio.

San Antonio de Bexar had long been the Spanish and Mexican Republic military center of Tejas, and Zachary Taylor's forces occupied it within three months of landing at Corpus Christi. Major Thomas T. Fauntleroy established Camp Bexar with two companies from the Second Dragoons six miles south of town on October 20, 1845. The following month, Fauntleroy went to take command of the one-company post at Austin while the regiment's second-in-command, Lt. Col. William S. Harney, became the senior officer in San Antonio. Harney vacated Bexar at the end of November, leading his dragoons on a reconnaissance of the Rio Grande. A small Second Dragoons force returned to San Antonio in July, 1846, but by then the city had been chosen as the gathering point for Wool's division, destined to become a three-thousand-man force of regulars and Arkansas and Illinois volunteers to operate against the Mexican state of Chihuahua. Wool arrived in August, 1846, and organized his division with the help of his chief quartermaster, Maj. Charles Thomas.[23]

Quartermaster General Jesup designated the tiny port of Lavaca, established on the coast 160 miles from San Antonio in 1841, as the Texas coastal transfer point for supplying Wool's division. Jesup had sent horses and mules overland from the Mississippi Valley to Taylor's army, as well as prefabricated wagons from Philadelphia by sea. Much of those supplies were usurped by Wool's force, thanks as much to the aggressiveness of his logisticians as to Wool's own reluctance to pass along any transportation that entered his area of command. The workhorse of the supply operation at Port Lavaca was a Pennsylvanian and 1824 West Point graduate, Capt. James Ramsay Irwin, a quartermaster officer destined to die in Mexico City in 1848. Irwin took charge of the Lavaca operation in July, 1846. In two short months he had sent to San Antonio 1,112 wagon loads of supplies from New Orleans and oversaw the assembly of 150 wagons by a small army of carpenters sent by sea for the job. At San Antonio, an Illinois volunteer quartermaster, Capt. James Harvey Ralston, set up a supply depot at the Alamo, repairing the Long Barracks and clearing the chapel floor of debris. In late September, 1846, Wool's Division of the Center set out from San Antonio to capture Chihuahua with San Antonio and Port Lavaca serving as his logistical base. Wool reached Parras in December, 1846, only to be ordered to march to join forces with Taylor at Saltillo, forcing him to shift his line of communication from San Antonio to Camargo. In December, 1846, Quartermaster General Jesup decided Port Lavaca had outlived its usefulness. The operation was shut down, and the quartermasters forwarded the remaining supplies to Brazos Santiago.[24]

Two additional Texas points saw limited use by the army during the Mexican War. In November, 1845, the Second Dragoons occupied Austin with a single company that camped in the city off and on until May, 1846, when the regimental commander ordered it to the Rio Grande. The Ordnance Bureau established a small weapons and ammunition depot in Galveston in 1846. It eventually ceased operations in May, 1849.[25]

The three years of federal military activity in Texas associated with the Mexican War had a significant impact on the state, although not even the quartermaster general could provide an accurate accounting of the sums the U.S. Army spent. During the war, the army created two major Texas ports, Corpus Christi and Brazos Santiago–Point Isabel, and was responsible for fostering the conditions leading to the founding of Brownsville, an important Rio Grande Valley city. Equally important, army logistics requirements brought steam navigation to the Rio Grande. Sea traffic from the Texas coast to the crucial port of New Orleans had been haphazard prior to the war, but afterward became almost a matter of routine, solidly establishing this line of communication and mails. Finally, the war settled the lingering security questions that followed the Texas Revolution, and brought the state under the protection of the federal umbrella.

The Mexican War was also a boon to Texas' population. Many veterans first exposed to the state during the war remained and became lifelong citizens. Typical of the type were John Vale and Jesus Sandoval. Vale served as a regular in the Second Dragoons, mustered out at war's end, became a mining engineer, and in 1873 was the customs collector at Roma. Coming from Mexico as a Quartermaster's Department employee in 1846, Sandoval remained in the Rio Grande Valley, gaining his citizenship in 1853. By 1875 he was a rancher near Brownsville.[26]

In the spring of 1848, as the victorious American army began to plan its redeployment from Mexico, the Texas legislature asked the U.S. Congress to pass a law establishing a chain of forts on the Texas frontier between the Rio Grande and the Red River. Approval of this request fundamentally altered the military geography of the region and began the true expansion of Texas' Anglo frontier into the relatively unoccupied north-central area and into the southwestern borderlands districts long dominated by Tejanos, the state's first true plainsmen. The original requirement for the location of military garrisons, and their subsequent expense, was relative to the frontier line and settlement patterns in Texas. The traditional view of geographers is that environment and rainfall were the key factors in determining frontier settlement, although recent scholarship has added transportation routes to the mix. In Texas, the area west of the 98th meridian (the area generally west of the San Antonio–Austin line) had a less than ideal twenty to thirty inches of annual rainfall and practically no existing roads. The majority of the Anglo population was therefore located east of this line, and settlement west of the line remained scarce throughout the nineteenth century.[27]

In the summer and fall of 1848, the army established the basic postwar military geography of Texas. As part of the Western Division headquartered in New Orleans, Texas became the Eighth Military Department. A force of 1,488 troops—14 percent of the regular army—was ordered to the state. That force included two-and-one-half infantry regiments, six dragoon companies, and one light and one heavy artillery battery, and was led by the department commander, Col. (Bvt. Maj. Gen.) William Jenkins Worth. A thirty-five-year veteran, Worth had seen action in the War of 1812, the Second Seminole War, and the recent Mexican War.[28]

The initial troops to take up station on the frontier were from the First Infantry Regiment. Most of the regiment's companies arrived by sea at Brazos Santiago from New Orleans on October 19, 1848, and joined with a battery of the Fourth Artillery at Fort Brown. The First Infantry's headquarters and three companies remained there while two companies pushed straight upriver to Davis' Landing on the Rio Grande, establishing the first of the new Texas forts there on October 26. The new post was soon known as Ringgold Barracks. Within two months the First Infantry also sent companies to San Antonio, the Sabinal River, Austin, and Fredericksburg. On November 5, 1848, six companies from the Second Dragoons arrived at Galveston by steamer from New Orleans, marched straight overland to Austin, and established a headquarters there called Camp Maxwell. Deploying from Camp Maxwell during November and December, 1848, the dragoon companies took up stations in the north-central frontier on the west fork of the Trinity River, the Brazos River, and Hamilton Creek. One company then went west to the Medina River while two companies went to the Rio Grande—first to Fort Brown and then up to Ringgold Barracks. The Eighth Infantry Regiment came down the Mississippi by steamer from Jefferson Barracks, Missouri, passed through New Orleans, and arrived at Port Lavaca on December 18,

1848, on the steamers *Telegraph* and *New Orleans*. Crippled by the death of 128 soldiers in a cholera epidemic that swept the Eighth Infantry camp at Port Lavaca, the regiment finished deploying to Camp Worth in San Antonio by January 17, 1849. Half of the regiment remained there through the summer. In May, two companies went to Fredericksburg and three marched to Austin. Additional companies spread out to posts on the Trinity, Sabinal, and Brazos Rivers later in the summer. Six companies of the Third Infantry—about half of the regiment—established a temporary camp in San Antonio in April, 1849, while departmental and regimental quartermasters organized the logistics for their march to El Paso, where in September, 1849, they established a post near a site that would later become Fort Bliss.[29]

From late 1848 to 1851 the army in Texas cobbled together a piecemeal barrier of company forts up the Rio Grande to Fort Duncan and northeast along the bare trace of settlement lines on the Brazos, Colorado, and Trinity Rivers. In 1851, Col. Persifor F. Smith, a Princeton-educated lawyer and Mexican War veteran, took command of all forces in Texas. After an extensive reconnaissance, Smith decided to reinforce the thin First Federal Line or Indian Frontier Line with a new system of forts, eventually called the Second Federal Line or Western Line of Defense. An outer line of forts at the edge of the Staked Plain (also known as the Llano Estacado) and on the Edwards Plateau, primarily manned by infantry a hundred miles in advance of the settlements, was supposed to provide warning when Indian raiders crossed from the wilderness into the Texas interior. Mounted troops on the inner line, where forage was considerably less expensive, were then to take up pursuit of the raiders. Additional posts were eventually added to guard the line of commerce of the San Antonio–El Paso military road.[30]

The fact that the defensive strategy underlying this two-tiered system of forts was not particularly effective for battling the Plains Indians had little bearing on the fact that the forts still had to be supplied. Texas quartermasters labored to develop a logistical system to meet the operational requirements under conditions that would have staggered their Napoleonic counterparts in Europe. The straight-line distance from the Texas coast to Fort Worth, for example, was nearly equivalent to the girth of France. Napoleon's supply line from Poland to Moscow in the 1812 campaign was slightly shorter than the supply route from the Texas coast to the post at El Paso.

The reality of such vast distances and expenses in maintaining lines of communication in Texas, and on the western frontier in general, seemed to come as a shocking surprise to congressional appropriations committees. As the army deployed along the post–Mexican War frontier, the quartermaster general's transportation expenses increased by 1500 percent over prewar levels. The $120,000 spent moving the army in 1844 rocketed to $1.9 million by 1849, with the overall Quartermaster's Department budget rising from $870,000 to $4.2 million. In 1845 the army had 847 mules for supply trains; in 1850 it had nearly eight thousand. Forage costs tripled during the same period, as did rents, and construction expenses increased by 500 percent. "Prior to 1845," Secretary of War Charles M. Conrad explained to Congress, "our frontier posts were all established either on the Gulf of Mexico, on Lake Superior, or on the headwaters of the Mississippi or its tributaries. They were all, therefore, accessible by water, and many of them situated in the midst of fertile and cultivated country." By contrast, in the immediate post–Mexican War era, the army had a dozen forts on the Pacific coast—where all labor and supply costs were exorbitant—and nearly fifty posts on the Great Plains and in the Southwest—far from navigable rivers and agricultural centers, and thus requiring expensive long-haul wagon freighting of supplies and material. "There is not," noted Quartermaster General Jesup, "as far as I can learn, a steamboat or railroad line, or even an ordinary turnpike road, in Texas, New Mexico, California, or Oregon."[31]

In April, 1849, the War Department officially designated San Antonio as the department headquarters, and the town became the hub of all army operations in Texas. Although not yet sponsoring a full-fledged depot, in June, 1849, the Eighth Infantry detached Lt. Lafayette B. Wood to manage the growing subsistence and ordnance stores in the town. On January 1, 1850, the Quartermaster's Department rented the Alamo compound for $150 per month from the Catholic Church, and an adjacent lot for twenty dollars from Samuel A. Maverick. Also in 1850, the quartermaster leased a stone building and a lot on the San Antonio River as the site of the Eighth Military Department's arms and munitions depot, constructed a large adobe building there, and hired four civilian workers. This ordnance depot was expanded in 1855 and called the Arsenal of Construction. In 1857 it was renamed the San Antonio Arsenal. This combination of spaces formed the heart of Texas quartermaster operations for the receipt, issue, and storage of supplies and ammunition for most of the antebellum period.[32]

By 1853 the Quartermaster and Subsistence Departments, along with the small ordnance establishment in San Antonio, spent $110,000 in gold and silver per year on employment, rents, and purchases of goods and forage—90 percent of it by the quartermaster. However, in 1852 and 1853, decisions by the department commander caused San Antonio to slip in importance and Bexar very nearly lost its dominant position to several competing rivals, including Indianola and Corpus Christi. In November, 1852, Department Commander Smith, by then a brevet major general, moved his headquarters from San Antonio to Corpus Christi—primarily for his own health reasons, preferring the coastal climate to that of central Texas. A debate arose within military circles in 1853 over the proper location for the Texas departmental depot. The Western Division commander finally tried to put a stop to it when he ordered the logistical operation at San Antonio to be transferred to Indianola.[33]

Beginning in 1849, San Antonio received the bulk of its military supplies by government wagon making the 130-mile trek from the coast at Indianola. Only three to five days by steamer from New Orleans, no port could rival Indianola as the gateway to army logistics on the Texas frontier. Located on the west shore of Matagorda Bay, "Indian Point" had originally served as a debarkation point for German colonists in 1845. The town founders, William C. Cook and Samuel A. White, had the town site surveyed in 1846 and changed the name to Indianola in 1849. Commercial seaport development, with a large dose of army supply traffic, expanded the site to include nearby Powder Horn Bayou. In 1850 the army began leasing buildings and a wharf from Cook and continued to increase operations during the remainder of the decade.[34]

The department commander ordered the Indianola depot improved in 1851, and by 1853 the port had a population of six hundred and was the principal transfer point for major supply depots at Austin and San Antonio. By then the army was leasing five large buildings and a wharf. In 1856 a military inspector declared Indianola indispensable, noting its good harbor and the fact that the semiweekly steamer to New Orleans stopped at Galveston. The Quartermaster and Subsistence Departments continued to increase their holdings, leasing twelve hundred dollars worth of buildings, and providing employment for forty-one citizens at $13,400 per year. The year 1856 also brought the beginning of a failed dream: a railroad to be constructed from Indianola to San Antonio.[35]

San Antonio's second rival, Corpus Christi, was no stranger to Mexican War regulars like department commander Smith, who had served with Zachary Taylor's army. Corpus Christi's founder, Henry L. Kinney, was politically influential, serving as a senator in the Texas legislature. An old Mexican War friend of President Taylor's, Kinney was being touted by Texas papers in 1849 as Taylor's choice to become the next minister to Mexico. In June, 1849, a Corpus Christi citizens' committee petitioned Secretary of War

Crawford to establish an army fort at their port. Crawford's reply deferred to the judgment of the department commander, who wished to put all troops possible on the frontier line. Kinney then hired J. H. Blood as his Washington agent to lobby Quartermaster General Jesup to build a supply depot at the port. The Quartermaster's Department soon rented buildings and established a small depot in Corpus Christi in November, 1850, intending to supply Fort McIntosh on the Rio Grande. However, due to the lack of transportation and water on the 140-mile route, it took more than a year to push the first train to the river. The depot did pass on rations received from Baltimore, New York, and New Orleans to several Nueces River posts, and sent quartermaster stores shipped from New Orleans to San Antonio. The fact that Corpus Christi became the department headquarters in 1852 did nothing to alter the difficult local conditions facing logisticians. These limitations included a deficit of animal forage—which had to be brought from New Orleans—and a shortage of water for both drinking and steaming. Sandbars at each end of Mustang Island limited supply vessels drawing more than six feet, and the flats of the bay near town restricted vessel draft to four feet. By 1853, the forty-five Corpus Christi citizens employed by the Quartermaster's Department—mostly teamsters—brought an annual wage of $13,000 in gold to the community. In 1856, the Quartermaster and Commissary Departments at Corpus Christi rented $3,696 worth of buildings and provided employment for 142 citizens—again mostly teamsters—with a payroll of $39,240 per year. A military inspector in 1856 reported that the cost of the depot was too extravagant considering the difficulties of the bay and the few posts the depot supplied.[36]

In the struggle to become once again the official military center of Texas, San Antonio had its champions. Included in their ranks were the two most influential military inspectors to tour antebellum Texas: Lt. Col. William G. Freeman in 1853, and Col. Joseph K. F. Mansfield in 1856 and again in 1859 and 1860. Freeman reported that supply operations in San Antonio "are probably more extensive than those of all other depots in Texas combined." The inspector added that Indianola was very remote from frontier forts, too damp for a major depot, and that forage and wood were expensive. "San Antonio, on the contrary," he wrote, "Is situated in a grain growing region where corn can be purchased at half the price it costs at Indianola, and wood and water are abundant." Furthermore, he argued that San Antonio's central location to Texas forts was an important advantage required of a supply depot.[37]

Mansfield, the inspector general of the army and the builder of Fort Brown in the Mexican War, reported in 1856, "It is beyond dispute that San

Antonio is the best position for the Head Quarters of this Department being the most central and convenient to all the other posts." Additionally, Mansfield called for the establishment of a large permanent depot at San Antonio. San Antonio's victory came in October, 1855, when the department headquarters returned to the town and the earlier decision to close the San Antonio depot was quietly shelved. "The new and more central position," trumpeted a Texas editor, "will be of great service to the State." Firmly reestablished as the supply and the operational hub of Texas in 1856, the San Antonio quartermaster, commissary, and ordnance activities employed 138 citizens at a cost of $39,000 per year.[38]

To support military operations in north-central Texas, army logisticians established a second interior supply point located at Austin. In November, 1848, two First Infantry companies began constructing stables and a square of large *jacal* (picket) buildings with board siding near the Colorado River on the northwest edge of town. Three companies from the Eighth Infantry continued construction when they occupied the post from July to September, 1849. To provide for the new posts established on the Trinity, Brazos, and Colorado Rivers, the Austin depot received rations directly from Indianola, 130 miles away, and sent its government wagon train eighty miles to the southwest on the seventeen-day round-trip to the San Antonio depot for quartermaster and ordnance stores.[39]

In 1853, the Austin depot—also known as Austin Arsenal—consisted of two large, wooden storehouses, a stone magazine, and a few quarters, all arranged in a square. Austin lost much of its significance with the closing of Forts Worth, Graham, Croghan, and Gates as the frontier line shifted west. More of a transfer point than an actual depot by 1853, its seventy-eight wagon government train furnished no posts with quartermaster supplies, but rations brought from Indianola were passed on to Forts Belknap, and Phantom Hill. Because the post supposedly belonged to the government, the quartermaster paid no rent. The average yearly local expenditure for forage and expenses was seventy thousand dollars, and the ninety citizens employed at the depot earned a total of $24,800 per year. By late 1854 the Austin post had all but ceased logistical operations.[40]

The supply system in Texas during the period 1849 to 1855 could be characterized as haphazard, by necessity mirroring the ad-hoc nature of the military decision-making process that led to the selection and life span of fort sites. The early Texas posts were supported with supplies transported from Indianola and Corpus Christi to the depots at San Antonio and Austin in undermanned government wagons—with only an occasional government contract being awarded to private Texas freighters. Additionally, for several years, posts on the eastern edge of the north-central Texas frontier received supplies shipped directly from New Orleans on hired wagons using transfer points at Galveston and Houston.

The first post on the north-central frontier, Fort Martin Scott, was established by the First Infantry near Fredericksburg in December, 1848, and generally received its supplies from San Antonio. Fort Croghan, located on Hamilton Creek near the upper Colorado River, was the next post constructed. It was supplied through Austin. Fort Graham, established near the Brazos River in April, 1849, received its quartermaster stores from San Antonio and its rations from New Orleans by hired wagon through Houston. The northernmost post, Fort Worth, established in June, 1849, had the same supply system as Fort Graham. Built in October, 1849, Fort Gates—situated on the Leon River—initially received its rations from New Orleans via Houston but switched to government wagons from Indianola in 1850. The difficulties of supplying these northern posts of the First Federal Line led Department Commander Smith to explore the possibility of expanding the small army depot at Preston, Texas—at that time used to support troops in the Indian Territory. Smith wanted to clear the great Red River log-raft blockage above Shreveport, Louisiana, and create a more efficient supply system based on steamboats floating all the way to Preston. Frustrated by the failure of efforts to adequately clear the raft, Smith abandoned the idea in 1853.[41]

The army established Fort Inge on the Leona River on the southwestern frontier in March, 1849, followed by Fort Lincoln near the Sabinal River on Seco Creek in July of the same year. Both of these posts were supplied by army wagons from San Antonio. This line expanded south in March, 1850, with Fort Merrill on the Nueces River northeast of Corpus Christi and, in May of 1852, Fort Ewell, located upriver from Merrill. Merrill drew quartermaster stores and forage from San Antonio and rations from Corpus, and acted as a subdepot for passing supplies on to Fort Ewell via a small government wagon train. Fort Lincoln was closed in the summer of 1852, and in June the southwestern line was extended farther west with the establishment of Fort Clark on Las Moras Creek. Fort Clark drew the bulk of its supplies from San Antonio but occasionally was ordered to draw rations from Corpus Christi—a trip that took its eight-wagon government train a month to complete.[42]

The period 1851 to 1853 brought a number of post closures on the north-central frontier and saw a radical shift westward as the Second Federal Line formed. Fort Martin Scott at Fredericksburg ended its life as a troop post, but served as a forage depot to provide hay and corn for government trains traveling to northern Texas forts. The first westward expansion came in June, 1851, as Fort Belknap was built on the Clear Fork of the Brazos River. A month later, Fort Mason began operations on the Llano River, followed in November by the forlorn and ill-chosen Fort Phantom Hill on the Clear Fork of the Brazos River. Fort Terrett on the North Fork of the Llano opened in February, 1852, followed by Fort McKavett on the San Saba River in March, and Fort Chadbourne near the Colorado River in October. San Antonio became the principal logistical depot for these new posts on the north-central frontier, with the exception of Fort Phantom Hill, which was supplied from Austin by government wagons. In March, 1852, the army closed Fort Gates. That closure was followed by the deactivation of Forts Graham, Croghan, and Worth between September and December, 1853, as units marched westward to provide garrisons for the new posts. In October, 1853, the state's military administration was redesignated the Department of Texas.[43]

Events at El Paso during the round of post closures serve as an example illustrating that Texas citizens would not hesitate to use their political influence to protect their commercial interests and their economic relations with the army. When the Third Infantry established Post Opposite El Paso in 1849, at that time in the Department of New Mexico, the regiment leased buildings at the site of Franklin, or Coons Rancho, from Benjamin Franklin Coons. The local senior officer, Maj. Jefferson Van Horne, soon decided that the lease, without adequate firewood, was far too expensive. Hoping to save money, Van Horne decided to move the garrison twenty miles south to the old presidio of San Elizario, where he already had two companies stationed at much less cost. Led by Chihuahua trader James W. Magoffin, local citizens petitioned the New Mexico department commander. The petition, which emphasized—with a good deal of justification—the constant threat of outlaws and Indians, rather than economic concerns, was bolstered by the arguments of the local army quartermaster, who did not like the flood-prone San Elizario site. That petition was successful. However, nineteen months later a senior officer of the Third Infantry once again recommended moving the garrison, challenging the military advantage of the Coons Ranch location, as well as the expense. Led by Simeon Hart, who had installed a mill and had a flour contract with the army, the local citizens launched a new petition to keep the fort—this time unsuccessfully. The post closed in September, 1851. Magoffin, Hart, and other landowners and merchants began an intense two-year campaign of petitions and letters, lobbying Pres. Millard Fillmore, Gov. P. H. Bell, and military authorities. Finally, in December, 1853, Secretary of

War Jefferson Davis, on Inspector General Mansfield's recommendation of military necessity, ordered that the post be reestablished. Four companies from the Eighth Infantry arrived in January, 1854, and leased the site for their garrison from James W. Magoffin.[44]

The period 1854 to 1859 brought not only an additional significant shift of the military line westward into the Trans-Pecos, but heralded a fundamental change in the system of supply transportation in Texas. On the north-central frontier, Forts Terrett and Phantom Hill closed in 1854, but in January, 1856, Camp Cooper opened on the Clear Fork of the Brazos River, followed in August by Camp Colorado near the Colorado River. The three-hundred-mile leap to the Trans-Pecos region began in October, 1854, with the establishment of Fort Davis on Limpia Creek in the Davis Mountains. Companion Trans-Pecos posts sprang up in rapid march order shortly after the leader of the Second Cavalry, Col. Albert Sidney Johnston, took command of the Department of Texas. In August, 1855, the army built Fort Lancaster on the banks of Live Oak Creek near Howard's Springs in the Pecos River valley. It was followed by Camp Wood on the upper Nueces River in May, 1857, and Camp Hudson on the Devil's River in June. Added to this line of posts designed to protect the military and commercial routes between San Antonio and El Paso were Fort Quitman in September, 1858, and Fort Stockton at Comanche Spring in March, 1859. The need for troops to man this expansion brought the 1855 closure of two southwestern frontier posts: Forts Merrill and Ewell. By 1856, a quarter of the U.S. Army—4,047 soldiers in two mounted regiments, four infantry regiments, and parts of two artillery regiments—occupied eighteen Texas posts. Although San Antonio furnished supplies for all of these new posts, the quartermaster no longer provided every mule and wagon used to move rations and stores. Beginning in 1855, nearly all supplies in Texas were moved by large-scale commercial wagon contractors, primarily George Thomas Howard in the antebellum era. The contract system remained in effect until the coming of the railroad and would, as explained later, have a substantial impact on Texas' economy. In addition to relying on contracted transportation to meet the logistics challenge, Secretary of War Davis experimented with camels in an effort to supply field operations in the arid Southwest. The army imported several dozen African camels to Texas in April, 1856, locating them at Camp Verde. In one sixty-mile field test between that post and San Antonio, six camels carried six hundred pounds each, for a total of 3,648 pounds, in two days. Two six-mule army wagons hauled the same load over the same distance in four days. On a similar test on muddy roads impassable to wagons, a camel train covered the route with an average load of 328 pounds each. These and other field tests in the Southwest, proved the potential of the camel, but the program came to halt with the start of the Civil War.[45]

Army quartermasters had to develop two supplemental logistical systems to supply posts on the Rio Grande. In the extreme west, Fort Bliss—located opposite El Paso, Mexico—was so far from San Antonio and the Texas coast that for much of the antebellum period it drew its supplies via the Santa Fe Trail from Fort Leavenworth, Kansas. The supply system that evolved for the lower part of the river, called the Rio Grande Line, was unique when compared to that of the west-Texas frontier and more closely akin to that of the upper Mississippi or Missouri River valleys in that the quartermasters could take advantage of waterborne logistics. The transport and depot system for the Rio Grande Line was an outgrowth of the basic network developed during the Mexican War. Steamers from the eastern seaboard and other points were off-loaded by lighter at Brazos Santiago or cross-loaded to river steamers for the trip upriver to Fort Brown. The Fort Brown quartermaster, with an annual operating budget of about twenty thousand dollars, forwarded supplies farther upriver on contract steamers, such as those operated by Mifflin Kenedy and Richard King, to Ringgold Barracks. Steamers operating from there could generally navigate the 103 miles northward to Guerrero, Mexico, from June to November. However, obstructions in the river above Ringgold Barracks usually required a shift to wagon or keelboat for the 120-mile land trip or 216-mile keelboat trip to Fort McIntosh, established at Laredo in 1849. In the early 1850s Fort McIntosh acted as a forwarding depot, maintaining teams of thirty to forty mules to transfer supplies a further one hundred miles to another 1849 post—Fort Duncan at Eagle Pass. Fort Duncan also purchased forage from the Mexican interior or had it shipped overland from Corpus Christi if bought in New Orleans.[46]

The sea base of the Rio Grande Line continued to be Brazos Santiago throughout the antebellum period. By 1853, the mountain of Mexican War stores had diminished and the island became more of a transfer point than a storage depot. The quartermaster employed three citizens, including a lighter pilot, and had on hand a small soldier guard detail to protect the wharf and five storage buildings. When returning to Texas through the Brazos, Mexican War veterans who recalled the great sprawl of ramshackle structures—which had been salvaged for lumber— were greeted by empty dunes. A "hotel" established in the hull of a wrecked steamer grounded on the beach, offered novel accommodations that included a bar and sleeping rooms. By 1856, a second wharf and the proper selection of supply vessels eliminated most of the old Mexican War requirement for lightering, although the quartermaster retained four civilian employees.[47]

With the development of the upper Rio Grande posts, Fort Brown became a supply depot in June, 1848. Fort Brown received its stores through Brazos Santiago and, for those shallow-draft vessels able to navigate the river, directly from New Orleans—a 628-mile trip by sea. As the Mexican War closed, great piles of surplus equipment from disbanding units were centralized for storage or disposition at Fort Brown. An artillery officer reaching the post by steamer in October, 1848 recorded: "All seemed chaos and confusion. The place had been made a dumping ground of the debris of Taylor's conquering army." As late as 1857, the Fort Brown quartermaster was still sorting through great stacks of shoddy, unmarked Mexican War supplies and ordnance, none of which could be foisted off on sharp-eyed regimental quartermasters.[48]

With the coming of the Civil War in 1861, the army was forced to abandon its Texas posts. This forced Texas' provisional government to provide forces for protecting the Indian frontier. The harsh realities of manpower, money, and logistics severely crippled efforts to furnish much more than a mounted regiment to guard the settlement line—a force less than half that fielded by the federal government during the previous year. Ironically, the provisional government, reluctant to relinquish authority to the Confederate central government, tried to convince Richmond to assume liability for protecting the Texas frontier, as Washington agreed to do after the territory's annexation. In the end, Texas was left to its own devices, spending eight hundred thousand dollars in the first ten months of the Frontier Regiment's operation. In general, compared to the more robust quartermaster system and fiscal resources of the U.S. Army, Confederate army and Texas state forces operating in the Southwest suffered continuously from the restrictions imposed by logistics. Like the campaigns of the Frontier Regiment, attempts by the state government to achieve military control over the Indian Territory faced the grim stricture of supply. The most ambitious enterprise in the Southwest—Brig. Gen. Henry Hopkins Sibley's 1861–62 campaign to extend the Confederate empire into New Mexico and on to California—largely came to grief when Sibley failed to capture the Fort Union, New Mexico, logistics depot, and his own supply train was destroyed near Glorieta Pass, New Mexico.[49]

In contrast to these Confederate logistical failures, Union forces managed to retain supply depots in New Mexico and Kansas and to launch limited coastal operations along the Gulf that were supplied by sea. The federal government returned to the Texas coast from October, 1862 to January, 1863 in a series of actions by a naval squadron under Commodore W. B. Renshaw that occupied Galveston, Corpus Christi and Indianola, while a column of California volunteers captured El Paso in December, 1862. Later, in the winter of 1863–64, the Army of the Gulf captured and occupied Brownsville, Brazos Santiago, Indianola, and a number of Texas coastal islands, and attacked Laredo. Meanwhile, the California column advanced down the Rio Grande as far as Forts Quitman and Davis, before pushing on to Fort Lancaster. Although the Army of the Gulf was withdrawn to participate in the Red River campaign, Union forces held on to El Paso and Brazos Santiago until the end of the war. At the end of the conflict, the federal government invaded the Texas coast with thirty-nine thousand troops in nine divisions and occupied dozens of communities in eastern, central, and southern Texas— literally seizing control of the state and its lines of communication.[50]

While the naval blockade and Texas coastal operations during the war did not compel the state to surrender, it did force Texas to maintain a significant force to guard against the threat. It also had an adverse effect on the morale of some Texas troops. Lieutenant Volney Ellis, for example, while serving in Louisiana with the Twelfth Texas Infantry, believed the federals would capture Hallettsville in 1863 and thus wrote: "My home and little family at once thrown outside the line of protection. Truly this is a gloomy picture. . . ." Worse yet, he had to console his wife and calm her fears of a slave insurrection and retribution in the event of a successful Union invasion. Federal operations also restricted coastal commerce. Texas' administration was forced to organize complicated procedures for moving cattle and cotton across the Rio Grande into Mexico—there to be traded via Havana under the Mexican flag, or under that of neutrals such as Great Britain, for delivery to New York and other eastern seaboard textile centers.[51]

At the end of the Civil War more than fifty thousand federal troops under Maj. Gen. Philip H. Sheridan marched into Texas from the east or landed on the Texas coast. The bulk of the force was initially deployed along the lower Rio Grande to show opposition to Archduke Maximilian's regime in Mexico. As French rule collapsed and the majority of Sheridan's volunteer regiments mustered out and returned home, Union forces remaining in Texas were committed to influencing domestic politics, enforcing federal laws, and protecting newly freed slaves—activities that took priority over frontier security, especially after passage of the Reconstruction Acts in March, 1867.[52]

This focus on civil-military affairs and internal security put half of the federal soldiers near major population centers in east and central Texas. At

Marshall, soldiers of the Eighth Illinois Volunteer Infantry found a barter economy, the citizens paying taxes in kind with bacon, beef, and produce. Near the Sabine River, when a Seventh Indiana Cavalry officer offered a farmer paper "greenbacks" for peaches and melons, the Texan "seemed very anxious to know whether such currency would pay his taxes." At Port Lavaca, Ohio volunteer infantrymen discovered government coffee and sugar to be as good as money when trading for melons and sweet potatoes. Although inflation had created a cash-poor Texas economy and wartime labor and material shortages had crippled goods production, many troops were proximate to fairly well-developed and undamaged lines of communication. This eased the burden of logistics in Texas for army quartermasters. However, general resentment toward occupation troops, coupled with legitimate concerns over the Indian threat on the frontier, prompted Gov. James W. Throckmorton to appeal to Sheridan and the secretary of war in September, 1866 to send troops to defend the western portions of the state. A skeptical Sheridan, believing the Indian dangers exaggerated and increasingly concerned over the lack of civil justice in the interior of Texas, eventually yielded to political pressure, committing the Fourth and Sixth Cavalry regiments to the frontier line in the late fall.[53]

By late 1866, army occupation in Texas covered much of the state east of the frontier line. This brought the reopening of the antebellum posts of Fort Brown, Ringgold Barracks, Fort McIntosh on the Rio Grande Line, and Camp Verde and Forts Martin Scott, Inge, Clark, Mason, and Bliss on the frontier. In spite of Reconstruction duties in east and central Texas in 1867, the army pushed the frontier operation westward by abandoning Fort Martin Scott and occupying Forts Belknap, Chadbourne, Lancaster, Stockton, Davis, and Camp Hudson. Additionally, two new posts were constructed: Fort Griffin on the Clear Fork of the Brazos in July, 1867, and Fort Concho on the Middle Fork of the Concho River in December. In 1868 the army closed Forts Belknap and Chadbourne but reopened the antebellum posts of Forts McKavett, Quitman, and Duncan and constructed a new post, Fort Richardson, on Lost Creek, a tributary of the Trinity at Jacksboro. Forts Inge and Mason were closed in 1869, followed by the abandonment of Fort Lancaster in 1871. However, the army continued to maintain the series of old antebellum posts and three new forts: Richardson, Concho, and Griffin. Fort Elliott, located on the North Fork of the Red River, was established in the far northeast Panhandle in February, 1875.[54]

New Orleans was the main supply depot for the Southwest during the period 1866 to 1874, generally forwarding supplies by water to the Texas coast. However, the waterborne route had its own vulnerabilities. This was demonstrated in the summer of 1871 when a cholera quarantine forced Texas ports to turn away New Orleans vessels, disrupting the state's logistical system. Along with the coastal transfer points at Indianola and Brazos Santiago, the most important supply depots in Texas were San Antonio, Austin, Fort Brown and Jefferson.[55]

In 1866 the army established a sizable quartermaster and subsistence depot at Jefferson in far northeast Texas that continued supply operations until it closed on May 31, 1870. Jefferson was a deepwater port created by the backwater of the great logjam on the upper Red River, which in turn filled Cypress Bayou. Operating out of three rented brick buildings, Jefferson received stores and supplies from New Orleans via an eight-hundred-mile water route up the Red River and Cypress Bayou, procuring shipments of rations from the East coast through Galveston to the rail terminus at Calvert. By the time it closed, the Southern Pacific had reached Marshall, just sixteen miles distant by wagon. Jefferson in 1870 mainly supplied rations to Fort Griffin and Fort Richardson by contracted wagon. Ironically, Corps of Engineers efforts to clear the great log raft on the Red River beginning in 1873 dried up the deepwater channel to Jefferson, making the depot useless for port activities by 1882.[56]

The Austin depot, reestablished inside the city in late 1865, received supplies at the Texas Central rail terminus at Brenham, 110 miles distant, as well as by contracted wagon direct from the coast at Indianola and from San Antonio. Austin supplied stores and rations by commercial freighter to Forts Griffin and Richardson, and to the temporary posts at Waco and Corsicana.[57]

Receiving stores and rations from New Orleans, the Fort Brown supply depot transferred goods by river steamer twice a month to the Rio Grande post of Ringgold Barracks and from there by wagon to Fort McIntosh, much as it did in the antebellum era. Fort Brown had three subposts: Clarksville, Point Isabel, and Brazos Santiago. Located at the mouth of the Rio Grande, Clarksville was a small customs house, Point Isabel was primarily a hospital site, and Brazos Santiago a storage and transfer point with a government wharf and warehouse.[58]

Union volunteer forces of the Fifty-ninth Illinois Infantry under the command of Col. P. Sidney Post occupied San Antonio on September 20, 1865. It would be an additional fifteen months— December 20, 1866—before regular army troops returned to the city. The first regular soldiers to take station were from the Thirty-fifth Infantry Regiment, commanded by Capt. and Bvt. Lt. Col. Edwin C. Mason. The great quartermaster and subsistence depot at San Antonio went into operation in late 1865, receiving its supplies by contracted wagon through Indianola. Renting over twenty thousand dollars worth of buildings per year, the depot in turn shipped by contracted wagon to the Austin depot, to the Texas interior, and to the frontier posts of Forts Griffin, Richardson, Concho, McKavett, Clark, Inge, Duncan, Stockton, Davis, Quitman, and Bliss. The only posts that San Antonio did not supply were those on the lower Rio Grande.[59]

San Antonio was subject to the same accumulation of shoddy war surplus as Fort Brown had been after the Mexican War. Seven years after the Civil War, one disgruntled inspector reported finding great "quantities of worthless articles . . . wagons, the hubs of the wheels of which seem to have been of the most perishable material . . . entirely useless . . . 150,000 lbs, of horse-shoes of such enormous sizes that they cannot be used . . . 8,000 pounds of so-called . . . paint, and which probably was never worth its transportation." The inspector also found barrels and buckets of such frail construction that they seemed like they were "of the kind made for children's toys."[60]

In the first several years after the war there was renewed debate within the army Quartermaster's Department as to the most suitable location for the Texas supply center. The arguments raised were similar to those voiced in 1853. Texas' chief quartermaster, Bvt. Lt. Col. James G. C. Lee, wrote an assessment in 1868 favoring San Antonio over Austin, Indianola, or Corpus Christi—all of which, in his opinion, had been tried in the past and "found impracticable." Lee described San Antonio as the hub of all points, adding, "transportation can always be obtained here, it being the great centre of freighters; not only for Texas, but Chihuahua, and in fact all northern Mexico." By 1870, the quartermaster general, Maj. Gen. Montgomery C. Meigs, settled the impasse by ordering the Austin depot closed and moved to San Antonio. He observed that "San Antonio is the natural center of interior commerce of Texas, and the proper point for the supply of the posts on the Indian and Mexican frontiers of that state."[61]

San Antonio emerged victorious once again when Congress in 1870 appropriated the money to build a large-scale permanent depot in the city. San Antonio depot construction finally began in June, 1876 and was finished in July, 1877. Known as the "Quadrangle," the massive logistics center became operational in 1877, allowing the chief quartermaster to close down operations at the Alamo compound and to transfer stores to the new depot. An upper story was added to the Quadrangle to house the Department of Texas headquarters in 1878. By 1891 the post, named Fort Sam Houston in 1890, had completed a modernization project to include a telephone system.[62]

In 1868, Quartermaster General Meigs returned to the late-antebellum policy of centralized freight contracting for moving army logistics. Harden B. Adams and Edwin de Lacy Wickes, of the San Antonio firm of Adams and Wickes, secured the major portion of the contract to supply Texas forts, retaining much of the monopoly for a decade. The post–Civil War logistical system in Texas roughly followed the model established in the antebellum years, although due to the unsettled nature of the country, it took a full decade to get it into efficient operation. In January, 1868, because of poor trail conditions and severe weather, freight contractors failed to deliver supplies to Fort Concho—leaving the post quartermaster with insufficient animal forage and the garrison without coffee, sugar, or flour in the dead of winter. Experiences such as this taught post commanders to stockpile enough supplies for several months. A second problem was the lack of maps, developed routes, and knowledgeable guides for trains. As late as 1872, an officer reported, "It will hardly be credited when I state that none of the teamsters in my train agreed as to the distances traveled daily, or which were the right roads between San Antonio & Fort McIntosh, tho' all but one had been over the road several times."[63]

Supplying operational mounted patrols in the field represented a different set of problems for logisticians. Combat patrols on the Texas frontier, as they were elsewhere on the western frontier, were limited in duration and range by the requirement for water and animal forage. In the antebellum era the use of pack mules on the Texas frontier was common. During the same period, patrols tended to be fairly small, averaging twenty-five soldiers, and generally were away from the fort—the logistical base—about two weeks. In the post–Civil War era, the army made more frequent use of long-range, large-column operations and had to overcome the logistical challenges associated with the forage requirements of several hundred horses. Cavalry columns working their way across the Staked Plains often were accompanied by a train of twenty to thirty wagons. Recognizing the difficulties of logistical sustainment for long-term campaigning in far-western Texas, a number of frontier commanders began the practice of establishing forward field supply bases prior to a campaign. Lieutenant Henry W. Lawton, the tireless quartermaster of Col. Ranald S. Mackenzie's Fourth Cavalry, established a forward supply base on the Salt Fork of the Brazos River for Mackenzie's 1871 campaign into West Texas, and built a second one on the Freshwater Fork of the Brazos for the 1872 campaign. During the Red River War of 1874–75, the Fourth Cavalry again used a field forward supply base on the Freshwater Fork of the Brazos, and Col. Nelson A. Miles established a supply dump for the Sixth Cavalry and Fifth Infantry on the North Fork of the Red River in December, 1874—a site that eventually became Fort Elliott.[64]

The army had about 15 percent of its force in Texas in 1873—4,450 soldiers in three cavalry and four infantry regiments stationed at fifteen posts. Major changes in Texas' logistical system came in fairly rapid order in the ten years between 1874 and 1884, brought on by the coming of the railroads and the end of the Indian wars on the state frontier. The Missouri, Kansas, and Texas Railroad had reached Denison by 1873, offering a fast, efficient means of transportation of troops and supplies into the Department of Texas. Within a year, the railroad had naturally combined with steamships to supply Texas forts. By 1875, rations were being sent by rail from New Orleans eighty miles west to Brashear City, Louisiana. There they were loaded aboard coastal steamers, which sailed 377 miles to Indianola. They were once again put on trains for the seventy-five mile trip to the rail terminus at Cuero, then moved by contract wagon eighty miles to San Antonio for redistribution to posts. From its origin at New Orleans, a single lot of rations took twenty-five days to travel 738 miles to Fort Clark or forty-six days to cover the 1,006 miles to Fort Stockton. Forts Griffin and Richardson received stores both by wagon from San Antonio and directly from St. Louis via the Missouri, Kansas, and Texas Railroad to Dension and thence by contracted wagon.[65]

In the end, both the railroad and nature combined to supplant the steamship with the iron horse as the crucial means of logistical lift in the Texas theater of operations. In September, 1874 a hurricane swept the south Texas coast, destroying the wharf and government warehouse at the reliable old logistics point of Brazos Santiago, ending its use. A year later, on September 16, 1875, a hurricane wrecked Indianola, all but ending the life of that once-crucial supply point. The supply depot at Austin ceased operations in early 1872, and the post of Austin was completely abandoned in August, 1875. San Antonio thus emerged as the sole center of logistics for the Department of Texas, although Fort Elliott—established in the far northern Panhandle in February, 1875—was supplied by Fort Leavenworth, Kansas, via railroad to Fort Dodge and by contracted wagon for the final 176 miles to the post.[66]

The railroad came to San Antonio in February, 1877. However, as it would be six more years before trains would cross west Texas, the quartermaster depot continued to maintain its contract system for long-haul commercial freighting. Although contracted Texas freighters distributed the majority of supplies to the forts, the depot retained a sizable army wagon train. The army used government wagons to sustain supply operations for the large army columns operating in the field and along the Mexican Border, as well as for moving unit equipment from post to post as regiments relocated. In 1879 the San Antonio depot had a train of four hundred mules, twenty-eight carts, and 128 wagons of various sorts. To operate this train required a trainmaster and 114 citizen employees, such as teamsters and herders, and a wagon maintenance crew of sixteen citizen blacksmiths, wheelwrights, and other mechanics. The annual pay of these 130 civilians amounted to $53,124. To feed the animals of this train, the chief quartermaster at San Antonio purchased $87,216 worth of hay, corn, and oats. It thus cost the army $140,340 to operate this wagon train out of San Antonio in 1879—most of it going directly into the local economy.[67]

Texas' Indian wars ended by the early 1880s. The power of the Comanche and Kiowa tribes was broken during the Red River War of 1874–75, and the few remaining hostile Apaches were pushed into Mexico by Col. Benjamin H. Grierson's final Trans-Pecos campaign in 1880.

Although Camp Peña Colorado opened in August, 1879, along the expected west Texas railroad route—as did Fort Hancock in April, 1881—the twilight of the Indian campaigns in Texas brought a host of fort closures: Fort Richardson in May, 1878; Fort Griffin in May, 1881; Fort Quitman in 1882; Fort McKavett in June, 1883; Fort Duncan in 1883; Fort Stockton in June, 1886; and Fort Concho in June, 1889. In January of 1883 the Southern Pacific Railroad traversed the entire Trans-Pecos, and by 1884 all of the remaining Texas forts were within short-haul distance of the rails, ending the great era of long-distance commercial wagon freighters in Texas.[68]

By 1889 quartermasters were moving 75 percent of army supplies in Texas by rail. Within six years, use of the railroad allowed the commissary general to end the practice of purchasing Texas cattle on the hoof and to ship frozen beef to every mess hall in the state. In 1889 Texas troop strength dropped to 1,904 soldiers—7 percent of the regular army—and military leaders, long arguing the centralized supply efficiency of large garrisons, pressed to consolidate units in fewer posts at regimental strength. This policy brought a new round of fort closures: Fort Elliott in October, 1890; Fort Davis in June, 1891 after three decades as a key military site; Camp Peña Colorado in January, 1893; Camp Del Rio in 1896, and Fort Hancock in December, 1895.[69]

By the end of the nineteenth century, Texas was home to 1 percent of the army—twelve hundred soldiers belonging to a cavalry regiment, an infantry regiment, and several artillery batteries. They occupied the interior posts of Forts Sam Houston and Clark; the Rio Grande posts of Forts Bliss, Duncan, McIntosh, Ringgold, and Brown; and the three Galveston-area coastal fortifications at Forts San Jacinto, Crockett, and Travis. In 1873 Congress had approved a policy of purchasing rather than leasing army posts and, after a quarter-century of legal wrangling, the federal government owned all of its Texas forts.[70]

Texas army logisticians, in building and maintaining a supply system to sustain the operational force, helped create a dozen Texas towns with a fort–satellite village relationship. They also directly affected the state's commercial and agricultural life. Between 1849 and 1900 the Quartermaster's Department expended over 32 million dollars in the state. As outlined in Table 3, 28 percent of these funds went for the purchase of animal forage, 21.2 percent to transportation, 13.5 percent to fort construction and repair, 9.9 percent to the salaries of citizen employees, 3.8 percent to buy horses and mules, 1.1 percent for rents and leases, and the remainder for miscellaneous expenses. Subsequent chapters will demonstrate how each of the areas of quartermaster activity made a significant and unique contribution to Texas' economy.[71]

The historical record indicates that quartermaster officers and other army logisticians in Texas were mostly honest and as efficient as circumstances permitted. Incidents of corruption were rare, most often involving suspected misuse or violation of army regulations rather than outright theft or graft. In 1851 Quartermaster General Jesup sent an inspector to Texas specifically to look for corruption and abuse, but the officer found little to report. Typical of the few cases on record is that of Capt. William K. Van Bokkelen, an 1843 West Point graduate and quartermaster of Indianola in 1857. Van Bokkelen was charged with a number of specifications. These included using his wagons and teamsters to move houses in the town, scheming with his civilian clerk to run a private partnership to contract rations for the army, and using his wagons to transport voters to get his friend the clerk elected as the county judge. The court-martial found him innocent of the major charges, but guilty on some of the minor facts of the case. Attaching "no design of wrong," the court sentenced him to a written reprimand, "believing the accused to have acted more from thoughtlessness than from any intention of wrong."[72]

A better-known illustration is the post–Civil War example of 2d Lt. Henry O. Flipper, the first African-American to graduate from West Point. In 1880 Flipper, a Tenth Cavalry line officer, drew the unlucky assignment of acting assistant quartermaster and acting assistant commissary of subsistence at Fort Davis. Flipper was but one of dozens of inexperienced young officers who had to perform this duty on the Texas frontier. In March, 1881, Flipper discovered he was short $1,440 in post commissary funds, which he believed may have been stolen by a servant. Flipper covered the deficit with a personal check, but during weekly inspections led the post commander, Col. William R.

Shafter, to believe that his status of accounts was in proper order. The deficit was discovered during an August, 1881 audit. Flipper's woes were compounded by the fact that he lacked sufficient bank funds to cover the check. Flipper was acquitted of embezzlement in the ensuing court-martial, but he was convicted and dismissed from the service for conduct unbecoming an officer because he lied to his post commander. This was one of many instances on the Texas frontier in which an untrained junior-officer logistician was held liable for irregular practices with government funds. In most cases it was a matter of carelessness or ignorance of regulations rather than out-and-out corruption.[73]

CHAPTER 3

Transportation

Prairie Schooners, Steamers,
and the Iron Horse

The Quartermaster's Department was the nineteenth-century army agency responsible for the movement of all material and personnel. Transportation costs, particularly on the prerail frontier, were an enormous burden on the quartermaster general's operating budget. Of the $32.2 million the Quartermaster's Department spent in Texas in the five decades between 1849 and 1900, about $6.8 million went toward transportation, representing 21.2 percent of total logistical expenditures, the second highest economic category after animal forage. This total expenditure reflects both government wagon and freight contracted for shipment by private companies. As illustrated in Tables 4 and 5, hired or contracted transport expenditures reached a total of $3.8 million or about 55 percent of the transportation total. Of that total, wagon contracts accounted for 74 percent, rail for 15 percent, and water transport for 11 percent of the contract dollar outlay.

WAGON FREIGHT

When Brig. Gen. Zachary Taylor's army arrived in Texas in 1845, just prior to the Mexican War, the state had little in the way of four-wheeled wagon transport, the two-wheeled *carreta* being the dominant form of hauling. To meet the needs of the war, the army imported several hundred Philadelphia-made wagons for operations. These were shipped disassembled and put together by a team of carpenters at Port Lavaca. Taylor's army used about 150 of these wagons and another 125 went to Brig. Gen. John E. Wool's Center Division forming at San Antonio. Taylor's quartermasters augmented their transportation requirements with Mexican ox carts and pack trains of up to fifteen

TABLE 4.

ARMY EXPENDITURES IN TEXAS FOR WAGON,
WATER, AND RAIL TRANSPORTATION
CONTRACTS, 1849–1897

Period	Texas Wagon-Freight Contracts	Steamship & Sail Contracts in and to Texas	Payments to Texas Railroads
1849–1861	$620,000	$192,000	$0
1869–1879	$2,000,000	$200,000	$50,000
1880–1889	$120,700	$33,800	$382,800
1890–1897	$75,800	$12,400	$137,900
Totals	$2,816,500	$438,200	$570,700

Source: Calculated from a survey of each year's "Report of the Quartermaster General of the Army" in the annual *Report of the Secretary of War,* 1849–1900.

TABLE 5.

ARMY FREIGHT SHIPMENTS IN TEXAS
WITH SAMPLE TONNAGES AND YEARS

Year	By Wagon	By Water	By Railroad
1849	80%	20%	0%
1850–1851	90% (2,663 tons)	10% (303 tons)	0%
1883	37% (1,824 tons)	6% (279 tons)	57% (2,804 tons)
1887	33% (1,961 tons)	5% (299 tons)	62% (3,792 tons)
1889	23%	3%	74%

Source: Calculated from a survey of each year's "Report of the Quartermaster General of the Army," in the annual *Report of the Secretary of War,* 1849–1900; from the National Archives, Record Group 92, Records of the Office of the Quartermaster General, Entry 1245, "Register of Contracts, 1871–1912"; and from the annual Senate and House of Representatives *Executive Documents,* "War Department Contracts."

hundred mules. With little Texas labor to be had, the army imported team-sters from the Mississippi Valley and from the eastern seaboard. One ex-ample serves to illustrate the scale of transportation requirements for the army when it crossed the border into Mexico. In October, 1846, a train of 150 wagons from Point Isabel to Monterrey hauled five hundred thousand ra-tions for Taylor's army—enough to feed his troops for ninety days, allowing an average of 10 percent for spoilage and waste. The army's use of imported four-wheeled, mule-drawn wagons fundamentally altered the traditional nature of freighting in Texas.[1]

After the Mexican War, the supply of Texas forts and the movement of army freight became a significant economic multiplier to Texas' growing long-haul wagon freight industry. One historical analysis of the 1850 census indicates that of San Antonio's 3,168 inhabitants, 170 were Hispanic surnamed "cartmen," 45 were Anglo-surnamed independent "wagoners" and "wagon masters," and 128 wagoners and wagon masters were working for the army Quartermaster's Department. In this census, 343 Bexareños were enumerated in the freighting occupation in San Antonio, about twice that of "laborer," and seven times that of other occupations such as carpenters, stonemasons, or clerks. On his trip through San Antonio in 1854, Frederick Law Olmsted observed that freighting goods from the coast to the city "forms the principal support of the Mexican population."[2]

Prior to the Mexican War, freighting in Texas was the province of the ox-drawn *carreta,* a ponderous, two-wheeled cottonwood cart six feet wide and fifteen feet long, perched on an oak axle anchoring ten inch-thick wooden wheels that stood seven feet high. The larger carts, pulled by six yoke of oxen, could haul about thirty-five hundred pounds. Smaller carts, with four-foot wheels and three yoke of oxen, hauled eight hundred pounds. Mexican carts continued in use but the war brought to Texas both the army wagon and the great American freighting wagons such as early versions of the post–Civil War "prairie schooner." The six-mule, three-and-one-half by ten-foot government wagon could haul two or three thousand pounds, depending on surface conditions, whereas the rugged four-and-one-half by twenty-four-foot commercial freighter hauled seven thousand pounds when drawn by ten mules.[3]

The threat posed by thieves and Indian raiders made freighting on the Texas frontier a dangerous enterprise if adequate security was not taken. A typical dozen-wagon train had a wagon master and twenty or so heavily armed drivers who were well versed in the drill of forming a circular corral with the wagons as a defensive measure for men and mules when halted. Freighters always tried to make the most of back-haul after delivery to a post. August Santleben, who reestablished the San Antonio–Chihuahua, Mexico, trade route after the Civil War, occasionally hauled government freight to forts. Santleben recorded that in 1872, after a delivery to Fort Davis, he took his empty wagons to the Pecos Salt Lake fifteen miles north of Horsehead Crossing, shoveled up fifty thousand pounds of surface salt, and sold it for a nickle a pound upon his return to San Antonio.[4]

There was an evolving pattern to army freighting in Texas. From 1848 to 1854, government wagons with soldier and civilian-hired teamsters moved the bulk of military cargo, with only an occasional civilian-contracted freight run. Beginning in 1855, one or two civilian contractors moved the majority of army freight, and in 1857 a single contractor hauled all of the army's Texas freight. In the post–Civil War years 1868 to 1880, two or three major civilian wagon contractors moved most of the long-haul government freight. After the period 1881 to 1884, when the railroad reached the vicinity of most Texas forts, contracted freighting was limited to five or six individuals who ran a short-haul wagon service from the rail terminus to the local post.[5]

When the army occupied the Texas frontier in 1849, the Quartermaster's Department made only two formal contracts for freighting: one with Henry P. Howard to transport twenty thousand rations from Port Lavaca to Austin, and another with George T. Howard to haul the Eighth Infantry's baggage from Port Lavaca to San Antonio. The army maintained a large supply of wagons and mules to conduct its own freighting, but Quartermaster General Jesup was trying to convince Congress that civilian-contracted wagon freighting would be less expensive and more efficient. Jesup and other officers argued that the army's lack of expertise, the drain on soldier labor, the cash investment required for wagons and draft animals, the maintenance cost, and the money required to feed vast amounts of winter forage to unemployed mules all placed an unnecessary burden on the government. One officer estimated that the cost of forage for the teams represented 40 percent of the cost of a freighting expedition. The Texas department commander, Col. Persifor F. Smith, fully supported the move toward civilian teamsters. He reported in 1852 that soldier wagoners were unreliable because "they get drunk, neglect their animals." As further evidence of their malfeasance, he cited the case of a group of soldier teamsters in Corpus Christi that had sold off the forage it was supposed to feed its teams.[6]

Radiating from the great quartermaster depot established at San Antonio in 1849, army mules and government wagon caravans plodded the rough tracks of Texas, moving cargo from the coast, trying to keep up with the demands of supplying the far-flung frontier posts. Most trains required an armed escort, which further eroded the combat power in understrength frontier companies. In 1850, Department Commander George M. Brooke extended army protection to private freighters by inviting their trains to accompany escorted army caravans and share in the shield of the military escort. The scale of the army supply operation is reflected in the 1851 report of Maj. Edwin B. Babbitt, the chief quartermaster at San Antonio. Babbitt, maintained 115 wagons, 344 mules, 125 horses, and 128 teamsters to meet the basic logistical requirements of the 2,819 troops in Texas. The government wagons and mules averaged eighteen trips during the year, hauling 1.9 million pounds of rations, stores, baggage, and supplies. The demands being greater than army resources, Babbitt had to hire a number of civilian freighters. It took ninety-eight two-wheeled ox carts to haul 254,900 pounds of forage and rations, and eighty-seven wagons from private contractors were needed to shuttle supplies to a large-scale expedition led by Capt. William J. Hardee operating between the Rio Grande and Nueces Rivers. During the period 1849 through 1851 the San Antonio depot moved more than 5.3 million pounds of supplies, but only about 12 percent of it was contracted to private Texas freighters.[7]

Despite Secretary of War Charles M. Conrad's reluctance to hire civilian contractors, the measure proved necessary to solve the most difficult logistical problem in Texas: furnishing Post Opposite El Paso, soon to be called Fort Bliss, located 585 miles and three months by wagon from San Antonio. For much of the antebellum period, Fort Bliss belonged to the military department governing New Mexico rather than Texas, and was supplied by the Santa Fe Trail from Fort Leavenworth, Kansas. However, in 1850, working in conjunction with a number of commercial trains opening a trade route from the Texas coast to Chihuahua, Mexico, the Texas quartermaster contracted to haul eight hundred thousand pounds of rations and stores to the post. The deal involved El Paso businessman Benjamin Franklin Coons, San Antonio merchants Nathaniel C. Lewis and John D. Groesbeeck, and L. G. Capers. The "Great Train" they formed consisted of several hundred wagons, 450 civilian teamsters, and 175 soldiers under the command of Bvt. Maj. John T. Sprague. Unfortunately, the supplies suffered about 40 percent spoilage during the three-month journey.[8]

In the summer of 1851, a 150-wagon government train commanded by Capt. Samuel G. French made a similar supply run to El Paso. French reported that smaller trains were more efficient, that civilian-contracted freighting was less expensive than government wagons, and that it was cheaper to supply El Paso via the Santa Fe Trail than through San Antonio. In addition to the $100,000 the government spent supplying El Paso, an additional $12,000 was expended on a contract to ship four hundred thousand pounds of freight brought in through Houston for Forts Gates and Worth. Alarmed at the growing $1.8 million bill for freighting to western posts, the secretary of war made every effort to cut costs. No contracts were let in 1852, and only a few small contracted trains made the trek to El Paso in 1853 and 1854—including one from San Antonio carrying two hundred thousand pounds.[9]

By 1855, Congress and the secretary of war had recognized the fiscal efficiency of civilian freighting, changing the pattern of supply in Texas and the western frontier to one of large-scale contract hauling with one or two bonded firms. This would remain the pattern until the coming of the railroad in the 1880s.[10]

Texas wagon freight contracts for 1855 reflect this policy change. The freighting titan of Majors and Russell, operating from Fort Leavenworth, received a two-year contract to move up to 2.5 million pounds to the primary western forts and to supply the Texas post of El Paso. Although the San Antonio quartermaster, Maj. James Belger, continued to piecemeal hire the occasional independent train, he let two major contracts to supply Texas posts—both requiring posted bonds of more than a hundred thousand dollars. The first contract, issued on May 29, 1855, went to George H. Giddings and J. R. Jefferson, who agreed to haul freight from Indianola to San Antonio, and from that depot to Forts Duncan, Inge, Clark, Davis, and Bliss, plus Fort Fillmore, New Mexico. The agreed price was commensurate with the distance to the posts. The second contract, issued on November 17, went to George T. Howard for moving army supplies in lots up to two hundred fifty thousand pounds on fifteen days' notice from the San Antonio depot to Austin, Forts McKavett, Chadbourne, and Belknap, and any other new posts established in Texas. Failure to deliver would result in a fine of three dollars per day for each thousand pounds. An interesting aspect of the close cooperation of Texas freighters is that two of the sureties on Giddings's bond were none other than his major competitors, George T. Howard and Duncan C. Ogden, who were to share 50 percent of the profit. Although Howard received the lesser of the two contracts for 1855, he soon emerged as the dominant army freighter in antebellum Texas.[11]

Forty-one-year-old George Thomas "Tom" Howard moved to Texas from Washington, D.C., in 1836. He rose to lieutenant colonel in the Texas army, was a veteran of the Plum Creek Fight and the disastrous Santa Fe and Somervell expeditions, and served in the Texas Volunteer Cavalry in the Mexican War. In 1848 he married the niece of an army surgeon, and in 1850 secured an appointment as the federal superintendent of Texas Indian agents, resigning the post in 1855. In 1840 Howard and his partner, Duncan C. Ogden, opened a trading store in San Antonio, an enterprise that functioned, as did all commerce in the Republic of Texas, on personal vouchers, discounted promissory notes, land script, and general credit. When the U.S. government paid off half of Texas' public debt of $10 million in 1850, the state was able to pay its debtors in cash. Howard collected $27,000 owed for services and supply to various Texas military adventures and promptly launched into major business enterprises, expanding his San Antonio store and buying thousands of acres of real estate. By 1856, Howard had—on a foundation of personal acumen, federal money, and army contracts—begun to establish the largest freighting enterprise in Texas prior to the Civil War.[12]

In 1856 the army added Forts Clark and Bliss to Howard's contract, and in 1857 it gave him one-year contracts for all the posts in Texas as well as the responsibility of moving supplies from the port of Indianola to the San Antonio depot. In 1857 Majors and Russell dropped Fort Bliss from their contract at Fort Leavenworth, leaving Howard a complete monopoly on army freight in the state. Howard ran nearly eight hundred ox and mule teams, averaging a profit of $30,000 to $50,000 per year, and by 1860 had $150,000 in real and personal property, as well as nine slaves. Howard retained his monopoly until December, 1860, when James Duff aced him out of the general freight contract, while Russell, Majors, and Waddell regained the contract for Fort Bliss.[13]

James Duff, a Scotsman, was a minor figure in army logistics in Texas until 1860. He had been the post sutler at Fort Belknap in 1856, providing moderate quantities of corn, hay, and flour to the post from 1857 to 1860. He also shipped corn to Camp Colorado and Fort Chadbourne, and flour to Fort Mason in 1857. In 1859 he shipped eight hundred head of cattle to Fort Bliss. In late 1860 Duff not only received a monopoly for freighting supplies to most posts in Texas, he contracted to perform the duties of quartermaster at the Indianola depot as well. With war clouds brewing, it is ironic that the army put the bulk of its logistical network in Texas directly under the control of a former enlisted deserter and zealous Southern sympathizer. The exodus of the army from Texas three months later ended Duff's monopoly but he went on to gain infamy as a state military officer. Duff was responsible for the wholesale hanging of Unionists in Fredericksburg, and his company murdered nine wounded German Unionist prisoners on the Nueces River in August, 1862. After the war, Duff fled to Denver, Colorado, where he became influential until word of his desertion and the details of the Dutch Battleground Murders became public. He then escaped to London, where he ultimately settled.[14]

In the wake of the Civil War, which shattered Texas' economy, the business of freighting in the state was eventually revitalized with the help of government contracts. Initially after the war the army had a surplus of war-weary wagons and, as it did after the Mexican War, conducted much of its own internal transportation. By 1868, the postwar reduction in funds and manpower led Quartermaster General Montgomery Meigs to reinstate the late-antebellum system of large-scale contracts for army freight in Texas. George Berg of Mora, New Mexico, gained the contract to deliver to Texas posts west of 105 degrees longitude, and the San Antonio firm of Adams and Wickes provided transport to the remaining Texas forts. From the port of Indianola in 1868 the army shipped 7.2 million pounds of freight to the San Antonio depot and 1.4 million pounds to the Austin depot. Five million pounds of supplies were transshipped from San Antonio to Texas forts, while Austin provided a million pounds. The army moved a total of 14.8 million pounds of freight in Texas in 1868—95 percent of it by contract freighters—for $500,000.[15]

Harden B. Adams came to San Antonio from New Jersey in 1850 at age seventeen, serving as a Confederate quartermaster major in the Civil War. In 1868 he formed a freighting partnership with Edwin de Lacy Wickes, who had made a sizable fortune in Chicago real estate. Adams and Wickes gained their first big army contract in 1868, executing their duties "with promptitude and vigor," according to the chief Texas quartermaster. The San Antonio firm soon became the dominant business force in army freighting in post–Civil War Texas, gaining a major contract every year over the next decade, and moving into real estate in the 1880s when the railroad superseded wagon freighting.[16]

Adams and Wickes had a few small rivals through the 1870s. Mifflin Kenedy and Richard King, of Kenedy and King, had a steamship contract on the Rio Grande and retained for several years the wagon contract to Fort McIntosh from their water terminus at Fort Ringgold. E. C. Dewey, W. C. Graham, and others secured small contracts for freighting from the expanding east Texas rail terminals. In 1875, for example, Edward Froboese underbid Adams and Wickes for the contract to supply posts in west Texas and along the upper Rio Grande.[17]

By 1881, most Texas freighting contracts were tied to transporting supplies from the nearest rail terminal to a post. The result was a return to a system of multiple contracts, rather than a large monopoly. Nine separate freight contracts provided for Texas posts. Fort Elliott, located in the far northern Panhandle, was supplied from Fort Dodge, Kansas; Fort Bliss from Las Vegas, New Mexico; Fort Davis from the rail junction at Fort Worth, and so on. The San Antonio depot still contracted to supply most of the

Texas forts, but the growth of railroads began to greatly reduce the cost of transporting freight by wagon.[18]

The end of long-distance army freighting in Texas came in 1884 when virtually every Texas post except Fort Elliott was within short-haul distance of a railroad. Four or five surviving freighters continued to make a living on these small contracts. The army paid $10,473 to Jackson E. Labatt for the eighty-five-mile run from Abilene to Fort Concho. August Santleben and Edward Froboese managed to earn $2,000 per year in 1885 and in 1886 engaged in local hauling around San Antonio for the quartermaster depot. Daniel Murphy and Sons earned $5,704 hauling army supplies over the twenty-four miles from the railroad at Murphyville to Fort Davis. By 1890, the army paid less than $5,000 for Texas wagon freighting, and small local contracts continued to be awarded on a minor scale until the turn of the century. Despite the meager profit involved, as was the case with Daniel Murphy, the relationship represented a continuation of the long-term commercial-military cooperative spirit in Texas, and highlighted the multiple roles contractors sometimes played.

Daniel Murphy came to Fort Davis in 1857, starting a 160-acre ranch near the post and opening a saloon and store. He quickly earned a reputation as a solid citizen, gaining the respect of the garrison, which continued after the Civil War. Murphy steadily expanded his real estate holdings. He eventually owned a sawmill in the Toyah Valley and a spring near the railroad. The latter was christened Murphyville in 1883 but was renamed Alpine five years later. Murphy sold the government a sizable portion of the land that became the eastern part of the Fort Davis military reservation, and donated a site in town to the Catholic Church. Largely because of the prosperity brought by the fort, Daniel Murphy joined the ranks of the local frontier elite, genially opening his home to soldiers and giving away four daughters in marriage to army officers.[19]

A number of factors affected the price of wagon transportation in Texas. In the early antebellum years the initial shortage of labor and wagons, coupled with the high risk of loss on the hazardous routes, made freighting relatively expensive. That expense soon leveled off thanks to the efficiency of competitive bidding, large-scale contracts, and the development of adequate road networks. Finally, and most importantly, railroads dramatically lowered the cost and all but destroyed long-haul wagon freighting in Texas.

The specific cost of wagon freighting in the state was primarily an exponent of the mileage or distance to be hauled. From 1849 to 1855 prices were based on fixed rate per hundred pounds for a known distance to a specified post. Agreements made during the era of large-scale general contracts (1855 to 1881) established a fixed price per one hundred pounds times one hundred miles for a series of posts—for example all posts west of San Antonio, or all posts between two stated lines of longitude. After 1881, when most freighting was between a nearby railhead and a fort, the contracts reverted to the older system of a fixed price per one hundred pounds for a specified short route to a named post.

Adjustments for inflation are not factored into the following examples of freighting prices. Although inflation did moderately affect the price of freighting, its overall significance was not extreme: about 16 percent of the comparative price between 1850 and 1890. The inflation rate for the 1850s was about 9 percent. It leaped to 42 percent during the Civil War years (1861 to 1865), causing a steep increase in transportation costs in the immediate postwar years. The bust cycle and economic panic at the beginning of the 1870s ushered in a decade-long deflationary period of a negative 35 percent, sinking the relative value of the dollar to a level near prewar prices. This deflation, and the minor inflation of the 1880s, represents a total inflation of about 16 percent between 1850 and 1890, the primary span of significant army activities on the Texas frontier.[20]

The cost of freighting in Texas is reflected in a number of general examples examined over the period 1849 to 1890. In 1849 it cost $2 per 100 pounds to move supplies from the Texas coast to San Antonio. In 1855 it cost $1.25 per 100 pounds to cover the 140 miles from the port of Indianola to the San Antonio depot, a price that remained steady throughout the 1850s. In 1868 it cost $1.70 per 100 pounds to move goods over the same route, a 27 percent increase over 1855. In 1873 the rate from Victoria—the terminus of the Gulf, Western Texas, and Pacific Railroad—to San Antonio was $1.08 per 100 pounds, a decrease of 14 percent over 1855. In 1881, the last year of contracted wagon shipments into San Antonio, wagon-delivered freight cost the army 64¢ per 100 pounds from Victoria, a decrease of 49 percent from 1855. Transshipping goods the 130 miles from the San Antonio depot to Fort Clark cost $1.43 per 100 pounds in 1856. The cost fell 24 percent, to $1.10 per 100 pounds, by 1859. In 1869 it cost $2.13 per 100 pounds to ship goods over the same route, up 25 percent. Costs were down again in 1875—by 29 percent to $1.02 per hundredweight. When the railroad reached Spofford Junction after 1883, the ten-mile trip cost 12¢ per 100 pounds, lowering the cost of moving goods to Fort Clark by wagon 92 percent from the 1856 price.

The army calculated that Fort Davis, located in remote west Texas, was 465 miles from the San Antonio depot. It cost $7.82 per 100 pounds to ship freight there in 1855. The price remained steady until the post–Civil War years. In 1878 it cost $7 per 100 pounds, a reduction of only 10 percent. By 1884, however, the twenty-four-mile short-haul from the railroad at Murphyville to Fort Davis cost just 19¢ cents per 100 pounds, a reduction of 88 percent from the era of long-haul wagon freighting.[21]

The post–Civil War garrison at Fort Concho, located 215 miles from San Antonio, was supplied in 1869 at cost of $3.50 per 100 pounds. By 1881, it cost 61 percent less: $1.37 per 100 pounds. When the railroad reached Abilene that same year, the eighty-five-mile wagon trip from the railhead cost just 86¢ per 100 pounds, a reduction of 76 percent from the 1869 price. When the railroad reached Ballinger in 1887, the cost of shipping goods to Fort Concho fell to 27¢ per 100 pounds, a 92 percent reduction from the original wagon-freight cost.

The last holdout for long-distance wagon freight was the isolated northern Panhandle post of Fort Elliott, established in 1875. The post was supplied from Fort Dodge, Kansas, 165 miles away, at a cost of $1.79 per 100 pounds in 1877. When the railroad reached Harold, Texas, in 1885, the 145-mile trip cost $1.60 per 100 pounds, an 11 percent reduction. In 1888 Fort Elliott was supplied from the railhead at Miami, Texas, a trip of eighteen miles that cost just 18¢ per 100 pounds, a reduction of 90 percent from the 1877 price.[22]

Texas wagon freighter August Santleben observed that in the early 1880s, when he realized the railroad would extend from San Antonio to El Paso, "I knew my freighting business would be ruined." He quickly sold off his long-haul wagons and animals. By 1888 the establishment of a rail terminus within twenty-five miles of every Texas post meant a reduction of the original pre–Civil War wagon transportation cost of more than 90 percent. In 1868 the Quartermaster's Department spent about $426,000 on wagon transportation in Texas. That figure shrank to only $15,824 by 1888, just 3 percent of the cost two decades previous. This drastic reduction was due primarily to the revolution in frontier army logistics brought by the iron horse. Congress, hoping to gain a budgetary windfall from the lessening requirements for wagon transportation, in 1890 directed the Quartermaster's Department to sell off the majority of the wagons, equipment, and animals it maintained to provide a field supply system for the frontier force. This lost capability, and the subsequent loss of expertise in field logistics, would prove an embarrassment when, at the end of the decade, the War Department struggled to transport and supply an army in a theater largely devoid of rail systems in the Spanish-American War.[23]

Of the $2.8 million the army spent for contracted wagon freighting in

Texas, about $620,000, or 22 percent, was in the antebellum years 1849 to 1860. A total of 137 contracts for wagon freighting were awarded to eighty different individuals, of which thirty-nine contracts to twenty-five individuals were issued during the antebellum years. In spite of Frederick Law Olmsted's observation that freighting was crucial to the economic survival of Texas' Hispanic population, only 3 percent of these army contracts went to persons with Spanish surnames. In effect, Texans of Mexican descent were limited to the labor and teamster levels of army contracted freighting in the state and, with few exceptions were, seldom directly involved in the upper levels of financial management and competitive bidding. Nevertheless, army dollars and military roads were a tremendous boon to the business of moving goods in Texas. More importantly, the general establishment of an efficient overland transportation network within the state, much of it a matter of military necessity, was an economic multiplier that brought an exponential benefit to every form of business in Texas.[24]

Texas-contracted wagon freighting was, for the most part, free of proven cases of corruption, although army officers were generally suspicious of civilian contractors. Quartermaster General Meigs complained in 1871 that Texas transport cost had increased because of straw bidding—a practice in which the lowest approved bidders would disappear, refusing contracts on "frivolous pretext," thus leaving the army stuck with the highest bidders. Lacking clear proof, Meigs did not go so far as to claim there was an outright conspiracy.[25]

The most serious charges of army contractor corruption on the Texas frontier were brought in 1871 and 1872. The scandal involved the largest army freight contracting firm, Adams and Wickes; the department commander, Bvt. Maj. Gen. Joseph J. Reynolds; and the talented but irascible leader of the Fourth Cavalry, Col. Ranald S. Mackenzie. The alleged corruption began in 1869 when Mackenzie, as commander of Fort McKavett, claimed that a load of corn delivered by Adams and Wickes did not meet government specifications. Department Commander Reynolds had his quartermaster pay the firm despite Mackenzie's protests. Later, in March, 1871, Mackenzie, then at Fort Richardson, claimed that wood and forage contracts awarded to Adams and Wickes by Reynolds were in excess of real requirements and were issued without competitive bidding. Mackenzie said he contracted for two thousand bushels of forage from another source in June, but that General Reynolds instructed him to cancel the order in favor of Adams and Wickes. Mackenzie refused and instead went over Reynold's head, reporting his suspicion of fraud to the commander of the military division.[26]

Mackenzie also leveled the more serious charge of bribery and influence, in that Adams and Wickes had given General Reynolds the deed to a house in San Antonio. Mackenzie claimed to have a copy of the deed, but would not, or could not, produce it. Reynolds, furious at the charges, retaliated by demanding Mackenzie's court-martial. The judge advocate general ruled that it was not expedient to pursue a trial, and the entire matter faded away with little additional publicity in January, 1872 when the Division of the Missouri commander, Lt. Gen. Phil Sheridan, sent Brig. Gen. Christopher C. Auger to replace Reynolds.[27]

STEAMBOATS AND SAIL

Besides being a prime customer in the development of commercial wagon transportation in Texas, the U.S. Army played a major role in the growth of water transport. The use of steamboats in the Mexican War was the most important innovation in the logistical aspects of warfare up to that time, freeing waterborne supply from the tyranny of wind and tide. To support the Mexican War, the Quartermaster's Department purchased thirty-eight sailing ships and thirty-five steamships. The high-tech steamers were cantankerous, and only half were still serviceable at the war's end, but they more than fulfilled their potential.[28]

The geography of the Texas coast and rivers offered a formidable obstacle to maritime efforts. Texas had no natural deepwater harbors; the good shallow harbors were hindered by treacherously shifting sandbars and unpredictable weather. The few navigable rivers had marginal and inconsistent water levels that were dependent on erratic rainfall.

Nevertheless, in 1837 Charles Morgan established a steamship run with two vessels plying between Galveston and New Orleans, and river steamers were put to good use on the lower Brazos and other east Texas rivers. Mexican businessmen attempted to use steamboats on the Rio Grande without success. Henry Austin, cousin to Stephen F. Austin, ran his *Ariel* between Matamoros and Camargo in 1829 and 1830, but gave up the Rio Grande as unprofitable after a year's effort. In the end, it was the U.S. Army that expanded the use of steamships all along the Texas coast and established the routine use of steamboats on the Rio Grande. Two months after Taylor's army arrived at Corpus Christi in 1845, the government-owned, 141-ton sidewheeled steamer *Neva* was consistently lightering cargo from the temporary depot on St. Joseph's Island across the bay to the army on the beach. All the while, the fleet of small sail vessels carrying supplies remained at the mercy of the sea and breeze. Assisting the *Neva* was the chartered 100-ton sidewheeler *White Wing*, which—to ensure the availability of a second steamer at the depot—the Quartermaster's Department had purchased for $7,500.[29]

The Quartermaster's Department experienced an extreme shortage of shipping to support the war. Boats were difficult to purchase, the owners figuring to make more by contracting than by selling outright. Contracted ships to supply the Mexican War were averaging $40 to $50 per day, with demurrage averaging $60 per day. In early July, 1846, Capt. John Sanders of the Corps of Engineers purchased for Taylor a number of shallow-draft steamers at Pittsburg, Pennsylvania— including the sidewheeled *Corvette*—and sent the boats to the Rio Grande. Sanders hired Mifflin Kenedy as the master of the *Corvette* for $125 a month, describing him as a young man "of the right stamp." Kenedy in turn recruited one of his former pilots, Richard King, to come to the Rio Grande and serve the Quartermaster's Department. These two army employees went on to found one of Texas' great business empires after the Mexican War.[30]

Meanwhile, Bvt. Lt. Col. Stephen H. Long of the Topographical Engineers supervised construction of a steam dredge and six sidewheeled government steam transports for use by the Quartermaster Corps. From Louisville came the *General Jesup* (374 tons, 250 tons burden), completed in February, 1847, for $13,227. The next finished was the *Colonel Hunt* (214 tons). From Cincinnati came the *General Hamer* (300 tons burden) in April, 1847, for service in the Gulf, while the *Ann Chase* (300 tons burden) went to New Orleans in June, 1847. The *General Butler* and *Colonel Clay* (350 tons burden each) were completed in October, 1847, and the steam dredge *Lavaca*, for that Texas bay at a cost of $18,392, was ready in March, 1847.[31]

Steamboats were efficient but dangerous, creating no small amount of anxiety among military travelers. At Corpus Christi, on September 13, 1845, the army was suitably impressed when the chartered steamer *Dayton* exploded, killing two officers and ten men of the Fourth Infantry. However, steam power was indispensable for maintaining the Rio Grande supply line. The first Quartermaster's Department steamboat to try the river was the *Neva*, arriving at Matamoros on May 24, 1846, with the First Artillery's baggage. As Taylor's supply line expanded upstream to Camargo, steamers followed, testing the limits of technology and the patience and skill of boat captains. A typical trip from the river's mouth to Camargo was four to seven days. Drawing less than two feet of water, the flat-bottomed *Colonel Cross* made the fastest steam run from the mouth to Camargo in sixty-one hours, fifty-five minutes, or two and one-half days, of which nearly eleven hours were spent at stops. However, not all trips were so fortunate. On October 1, 1846, the *Major Brown*, 150 feet long, forty-six feet wide, and drawing three and one-half feet of water, ascended the rapids at Roma and went to Laredo. It was stranded there for two years when the river fell.[32]

The *Colonel Cross* made a trip up the Rio Grande in the summer of 1846 that is illustrative of the difficulties encountered navigating the treacherous river. At sunrise on August 26, 1846, the steamer departed the mouth of the river, starting for Camargo with four hundred volunteers from the First Mississippi Rifles. A few miles upriver, the boat stopped long enough for the soldiers to bury a comrade who had died of illness. After numerous interruptions along the way, the steamer arrived at Matamoros on the morning of August 28. The boat lost another day when an army officer discovered there was an illegal shipment of liquor aboard, which led to the firing and hiring of a new master. The *Colonel Cross* finally got underway again at 10 P.M. on August 30, but soon destroyed a paddlewheel when it was pushed against the bank by a strong current. After a day spent constructing a new wheel, the boat again resumed its journey, only to lose a rudder when it was rammed by another steamboat. After six hours of repairs and another six hours of steaming, the boat ran a sharp turn in the dark and crashed into an overhanging tree limb, smashing up part of the pilothouse and a few staterooms. The new master decided never again to run at night. Two "man-overboards" and numerous wood stops later, the *Colonel Cross* arrived at Camargo on the evening of September 4 after ten blistering days on the Rio Grande.[33]

By the end of the Mexican War, the concept of steamer travel on the Rio Grande was firmly established. It soon became a crucial element in supplying forts along the river, and an important Texas business. Throughout the period 1850 to 1890, supplies came by sea to Brazos Santiago or direct to Fort Brown, and were moved upriver by contracted steamer to Ringgold Barracks. From 1850 to 1854, and again in the early 1870s, supplies were passed upriver from Fort Ringgold by keel boat, or overland by contracted wagon to Fort McIntosh at Laredo, and to Fort Duncan at Eagle Pass.

During the three decades after the Mexican War, Kenedy and King was the dominant force behind steam transportation on the Rio Grande. As previously mentioned, the army brought Mifflin Kenedy and Richard King to Texas during the war, and they remained to become powerful businessmen, the genesis of their empire coming in 1849, when the Quartermaster's Department sold off its Mexican War steamers at Brazos Santiago. King bought the war-weary *Colonel Cross*—built four years earlier for $14,000—for a mere $750. Other river captains purchased a half-dozen army steamboats at similar bargains. M. Kenedy and Company, formed in February, 1850, with two other partners, soon drove its competitor's cranky wartime steamers from the river by having two King-designed boats built in Pittsburg, Pennsylvania. Arriving in August, 1850, the 150-foot, 500-ton, sidewheeled *Grampus* was the "outside" boat, moving cargo from Brazos Santiago ten miles upriver to the company's new terminal at White Ranch. From there the sternwheeled "inside" boat—the agile, shallow-draft, 200-ton *Comanche*—delivered cargo as far as the head of navigation at Roma. The low prices, efficient cargo system, and reliable boats of Kenedy, King, and their partners put the remainder of the independent river captains out of business within two years. On February 10, 1851, the army's general contract for Rio Grande water transportation went to M. Kenedy and Company. The original contract called for transporting animals, men, and supplies from Brazos Santiago to Fort Brown or return at a charge of $3 per soldier, $5 per horse, and 30¢ per 100 pounds of freight. The army paid $8 per soldier, $12 per horse, and $1 per 100 pounds of freight for the run from Fort Brown to Ringgold Barracks.[34]

Richard King took a personal interest in the military business, taking care to seek and maintain cordial relations with army officers and quartermasters. Although the army contracts were not the foundation of the business, King believed government freighting could be counted on for a steady, dependable profit. M. Kenedy and Company retained the Rio Grande general contract for the army until 1855, reducing the Fort Brown–Fort Ringgold run to $5 per soldier, $7 per horse, and 75¢ per 100 pounds of freight. Although company records are sketchy, it appears that M. Kenedy and Company earned a net profit of $18,000 in 1855, making twenty-one commercial and army contract trips on the river. In mid-1855 the general two-year contract went to J. P Armstrong, but Kenedy and King secured seven specific one-time contracts between 1856 and 1860. The contracts called for hauling $10,000 worth of supplies and soldiers, mostly on King's *Ranchero*. By 1857, the company's general profit was $40,000 per year. The army ceased letting general steamship contracts on the river in 1857, but returned to the system again after the Civil War. During the Civil War, Kenedy and King steamboats hauled Confederate goods and—when the Union captured Brownsville in November, 1863—were pressed into service for the Union army. In 1866 Kenedy and King, to ensure a monopoly on the Rio Grande, bought all steamers afloat on the river. The first postwar army contract, issued in 1869, once again went to Kenedy and King and their four operating boats: the *J. San Roman, Tamaulipas I* and *II,* and the *Matamoros II.* Operating first as Kenedy and King and then as King, Kenedy, and Company, they retained the general contract until 1874, when the firm dissolved with capital stock worth $250,000.[35]

H. K. Hazlett took over the general steamer contract in 1875 but lost it the following year to Charles Best. From 1876 to 1880 the army did not let an annual contract for the Rio Grande, but the U.S. Navy wrote an odd footnote to steamer history on the river by stationing a gunboat at Brownsville during this period. The side-wheeler USS *Rio Bravo* patrolled the lower Rio Grande from October, 1875, to April, 1879, for the purpose of interdicting Mexican cattle thieves and as a show of force against revolutionaries. It accomplished neither. Perhaps patrolled is too generous a term as the vessel had a four-foot draft and spent the majority of its four years tied to a wharf. However, it did have two small, steam-driven launches that occasionally did useful work.[36]

The army returned to the annual contract system in 1881 when William Kelly and his 100-ton, wood-burning stern-wheeler *Bessie,* gained and held the monopoly until 1889. A former Union army river master and Kenedy and King skipper, Kelly and several business partners bought four Kenedy and King river steamers in 1874 and created the Merchants Steamboat Line. The reduction of the Texas military force and the coming of the railroad quickly cut into Kelly's profits. He made only $18,000 from the army in his nine years of operation, averaging only $2,000 per year. For example, Kelly's rates in 1886 for the Fort Brown–Fort Ringgold run were $12 for an officer, $6 for an enlisted man, and 60¢ per 100 pounds of freight. By 1895, Rio Grande steamer traffic had declined to the point where the department commander, Brig. Gen. Zenas R. Bliss, reported, "There is but one boat on the river, and, owing to the high charges of the Mexican authorities, it does not land on the Mexican side, except occasionally when there is enough freight to warrant the payment of $100 for the privilege." An officer who rode the *Bessie* down the twisting river from Fort Ringgold in 1896 recalled how often the wind and current would sweep the stern about in a bend, nosing the bow of the boat into the bank, sending her careening backward downstream. At the next bend the captain would nudge the stern to the bank, letting the current bring the boat about to point the bow once again properly downstream, a maneuver repeated so often the officer reported "she waltzed us all the way to Brownsville." Kelly was the last of the Rio Grande steamship operators, running his *Bessie* on the river until 1904.[37]

While the Rio Grande steamer contracts had a direct impact on Texas' economy, the army also had general sea-transport requirements to the Texas coast that contributed to the state's Gulf commerce. As a post–Mexican War example, between April and September, 1849, fifty-eight sail and steam vessels hired by the Quartermaster's Department unloaded 6,563 tons of supplies along the Texas coast, with $595,000 worth of goods being warehoused at Brazos Santiago. To support the army in Texas in 1853, nineteen schooners, brigs, and steamers landed at Indianola, Corpus Christi, and Brazos Santiago, bringing 908 soldiers and 12,077 barrels of stores at a contract cost for sea transport of $34,000. Representative of these contracts was the schooner *Blooming Youth* from Baltimore, which carried 1,150 barrels of rations to Corpus Christi in April, and 1,800 barrels to Brazos Santiago in October— two round-trips worth $4,475 to skipper J. W. Brown.[38]

In 1858 the Quartermaster's Department let a single contract for the New Orleans–Texas coast run for supplies and troops. The first general contract, issued for $3,000, went to Harris, Morgan, and Company, which operated the steamers *General Rusk* and *Mexico*. Charles Morgan had been a pioneer in Texas coastal steamships, a developer of Indianola, and his Morgan Line dominated Texas coastal shipping under various company names until the 1880s.[39]

The general contract for the New Orleans–Texas coast run was continued in 1870 with an agent of Charles Morgan, Charles A. Whitney and Company of New Orleans. Whitney and Company held the contract for sixteen years until 1886, when it went to another Morgan business, Morgan's Louisiana and Texas Railroad and Steamship Company. In the 1886 contract, the Morgan company agreed to transport freight from New Orleans to Corpus Christi at a rate of 60¢ per 100 pounds, $25 for officers, $12 for enlisted men, and $15 for animals. The last year a general contract was issued for the Texas coast run was in 1887. That contract was issued to the Southern Pacific Company's water-transport division, which in fact was the old Morgan Line until it was purchased by the railroad company.[40]

Army waterborne logistics originated Rio Grande steamship travel and contributed to the development of Texas ports such as Indianola, Corpus Christi, Port Lavaca, Galveston, and Brownsville. Port facilities such as wharves and storehouses were financed or leased by the army, which in turn led to additional commercial growth. As demonstrated in Table 5, water transportation in the post–Mexican War years accounted for 10 to 20 percent of army freight expenditures in Texas but was eventually rendered obsolete by the coming of the railroad.

RAILROADS

In the five years before the Mexican War, total military transportation costs were about $150,000 per year. The cost of military transportation rose to $2 million per year after the war as units deployed into the vastly expanded theater of operations in the West where, as Quartermaster General Jesup observed in 1851, there was a dearth of transportation routes and systems. Estimating that half of the entire quartermaster budget went toward moving, rather than purchasing, material, Jesup calculated that transportation costs could be cut in half if an efficient railroad system was built in the West. The following year, 1852, Jesup reported to Congress that a railroad from the Mississippi River across northern Texas, "would quadruple our military power in that quarter." Jesup went on to point out that the railroad would become essential to defending newly acquired Pacific coast and that, from a military perspective, the construction of a railroad to bind together the nation, "would be more important than any other in which the government could engage."[41]

Attempts to develop railroads in Texas began in 1836, but faltered from lack of financing and public interest. The first railroad in the state, a twenty-mile local line near present-day Houston called the Buffalo Bayou, Brazos, and Colorado Railroad, began operating in 1853. An army officer's wife riding this line in 1859 recorded, "The best thing I can say of it was, it was very short." At the start of the Civil War, ten small railroads operated in Texas over 468 miles of rail, most of which fell into disrepair during the conflict.[42]

In 1853 Congress, recognizing the need for a transcontinental railroad, authorized funds for army engineers to begin a search for the best route west from the Mississippi River. In Texas, beginning in February, 1854, Capt. John Pope and a party of seventy-five men surveyed a route along the thirty-second parallel from New Mexico across the northern Llano Estacado to the Red River at Preston, Texas. Pope's general knowledge of western Texas was built upon earlier army wagon road reconnaissances by officers such as Capt. Randolph B. Marcy, Lt. Col. Joseph E. Johnston, and Lt. William H. C. Whiting. Pope was enthusiastic about the potential of the rail route, as were nearly all of the other surveyors for their own routes. Although Secretary of War Jefferson Davis favored the southern route through Texas, in the end there was enough political support for other paths along the 35th, 38th, and 41st parallels, that the issue was tabled until after the Civil War.[43]

Railroad construction began in earnest in the West shortly after the war ended. Crossing the northern Great Plains, the Union Pacific became the first transcontinental railroad in March, 1869. It was another decade before rails stretched across Texas.

By 1873, the Houston and Texas Central Railroad reached from Houston to Dallas, the Texas and Pacific Railroad ran from Texarkana to Dallas, and the Missouri, Kansas, and Texas Railroad connected Denison to Kansas. However, all three had to struggle to overcome the financial constraints of the Panic of 1873. Eventually three railroads would compete to be the first to reach San Antonio. In 1870 Charles Morgan bought the bankrupt San Antonio and Mexican Gulf Railroad, which had reached from Port Lavaca to Victoria in 1866. Morgan's rails reached Cuero but got no farther because of a lack of funds. Financial titan Jay Gould gobbled up a number of Texas railroads in the 1870s and his International–Great Northern Railroad slowly pushed from Austin toward San Antonio by 1876. The victor in the race to San Antonio was, ironically, the first Texas railroad company—the tiny Buffalo Bayou, Brazos, and Colorado Railroad, which was acquired in 1870 by Thomas W. Peirce and associates, and renamed the Galveston, Harrisburg, and San Antonio Railway Company. After a six-year struggle against yellow fever, swollen creeks, and financial strains, Peirce's first freight train reached San Antonio on February 15, 1877. It was followed by Gould's International-Great Northern from Austin in February, 1881, which, by December, stretched to Laredo, where it connected with the Mexican Central Railroad to Mexico City. The San Antonio connection allowed the army to send much of its supplies directly to its Texas quartermaster depot from major supply centers such as St. Louis, avoiding the delays and risks of Gulf coast shipping. In 1881 Collis P. Huntington bought controlling interest in the Galveston, Harrisburg, and San Antonio, and began pushing its rails west toward the Rio Grande, while at the same time his Southern Pacific reached El Paso from San Francisco. To provide security for the survey and construction parties working across the Trans-Pecos, the Texas department commander furnished company-sized cavalry escorts from Forts Clark and Davis. The two lines connected near the mouth of the Pecos River on January 12, 1883, completing a railroad across Texas and becoming the Southern Pacific's Sunset Route, the first of the Southern intercontinental lines. By 1898, ten major rail systems operated in Texas with 13,825 miles of rails.[44]

As illustrated in Table 4, the army paid railroads in Texas over a half million dollars from 1869 to the turn of the century. This represents 19 percent of the post–Civil War army transport costs in Texas. After 1880, the railroad was the predominate method of moving supplies and the associated expenses outstripped both wagon and water transport. As the examples in Table 5 demonstrate, by the early 1880s the army in Texas moved half of its supplies by rail. The figure grew to three-quarters by the end of the decade.

In general terms, Texas' railroads reduced the army's cost of transporting supplies to forts by 80 to 90 percent when compared to wagon freighting expenditures in the prerail era. During the 1870s the average rate for a railcar hauling 20,000 pounds of freight was 8¢ to 10¢ per 100 pounds per 100 miles. In 1875 the cost of wagon freight from San Antonio to Fort Clark was $1.02 per 100 lbs. When the railroad finally reached within ten miles of Fort Clark in 1883 the army still had to pay 12¢ cents per 100 pounds for the short wagon haul. However, when added to the 10¢ per 100 pounds to ship to the terminus by rail, the total cost for rail and wagon-freight shipments to Fort Clark from San Antonio was about 22¢ per 100 pounds—a total reduction of 81 percent over 1875. At remote Fort Davis in 1878, the price for wagon freight all the way from San Antonio was $7 per 100 pounds. By 1884, the twenty-four-mile wagon short-haul from the railroad at Murphyville to Fort Davis was only 19¢ per 100 pounds. When this was added to the 46¢ per 100 pounds to ship supplies by rail to Murphyville, the total cost to the army was about 65¢ per 100 pounds—91 percent less than in 1878.[45]

With the boom of land-grant railroads in the West after the Civil War, for nearly a decade the army received free rail transport in exchange for the federal government's deeds of land to the railroad companies. The railroads would in turn sell off the lots along their tracks to finance construction. However, in Texas the federal government had no public domain and thus the 30 million acres granted to railroads by the Texas legislature did not translate into a free ride for the army, as it did on other parts of the frontier. The terms of the state's annexation and the lack of federal domain proved to be as much a financial burden to the army as they had been with the selection of fort sites and the problem of finding Indian reservations.[46]

For a short period the army had free transport on several Texas railroads. In various parts of the country during the Civil War military railroad engineers built or reconstructed fifty railroads, one of which was at Brazos Santiago and another at Indianola. At the end of the war the Quartermaster's Department sold off 433 engines, 6,605 rail cars, and 2,630 miles of track, much of it on credit in trade for army transportation. In 1866 the San Antonio and Mexican Gulf Railroad bought $48,775 worth of track and equipment on transportation credit, and in 1868 Charles Morgan's Indianola Railroad bought the Brazos Santiago strip for $5,000 in cash and $20,000 worth of free army transport. Morgan bought the San Antonio and Mexican Gulf in 1870, cleared its debt in June, 1871, and discharged his Indianola Railroad debt in May, 1873.[47]

The war-worn nature of equipment bought by these Texas railways was evident to federal soldiers arriving in the state at the end of the conflict. A Fourth Cavalry trooper taking the "one horse rail-road" from Indianola in late 1865 observed, "It got stuck . . . every once in a while and the men had to jump off and giver her a lift . . . when the thing did go a little decent it only moved about as fast as a good pair of horses." A Sixth Cavalry soldier taking the San Antonio and Mexican Gulf from Port Lavaca to Victoria in 1866 noted that the train was a "wheezy old locomotive," and recalled that "All hands got out and pushed at times." He added dryly, "The natives, when in a hurry to visit Lavacca, either rode horseback or walked." A Sixth Cavalry officer riding the same train in 1866 remarked it covered twenty-eight miles in eight hours, "My men getting out now and than to catch rabits along the route and than catching the train again without any difficulty." By 1882 the Texas rail system had improved to the point that an infantry lieutenant proudly reported the swift move of his company by rail from Fort Clark to El Paso on a circuitous route covering about double the straight-line distance. They boarded the train at Eagle Pass Junction, went through San Antonio to the Colorado River, then north to Fort Worth, and finally west to El Paso. In 1884 a cavalry lieutenant recorded that it took just six days to complete the train trip from Baltimore to Marfa, the rail stop for Fort Davis. The rail system unquestionably eased the danger and burden of traveling for army families. After experiencing rough wagon journeys on the Texas frontier in the 1870s, an Eighth Cavalry officer's wife returning to the state in 1885 wrote, "On arriving in San Antonio, instead of a tedious ambulance-ride awaiting us, we went by rail to Fort Clark, which we reached in a few hours."[48]

In 1883, the first year an extended rail network operated across Texas, the army spent $967,631 for railroads to move 152.6 million pounds of freight and 65,166 passengers in the continental United States. The army in Texas, with eleven posts and 2,842 troops, spent $31,323 on rail transportation to move 4.5 million pounds of freight and 2,449 passengers. The following year, the army in Texas moved 5.6 million pounds of goods and 1,220 passengers by rail at a cost of $42,454—of which $34,992 was paid to the Galveston, Harrisburg, and San Antonio Railway Company. Army rail freight shipments in Texas in 1885 doubled to 10.3 million pounds, the number of passengers remained steady at 1,263, and expenditures rose to $81,006, with $43,309 going to the Galveston, Harrisburg, and San Antonio. By 1889, Texas had decreased its troop strength to 1,904 soldiers in ten posts and cut its rail costs to $30,737.[49]

In addition to taking advantage of the railroad to supply fixed garrisons, army quartermasters in Texas experimented with using the rail line to resupply mobile field forces. In April, 1885, when the Tenth Cavalry relocated to Arizona, the cavalrymen marched near the Southern Pacific line where it was supplied by a train carrying cooking wood, forage, and water for the two thousand horses and mules in the column. A soldier who participated in the march remembered that "The water alone for the trip cost the Government $1,200."[50]

These figures indicate that the army was very quick to take advantage of the rail network connecting its far-flung posts and, in the process, make a substantial economic contribution to Texas railroad lines. In addition, the railroad's expansion fundamentally altered the army's century-old policy of dispersing frontier garrisons to small temporary forts. The change to larger permanent posts in turn meant a boon to Texas' industry, bringing a reliable long-term market to the communities in which troops were concentrated while at the same time crippling the satellite communities near the posts abandoned in the move toward consolidation.

Lieutenant Gen. William T. Sherman wrote in 1871, "The rapid progress of the railroads in Texas, and of those leading from the Missouri towards Texas, changes the whole problem of supplies; and the use of troops on that frontier will be greatly facilitated by these railroads." A decade later, as the last cross-Texas railroads neared completion, Sherman called for a reorganization of the frontier army, taking soldiers out of the "decay of temporary quarters" and moving them into well-built permanent garrisons concentrated near the rail lines.[51]

CHAPTER 4

Forage
Corn, Hay, and Oats

As illustrated in Tables 3 and 6, the army's purchase of $9 million worth of forage—the corn, oats, and hay that fed horses and mules—was the largest single category of expenditures for the Quartermaster's Department in Texas, and had the greatest immediate impact on the state's struggling frontier economies. Like the fixed ration for soldiers, the army developed fixed standards for forage. In the 1850s, for example, the maximum allowable ration of forage for a horse or mule was fourteen pounds of hay and twelve pounds of corn or oats per day. Although the hay allowance was usually available, most army animals in Texas received only half of the corn ration—about ninety bushels a year—because of economic constraints in garrison and difficult transportation conditions in the field.[1]

From 1847 onward, the army standard for a bushel was 56 pounds of corn and 32 pounds of oats, while a ton of hay ranged from 2,000 to 2,240 pounds. To guide quartermasters in local purchases along the border, the army officially established the Mexican *fanega* of corn at 2.5 bushels or 140 pounds. Forage in Texas was expensive but reasonable when compared to other military departments. A Quartermaster's Department analysis in 1850 determined that to feed one horse for one month in Texas cost $10.30, whereas it cost $27.24 in Oregon and $7.54 in the Northeast.[2]

Texas corn, oats, and hay were not available in the quantities or locations required during the Mexican War, so the army imported the bulk of its forage by sea from New Orleans through Brazos Santiago. However, when it deployed to the Texas frontier in 1849, the army began to purchase vast quantities of local Texas forage. Table 6 breaks down the $9 million the army spent on forage in the state during the last half of the nineteenth century. Just over 50 percent of the total went for corn, while the remainder was split equally between hay and oats. As is evident in Tables 6 and 7, oats were not

TABLE 6.

ARMY QUARTERMASTER EXPENDITURES IN TEXAS
FOR ANIMAL FORAGE, 1849–1900

Category	Period 1849–1861	1867–1879	1880–1889	1890–1900	Total
Total army spending for Texas forage	$1,196,000	$4,614,000	$2,500,000	$742,000	$9,052,000
Army purchase of Texas corn (in bushels)	520,700	1,655,000	1,650,000	372,000	4,197,700
Army purchase of Texas oats (in bushels)	16,000	1,355,000	899,000	590,000	2,860,000
Army purchase of Texas hay (in tons)	20,700	89,300	53,000	37,000	200,000

Source: Calculated from each year's "Report of the Quartermaster General of the Army," in the annual *Report of the Secretary of War,* 1849–1900, and from the National Archives, Record Group 92, Records of the Office of the Quartermaster General, Entry 1245, "Register of Contracts, 1871–1912." The records are incomplete for Texas quartermaster dollars spent on forage in 1890–1900, but the decade figure was estimated using linear regression analysis for the known years of that decade to calculate the total.

TABLE 7.

AVERAGE PRICES PAID BY THE ARMY FOR TEXAS FORAGE, 1850–1890

Year	Corn per 56 lb. bushel	Price Range, Corn	Oats per 32 lb. bushel	Price Range, Oats	Hay per ton	Price Range, Hay
1850	$1.31	$1.05–3.00	no purchases		$10.00	$3.19–40.00
1852	$1.60	$0.90–2.40	$1.60	$1.60	$8.28	$3.40–15.00
1854	$1.35	$1.26–2.00	no purchases		$13.70	$7.35–19.95
1856	$2.34	$0.94–2.84	no purchases		$12.25	$7.75–14.25
1858	$1.40	$0.72–2.90	no purchases		$11.50	$6.84–29.40
1860	$1.93	$1.38–2.16	no purchases		$15.00	$8.84–35.00
1871	$1.78	$1.11–2.20	$0.81	$0.42–1.60	$9.40	$7.35–18.00
1884	$0.93	$0.73–1.40	$0.82	$0.59–1.17	$11.70	$10.80–19.50
1889	$0.63	$0.57–1.28	$0.45	$0.18–0.80	$9.20	$7.80–27.00
1890	$0.71	$0.48–1.08	$0.50	$0.39–0.77	$9.40	$6.80–22.00

Source: Calculated from a survey of each year's "Report of the Quartermaster General of the Army," in the annual *Report of the Secretary of War,* 1849–1900, and from the National Archives, Record Group 92, Records of the Office of the Quartermaster General, Entry 1245, "Register of Contracts, 1871–1912."

a common Texas crop during the antebellum period, and the Texas quarter-master often imported them from New Orleans or Mobile, Alabama. The purchase of hay was greatly reduced because soldier labor was often used to cut native prairie grasses, and units established grazing camps for horse herds. The army purchased forage in two ways: by small piecemeal local purchases, and by bulk contract with delivery guaranteed by a surety bond. The cost of forage was tied directly to drought conditions and to the distance it had to be hauled. In 1851, for example, the quartermaster at the San Antonio depot was able to bulk purchase seventy-one thousand bushels of corn from local farmers at an average of $1.16 per bushel, while at Fort Graham, which had few nearby farmers, contracted corn cost $1.76 per bushel. The establishment of a frontier fort usually drew farmers into an unsettled area because the post provided a ready economic opportunity. However, in the early 1850s, many of these frontier subsistence farmers had little surplus forage available for the army.[3]

As can been seen in Table 7, the price of army corn rose about 47 percent during the 1850s. The national inflation rate accounts for about 9 percent of this rise. While the cost of corn did tend to decrease at posts near the settlement line, the real culprit was the increased cost of transportation as the army began to establish more posts on the distant Trans-Pecos frontier. By 1860, half of the army's nineteen Texas posts were far beyond the farmers moving slowly westward in their wake, therefore requiring extensive overland wagon transport for corn forage. Texas corn prices were 400 percent above the national average by 1871, but the army in Texas paid about fifteen cents a bushel less than was typically paid in 1860. If the massive wartime inflation rate of 42 percent is factored in for the 1860s, Texas corn in 1871 cost the army about half of the 1860 per-bushel price. By 1881, Texas corn sold at 180 percent above the national average, with the army in Texas paying 33 percent less per bushel than it had ten years earlier. Improved transportation, increasing settlement, and deflation of a negative (minus) 35 percent account for this change. By 1890, the full use of railroad transportation and widespread settlement put Texas corn at only 30 percent above the national average, making it relatively inexpensive for the army. In contrast, Texas hay during the period 1850 to 1890 remained on par with the national average cost per ton. Prices remained relatively stable throughout the period, with the range of prices almost entirely dependent on the distance to be transported.[4]

The economic impact of forage purchases tended to be more significant at the micro (local) level, than over the entire agricultural macro-system in

Texas. In 1851 the army bought 1.4 percent of the corn and 13 percent of the hay produced in the state. However, the triangle of Fort Croghan and the quartermaster's depots in San Antonio and Austin purchased 14 percent of the corn and 48 percent of the hay grown in the thirteen counties contiguous to those posts. The San Antonio quartermaster's depot in Bexar County purchased the equivalent of 86 percent of the corn and 88 percent of the hay grown in the county in 1851, while the Austin depot purchased 60 percent of the corn and the equivalent of one hundred times the amount of hay grown in Travis County. The isolated posts in west Texas provided a distant market for the frontier settlement line, located several hundred miles to the east. For example, Fort Davis in the Trans-Pecos purchased for its own needs and stocked forage for expeditions on the El Paso road. Between October, 1854, and March, 1856, the post quartermaster purchased $92,472 worth of forage. With few farmers in the immediate vicinity, the majority of it had to be hauled from the settlement line more than three hundred miles to the east. Mexico also benefited from army forage purchases. In the antebellum era, Fort Davis and the Post Opposite El Paso (later called Fort Bliss) often purchased corn from Chihuahua, Mexico, because it was much closer than the Texas settlement line. The transportation advantage became painfully apparent when the governor of Chihuahua briefly forbade the export of corn in 1854. The decree, reported the department commander, ". . . made solely to annoy us, will embarrass our supplies of forage." The effect of the temporary embargo made the army further encourage agricultural settlement in the Trans-Pecos in order to make the posts more self-sufficient through local markets.[5]

By 1860, Texas corn production had tripled to 16.5 million bushels and 11,865 tons of hay, the army purchasing 0.25 percent of the corn crop and 23 percent of the hay grown in the state. Once again, the local county picture is significant. For example, Ringgold Barracks in Starr County purchased four times the amount of corn and two hundred times the amount of hay grown in the county. The far frontier posts of Forts Davis, Stockton, and Clark and Camp Wood contracted for twenty-seven thousand bushels of corn, yet little was reported produced in the local counties of these forts.[6]

The general pattern of army forage purchases in the 1850s remained the norm in Texas throughout the remainder of the nineteenth century. Unlike transportation contracts, which by 1856 were awarded to a few large-scale contractors that serviced all of the state's forts, forage purchases involved multiple small- and medium-scale sources for each post. Typical was the case of Fort Inge in 1858. The post quartermaster reported purchasing hay from sixteen different farmers and issuing a single-source contract for corn. In addition to the contractors, the quartermaster made a multitude of open-market piecemeal purchases. While Fort Inge in 1858 was typical of the period, Edwin D. Lane was the single source of supply for thirty-three thousand bushels of corn shipped to Forts Mason, McKavett, and Chadbourne, and Camp Colorado. The next year, the quartermaster returned to a multisource system. At times, such as the great Texas frontier corn-crop failure in 1860, the army had to revert to importing additional corn supplies from New Orleans and Mexico. Altogether, the army let more than 180 contracts to state farmers to supply forage to Texas posts during the 1850s.[7]

In 1870 the army purchased 1.2 percent of the Texas corn crop and 67 percent of the hay. However, the San Antonio depot and Fort Concho purchased the equivalent of 86 percent of all the corn grown in Bexar County, while Fort Brown purchased an amount equal to 114 percent of the corn raised in Cameron County. In 1880 the army purchased about 0.54 percent of the corn and 8 percent of the hay grown in Texas, while Fort Brown contracted the equivalent of only 4 percent of the rapidly rising hay production in Cameron County. In 1890 army forage purchases dropped to 0.06 percent of the corn and 0.8 percent of the hay in Texas. The figures indicate that the major impact of the army's purchase of forage in Texas occurred in the period 1850 to 1880.[8]

A survey of the average per-capita consumption of corn gives an indication of the impact of the army on the Texas corn market. The typical Texas civilian horse or mule consumed about 7.5 bushels of corn, and his human master consumed 13 bushels. Based on total Texas corn production and population in the period 1850 to 1900, the average annual consumption rate per-capita for civilians was 26 bushels. During the same period, the average annual soldier population in the state was 2,914, and the army purchased 348 bushels of corn to support each soldier. Compared to his civilian counterpart, the soldier required thirteen times the amount of corn, thus making a substantial contribution to the Texas corn market.[9]

Rather than risk the variable of weather in a demand-driven market, the quartermaster at each post generally made six or eight contracts for delivered forage, arranged several months before the planting season in order to get a reasonable price. Many contracts were drawn with local small farmers, but very often the larger ones were with middlemen, who would then post a bond of about half the value of the contract, arranging for transportation and consolidating the required amount of corn or hay from a wide number of sources. A representative small contractor, before he was killed by Indians in 1861, was Julius Sanders, one of the first corn growers to settle near Fort Inge when the post was founded in 1849. Sanders sold at least $1,686 worth of his surplus forage to the army in the 1850s. While the amount may seem paltry in the macro-scale of Texas logistics, it was enormously significant to farmer Sanders. It represented three years of wages in the scale of the period, and in fact was equivalent to 45 percent of the $3,750 worth of real and personal property listed for Sanders in the 1860 census.[10]

Characteristic of a forage middleman was Juan Galván, who secured several contracts in 1871 for $14,000 worth of hay and corn for Forts Ringgold and Brown. Middleton Tate Johnson was a larger-scale middleman. Johnson was a legislator in the Republic of Texas, a Mexican War volunteer veteran, and friend of Texas department commander Col. William J. Worth. Johnson helped the army select the site of Fort Worth in 1849, and was instrumental in establishing Tarrant County. He owned Johnson's Station, the social-political hub of north-central Texas in the early 1850s, and in 1860 married the widow of a Second Dragoons captain. During the period 1852 to 1858, Johnson contracted with the quartermasters at Fort Belknap and Camp Cooper for $47,450 worth of forage, the equivalent cash value of fifteen thousand acres of Texas land in that era.[11]

Johnson was scrupulous and honorable in his forage business with the army at a time when other contractors were careless of their obligations. An army surgeon at Fort Concho in 1879 observed that the contractor there delivered hay so dirty that cavalry officers refused to feed it to their horses. Even though the mountain of hay sat rotting, the following year the same individual was again awarded a hay contract. "There are very few things the Government undertakes," wrote the surgeon, "but what it gets swindled in the execution." In 1883 the quartermaster at Camp Peña Colorado rejected an entire delivery of forage from this same contractor.[12]

In an attempt to take advantage of the opportunities of centralized distribution brought by the railroad, Texas' chief quartermaster experimented in 1888 with a single $250,000 contract for all the army forage in the state. The contractor failed to deliver, forcing the army to make more expensive open-market purchases and return to a divide-the-risk strategy with ninety-eight forage contracts the following year.[13]

Although the cost of transportation to remote forts increased the expense of corn and hay, in general the forage contract system in Texas worked well and contractors usually met their obligations, delivering forage at or below the open market price. The contracts provided a steady flow of army dollars into frontier agricultural economies, spreading the wealth through a multitude of small contracts rather than allowing one or two individuals to monopolize the market. Contractors often went out of their way to maintain good relations with the army. Cesario Torres, for example, delivered his load of five hundred bushels of corn to Camp Peña Colorado in 1883 and offered a sugar-cured ham and thirty pounds of fine corn meal as a present for the post commander. Another example is that of a former dragoon sergeant who, while ranching near the Red River in 1872, sold open-market forage to the Fourth Cavalry at prices well below average in an effort to encourage the soldiers to protect his ranch from Indian raiders.[14]

CHAPTER 5

Real Estate

Fort Leasing, Purchase, Building, and Repair

Unlike in other western states, when Texas achieved statehood there were no parcels of federal land within its borders that could be used as forts or Indian reservations. This was a legacy of the Spanish colonial and Mexican federal experience when provinces, rather than the central government, controlled public lands. The fact that the federal government owned no land within this vast theater of operations repeatedly frustrated department commanders and chief quartermasters who were required, at increasing expense, to lease fort sites and rent building spaces to conduct government business. Nineteenth-century leases and rental fees, although reasonable, eventually came to just over $367,000—about 1 percent of the quartermaster's budget for Texas. The state constitution contained a provision allowing the federal government to condemn land for its use, but local juries usually determined the fair-market value. After the Civil War, when Congress authorized the outright purchase of Texas posts, it required two or three decades of legal haggling and lawsuits before the government was able to acquire valid deeds to its forts.[1]

When the army began operating on the Texas frontier after the Mexican War, it had to lease from private individuals both depot buildings and post sites. On January 1, 1849, for example, Maj. Edwin B. Babbitt, the San Antonio quartermaster, leased the Alamo as a storage building from the Catholic Church for $150 per month. Babbitt, acting in good faith, had the building repaired by adding the now distinctive curvilinear upper gable, as well as upper flooring, windows, and a new roof, none of which was present when the site became a Texas shrine in 1836. The army continued to lease the Alamo until 1877, prompting one regular-army soldier, coming to Texas in the wake of the Civil War, to reflect when he saw it in 1866, "To the everlasting disgrace of Texas, no noble monument marks the spot; in fact when I first saw it, it was part of a livery stable."[2]

As another illustration, beginning in 1856 the army paid $445 per month to San Antonio merchants James and William Vance to lease a large building for a troop barracks and a neighboring two-story stone house for the department headquarters. Both buildings were located on what is now the site of the Gunter Hotel.[3]

Each building and post in the state was a separate contract and each seemed to have its own characteristics and quirky history—as individualistic as the Texans with whom the local quartermaster conducted negotiations. Take, for example, William C. Cook, the cofounder of Indianola, who leased the army his wharf and warehouse at that port in 1850 for $50 per month, but refused any but a year-to-year contract. The next year he raised the rent to $80, and by 1860 was charging $140 per month, making more than $11,000 for his decade-long arrangement with the government.[4]

Other Texans, such as Samuel A. Maverick, were less mercenary with the army. They did as much as possible to stabilize the lease arrangements and encourage soldier occupation of their frontier land. This led to increased settlement and ultimately enhanced the value of other real estate in the vicinity. Colonel Persifor F. Smith set the standard as department commander in 1852 when he directed that post leases should be for $50 per month and should include the right to cut wood. In July of that year, Maverick leased the army 3,000 acres on Las Moras Creek for Fort Clark, signing a twenty-year contract that met those terms. His 1856 lease for Fort Chadbourne included woodcutting rights and charged just $25 per month. In December, 1852, David Murphee agreed to a five-year lease with wood rights at $50 per month for Fort Inge's 4,500 acres. Obtaining a lease for Fort Davis's site on Limpia Creek was initially complicated by a claim dispute between John James, James W. Magoffin, and other parties. The army eventually decided in favor of James and leased the post site from him in October, 1854. However, James soon filed suit in San Antonio to gain payment for $20,000 worth of timber the army cut to build the fort, a claim that was settled for $1,000 in 1860. In October, 1856, James signed a twenty-year lease with wood rights for Fort Davis's 300 acres for $25 per month. James agreed to a subsequent contract in 1859 calling for $50 per month with wood rights for the 640-acre Camp Hudson site on the Devil's River. In 1860 the army signed a twenty-year lease for Fort Duncan's 3,000-acre site with San Antonio merchant and banker John Twohig for $130 per month. At a number of other forts—such as Worth, Gates, Martin Scott, and Ewell—commanders simply assumed a sort of military squatter's rights or gained tacit approval to occupy the land without a lease arrangement.[5]

In some cases these relatively uncomplicated and inexpensive frontier fort leases continued after the Civil War. John James once again leased the army Fort Davis, this time settling on a fifty-year contract calling for $75 per month. Twohig leased Fort Duncan for $75 per month, as well as Camp Del Rio for $19 per month. The Adams and Wickes freighting company leased the army 1,400 acres for Fort Concho for $200 per month, while Cesario Torres leased out Camp Langtry for $8 per month. Beginning in January, 1877, the army rented Fort Elliott for $2 per year, $1 going to the state government and $1 going to the Houston and Great Northern Railroad Company. In 1873 Peter Gallagher finally insisted on a formal lease arrangement with the army for Fort Stockton, which was reoccupied in 1867. The Texas chief quartermaster signed the lease on September 17, 1873, agreeing to pay $600 per year for 976 acres, including water rights from Comanche Spring, and an additional $200 per year for a 25-acre post garden located four miles northeast of the fort.[6]

Not all lease arrangements were so agreeable. The Rio Grande forts tended to have their own peculiar complications because of vague titles and Spanish land grants issued before the Texas revolution. Additionally, the absence of wood rights and suitable timber along the river made fuel more expensive. On the upper Rio Grande at Fort Quitman, five or six different landowners waged a twenty-five-year legal squabble over the right to collect lease money. The eventual victor was Maj. Anson Mills of the Tenth Cavalry, who won a settlement in 1884 calling for the payment of $2,700 for rent due from 1868 to 1877. Another example, this one on the lower Rio Grande, is that of Ringgold Barracks. Henry Clay Davis, who had forage contracts with the quartermaster, also owned the site of the post. He leased it to the army in 1853 for one year at $50 per month, and was awarded $6,000 worth of back rent to 1848. The army renewed the contract the next year, agreeing to five more years at the same rent. The army later abandoned the site, but briefly returned in 1859 during the Cortina troubles. Davis demanded $200 per month rent and $400 back rent. Lieutenant Col. Robert E. Lee, the department commander, responded by ordering his quartermaster to find a new site nearby. However, the officer, searching Starr County and Mexican records, discovered that Davis's ownership claim had been challenged two years earlier and that Davis was embroiled in a district-court suit. The Civil War interceded before these complications could be sorted out, and the issue remained unsettled. The army finally gained control of the post in 1878 by having the land condemned to federal ownership.[7]

At Fort Griffin in northwest Texas, land control and lease disputes between army commanders and local developers led to ill-will and, eventually, to a negative impact on the commercial potential of the satellite trading village known by the same name as the fort. The army occupied the post, located on the Clear Fork of the Brazos River, in 1867 without a lease arrangement. A year later the post commander wanted to expand the military reservation to include a buffer against the saloons springing up on the post boundary. The Texas chief quartermaster's records review showed that the heart of the fort was on an old Peters Colony parcel of land that had been purchased in 1858 by one of the stockholders, D. M. Dowell of Louisville, Kentucky. In 1874 the army notified Dowell it had built the post on his land. He not only tried to make arrangements for a lease, but entered into a town-development scheme with two local land speculators. This idea did not please army officers at Fort Griffin who, in 1872, had declared the area along the post's perimeter known as the "Flat" a part of the government reservation and chased off the gamblers, liquor sellers, and harpies. The Flat's rebirth as the village of Fort Griffin followed a town-site survey in 1874 that resulted in lot sales and the return of grog shops along the river. After a false start at a lease arrangement and a good bit of legal confusion and doubt as to Dowell's clear title, the Fort Griffin commander evicted all residents and squatters within the military reservation and Dowell's land-claim boundary. The result of this dispute was uncertainty over the town's future. The uncertainty reinforced the town's somewhat dubious reputation, leading to a regional vote in favor of establishing the county seat at Albany, which eventually gained the railroad. In 1875 the army finally began paying Dowell for his lease, but his anticipated town-development windfall failed to materialize.[8]

In contrast to the sniping over Fort Quitman, Ringgold Barracks, and Fort Griffin, the arrangements at Fort McIntosh were more cordial. In 1853 Don Dolores Garcia leased the twenty-five-hundred-acre post to the army for ten years for sixty-two dollars per month, receiving back rent for the previous five years. The army left in 1858, returning a year later to be welcomed to a new, free five-acre camp in exchange for giving the city of Laredo the buildings at the old star fort. Then, in 1860, Don Thomas Trevino, representing the city, signed a twenty-year lease for the old site for fifty dollars per month. In September, 1874, the city gave the federal government the post—a gift Congress approved in March, 1875.[9]

Army lease dollars could be crucial to the financial health of local businessmen, as was the case with Benjamin Franklin Coons. Coons established his store and "Coons Ranch" opposite El Paso, Mexico, in 1849, and leased the army several buildings and a six-acre site for a post. When the troops pulled out in 1851, Coons's loss of the $350-per-month lease money forced him into foreclosure and forfeiture of his land titles.[10]

In 1854, Quartermaster General Jesup, alarmed by the exorbitant cost of leases and rents in Texas, called for Congress to authorize the purchase of fort sites in the state. Within three years Congress appropriated $150,000 for Texas fort purchases, but the Civil War intervened before any transactions could be completed. The post–Civil War quartermaster general, Maj. Gen. Montgomery C. Meigs, raised the same issue in 1871 and 1872. Finally, in March, 1873, Congress passed a public law authorizing the purchase of Texas forts. An engineer board study the following year recommended the purchase of eleven Texas posts for $106,000. However, the legal negotiations and appropriations for each specific fort had to be dealt with in turn, and it was not until March 3, 1875, that Congress approved the first three purchases: $25,000 for Fort Brown, and $10,000 each for Fort Duncan and Ringgold Barracks.[11]

Not surprisingly, Congress and landowners had remarkably differing concepts about the relative worth of the real estate. At Fort Duncan, John Twohig wanted $358 more than Congress allowed, which meant a new appropriation and endless delay. The title for Fort Ringgold remained in litigation, so no action could be taken. By the following year, Twohig wanted yet another $10,000 more than Congress offered for Fort Duncan, and a district court fixed the price of condemning Fort Ringgold at $20,000—which the army eventually paid in April, 1878. In 1880, after seven years of delay, Congress approved $200,000 to buy Rio Grande posts but then put a hold on the money until army engineers could determine how construction of railroad lines in the state would affect the need for Texas forts. By 1882, Twohig had increased his demand for Fort Duncan to $36,000. An indignant secretary of war deemed the price "exorbitant," and ordered the post abandoned. This brought Twohig's price down to $20,000 by 1889, which the government finally paid. The deed was transferred to the army on March 31, 1894—twenty-one years after the process began.[12]

The most interesting of the fort-purchase controversies involved Fort Brown. The army built the fort in 1846 during the Mexican War, occupying it for three decades without paying rent or entering into a lease. The site was part of the 1781 Espirtu Santo Grant given by the Spanish to Don Blas Maria de la Garza, who passed it on to his niece, Maria Josefa Cavazos, in 1802. In

November, 1853, the secretary of war used Texas' constitutional statues to condemn the land for federal use, but the army was unwilling to pay the jury-assessed value of $50,000. As part of the post–Civil War move to purchase Texas fort sites, Congress appropriated $25,000 for the purchase in 1875, but the Cavazos heirs spurned the offer in 1877 and told the army to clear off of their property. The following year the United States initiated a new suit to condemn Fort Brown as federal property. The Supreme Court confirmed the Cavazos title in 1879 and by 1881 the federal government had lost the suit to condemn the land. The government reopened the case and a Texas judge ruled it could buy the property if it honored the family's demand for $160,000 in purchase price, back rent, and interest from 1846. Congress appropriated the money in 1885, cleared the title in 1887, and paid the Cavazos family in April, 1895. The state government ceded jurisdiction to the federal government two months later. Finally, after twenty years of legal wrangling, the army owned Fort Brown.[13]

Other fort purchases, such as those in San Antonio and El Paso, were much less complicated because of the cooperative involvement of the city fathers. The federal government came to own the 19 acres of San Antonio Arsenal in 1859 through local land donations and simple purchase arrangements. The 937 acres on which Fort Sam Houston sits began with donations of 92 acres for a quartermaster depot site by San Antonio in 1870, 1871, and 1875. The army purchased 50 additional acres from 10 individuals for $41,000 in 1882 and 1883, and condemned 19 acres in 1883, followed by another 361 acres in 1903. In 1886, the army purchased an additional 310 acres for use as a drill field.[14]

Fort Bliss was also purchased in piecemeal lots, demonstrating a high degree of common cause between the city government, local commercial interests, and their representatives at the national level. After leasing one site from James Magoffin for $2,760 annually, and a later site at Concordia Rancho for $2,500 per year, Congress in 1879 approved the purchase of a 135-acre fort site near Simeon Hart's Rio Grande mill for $40,000. The title transfer was completed in 1886. The department commander, Brig. Gen. David S. Stanley, then lobbied the war department for an expanded post on a healthier site, while El Paso Rep. Samuel W. T. Lanham and Sen. John H. Reagan introduced concurrent bills in Congress. In March, 1890, Congress approved the establishment of a new post on La Noria Mesa, four miles north of the river, with $150,000 allocated for building construction but no funds for land purchase. Local businessmen formed the El Paso Progressive Association, raised $8,700 in contributions from citizens, banks, and companies, bought 1,000

acres for the army, and drilled a well on the site. When a quartermaster inspector insisted on 50 additional acres for a buffer to keep grog shops and
undesirables off the mesa, the citizens' committee once again raised the funds
and purchased the required land. The quartermaster general then sought an
additional 200 acres for a railroad siding, a demand that was again met by an
increasingly frustrated citizenry with $6,825 in donations from railroad and
real estate investors. Finally, satisfied with the city-donated 1,266 acres the
citizens' committee had purchased from six different landowners, the army
began construction on the site in September, 1892.[15]

In several cases, the fate of property abandoned by the army had an
economic impact on the local community. In 1888, for educational purposes,
the United States gave the city of Austin the old Arsenal Block between Red
River and Third Streets. In 1890 Congress authorized the public sale of the
old Fort Bliss, which was sold off in twenty-five lots for a total of $15,000
between 1895 and 1900 to finance a road to the new Fort Bliss. In 1894 the
site of the old Fort Bliss cemetery was given to the city of El Paso for use as a
park.[16]

By the turn of the century, the federal government owned all of its posts
in Texas, purchasing San Antonio Arsenal (1859), Fort Sam Houston and San
Antonio Depot (1870–1903), Fort McIntosh (1875), Fort Ringgold (1878),
407 acres of Camp Del Rio (1882), 300 acres of Fort Davis (1883), Fort Clark
(1883), Fort Hancock (1884), Fort Bliss (1892), Fort Duncan (1894), Fort Brown
(1895), and several coastal forts around Galveston (1898–1900).[17]

Fort sites were generally selected with priority given to military neces-

TABLE 8.

ARMY QUARTERMASTER EXPENDITURES IN TEXAS

FOR RENTS, LEASES, PURCHASES, REPAIRS,

AND CONSTRUCTION, 1849–1900

Category	Period				Total
	1849–1860	1869–1879	1880–1889	1890–1900	
Buiding repair & construction	$191,900	$2,484,100	$727,100	$965,500	$4,368,600
Rents & leases	$149,200	$125,900	$57,400	$34,500	$367,000
Fort Purchases			$85,665	$330,000	$415,665
Total	$341,100	$2,610,00	$870,165	$1,330,000	$5,151,265

Source: Calculated from each year's "Report of the Quartermaster General of the Army," in the annual
Report of the Secretary of War, 1849–1900.

sity over the convenience of construction or pork-barrel considerations regarding the impact on the local economy. Fort Ewell, founded in 1852, is a case in which military necessity outweighed convenience of construction and perhaps even common sense. Fort Ewell protected the important Nueces River crossing of the San Antonio–Laredo road. However, it was located ten miles from the nearest timber, surrounded by salt marsh, prone to severe flooding, and lacked forage or grazing grass. One inspecting colonel observed, "A less inviting spot for occupation by troops cannot well be conceived." This sentiment was echoed by a lieutenant stationed at the post. He remembered it as, "The most unhealthy and comfortless of all our frontier posts." Mercifully, the army abandoned Fort Ewell in October, 1854. Another poorly sited post was Fort Phantom Hill, founded in 1851 between the Clear and Elm Forks of the Brazos River, four miles from potable water, and forty miles from timber. An 1853 inspector urged the post be moved to an alternate location, adding, "It would really be a charity to remove the garrison."[18]

Once a fort site was chosen with an eye toward water and the availability of natural construction material, the next stage was to select building locations. In Texas, the buildings were seldom arranged for local defense but rather, as the department commander explained in 1852, "The main object in arranging the buildings for cantonments is the health and discipline of the troops." His instructions to subordinate commanders included placing barracks to face the prevailing wind, and to build stables at the foot of slopes to take advantage of proper drainage.[19]

The establishment of each fort had an immediate impact on most nearby communities in the form of a ready commodity market, increasing retail sales, but not necessarily improving the income of the local labor pool. The completion of the lease arrangement in the 1850s and 1860s meant construction by troop labor, often under the supervision of one or two hired citizen specialists. In the late 1860s the pattern began to change to an arrangement favoring contracted private construction projects augmented by troop labor.

Lieutenant Parmenas Taylor Turnley of the First Infantry recorded while establishing Fort Duncan on the Rio Grande in 1849, "No building timber existed anywhere within a hundred miles." Soon finding a good local source of sandstone, Turnley said he "Got a dozen soldiers, whose trade had been stone work, to quarrying stone, others hauling it, and still others went to work putting up a stone storehouse and hospital." Three years later, while serving as the quartermaster opening Fort Terrett on the Llano River, Turnley wrote, "Stone and timber could be had within six miles from the site, and we went to work cutting and hauling logs to put up buildings." Another lieutenant at the site at the same time recorded, "The troops had to cut logs, make shingles, quarry and lay stone, and, in fact, do all of the work necessary to house themselves and the officers."[20]

In 1849 the troops at Fort Lincoln spent most of their first year at the post involved in construction duties, building all sixteen buildings and a corral for less than $2,000. In 1853 the soldiers at Forts Mason, McKavett, and Terrett spent their first three months on the frontier building rather than patrolling. At Fort McIntosh in Laredo, the Fifth Infantry spent the first two months of 1853 constructing a small star-fort field fortification with two corner bastions—real military labor supervised by Maj. Richard Delafield, a future chief of engineers. Considering the state of peace with Mexico, a visiting inspector scoffed at the necessity of the fortification, observing dryly, "The same labor would have put the men in comfortable quarters."[21]

The exclusive use of troop labor for post construction was army policy in the antebellum period. In the wake of the post–Mexican War territorial expansion and the alarming exponential increase in army expenses, Secretary of War Charles M. Conrad, a lawyer without military experience, took strict measures to curb what he termed, "instances of reckless extravagance." Conrad issued field commanders a directive in which he personally reserved the approval of all permanent construction. Hospitals, buildings, quarters, or barracks at frontier posts were to be temporary structures "of the cheapest kind," constructed only with soldier labor. Throughout the 1850s his successors continued Conrad's policy of soldier labor and temporary construction.[22]

Whatever savings were achieved by using soldier labor came at the expense of training efficiency and soldier morale. A Sixteenth Infantry soldier who served in Texas complained, "There is more laboring than soldiering in the U.S. Infantry." An antebellum officer anonymously but publicly railed against the destructive effect of soldier labor, writing: "Esprit du corps and individual efficiency . . . destroy both by scattering the army in squads, employing soldiers to build quarters . . . by putting them at every labor known in civil life without the pay therefor; those not so employed having to do the duty of those that are; the civilian, working by his side, receiving five times his pay for lighter labor, thus breaking down in every possible way his individual as well as professional pride." An antebellum inspector found that the high desertion rate in Texas was directly related to fort construction. "The officers," he reported, "attribute this defection, in most instances, to the dissatisfaction of the soldiers at being put to mechanical labor, constructing adobe houses &c. To such employment they exhibit the greatest repugnance, regarding it as a violation of their contract of enlistment. . . ." As for the impact on training, he added, the requirement to have the troops construct forts resulted in a "serious detriment of their military instruction, and this remark is applicable, in a greater or less degree, to nearly every garrison in Texas."[23]

In the early 1850s Congress denied authorization for most items associated with completing basic construction. One officer wrote of a Texas post in 1852, "As the government refused us everything except iron and nails, the officers had to furnish, at their own expense, doors, sash, and glass." To escape the ninety-nine degree heat at Fort McIntosh in 1856, members of the garrison had to purchase out of their own pockets the corner posts and lumber needed to erect a brush arbor shade over their tents. At the same time, officers at Fort Duncan spent their own money to repair their quarters. A sergeant at Fort Duncan built a set of stone quarters for his family out of personal funds, as did several officers. When the adjutant general of the army reminded the Texas department commander that he was not authorized to use public funds to purchase glass, doors, or hinges, Bvt. Maj. Gen. P. F. Smith fired back a letter calling the measure an unrealistic "absurdity."[24]

Common threads in U.S. military and political policy from 1848 through the 1870s included the lack of funding, uneven fiscal application, the useless expenditure of resources through administrative inefficiencies, and the failure to engage in long-range planning. Simply put, neither politicians nor military authorities had a master plan. The results translated into frustration and waste at the practical level. One large stone building at Fort Clark, nearly completed in 1853 after five months of work by the troops, was abandoned and eventually fell into decay because the quartermaster could not authorize funds to purchase shingles for the roof. That same year, the stone barracks at Forts McKavett and Terrett had the potential for comfort but because of the absence of funds lacked flooring, windows, and doors.[25]

The end result of erecting soldier-constructed buildings on a shoestring budget was entirely predictable: shabby living and shoddy facilities, such as the troop barracks at Ringgold Barracks which an inspector in 1853 called, "wretched hovels not fit for occupancy," and those at Fort Inge, described as being "in a wretched state of delapidation." In 1850 the post doctor at Fort Martin Scott described his medical facility as "a miserable thing made of round logs chinked with mud and clay covered with a [tar]paulin and designated by the proud name of *Hospital.* It has a hole in each end for the purpose of windows without frame sash or glass, but a piece of woolen blanket a foot and half square which serves for all." Lydia Lane, an officer's wife at Fort Inge in 1854, described her soldier-built *jacal* quarters as being "almost ready to tumble down . . . in an advanced stage of decay. A high wind might easily have blown it over."[26]

Similar to the experience of the Spanish colonial army, the U.S. Army on the Texas frontier had a wide inventory of building techniques, each dependent on the availability of manpower and local material. Making use of all types of material—from adobe brick to dressed stone—the army in Texas constructed nearly every form of structure, from rickety *jacal* shelters to formal stone hospitals. Until the late 1870s and the coming of the railroad, sandstone, adobe brick, cedar and oak pole pickets, thatch, and cedar shingle prevailed in southwest Texas and the Rio Grande forts. Adobe, quarried limestone, and pickets were common in the Trans-Pecos. Soldiers in north-central Texas used stone, horizontally laid pine and elm logs, and, on rare occasions, milled lumber.[27]

The doctor at Fort Martin Scott described a building of horizontal log construction, whereas Lydia Lane's quarters were of the more common *jacal* or picket vertical construction. Lieutenant Dabney Maury, Lydia Lane's neighbor in 1854, said of this type of typical west Texas frontier building, found in places where good lengthy timber was scarce: "At Fort Inge they were made of poles set in trenches close together, the many open chinks being daubed with mud. The roofs were thatched, and the floors were of course boards sawed by hand. All was as unsightly as it was comfortless." In describing her 1856 quarters at Fort Clark, Lydia Lane noted: "The walls were built of green logs with the bark left on them, and they were set up on end—not like the usual log cabin. The Mexicans call a house of that kind a 'jacal'. . . . The walls were seven or eight feet high, and supported a slanting roof . . . with an enormous chimney, built of stone, in the middle of it. The spaces between the logs were chinked with mud, or plaster . . . no ceiling— nothing but the shingles over our heads. . . ."[28]

Jacal, palisado, and *chamacuero*—picket or palisade vertical construction—had been a traditional alternative south and west Texas building method since the Spanish colonial era, and remained so after the Civil War. A Sixth Cavalry trooper said of his seven-foot high, fourteen-by-twenty-foot rectangular "picket" barracks at Jacksboro, Texas in 1866: "The building of one was simple; a trench of proper size was dug, say one foot wide and deep, four extra-sized posts were placed at the corners, then the remainder of the 'pickets,' usually from four to six inches through, were sawed a proper length and set in the ditch or trench, side by side, a 'plate' was spiked on the top, a roof, slightly inclined, was made by laying poles side by side, the interstices filled with twigs, and the whole covered thickly with dirt. The spaces in the walls were 'chinked' with chips and plastered with mud; doors made of boxes from the Quartermaster's Department were hung, and with a rude chimney and capacious fireplace, a house was finished in no time." *Palisado* construction was similar, but with one refinement: Rather than buried in a setting trench, the vertical posts or boards were tied or nailed to a log-based sill resting on the ground.[29]

Not all army-constructed buildings were so poorly conceived and executed. In 1853 the buildings at Fort Martin Scott were in good order and well-preserved, as were the comfortable stone buildings constructed by soldiers at Fort Mason.[30]

In spite of the soldier labor and minimum expenses dictated by army policy, the construction of Texas forts on the antebellum frontier did bring a minor amount of direct economic input to the retail markets of local communities. Altogether in the antebellum era of 1849 to 1860, the chief quartermaster authorized the purchase of just over $191,000 worth of building material in Texas. Major Babbitt, quartermaster at the San Antonio depot from 1849 to 1851, purchased $15,000 worth of materials from local businessmen. He bought 249,000 board feet of lumber, paying an average of $50 per 1,000 feet in 1850 and $31 per 1,000 feet by 1851. Babbitt also bought 316,000 shingles at an average price of $5.80 per thousand, and 5,800 adobe bricks at $1.22 per hundred. The Fort Graham quartermaster in 1851 purchased lumber from a mill on Porter's Bluff on the Trinity River, 120 miles away, at a delivered cost of $60 per 1,000 feet. He also contracted with J. C. Brice for twenty thousand clapboards at $2.50 per hundred, and for 150 bushels of lime at 50¢ a bushel.[31]

Typically, as at Forts Mason and McKavett in 1853, the troops collected the timber used in the construction of buildings, sawing it into lumber by hand. However, the five Fifth Infantry companies building Fort Phantom Hill in that same year carried a portable horse-powered sawmill from the Indian Territory, cutting six hundred feet of boards per day, versus a rate of forty feet by hand sawing.[32]

Most Texas posts made minor acquisitions of building material during the period 1849 to 1853. These open-market purchases helped the small lumber mills developing in the region. From 1851 to 1853, Fort Worth purchased pine lumber from mills located 160 miles to the east at $15 to $30 per thousand feet. The price was $60 per 1,000 feet if delivered to the post. The village of Dallas, 38 miles to the east, offered mixed oak and elm lumber at $20 per 1,000 feet, as well as cedar shingles at $5. The Austin depot bought pine lumber in 1851 for $25 per 1,000 feet, while cedar shakes and even bricks were available at a mill within 35 miles. Mills in Bastrop were advertising squared lumber at $25 per 1,000 feet, with planks and sheeting for $12.50 per 1,000 feet. Fort Gates bought lumber from Bastrop, which was 85 miles away, for $20 per 1,000 feet when hauled in government wagons. The cost of transportation doubled or tripled the expense of lumber for many posts. Fort Croghan, located 90 miles from the mill, bought Bastrop lumber for $45 per 1,000 feet delivered. On the southwestern frontier and Rio Grande Line in 1851, Fort Inge purchased $1,000 worth of locally-made cypress planks at $20 per 1,000 feet, but had to buy milled lumber from Bastrop, 165 miles away, at a delivered price of $75 to $80 per 1,000 feet.[33]

Corpus Christi had good brick at $4.50 per thousand in 1851, however, other posts in southwest Texas and on the Rio Grande found it nearly impossible to purchase local lumber and were forced to import their requirements. From 1849 to 1851, sawed lumber imported from Florida sold at Corpus Christi for $21 per 1,000 feet, while shingles were advertised for $4 per thousand. Fort Merrill shipped imported lumber through Corpus Christi at a delivered price of $30 per 1,000 feet. On the Rio Grande in 1851, Fort Brown's quartermaster salvaged lumber from the Mexican War buildings torn down at Brazos Santiago, Point Isabel, and the mouth of the river. He also obtained local brick at $4 per thousand, but paid $28 per 1,000 feet for new lumber shipped from New Orleans. Upriver at Ringgold Barracks, quartermasters also used boards salvaged from Mexican War–vintage buildings on the coast and imported lumber from New Orleans. The price of imported lumber naturally increased the farther upriver it had to be sent. Lumber from New Orleans was shipped up the Rio Grande to Fort McIntosh for $65 per 1,000 feet, while Fort Duncan paid $80 per 1,000 feet for lumber from New Orleans and Florida, and $10 per thousand for shingles.[34]

Compared to the purchase of construction materials, the army dollar accounted for little in the antebellum Texas labor market. Typically during the period 1849 to 1860, a quartermaster hired one or two civilian specialists, such as a stonemason or carpenter, for a few months to provide technical expertise to the troops constructing a post. Between 1849 and 1851, the quartermaster at Fort Graham hired a few citizens to build several small buildings and a kitchen for the hospital, while Fort Gates paid civilians to put up two temporary quarters. Fort Inge hired a stonemason in 1851 at $40 per month for three months to build chimneys for troop-constructed buildings. Fort Lincoln also hired a stonemason for chimneys, while Fort Merrill employed a carpenter and mason to supervise soldier construction, and Fort Phantom Hill hired only a carpenter. In 1853 Phantom Hill paid a stonemason $45 per month and a ration per day, while a carpenter at isolated Fort Belknap cost the quartermaster $75 per month. From October, 1852, until construction of Fort Chadbourne was completed in 1853, the quartermaster hired a citizen master carpenter for $60 per month and a daily ration, and a stonemason for $40 and a ration.[35]

The Rio Grande posts seem to have required more civilian labor than did the frontier forts. Between 1848 and 1851, half of the buildings at Fort Brown were built by citizen labor. Fort Duncan hired a group of laborers to help build an adobe hospital, a stone magazine, and the stables in 1849 and 1850, and three-quarters of the buildings at Ringgold Barracks were built by civilians hired during the same period. Fort McIntosh was the exception to the Rio Grande forts, hiring only a stonemason and two carpenters to supervise soldiers. However, the civilians quit the post in April, 1851, prompting the quartermaster to complain that "Public work at the post . . . has ceased for want of a directing master-workman." That construction should stop for want of supervision seems odd considering the number of West Point–trained officers present among the two First Infantry companies at Fort McIntosh. Graduates of antebellum America's premier engineering school, such as post commander Capt. Sidney Burbank, should have been capable of overseeing the construction of a few temporary buildings.[36]

By 1856, fiscal constraints had all but ended the practice of hiring one or two civilian construction supervisors at Texas frontier forts. An inspector that year reported that the majority of the state's posts had no citizens employed in building and construction.[37]

The general pattern of quartermaster expenditure for frontier post construction in antebellum Texas was an initial start-up cost of a few thousand dollars, followed by a yearly maintenance allocation of a few hundred dollars. Fort Inge, built between 1849 and 1853 at a cost of $1,680—including lumber, roof shakes, and the hire of a stonemason for three months—received practically no repair funds afterward. From 1852 to 1857, Fort Clark received $13,867 for initial construction, followed by a total allocation of only $349 in the years 1858 to 1861. The Austin depot spent $8,821 on construction between 1849 and 1852 but garnered only $863 for maintenance and repair operations during the subsequent three years. Fort McKavett was an exception, spending $152 during its first five years of operation, 1852 to 1856, and then receiving $1,534 for a building program in 1857 and 1858. The Trans-Pecos forts were fiscal orphans. The chief quartermaster allocated only $367 for Fort Davis between 1854 and 1861, while Fort Quitman, founded in 1858, received $358 during its three years of operation. The chief Texas quartermaster gave Fort Bliss $20.12 in 1858, and an additional $519 over the next two years. The most impoverished post in the antebellum years was Fort Stockton, which was awarded $4.18 for start-up costs in 1859, followed by an additional 75¢ for repairs in 1860.[38]

Compared to the frontier line, the Rio Grande forts were affluent. The most expensive post in antebellum Texas, Fort Brown, which was built between 1848 and 1852, had a construction fund of $37,497. The post then received a yearly average repair allocation of $620 through 1861. Ringgold Barracks spent $2,865 on initial construction between 1848 and 1850, then drew an average additional annual allocation of $102 until the Civil War. From 1849 to 1851, Fort McIntosh spent $2,508 on building the initial post infrastructure, then received an average of $222 per year afterward. The chief quartermaster allocated Fort Duncan $9,615 during the period 1849 to 1851, and an ample average of $372 per year for the remainder of the decade.[39]

Army leadership recognized the difficulty of properly housing troops in an immature theater of war such as Texas, approving an experiment in the mid-1850s to help solve the problem. Captain Parmenas Turnley, after spending years trying to find suitable material for constructing temporary army buildings on the Texas frontier, designed a portable cottage system that could be transported in a common army wagon. Designed in 1854, Turnley's Cottage, as it was known, could be erected in half a day and came in two sizes: 30 by 15 feet and 40 by 18 feet. However, the prefabricated buildings had their limitations. In June, 1856, twelve sets of Turnley quarters were damaged while being shipped to Fort Clark. That same month, Fort Lancaster installed six Turnley buildings: three barracks and three sets of officers' quarters. All of the buildings had likewise been damaged while being transported, prompting an inspector to label them "too delicate" for frontier use.[40]

Altogether, the Quartermaster's Department expended about 9 percent of its Texas budget—a total of $341,100—on rents, leases, repair, and construction during the period 1849 to 1861. Of that amount, 44 percent ($149,200) went toward rents and leases and 56 percent ($191,900) toward building construction and repair. The majority of the funds were decentralized disbursements to a wide variety of individual craftsmen and businessmen, rather than to a few major commercial monopolies.[41]

The initial stages of the army's post–Civil War occupation of Texas were a repetition of the antebellum pattern of using troop labor for post construction. In 1867, a Sixth Cavalry troop arrived at Buffalo Springs and, instead of patrolling for Indian raiders, the soldiers set about building corrals, stables, a dam, a bridge, and temporary quarters. This provoked one aggravated cavalry recruit to remark, "It had pretty nearly dawned on my mind by this time that the frontier troops in our army were simply 'armed laborers,' nothing less, nothing more."[42]

However, to complete the construction of Buffalo Springs, the Texas chief quartermaster sent a civilian labor force of eighty-eight carpenters, masons, and other craftsmen in the summer of 1867. The quality of the hired civilian workforce left something to be desired, being consistent with the transient nature of the work and the inherent risks of the frontier. According to a sharply critical cavalry sergeant at Buffalo Springs, civilian laborers there "Did absolutely nothing; just put in their time and were in each other's way." The risks incurred by citizens seeking army jobs on the frontier became painfully apparent in July, 1867, when the tiny garrison was attacked by Comanche Indians. When the civilian laborers rushed for the safety of the post from their construction camp, the warriors mistakenly believed them to be army reinforcements. Instead of assaulting the fort, they conducted a two-day siege, during which the soldiers armed the civilians with the few sabers that could be spared. By November, 1867, the chief quartermaster increased the citizen workforce to 110 craftsmen and laborers. In the end, Buffalo Springs became an example of the deficit of long-range planning at department headquarters. After six months of toil and the expenditure of $30,282 on civilian wages and $5,680 for material and assorted other requirements, the army had spent a total of $35,962 on the post—which it promptly abandoned on November 20, 1867.[43]

The same Sixth Cavalry troop that had to abandon the results of its hard labor at Buffalo Springs marched to garrison Fort Richardson at Jacksboro. There the barracks had been contracted for civilian construction but were incomplete when the troop arrived. "We at once commenced erecting our temporary barracks," recalled a cavalryman, "but owing to the scarcity of materials . . . they were, when finished, neither elegant nor waterproof."[44]

In spite of the continued use of soldier labor for fort building, the army in the post–Civil War era began to make more extensive use of citizen labor. A Fort Richardson soldier reported about 150 citizens were employed in the building program, "Doing such work as is usually performed on government enterprises—that is to say, doing the very least amount of work in the greatest given amount of time." From December, 1867, to June, 1868, the Quartermaster's Department paid these civilian employees $53,873 in wages and purchased materials worth $16,729 for the post's construction.[45]

At Camp Wilson, later called Fort Griffin, the chief quartermaster hired twenty-seven civilian construction employees between August and November, 1867, paying wages of $17,902 and purchasing $4,000 worth of materials for establishing the fort. The chief quartermaster sent a portable sawmill to Fort Davis in August, 1867. It went into operation the following month with the arrival of a workforce of 122 civilians that included forty masons and forty-three carpenters. Although the number of workers fell to ninety-six by December, 1867, in six months they were able to cut seventy thousand shingles and 89,317 board feet of lumber. The cost of civilian employment for the first six months at Fort Davis came to $29,671, with the quartermaster purchasing $9,660 worth of materials. The result of this expenditure was four partially completed buildings. Fort Stockton's lumber mill also arrived in August, 1867, but the supervising quartermaster there discovered there was no wood to cut into boards. A citizen workforce of 119 laborers drawing $5,696 in wages per month made adobe bricks while the quartermaster was forced to purchase $3,109 worth of lumber and $1,314 worth of shingles from Uvalde suppliers located three hundred miles away.[46]

During the twelve months from June, 1867, to June, 1868, the Texas frontier fort-building program, excluding the Rio Grande Line, spent more than $386,058 on citizen employment and $79,496 for materials—the equivalent of twice the total building and repair funds expended during the thirteen years of antebellum Texas operations. Texas quartermasters spent 68 percent of the entire army's 1868 construction and repair budget. In the first five years after the Civil War, 1865 to 1870, quartermasters expended $1,355,153 on Texas fort construction as old antebellum posts were refurbished and several new posts were constructed. This money was a benefit for Texas construction craftsmen and labor, particularly in the hard-pressed Texas economy of the Reconstruction era. During those same five years, Fort Bliss spent $9,344, while Fort Brown expended $300,670. Between 1867 and 1870 the Austin depot spent $337,581, Fort Davis $98,891, Fort Stockton $108,963, and Fort Concho $96,883. Between 1868 and the end of 1870, Fort Quitman spent $4,803, Fort Clark, $13,200, Fort McKavett, $16,885, and Fort Duncan $20,655. The repair and new construction programs for Ringgold Barracks and Fort McIntosh did not get underway until 1869 and 1870, with the former receiving $20,530 and the latter $13,625. However, to finance this construction on the Rio Grande the department quartermaster had to cut funds for the Trans-Pecos frontier, halting many construction projects in March, 1869. The civilian force at Fort Davis dropped from over a hundred to just eighteen. One citizen worker there complained that the army had to "Abandon the buildings nearly completed to the drenching rains and driving storms

. . . had the work . . . progressed . . . the early Autumn would have found the Post completed." The labor shortage caused construction of nine sets of quarters on Fort Davis's "officers' row" to drag on until January, 1871.[47]

Although the post–Civil War construction program was sufficient to create reasonable living conditions at the posts, there were cases, such as at Buffalo Springs, where the lack of a grand design or long-term planning created a waste of resources, time, and money. Other factors, such as the system of financing construction and the high turnover rate of post commanders, also contributed to inefficiencies in the building program. Congressional appropriations for specific buildings at specific posts allowed local quartermasters little flexibility. When money was available, post commanders, changing at a rapid rate, often altered the direction and priorities of the local construction program. The case of Fort Concho during the period 1867 to 1872 illustrates both points.

Texas' chief quartermaster paved the way for the construction of Fort Concho in the summer of 1867 by sending a sawmill and civilian workforce from San Antonio. For various reasons, the sawmill did not get into operation until November. The citizen laborers spent the intervening three months cutting stone by hand and chopping raw timber to feed the mill when it began to function. In November a board of officers changed the fort site, moving it from the south bank of the North Concho to the conflux of the North and Middle Concho Rivers. Because of a shortage of wagon transportation, none of the cut material could be moved to the new fort site. Although no buildings were completed, the army still had to pay $27,347 in wages to the citizen employees, leaving it little to show for the outlay.[48]

Captain David W. Porter was the quartermaster responsible for supervising construction at Fort Concho. This was typical of the way the army handled its building program on the Texas frontier. Rather than award a general contract for construction, a local quartermaster officer served in the role of general contractor, purchasing materials, organizing transportation, and hiring a civilian labor foreman to oversee the workforce. Porter had to haul some of the building supplies to Fort Concho by ox cart from the Texas coast—supplies that subsequently sat idle because of the difficulty he encountered in bringing enough labor to the remote site. By January, 1868, he had managed to lay the foundation for just one permanent building, the commissary storehouse. An increase in the workforce in the summer of 1868 brought additional progress, and by the time Porter died in October, 1871, the post had a stone corral and eight stone buildings—including two company-sized barracks, officers' quarters, quartermaster storehouses, and a hospital. Unfortunately, the 1872 building program floundered because of bureaucratic confusion. Workers had completed one additional building and portions of four more were in various stages of construction when, in February 1872, the project was once again halted and the citizen labor force discharged because Congress failed to allocate additional funds. The post surgeon found the entire system wasteful. Considering the "Misguided policy of the holders of the purse strings," he wrote, ". . . Mechanics have been collected far and wide in the country, at great trouble and expense, they have been kept but half employed during the winter, in preparation for the more favorable building season, and yet, as that season opens, they are discharged and scattered, for the want of a small appropriation. After a few months, work may go on again, but the men will be far from where they are needed, the material will have deteriorated, the favorable season wasted, and the stigma of waste and extravagance fastened stronger upon the army by this illusion, and yet the subject is beyond army control."[49]

A final factor reducing the efficiency of fort building on the Texas frontier was the high turnover rate of post commanders. Between 1867 and 1871, Fort Concho had twelve different commanding officers. The impact on the building program was recorded by post surgeon William M. Notson: "The different views of the separate commanders as to the detailed manner by which that result should be accomplished, has uniformly caused much time and labor, and of course money, to be expended by the power of the hour, in undoing some of the labor of his predecessor."[50]

The last of the important new forts built on the Texas frontier came in 1875 when, in April, Congress appropriated $70,000 for Fort Elliott, a six-company post at McClellan's Creek. After discovering there was a local source for timber, the quartermaster general released only $40,000 for the fort's construction.[51]

In general, by the mid-1870s, the construction and improvement program heralded a dramatic improvement in the living conditions of many Texas army families. At Fort Clark in 1876, two decades after Lydia Lane complained about her *jacal* hovel there, Frances Boyd, the wife of an Eighth Cavalry lieutenant, described her quarters enthusiastically as "A very comfortable little house, built of limestone, and charming as to exterior . . . double parlors on the ground floor and two large bedrooms above."[52]

The building of a modern and permanent San Antonio depot in the 1870s is also illustrative of the local lobbying, War Department infighting, legal wrangles, and bureaucratic frustration associated with army construction in the aftermath of the Civil War. In 1870 San Antonio made the first of three land donations to the Quartermaster's Department so it could build a permanent, large-scale depot in the city. The titles languished under review for two years at the Justice Department while, in 1871, Quartermaster General Meigs secured Secretary of War William W. Belknap's approval to spend a hundred thousand dollars of quartermaster funds on the project. In 1872 the attorney general finally approved the titles for the quartermaster depot, but on May 18 Congress passed an appropriations bill that gave it special authority for approval of any army permanent structure costing more than $20,000. Secretary Belknap, who had opposed the San Antonio project all along, ordered a halt to planning for the depot there and returned the money to the Treasury Department. The commanding general of the army, Lt. Gen. William T. Sherman, also opposed the depot but publicly grumbled that the requirement to gain special approval from Congress caused "Much embarrassment and probably waste of money."[53]

On March 3, 1873 Congress passed a new appropriations bill authorizing $100,000 for the San Antonio depot. Secretary Belknap, still unconvinced of the need for the supply center and wanting to use the money to buy other Texas fort sites, ordered Quartermaster General Meigs to take no action. Meigs countered Belknap's shortsightedness by publicly pointing out that San Antonio was Texas' natural transportation hub and that the army spent $25,000 per year in rents in the city. Meigs declared that building the depot was of "great importance and economy," as well as an embarrassment because the city had given the land after the War Department promised to build a depot on it. Meanwhile, the San Antonio city council took action, raising $1,000 to send a local merchant—West Point graduate, former regular army officer, and Confederate Col. Thomas Greenhow Williams—to Washington to lobby for the depot. Backed by Texas' congressional delegation and a petition signed by 496 San Antonians, Williams made several trips to the nation's capital, eventually gaining adequate support from army leaders and legislators. Acting on a bill introduced by Sen. James Glanagan, Congress reappropriated the $100,000 in March, 1875, and in May Secretary Belknap, facing increasing political pressure from the Texas delegation, finally relented, giving Meigs permission to continue the process of building the depot. Meigs soon discovered that the construction estimates exceeded by $20,000 the original $100,000 appropriation, forcing him to halt the project and seek bids for a commercial contract within the appropriated amount. The San Antonio firm of Ed. Braden and Company, owned by Edward Braden and J. W. Angus, was awarded the contract in June, 1876, and began work under the military supervision of Capt. George W. Davis of the Fourteenth

Infantry. By the end of June, construction of the "Quadrangle," as it came to be called, was well underway. The foundation was in place by November, and parts of the walls reached as high as eighteen feet.[54]

Built on an 8.94-acre site on Government Hill, the interior depot plaza contained 7.36 acres, with a total of 1.81 acres under roof, providing over a million cubic feet of storage space. Constructed from locally quarried stone, the massive, cream-colored limestone walls originally formed a rectangle 624 feet long and 499.5 feet wide, with an entry sally port in the two-story south wall. As a fire-fighting measure, an eighty-seven-foot stone watchtower with a Seth Thomas clock held a six-thousand-gallon iron water tank that was filled by steam pumps. The work from the original plan for the San Antonio depot was completed in July, 1877, allowing the chief quartermaster to close operations at the Alamo compound and to transfer supplies and stores to the new depot. After the initial structure was completed, the quartermaster general received an additional $20,000 appropriation and ordered the second story of the south front to be extended by adding sixteen rooms to house the headquarters for the Department of Texas, thus saving the cost of rent for downtown office space. The additions were completed in February, 1878, for $19,952, and the Quadrangle became the army's logistical and operational center in Texas.[55]

Aside from the San Antonio depot project, Texas' chief quartermaster spent $2.4 million on Texas fort construction and repair in the 1870s. In 1870 Texas received 50 percent of the army's construction and repair budget. That figure fell to 19 percent in 1873 and to 12 percent in 1874. By 1874 the Texas building boom was over, the annual expenditure for the state being only $84,549 that year.[56]

Fort construction and repair expenditures in the 1880s generally took the form of maintenance upkeep expenses and modest spending on new buildings at each post, rather than the larger scale fort-building projects of the 1870s. In 1880, for example, the long-serving Texas chief quartermaster, Maj. and Bvt. Brig. Gen. Benjamin C. Card, spent $5,137 repairing various post hospitals and $2,491 on the construction of a twelve-bed hospital in San Antonio. In addition, Card spent $22,857 on repair and construction of barracks and quarters at Texas forts, of which $1,528 went toward skilled labor, indicating Texas troops still did much of the repair work themselves. A typical expenditure was $867 for adding a room to the commanding officer's quarters at Fort Duncan. The most expensive project in 1880 was $3,418 for two new cavalry stables at Fort Davis. Card also wanted to institute a system of using portable buildings similar to the earlier Turnley Cottages at Texas posts, but the economy measure was not acted on by the army's leadership.[57]

Responding to pressure from the surgeon general, who reported finding increasing evidence of the health risks in water and sewage sources, Congress in 1884 began a system of regular appropriations to improve the water supply and sewage systems at forts. In Texas that year, Forts Davis, Brown, and McIntosh received a total of $6,000 to upgrade their systems and improve soldier health.[58]

The year 1884 also brought several new major military projects to Texas. Congress approved the spending of $9,831 on quarters and a corral at Fort Bliss. Camp Rice, an 1881 subpost of Fort Davis, became an independent post soon to be called Fort Hancock thanks to an expansion program of $47,200 for quarters and other buildings. In July, 1884, Congress appropriated $75,000 seed money for the construction of San Antonio Barracks at the developing Post of San Antonio—a $175,000 project begun in late 1886. In addition to the San Antonio project, the Texas chief quartermaster in 1887 spent $31,705 on repairs and construction, of which $5,093 went to citizen labor and specialists such as carpenters and stonemasons.[59]

Frustrated with the meager average of $40,000 he received for Texas building and repair, Department Commander Stanley reported in 1887: "The barracks and quarters at all the posts in this department, excepting at San Antonio and Fort Hancock, are old and of very faulty construction. . . . Improvements and large repairs upon the decaying buildings are very essential. The allowance of funds from the Quartermaster's Department . . . will not suffice to keep pace, by repairs, with the ravages of time."[60]

Although stymied by the slow pace of appropriations, General Stanley could take satisfaction in the progress of the Post of San Antonio. The Staff Post, fifteen sets of quarters designed by English-Texan Alfred Giles, was built at San Antonio in 1881. The mid-1880s brought a second major construction project calling for construction of an administration building, eight barracks, and eleven sets of officers' quarters for the fort. Called the Infantry Post, the San Antonio Barracks project began in 1886. The contract for the barracks went to P. T. Shields for $9,545 each, while five officers' quarters and outbuildings went to J. G. Marshall for $31,012. Ed Braden Jr. of San Antonio contracted for all of the plumbing for the buildings at $3,500. By 1889, two barracks and five sets of officers quarters had been completed at a cost of $51,002. Additional appropriations in the amount of $51,109 were approved in 1889 for the construction of seven officers' quarters, a bakery, and an ammunition magazine. Finally, in 1891, Congress appropriated $57,266—

the remainder of the funds needed for building what became Fort Sam Houston.[61]

Aside from the separate appropriation for the San Antonio Barracks, Texas' chief quartermaster expended $727,100 for construction and repair during the 1880s, much of it contracted to local commercial firms—a change from the pattern of the 1870s, when a quartermaster officer served as the general contractor for post construction.

In 1892, moving Fort Bliss four miles north of the border generated $167,704 worth of construction contracts for a brick double barracks, a mess hall, a hospital, a stable, storehouses, and thirteen sets of quarters. Although it was the largest project in El Paso history to that point, many of the contractors and much of the skilled labor came from other areas. Construction began in September, 1892, with the initial work completed by February, 1893. F. L. Stevenson of Dallas built the barracks, George H. Evans of Topeka, Kansas, secured the contract for the quarters and other buildings, and Charles Schumme of San Antonio installed the sewer system. Three El Paso firms earned contracts for the new post: Hammer and Caples for plumbing, Davis and Symons for steam pumps and iron mains, and E. S. Newman for the water wells. In addition to the local contractors involved in the project, most of the unskilled laborers in the 240-man building crew came from the El Paso area. While not all of the contracted money flowed into the local commercial market, the project did help soften the severe economic impact of the Panic of 1893.[62]

A year after Fort Bliss was built, the new construction authorization for the entire Department of Texas was a meager $14,693. Repairs came to $20,152, with an additional $5,772 appropriated for hospital repair. With the exception of the coastal fort program, the same basic pattern held for the remainder of the 1890s. In 1897, for example, Just $11,095 was appropriated for new construction in Texas, while posts received $22,664 for repairs and $2,350 for hospital repair. Congress also approved an additional $4,000 for a military road from El Paso to the new Fort Bliss.[63]

Ironically, naval events in the late 1880s and 1890s brought an additional minor boon to army construction in the state. As a result of the 1886 Endicott Board, Congress became acutely aware of the poor state of the nation's coastal defenses in light of the world's powerful new steel navies. However, funding to construct a modernized coastal fortress system was slow to materialize until the threat of a war with Spain, which produced a $15 million program that included a modest commitment for the Texas coast. In 1897 Congress authorized $71,000 for a contracted project for coastal battery construction at Galveston beginning with Fort Point, which soon was re-named Fort San Jacinto. Starting with a concrete torpedo casement completed in June, 1897, the project consisted of a group of wooden buildings with electricity, including a one-battery barracks, mess hall, and two officers' quarters, all of which were finished in December, 1899. An additional $14,060 was added to the contract for a barracks and buildings at Camp Hawley, along with $3,332 for a wharf at Bolivar Point. In April, 1900, construction began on a $67,832 building project at Fort Crockett on the Galveston beachfront. The foundations had just been started when, on September 8, 1900, a hurricane swept away the buildings at Fort San Jacinto and Camp Hawley and destroyed the work done at Fort Crockett. The batteries were subsequently abandoned. In March, 1901, Congress appropriated $992,000 for repair of the forts. That project was completed in 1906, although only Fort Crockett was regarrisoned in 1911.[64]

Lieutenant General Sherman wrote in 1882 that the railroads had made possible a concentration of frontier garrisons, calling for the end of the policy of temporary quarters and for the establishment of permanent posts. "The time is now," he wrote, "for a radical change in our whole system of piece-meal work in quartering troops. . . . For a hundred years we have been sweeping across the continent with a skirmish line, building a post here and another there, to be abandoned next year for another line. . . . Many of them are now worse than useless; built of the rawest materials, mere shelters against the winter's storm." Sherman included in his report to Congress that year a list of posts he wished to keep permanent; San Antonio was the only one in Texas. He proposed keeping Fort Elliott for ten years, and expressed a desire to abandon the rest of the Texas posts.[65]

Much of Sherman's idea of the efficiency of concentration reached fruition by the end of the nineteenth century. In 1896, of seventy posts in an army of 25,426 soldiers, only six (8.5 percent) were one-company forts, while twenty posts (28 percent) housed eight or more companies. The army's leaders were finally achieving the concentration they had so long sought. Texas went from thirty-two posts and stations in 1868 to only seven in 1896. The majority of the 1,913 troops in the state in 1896 were stationed in multicompany posts: eleven companies at Fort Sam Houston, six at Fort Clark, three at Fort Bliss, and two each at Forts McIntosh, Ringgold, and Brown. Only Fort Duncan at Eagle Pass remained a one-company outpost in the earlier tradition of the Texas frontier.[66]

Because Texas had no federal land, the army was required to lease its fort sites and pay a premium for wood rights and other amenities. Not until after the Civil War was a program of fort purchase vigorously pursued and, because of legal and title complications, that took three decades to complete. The Texas fort-building program moved through a series of patterns. The 1850s saw a policy troop labor and minimal costs. In the late 1860s fort construction was accomplished by a combination of troop and civilian labor, supervised by a quartermaster officer acting in the role of a general contractor. Construction of the San Antonio depot beginning in 1876 inaugurated the system of general commercial contracting for a complete project, a system that was extended to fort expansion in the 1880s. In the process of this transition, the army spent $217,800 on rents and leases, $415,665 on the purchase of fort sites, and $4,176,700 on post construction and repair. The greatest economic impact was felt by Texas' struggling economy during Reconstruction. Altogether, the army pumped $5.1 million into the state's economy through leases, rents, purchases, and building repair between 1849 and 1900, spending 93 percent of that money after the Civil War.

Taylor's Army of Occupation at Corpus Christi, October, 1845. *Brigadier Gen. Zachary Taylor's Mexican War regular forces occupied Corpus Christi for six months, boosting the port's civilian population from a few dozen inhabitants to more than two thousand. From November, 1852, to September, 1855, Corpus Christi served as the military headquarters for the Department of Texas. This sketch shows an infantry regiment drilling to the center right of the tents, a steamer underway in the bay, and a wagon column approaching the camp from the north. The original sketch was by Capt. Daniel P. Whiting, Seventh Infantry. This print on stone is by C. Parsons, and was lithographed and printed in color by G. & W. Endicott in 1847. Courtesy Prints and Photographs Division, Library of Congress, negative number LC-USZ62-126*

Port of Galveston, 1845. *The 1898 completion of a three-decade project to transform Galveston to a deepwater port was the greatest triumph of the U.S. Army Corps of Engineers in nineteenth-century Texas. The original image is a wood engraving in the* Illustrated London News, *January 4, 1845. Courtesy Prints and Photographs Division, Library of Congress, negative number LC-USZ61-293*

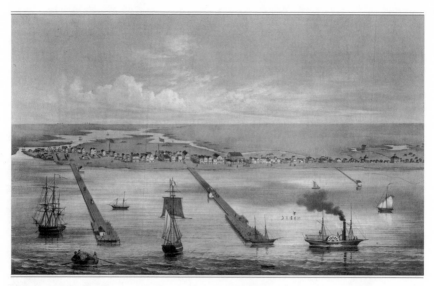

View of Indianola, September, 1860. *This is the "Powder Horn" extension of the original town founded three miles up the bay in 1846 and named in 1849. Indianola was the great gateway to military logistics on the Texas frontier, and for most of the antebellum era the army leased a wharf and warehouse at the site. From this port, army quartermasters and contractors moved supplies by wagon to frontier forts and to major depots such as San Antonio or Austin. Most of the town was destroyed by a hurricane in September, 1875. The original image is a hand-colored lithograph by Ed Lang after a drawing by Helmuth Holtz done from the royal yard of the bark Texana. Courtesy Prints and Photographs Division, Library of Congress, negative number LC-USZ62-1324*

Fort Brown, 1861. *Built opposite Matamoros by the Seventh Infantry as Fort Texas in March, 1846, this post served as a supply transfer point for the Rio Grande forts throughout the last half of the nineteenth century. The postwar satellite village of Brownsville became a major trading hub of the lower Rio Grande and northern Mexico. Engraving from* Harper's Weekly, *March 23, 1861. Courtesy University of Texas, Institute of Texan Cultures, San Antonio, negative number 92-131*

Point Isabel, 1861. *Established on the site of the Mexican village of El Frontón de Santa Isabel in March, 1846, Port Isabel and Brazos Santiago, located three miles across the Laguna Madre on Clark Island, served as the key logistical complex for the Mexican War and the cornerstone of military supply on the Rio Grande during the antebellum and post–Civil War eras. Army depot operations ceased at Brazos Santiago after a hurricane wrecked the wharf and warehouse in September, 1874. This engraving from* Harper's Weekly, April 13, 1861, *shows the side-wheeled steamer* Daniel Webster *sailing with U.S. troops aboard during the federal exodus at the start of the Civil War. Courtesy University of Texas, Institute of Texan Cultures, San Antonio, negative number 72-337*

Military Plaza, San Antonio, 1880s. *According to the 1850 census, overland freighting was the most important occupation of San Antonio citizens, and in 1854 Frederick Law Olmsted reported that freighting "forms the principal support of the Mexican population." In 1870, the quartermaster general of the army, Maj. Gen. Montgomery C. Meigs, observed, "San Antonio is the natural center of interior commerce of Texas. . . ." Until the coming of the railroad, San Antonio was the hub of frontier roads and the most important wagon freight center in Texas, making the city crucial to army quartermaster operations in the department. This 1880s photograph of a variety of light wagons in the plaza is from the* San Antonio Light *Collection. Courtesy University of Texas, Institute of Texan Cultures, San Antonio, negative number 1226-R*

The Alamo as a Quartermaster Depot, ca. 1868. *When Army quartermasters used the Mission San Antonio de Valero as a Mexican War supply depot in August–September, 1846, they repaired the Long Barracks and cleared debris from the shrine or church floor. In 1849 the Quartermaster's Department leased the Alamo compound for a depot, using it until 1861 and adding to the shrine the distinctive curvilinear upper gable, upper flooring, and a new roof—none of which was present during the 1836 siege. After the Civil War, the Alamo again served as an army supply depot until 1877. This prompted one soldier to record of the shrine of Texas liberty in 1866: "To the everlasting disgrace of Texas, no noble monument marks the spot; in fact when I first saw it, it was part of a livery stable." This photograph, probably taken in 1868, shows an army wagon pulled partially into the shrine and two more waiting in Alamo Plaza. The building to the left was originally the mission convent. Photograph from Catholic Archives, Austin. Courtesy University of Texas, Institute of Texan Cultures, San Antonio, negative number 82-489*

The Quadrangle, San Antonio, 1937. *Purpose-built in 1876–77 as the San Antonio Depot, the hundred-thousand-dollar project constructed by the San Antonio firm of Ed Braden and Company produced the first modernized quartermaster depot in Texas. The seven-acre quadrangle compound in the lower half of this photograph has at its center an eighty-seven-foot stone tower, which held a six-thousand-gallon iron water tank that used*

steam pumps to feed water to fight fires in the depot's one million feet of storage space. The second story of the south front, shown at the bottom of the photograph, was added in 1878 to house the Department of Texas' military headquarters. This 1937 aerial view is from the San Antonio Light *Collection. Courtesy University of Texas, Institute of Texan Cultures, San Antonio, negative number 2231-H*

The Army Wagon. *The ubiquitous six-mule army wagon moved tons of government freight on the Texas frontier. Ten feet long and hauling but two thousand pounds, the army wagon was no match for the rugged twenty-four-foot, ten-mule wagons used by some Texas commercial freighters to carry up to seven thousand pounds of army contract cargo. This pattern of the army wagon, manufactured from the early 1850s, has a rear brake—a feature added after 1862. The six-mule army wagon was replaced by a lighter four-mule version in 1878. Courtesy National Archives and Records Service, Washington, D.C., negative number 111-SC-91012*

U.S. Army Freighters, Fort Clark, 1885. *This image of long-haul wagon teamsters disappeared from the Texas frontier within a few years after this picture was taken. The railroad, which had already crossed the Trans-Pecos two years prior to this photograph, soon reached Spofford Junction near Fort Clark. These teamsters have a six-mule army wagon and are armed with the U.S. Model 1879 Springfield carbine. The cartridge belt hanging from the tree appears to have a Model 1883 buckle. On top of the wooden barrel above the left shoulder of the seated teamster is a typical field coffee grinder. This photo by Form & Lang at Fort Clark was originally in the collection of Sam Nesmith. The University of Texas, Institute of Texan Cultures, San Antonio, Texas, courtesy Sam Nesmith, negative number 75-335*

Wood Haulers, Fort Davis. *Army quartermasters bought 1.5 million dollars worth of firewood and charcoal from nineteenth-century Texans. This photograph is of a wood wagon at the steps of the post hospital in the late 1880s. Courtesy National Park Service; Fort Davis National Historic Site, Texas; negative number HD-46-6*

Fort Davis under Construction, 1867. *Not until the post–Civil War era did Congress approve significant funds or adequate civilian construction labor on the Texas frontier. In this pen-and-ink sketch titled "Construction of the Second Fort Davis," taken from a front cover of* Harper's Weekly *in October, 1867, the 1856 post undergoes a major building project, part of a 1.3 million dollar, five-year construction program for Texas after the war. A workforce of 122 civilians began building in the summer of 1867. The view is from the north side of the post and shows construction starting on "officers' row" on the left. The line of roofless structures in the center is the ruin of the original Eighth Infantry barracks. The older antebellum buildings are in the vicinity of the flagpole. Courtesy National Park Service; Fort Davis National Historic Site, Texas; negative number F-81*

Fort Davis under Construction, 1871. *In this photograph of "officers' row," the darker set of quarters on the left of the line is under construction. It is lacking a porch, door fixtures, windows, and whitewash. The decayed roofless building behind it is an original antebellum barracks. Courtesy National Park Service; Fort Davis National Historic Site, Texas; negative number HG-2*

Fort Davis Hospital under Construction, 1871. *Typical of the immediate post–Civil War period on the Texas frontier, Fort Davis had ten different commanders in the four years spanning 1869 to 1872. This instability had a negative impact on long-term planning and the details of post construction. This flawed original photographic image is of a hospital building under construction behind "officers' row." The project subsequently was abandoned before completion, dismantled, and moved west to "Hospital Canyon" about 1875. Courtesy National Park Service; Fort Davis National Historic Site, Texas; negative number HG-10*

Steamer *Bessie* on the Rio Grande, 1890. *Army quartermasters supplying Taylor's army during the Mexican War created the steamship business on the Rio Grande in 1846 and subsequently contracted steamers to furnish posts along the river until the end of the 1880s. Owned by William Kelly, the 100-ton sternwheeler* Bessie *is shown here unloading cargo at Fort Ringgold in Rio Grande City. Kelly and his* Bessie *had the army water-freight contract on the river from 1881 to 1889. Kelly*

was the last of the Rio Grande operators, running his boat until 1904. Courtesy National Archives and Records Service, Washington, D.C. American West photo number 29 [negative number 92-F-95-19A]

CHAPTER 6

Additional Expenses

Fuel, Rations, Beef, Horses and Mules, Military Cemeteries, and Sutlers and Post Traders

In addition to large ticket items such as forage, transportation costs, post rents, leases, and building programs, logisticians had to make fiscal arrangements for a number of lesser but vital aspects of providing for the army in nineteenth-century Texas. Although of narrower impact and scale than such items as transportation contracts, these additional economic areas were important to the Texans involved in the transactions and served to put army dollars into frontier development.

FUEL

The wood and charcoal used to cook soldiers' rations and to heat their barracks became, like every other aspect of support for the army, a source of $1.5 million worth of commerce for Texans and an expense to the federal government. Beginning in 1845, locally purchased charcoal and hardwood such as mesquite or oak, rather than imported coal, was the principal source of fuel for soldiers in Texas. The quartermasters in Taylor's army at Corpus Christi preparing for the Mexican War in 1845 paid Henry L. Kinney $1.50 per cord for wood taken from his lands. Seven years later, Kinney charged the small army garrison at Corpus Christi $5 per cord for wood that was cut and delivered by his workers.[1]

The army standard for hardwood in 1858 was a cord five feet wide, four feet high, and twelve feet, nine inches long. This cord of 255 cubic feet was considerably larger than a modern cord of wood, which measures 128 cubic feet. Like the specific allowance for rations, forage, and other classes of supply, the quartermaster general established complicated guidelines for the exact amount of wood authorized to soldiers based on rank, the season of the year, and the latitude of the post. In the regulations of 1881, for example, an enlisted soldier in a Texas barracks south of thirty-six degrees latitude was allotted a twelfth of a cord per month from May to August, and a sixth of a cord per month from September to April. A captain with two rooms and a kitchen could have three-fourths of a cord and three cords respectively.[2]

The relatively mild Texas climate and the ready availability of wood kept expenses to a minimum. Nevertheless, in the antebellum period from 1849 to 1861, Texas quartermasters purchased more than $61,000 worth of fuel in the state: about twelve thousand cords of wood at an average price of $3 to $5 per cord, and ninety-six hundred bushels of charcoal at 16¢ to 25¢ per bushel. Between 1867 and 1900, the army in Texas bought 350,000 cords of wood for $1.4 million at a typical price of $5 per cord, and 273,000 bushels of charcoal for $115,000, at a price of 30¢ to 40¢ per bushel.[3]

As with forage, some fuel was contracted and much was purchased on the open market. A number of the leases on frontier posts gave the soldiers the right to cut wood. At Fort Inge in 1853, wood rights were included in the lease, while at Fort Terrett an army inspector reported the four infantry companies at that post used an average of 561 cords of wood per year at a cost of $2.75 per cord. The San Antonio depot and all of the Rio Grande posts were far from direct sources of wood and routinely contracted for delivery. In 1871 Texas quartermasters let eighteen contracts for a total of seventeen thousand cords of wood at an average price of $5.16 per cord, as well as fourteen contracts for a total of 13,700 bushels of charcoal at an average price of 48¢ a bushel.[4]

Officers serving on a post Receiving Board inspecting delivered goods had to keep an eye out for the sharp practices of wood contractors, just as they did for forage sellers. Charles Judson Crane recalled that while he was serving as a lieutenant in the Twenty-fourth Infantry at Fort Duncan in 1878, wood contractors were adept at hollow-stacking cords of wood and cheating the government by 10 percent. Later, at Camp Peña Colorado in 1880, Crane discovered a contractor trying to supply cedar instead of the contracted hardwood. Crane noted that this same contractor and his two brothers made a practice of boxing-in bids. All three would submit on a government contract, one high, one in the middle, and one low. If no one else bid between their layers, they would withdraw the lower bid and forfeit a penalty in order to gain the higher profit. Crane viewed the practice as "cold blooded treatment of the Government."[5]

As Texas' population expanded and the drain on local fuel supplies increased, the commodity became difficult for the army to purchase. In 1887 the department commander reported that "Wood is also becoming scarce and dear." By 1896, softwood fuel for Fort Ringgold was $7.25 per cord, the second highest price paid anywhere by the army. As a result of these shortages, the army in Texas was forced to import more and more coal by sea and railroad. In 1885 only 1 percent of the Texas quartermaster's fuel costs were devoted to coal, but by 1890 coal use had grown to 21 percent of the fuel budget.[6]

RATIONS AND BEEF

The commissary general of subsistence, rather than the quartermaster general, was the nineteenth-century officer responsible for procuring food for the army. The army defined a ration as the set amount of food allotted to one soldier for one day. The cost of a ration in Texas was about 27¢ in 1856, 23¢ in 1868, 16¢ in 1874, and 49¢ in 1882. The precise contents and weights of components of the ration changed during the century, but generally consisted of a pound and a quarter of fresh or salted beef, three-quarters of a pound of bacon or pork, and similar small portions of flour, bread or cornmeal, peas or beans, rice or hominy, sugar, and coffee beans or tea. Whenever possible, soldiers and their families supplemented the ration with fresh vegetables from personal or company gardens, by fishing or hunting wild game, or by the local purchase of eggs, butter, ham, and other farm products. On at least one occasion an inventive officer's wife even made ice cream from Texas hail. At various periods army regulations allowed a commander to issue to his enlisted soldiers a one-gill whiskey ration, if such was required because of excessive fatigue or exposure.[7]

The Subsistence Department bulk-purchased the great majority of the ration from large trading hubs in the East and Midwest. However, local contracting of fresh beef and the piecemeal purchase of farm products did have an economic impact on Texas frontier communities.

During the Mexican War, Taylor's little army of six thousand at Monterrey consumed about two hundred thousand rations per month, most of which came to Texas by sea from bulk contractors at depots in New York, Baltimore, New Orleans, and St. Louis. However, a few Texans became involved in fresh beef contracting during the war. Henry L. Kinney, Taylor's landlord at Corpus Christi and his mule contractor at Camargo, also became a beef contractor for Maj. Gen. Winfield Scott during the Mexico City campaign. Ironically, Kinney bought most of the beef in Mexico, much of it from General Santa Anna's ranch near Veracruz.[8]

From the end of the Mexican War to the Texas railroad era of the 1880s, the pattern of bulk purchase and import of rations coupled with the local purchase of fresh beef remained the Subsistence Department's standard practice. While the bulk import of rations was a loss to the Texas farmer, it was a powerful boon to Texas seaports and sailors involved in receiving army supplies. It was also a source of commerce for the overland freighters who contracted to haul tons of beans, bacon, and hardtack across the state.

An examination of a few sample details offers an insight and appreciation of the scale of the enterprise, and the port, storage, and transportation requirements for army rations in Texas. From October to June, 1848, the army shipped 1,484 barrels of pork, 43,358 pounds of bacon, 72,986 pounds of bread, and 94,968 pounds of sugar to Brazos Santiago from New York and New Orleans. In 1856, the eighth year of army operations on the Texas frontier, the army imported 2,000 barrels of pork, 300,000 pounds of bacon, 280,000 pounds of bread, and 5,500 barrels of flour into the state.[9]

Between 1853 and 1856, sixteen ships from Baltimore and New York carried 18,343 barrels of army rations to the port of Corpus Christi, fourteen ships carried 16,750 barrels to Indianola, and seven ships transported 5,861 barrels to Brazos Santiago.[10]

Every one of these 40,954 barrels of army rations had to be brought through a Texas port, unloaded by a Texas laborer, hauled by a Texas freighter, and stored in a building leased from a Texan by the army. This hauling, loading, and storing was expensive. As early as 1849, Commissary General George Gibson complained of the cost and spoilage waste of bulk contracting and long haul, preferring, on the frontier especially, an open-market purchase system. Two fundamental problems prevented taking advantage of the efficiency of local markets. First, the army, beginning in 1818, was required by law to use a centralized bid and contract system. Second, the Texas market could not provide many items in sufficient quantities or at a price that would compete with the eastern seaboard's commercial network. In September, 1849, subsistence officers trying to supply the northwestern Texas frontier advertised for a month in several newspapers from Austin to Houston, welcoming bids for locally produced ration elements, including 15,000 pounds of bacon, 24,000 pounds of sugar, and 1,200 barrels of flour. The Commissary Department was unsuccessful in acquiring a local Texas source for the rations.[11]

In 1855 the bids for bulk rations from Baltimore and New York were so high that the commissary general refused to let general contracts, and instead advertised for smaller piecemeal contracts in San Antonio, Brownsville, and Corpus Christi. The results were initially disappointing because fresh beef, flour, and beans seemed to be the only portion of the ration that Texans could provide, and even those in limited quantities. W. H. Hughes provided flour to Fort Belknap and Camp Cooper, while Simeon Hart and James Magoffin supplied flour and beans to Fort Davis. After the army stationed troops in the area in 1849, Hart had established his business, known as Hart's Mill, on the Rio Grande near Magoffinsville, which later became El Paso. Hart had a limited contract in 1850 and 1851 to supply flour for 11¢ a pound to the Post Opposite El Paso, San Elizario, and Doña Anna, New Mexico, although he had to import much of it from his father-in-law's mill in Chihuahua, Mexico. Altogether, from 1855 to the start of the Civil War, the commissary general secured only twenty-one Texas contracts for flour and beans for Texas posts. Typically in this period, flour at distant Fort Davis cost $12.50 per hundred-pound barrel, while at Fort Belknap it ran $5.75 to $8.50 per barrel. A representative flour contract at a single-company post was about thirty thousand pounds for $2,400. One quartermaster, acting on his own initiative during an 1851 trip to El Paso, experimented with ten pounds of canned meat biscuit he purchased from Gail Borden in Galveston. Based on "its convenience and palatable qualities," he recommended to the quartermaster general that the army adopt the Texas product as part of the government ration. In spite of the favorable endorsement, Borden's meat biscuit was not added to the ration.[12]

In order to reduce the cost of feeding soldiers on the frontier, Secretary of War Charles Conrad instituted the army farm program in 1851, a revitalization of an earlier policy from the period 1818 to 1833. He ordered that each post establish a kitchen garden, which was a common practice anyway. Furthermore, he directed that the western departments begin a system of "farm culture" or "field cultivation" in which soldiers would grow forage and bread grains on a large scale under the direction of the post commander and subsistence officer. Commanders were required to submit quarterly progress reports to the War Department and were held responsible for the improper management of their farms. A few posts started farms, but many frontier commanders simply ignored the order, which would have further drained their meager manpower. Major General Scott, the old warhorse and senior army officer, completely opposed the measure as an impediment to unit discipline, considering the project an infringement on the agricultural incentives that brought civilian farmers to the settlement line. Although some post gardens were continued with success in Texas and New Mexico, on the whole the farm culture experiment was a short-lived failure that Secretary of War Jefferson Davis quietly terminated in 1854. While not officially required, many post commanders attempted to maintain garden plots for several reasons. First, the variety of fresh produce was a welcome supplement to the monotonous issue ration, improving soldier health and morale. Second, post-grown fruits and vegetables such as potatoes and melons could substitute for a percentage of the ration's bulk, which helped offset the cost. The money saved, or the unused portion of the ration subsequently resold, helped finance the post fund, which was used to purchase items such as library books, magazines, sports equipment, and tableware for the units. In spite of the best intentions, maintaining a post garden could be a challenge, particularly in the arid Trans-Pecos. At Fort Davis in 1868, for example, late planting of the post garden with the wrong type of seeds produced little results. The following year the civilian hired to oversee the project was fired for stealing seeds, and the 1870 plot was ruined by drought and a shortage of labor. Finally, beginning in 1871, the post garden yielded an ample supply of melons, potatoes, and vegetables—until it was destroyed by a grasshopper swarm in 1873.[13]

After the Civil War, Quartermaster General Meigs, to avoid expensive transportation costs, continued to insist that rations be purchased as close to the western forts as possible. The main depots for the West were New Orleans, St. Louis, and Chicago. By the mid-1870s, the commissary general continued to experience difficulties economically contracting bulk rations in Texas, although portions of the required flour—at $4.20 per hundred pounds —cornmeal, beans, vinegar, and salt could be acquired within the state, and fresh beef was plentiful. Inferior Texas mills and poor milling resulted in undesirable flour, although good floor was purchased by Fort Richardson at $8 per hundred pounds from the Lone Star Mills at Denison and from another mill in Dallas. By 1877, the Subsistence Department continued to import the majority of flour by railroad from St. Louis at less cost than local purchase. The network of railroads reaching Texas army posts by 1883 meant that, except for fresh local vegetables and beef, nearly all bulk rations could be purchased cheaply and transported quickly to the state from the major eastern and Midwest market centers.[14]

Although Texas' economy gained only marginally from the direct contracting of rations, each year the soldiers continued to spend cash in local markets for ration supplements. A soldier noted of the village of Jacksboro shortly after the establishment of Fort Richardson, "the place already showed signs of having received an impetus . . . the increased number of 'groceries' bore evidence of the 'enlightened' tastes of the augmented population." In 1854 Reading W. Black opened a small store on the frontier near Fort Inge. Black's diary entries are full of references of the visits of soldiers to his store, such as "2 Seargeants up here to dinner," or "several officers & one company got in . . . sent up here after things," or "Soldiers here after potatoes." Black's store became the nucleus of the town of Uvalde, and he became the most prominent member of the county, thanks in part to the commerce of the nearby garrison. Texas wagon freighter August Santleben records that, after the Civil War, he took the large numbers of wild apples and potatoes that grew on his ranch and sold them at Forts Davis and Stockton. The apples sold for $10 a crate, and the egg-sized potatoes went for 10¢ a pound, his largest transaction being $2,000 worth to the post sutler at Fort Stockton. In 1887, the inspector general estimated that Texas troops spent $12,275 from their own pockets on Texas potatoes and onions for their company messes.[15]

Uvalde merchant Reading Black's diary entries for July 10 and 13, 1855, read: "Cap King got in about 10 oclock & the whole command went on to the Frio we killed a beef for them," and, "Lieut Holiber come up here in the morning bought a beef paid $20 for it."[16]

These diary entries are indicative of open-market piecemeal purchases of fresh beef for the army. With an average Texas garrison of only three thousand troops, army beef consumption was not particularly weighty in the massive balance of the Texas cattle industry. In 1851 the two-company post of Fort Lincoln purchased an average of about three hundred pounds of fresh beef a month at 7¢ to 12¢ per pound—a yearly expense of less than $400. Nevertheless, these type of piecemeal purchases were apparently important to merchants like Reading Black, who was struggling to establish a trading enterprise and to build a town on the Texas frontier during the antebellum era.[17]

It was also important to the Texans who signed the 135 contracts to supply army beef in the years 1849 to 1860. The number of contracts and the diversity of suppliers indicate that although a few individuals routinely provided to a single post, no one individual or company had a monopoly on fresh beef during the era. Nicholas Chano had the most consistent contract, furnishing beef to Fort Brown every year from 1850 to 1859. Louis Martin cast the widest net, providing beef to Camp Colorado, and Forts Chadbourne, McKavett, and Mason in 1856 and 1857. Martin, a German immigrant and the first sheriff of Gillespie County, came to Fredericksburg in the 1840s, establishing a farmstead settlement in 1853 that became known as Hedwig's Hill near the Llano River in the vicinity of Fort Mason. With the army's help, Martin's net worth had grown from $1,500 in 1850, to $9,000 in 1860. During the antebellum period the army averaged eleven beef contracts per year. John Moore's 1859 contract to provide Fort Davis with 160 head for about $2,800, or 5¢ pound is a representative example. Overall, the army in Texas in 1859 accounted for nearly 29 percent of all the service's beef contracts, amounting to 1,760 head of cattle for a total of $30,000—a small portion of the 2.7 million head estimated to be present in the state at the time.[18]

Union forces operating in the West during the Civil War bought about ten thousand head of stolen Texas cattle from Comanche Indians, while Tejano partisans on the southern Rio Grande who were sympathetic to the Union cause stole cattle from Texas ranchers to sell for $5 a head to federal forces occupying Brownsville. After the war, the army returned to its previous pattern of awarding small-scale competitive bidding contracts to sources as near as possible to the post being supplied. Texas, with 2.9 million cattle in 1870 and 3.3 million in 1880, had the lowest contract beef prices for the entire army, averaging 5.8¢ per pound during the period 1866 to 1890, while the overall army average was 9¢ or 10¢ per pound. Texas had a great advantage over other army areas of operation such as Arizona, where the demand so outstripped the supply that fresh beef cost the army 12¢ a pound in the 1870s.[19]

The problem of expensive logistics for western Texas frontier posts remained a challenge for the Subsistence Department. An increase in cattle production in the Trans-Pecos in the 1870s lowered the cost of supplying posts such as Fort Davis or Fort Stockton, where ranchers George M. Frazer and Charles H. Mahle contracted beef at 6¢ per pound. However, the threat from Apaches and the lack of desirable range along the arid reaches of the upper Rio Grande kept the price of beef at Forts Bliss and Quitman upward of 11¢ per pound. A typical standard for the more remote and arid regions of west Texas can be seen in E. M. Herrford's three contracts in 1884 to supply the one-company post of Camp Peña Colorado with a total of 4,715 pounds of fresh beef at 11¢ per pound, for a total of $518.[20]

For Arizona and New Mexico, the coming of the railroad lowered the price of beef by decreasing the transportation cost for imported cattle. Conversely, the improved railway network in Texas in the mid-1880s initially drove up the cost of beef because the increase in exporting raised Texas cattle prices. In Texas, the average price of beef per pound paid by the army jumped from 5.4¢ in 1883 to 8.9¢ in 1884, eventually stabilizing at 7¢ in 1889.[21]

The railroad's most dramatic effect on army beef in Texas was in allowing the Subsistence Department to switch from multiple contracts for local fresh beef to centralized, large-scale contracting of frozen beef at six cents per pound. By 1895, the commissary general reported that his department made every attempt possible to purchase "chilled beef," shipping it to forts in bulk by railroad.[22]

In addition to a direct monetary input, various army operations also made a contribution to the Texas cattle industry. While soldiers on the march often stole and ate beef to supplement their meager government rations, they also recovered stolen cattle from thieves, escorted cattle drives through hazardous areas, and tried to contain Mexican cattle smuggling. On July 14, 1870, for example, Capt. Wirt Davis and a Fourth Cavalry detachment from Fort Griffin pursued and attacked a band of Comanche cattle thieves near Mountain Pass, recovering 150 stolen cows. On October 25, 1873, near Little Cabin Creek, a Sixth Cavalry detachment under Lt. John B. Kerr attacked a band of Indians and recovered 200 head of cattle. Beginning in 1870, the Texas department commander authorized local commanders to furnish escorts to cattlemen. The garrison at Fort Concho routinely established an escort to protect cattle herds crossing the dangerous strip on the Goodnight-Loving Trail between the Concho River and Horsehead Crossing on the Pecos River. From June to August, 1872, Capt. Joseph Rendlebrock and a detachment from the Fourth Cavalry and Forty-first Infantry at Fort Concho convoyed nine separate herds without a loss. As an aid and escort to the inspector of customs in July, 1878, Sgt. A. K. Paugh and a detachment from Company F, Eighth Cavalry, at Fort McIntosh participated in a successful expedition along the Rio Grande that seized fifteen hundred head of smuggled cattle.[23]

HORSES AND MULES

In addition to cattle, the army also made a contribution to Texas' horse and mule business. When Taylor's army camped at Corpus Christi in 1845 prior to the Mexican War, some of the southern officers brought their expensive thoroughbreds for horse racing, but many soldiers bought cheap Texas mustangs for amusement and convenience as few considered them capable of performing serious military work. Lieutenant Ulysses S. Grant, for example, bought three Texas ponies that quickly disappeared thanks to a careless herdsman. Grant, who was known as a penny-pincher, became the butt of a joke when members of the sporting set laconically observed that the dour Grant had lost "five or six dollars' worth of horses the other day." An indignant

Grant recorded, "That was a slander; they were broken to the saddle when I got them and cost nearly twenty dollars."[24]

It was the sharp practice of some Texans and Mexicans to sell a wild horse to an unsuspecting soldier. The unfortunate buyer would last about half a ride before winding up on his backside in the chaparral and the mustang would run off to its former master to be resold to another victim.[25]

At the start of the Mexican War, Quartermaster General Thomas Jesup, who established policies for the army's purchase of animals, believed that Texas and Mexican mules were of limited value for army supply work, and that grass-fed western horses were inferior for cavalry and artillery purposes. The Quartermaster's Department began to scour the Mississippi Valley for enough animals to support the war. Captain Simon H. Drum, for example, purchased eight hundred horses and mules in Cincinnati for Taylor—animals that were eventually diverted to Wool's Center Division, which was organizing at San Antonio. In August, 1846, Drum took the animals by two steamers down the river network to Alexandria, Louisiana, where he marched them overland to San Antonio, arriving on October 7, 1846, having lost only seven mules and thirty horses to fever, screw-worms, and stampedes.[26]

Moving horses and mules by sea into the theater of war was a complicated, expensive, and sometimes dangerous undertaking. Ringgold's Artillery brought 150 horses from Baltimore on the sailing ship *Hermann* in October, 1845. The horses, quartered in makeshift stalls below decks during the forty-nine-day voyage, were suspended in canvas belly-slings to keep them from being thrown to the deck by the ship's pitching. Rough weather in the Gulf excited the animals to the point where one artillery officer recalled, "I thought the horses would kick the vessel to pieces." When discharged at St. Joseph's Island off Corpus Christi, the horses were swung from a yardarm and lowered into a boat, eventually swimming across the bay to Taylor's camp on the beach. In August, 1846, a troop steamer from New Orleans bound for Brazos Santiago hit a storm in the Gulf. The ten horses and mules aboard went wild with fear and broke loose, destroying cabins and tearing furniture to pieces before the animals could be thrown overboard. By March, 1847, the Quartermaster's Department had designed a system of portable stalls that could go in the holds of ships to lessen the danger of transporting animals by sea. However, once a ship reached Texas, there remained the problem of safely unloading the animals. Representative of the experience was that of a dragoon officer, Lt. Richard S. "Dick" Ewell, who sailed from New Orleans with two hundred horses and was forced to wait offshore at Brazos Santiago for twelve days before the Quartermaster's Department could unload his vessel.[27]

The shortage of horses was acute enough to warrant a policy change. In early 1846 the Quartermaster's Department authorized the local purchase of Texas horses for field artillery batteries. A similar problem existed with mules. More than a thousand American mules were imported to Texas to draw wagons for Taylor's army—at a cost of $200 dollars each. In an effort to cut costs, Henry L. Kinney, Corpus Christi's founder, was hired to serve as Taylor's mule contractor at Camargo in late 1846. Kinney obtained more than a thousand Mexican mules for pack trains. The smaller animals, which he purchased for $10 and sold to the government for $15 to $20, could carry about three hundred pounds and last about six weeks before breaking down. At Camargo, six forges and twenty blacksmiths worked around the clock to provide the iron shoes needed for the animals.[28]

In the summer of 1847, local entrepreneurs were going into Mexico to buy herds of mules to sell to the Quartermaster's Department at $18 per head. At first there were plenty of mules on hand, but toward the end of the summer the Mexicans were driving mules well into the interior to keep them out of American hands. By October, the few local mules left for purchase along the Rio Grande sold for $100 per head.[29]

When the army deployed on the Texas frontier at the end of the Mexican War, the Quartermaster's Department resumed the practice of importing horses and mules from the Mississippi Valley, although it did occasionally purchase Texas animals. After the Civil War, during the years 1866 to 1871, the army had in service each year about 9,000 horses and 15,000 mules, of whch 3,000 horses and 3,000 mules were used in Texas. The quartermaster general's reduction of mule trains in 1871 limited total army mules to a ceiling of 10,500. The debate over the use of local versus imported animals for Texas service continued until the end of the nineteenth century. Typically, an army inspector in 1853 noted that it was "the general opinion of the officers in Texas that the horses of the country are better adapted to the mounted service than those purchased out of the State." Echoing this sentiment three decades later, an officer insisted that horses for the Department of Texas should be bought in the state because they were cheaper and already acclimated. "At least 50 per cent. of the horses shipped here from the North are not fit for the service for a year afterwards," he wrote, "and fully 20 per cent. have to be condemned from the effects of acclimating fever." However, another inspector had little regard for range horses, observing that animals of the "broncho strain" were difficult to train for the cavalry. After a few day's rest, he noted, their "broncho tricks will reappear," and a very high number had to be condemned for "viciousness."[30]

The high standards set by the Cavalry Board created an additional problem for the army when it sought to purchase Texas horses. The original postwar formula was a complicated set of geometric measurements comparing a ratio of the length of the head to the line of the withers (the shoulders), the hock and hoof line to that of the shoulder to haunch, and so on. These standards were apparently difficult to apply to western mounts. From November, 1871, to February, 1872, for example, a board of officers led by the San Antonio quartermaster spent four months traveling to local ranches in search of mounts for the Ninth Cavalry. The board inspected 587 horses,

TABLE 9.

DEPARTMENT OF TEXAS HORSE

AND MULE PURCHASES, 1849–1900

Period	Total $ Paid	Total Animals Purchased	Horses Purchased	$ Amount Horses	Mules Purchased	$ Amount Mules
1849–1861	$140,100	2,273	664	$55,400 (Av. $83)	1,609	$84,700 (Av. $52)
1866–1879	$825,400	7,599	5,686	$598,400 (Av. $105)	1,913	$227,000 (Av. $118)
1880–1889	$157,700	1,251	704	$91,800 (Av. $130)	547	$65,900 (Av. $120)
1890–1900	$120,700	1,073	892	$97,800 (Av. $109)	181	$22,900 (Av. $126)
Totals	$1,243,900	12,196	7,946	$843,400	4,250	$400,500

Source: Calculated from a survey of each year's "Report of the Quartermaster General of the Army," in the annual *Report of the Secretary of War,* 1849–1900.

TABLE 10.

ARMY SALES OF HORSES AND MULES IN TEXAS,

1866–1900

Period	Total $ Received	Total Animals Sold	Horses Sold	$ Amount Horses	Mules Sold	$ Amount Mules
1866–1879	$245,98 6[*]	7,316[*]	4,165	$108,456 (Av. $26)	2,715	$126,312 (Av. $46)
1880–1889	$74,389	2,016	1,140	$42,145 (Av. $37)	876	$32,244 (Av. $37)
1890–1900	$26,785	863	543	$156,154 (Av. $30)	320	$11,631 (Av. $36)
Totals	$347,160	10,195	5,848	$165,755	3,911	$170,187

Source: Calculated from a survey of each year's "Report of the Quartermaster General of the Army," in the annual *Report of the Secretary of War,* 1849–1900.
[*]Includes 436 oxen sold for $11,218 during this period.

finding only ninety-nine they could purchase to standard. Eventually, in 1876, board guidelines were simplified to included five- to nine-year-old geldings of hardy colors, from fifteen to nineteen hands high. As an exception, Texas-purchased horses could be fourteen and a half hands high.[31]

The military purchase of Texas horses and mules was not a particularly significant economic multiplier in the state. As can be seen in Table 9, the army purchased about twelve thousand Texas animals at a cost of $1.2 million. Purchases in the antebellum era represented about 0.2 percent of the horses and 2.5 percent of the mules in Texas. The high point for army purchase of Texas horses, 1866 to 1879, represented only 0.7 percent of the animals in the state at that time. Animal purchases in Texas during the same period represented 22 percent of all of the horses and 15 percent of all the mules bought by the entire army in every state. In other words, at the high-water mark, the army bought less than a quarter of its animals in Texas. In an odd footnote to history, the British army, facing a shortage of ox-drawn transportation for its 1879 Zulu campaign in southeastern Africa, sent an officer to purchase four hundred Texas mules for that military adventure. At any rate, the U.S. Army sold off horses and mules at public auction when the animals reached the end of their useful military lives. This practice provided a cheap source of animals and a considerable number were sold in the state as demonstrated in Table 10. The greatest impact on Texas sales occurred in the antebellum era, when army sales represented 0.5 percent of the horses and 2 percent of the mules in the state.[32]

MILITARY CEMETERIES

As a matter of custom rather than official policy, deceased soldiers and family members were buried in the small cemeteries associated with Texas posts from the time the army first arrived in Texas during the Mexican War. The cost of upkeep or beautification of these plots was largely a matter of soldier labor, and thus accounted for only minor incidental expenses. During the Civil War, military cemeteries achieved national attention. In 1862 Congress passed legislation creating the basic concept of national military cemeteries, giving to the Quartermaster's Department the responsibility and funding to construct and maintain the sites, as well as furnish the necessary headboards to mark graves.[33]

The general system of national cemeteries remained haphazard during the war. However, faced with the monumental task of recovering and re-interring several hundred thousand Union war dead when the war ended, the quartermaster general created a special Cemeterial Branch of the Quartermaster's Department to oversee the effort. In 1867 Congress appropriated funds for land purchases and long-term maintenance and care of the sites. By 1870, the Quartermaster's Department had established seventy-three national cemeteries with 299,696 Union graves at a cost of $3.4 million. The rapidly deteriorating wooden headboards were replaced with zinc-coated cast-iron after the war, and then with marble or durable stone in 1873, the same year that Congress granted burial rights to honorably discharged veterans. At this same time, rather than continue to maintain cemeteries at abandoned forts, the quartermaster general began reinterring remains at the nearest national military cemetery. This practice continued well into the twentieth century as the remains of soldiers and family members buried at obsolete posts were transferred to Fort Sam Houston until after the Second World War.[34]

When the national cemetery program was initiated in Texas in 1867, the Quartermaster's Department initially selected three sites: Galveston, Brownsville, and San Antonio. The Galveston cemetery, located on two and a half acres between Broadway and Avenue K, was established with 137 graves in 1867. By the following year, the Quartermaster's Department had spent an estimated $3,500 on wooden headboards, picket fences, walks, and carriage drives, and opened 383 graves, of which 38 contained the remains of unidentified soldiers. In addition to 231 bodies from Galveston, the remains of soldiers were brought from Port Lavaca, Green Lake, and Victoria. Galveston was removed from the national cemetery system in 1869 because the government was unable to obtain clear title to the land.[35]

The Quartermaster's Department received title to 1.09 acres on Sulphur Springs Road in San Antonio on November 15, 1867. The site was located on Powder House Hill, one mile east of the city on property donated by Mayor W. C. A. Thielepape. Interment of 168 Union bodies recovered from graves on the Medina River, Salado Creek, and from city cemeteries in Austin and San Antonio began in December, 1867, and was completed in April, 1868. The Quartermaster's Department built a wooden lodge, stone walls and walks, planted trees, dug a well, and placed stone markers on the graves for $14,669. By 1871, the cemetery had gained an additional 1.89 donated acres and increased to 281 graves, of which forty-one contained "unknowns." Its average yearly maintenance expense was $500 to $800. In 1875 the chief quartermaster finally received authorization to appoint a full-time superintendent for the site. Appointments of this type usually went to Union Civil War veterans. Although the first superintendent, Thomas A. Fitzpatrick, was from

Alabama, he had served in the war as a sergeant in the 18th Pennsylvania Volunteer Cavalry. The cemetery slowly expanded to 3.63 acres as Texas forts closed and post cemeteries, such as the one at Fort Concho in 1897, were removed to San Antonio. The exception was that of Fort Elliott in the far northern Panhandle. Bodies interred there were taken to Fort Scott, Kansas, when the post closed in 1890. After 1875, the budget and expenditures for the San Antonio cemetery remained steady at a few hundred dollars per year.[36]

The twenty-five-acre national military cemetery at Brownsville was established at Fort Brown in February, 1868. The remains of 920 Union soldiers, including 305 unknowns, were gathered from White Ranch, Point Isabel, Brazos Santiago, Redmond's Ranch, Ringgold Barracks, Victoria, Roma, and Corpus Christi. The land was originally acquired by public condemnation in 1872 but, as did its parent site of Fort Brown, remained in litigation until 1895. By 1871, the Quartermaster's Department had spent $10,212 on the construction of walks and drains, tree planting, cannon monuments, flagstaffs, and a wooden lodge. One inspector observed that the lodge was "a dingy red color . . [that] resembles a way-side tavern & is not creditable." Various detailed army officers supervised the cemetery until February, 1872, when Martin Schmidt became its first superintendent. In 1873 the cemetery had 2,697 graves, of which 1,409 were unknowns, and annual expenses were about $800.[37]

The dollar impact of military cemeteries in Texas—about fifty thousand—is so modest in scale that it would merit little discussion were it not for the fact that it serves as yet another example of the idea that every aspect of a soldier's life *and* death was an expense to the government and a boon to the state's commerce.

SUTLERS AND POST TRADERS

Sutlers of the antebellum era and post traders after the Civil War acted as specialized merchants, victuallers, bankers, and postmen, providing invaluable services and amenities for the frontier soldier and his family. Despite a public reputation for price gouging and shady practices, the majority of sutlers appear to have been hard working and relatively honest. The prices they charged reflect the expense of frontier transportation, a high ratio of goods spoilage, and the certain risk of credit sales to soldiers in an army with a 30 percent desertion rate. There were other risks as well. At Fort Graham, in July, 1850, a board of officers court-martialed five soldiers for robbing the sutler's store. The sutler's store was often the focal point for garrison society and for local frontiersmen, as well as functioning as a crucial supply point for travelers. One scholar observed that the army sutler was, in many respects, the adventuring advance guard of the mercantile and merchant class.[38]

Army regulations of 1821 created the position of the post sutler, to be appointed by the secretary of war, and regulated locally by four officers from the fort who formed a Council of Administration. While the sutler had a monopoly on mercantile sales within the post, he faced the sudden cancellation of his license due to a change of administration and a new order of political patronage. The post council fixed prices at the fort, with the sutler paying a tax into the post or regimental band fund at a rate of ten to fifteen cents per soldier present in the garrison each month. In the spectrum of post society in the antebellum days, the sutler had somewhat the status of an officer or gentleman, but after the Civil War he was often considered more in the order of a camp follower.[39]

In 1845 sutlers followed Taylor's army onto the beach at Corpus Christi, generating plenty of soldier complaints of high prices, which they apparently readily paid to improve their diet and comfort. Records reveal potatoes at five dollars a barrel, onions at six dollars, butter for fifty cents a pound, and eggs at fifty cents a dozen. The gouge was regulated by the natural law of supply and demand. When the army moved forward to Matamoros and the Rio Grande in 1846, it served as a ready market for the local border Mexicans and Tejano merchants who furnished ample and inexpensive goods and food in competition with the sutlers. Eggs, for example, were 25 percent cheaper than at Corpus Christi, and inexpensive loaves of Mexican sugar were extremely popular.[40]

After the Mexican War, in September, 1849, Secretary of War George W. Crawford issued orders changing army regulations, henceforth forbidding post sutlers to keep "ardent spirits, or other intoxicating drinks." Nevertheless, some post commanders tolerated the practice throughout the decade. In 1856 Fort McIntosh's commander disregarded the regulation because he believed his soldiers were better off drinking at the sutler's store on post than in the numerous grog shops hovering nearby. The selective enforcement of the regulation prompted the secretary of war to issue a stern reminder in 1859, threatening legal punishment for officers who did not enforce the policy.[41]

In addition to the moratorium on hard liquor, in the late antebellum period there were a number of rules governing the soldiers' relationship with the sutler. The ten-cent head tax per month has already been mentioned. To advance an enlisted man credit that exceeded one-third of his monthly pay required the permission of the soldier's company commander, and in no case could credit be greater than half the soldier's pay. Three days before payday the sutler had to present a record of his accounts against each soldier to the company commander. If a soldier died or deserted, the sutler, with adequate proof, could collect the debt from pay due the soldier at the pay table.[42]

Sutler appointments were usually formal affairs, supposedly controlled by the regimental commander. However, some were certainly by happenstance, as was the case at Fort Worth in 1849. Shortly after camping on the Trinity River, the post's founder, Capt. Ripley A. Arnold, saw a recently arrived Tennessee emigrant, Press Farmer and his family, living in a nearby tent. Arnold and Farmer struck up an acquaintance and Arnold offered Farmer the job of sutler to Arnold's dragoon company. Soon thereafter, Fort Worth's first merchant was in business. A more typical example occurred in 1856. To secure his position with the newly arriving Second Cavalry in January, 1856, sutler Edwin D. Lane rushed out from San Antonio to meet Col. Albert Sidney Johnston, who was still on the march toward Fort Mason. Through this display of initiative and enthusiasm, Lane achieved his position as sutler to the Second Cavalry.[43]

Lane, from Fredericksburg, was an experienced sutler, having taken over at Fort Terrett in February, 1853, after the post council fired sutler William Doak for his lax business practices and failure to forward supplies for five months. Lane's partner, San Antonian Thomas K. Wallace, had a brother who was an army captain and, along with another brother, had been the sutler at Fort Duncan in 1851. A First Infantry lieutenant stationed there at the time recorded: "They were both clever gentlemen, and added much to the society of the post. The store was well supplied with everything usually found in a country store, and the officers and soldiers could procure such articles as they required at reasonable prices. Attached to the store was the sutler's private office, which was very generally used as a club room. . . .The officers, at their own expense, erected a billiard-room."[44]

At Fort Ewell in 1853, an inspecting officer found the sutler's store was "tolerably supplied," but that the difficulties of transportation made items expensive, "Being generally an advance of 80 per cent over New York prices." In 1856 an inspector found that most sutlers sold liquor at Texas posts, specifically citing sutlers Alexander Young at Fort Davis, and Howard and Lane at Forts Chadbourne and McKavett, as being typical of all Second Cavalry suppliers. However, the Eleventh Infantry commander at Fort Mason did not allow sutler James Duff to sell spirits, and the commanders at Forts Clark and Lancaster withheld the privilege from sutlers Lepier and Dunlap.[45]

In 1866, Congress abolished the practice of appointing post sutlers and ordered the Subsistence Department to furnish such necessary articles as matches, combs, writing paper, and soap to soldiers at cost. The new policy cost the quartermaster general $3 million per year, and he could make required items available only in limited quantities, certainly inadequate to meet the needs of the troops. The following year, Congress excluded most frontier posts from the provisions of the act, allowing more than one trader at western forts and temporarily ending the old single-source monopoly. For example, three traders competed for soldier dollars and credit at Fort Davis in 1868. In 1870 Secretary of War William Belknap succeeded in getting the open act rescinded, allowing him to license a post trader at any fort not in a town or city. Belknap was soon to suffer severe censure, resigning in the midst of an impeachment move for allegedly accepting bribes in exchange for post trader positions. Indeed, the clerk for Jim Trainer, the post trader at Fort Concho, recorded in his diary in November, 1870: "Mr. Trainer is still absent in Washington, looking after the sutler appointment of post traders in consideration by Secretary of War Belknap. And the person who will give him the most money will secure the appointment. I understand that Trainer has already paid about $3,000 and now Belknap wants his purse lined with $4,000." Although the evidence against Belknap was hearsay, the scandal tainted the image of post traders and brought with it a general suspicion of corruption, graft, and ill-gained patronage. In 1869 Fort Richardson's post trader was suspected of cheating soldiers by using a rigged billiard table. The post trader at Fort Davis in 1875, a Belknap appointee, was universally unpopular with the garrison on general principle. At the same time, Fort Stockton's post trader lost his license and the regard of post society for maintaining his friendship with a married captain who had been ostracized after a scandal involving another officer's eighteen-year-old daughter.[46]

Initially, under the new postwar regulations, the post trader had fewer restrictive controls when compared to the prewar sutler. In addition, he did not have to pay a head tax, although he did lose the privilege of collecting debts at the paymaster's table. The 1872 regulations brought back the local post officers' councils to protect soldiers from price gouging.

One veteran trooper, expressing the collective wisdom of the barracks, opposed the elimination of the regimental sutler: "The sutler, under the regulations of the old army . . . upon the whole, he was not a necessary evil, but a real convenience to both officers and men. . . . First-class merchants . . . conducted the business in a legitimate manner . . . But the regular sutler was discontinued . . . succeeded by a class of small dealers officially known as 'post-traders' . . . much to the detriment of the service and to the comfort and morals of the men."[47]

The primary problem was not in the basic structure of the system but in its administration. The post trader could steeply discount the paper money paid to the soldiers and charge up to 10 percent interest on credit given to the troops. Barracks rumormongers sometimes suspected officers of the Council of Administration of being subject to undue influence from the post trader in the form of extra favors, free whiskey, free lunches, and of getting a discount on trader prices. A soldier at Fort Richardson observed on payday what he called "the evil of credit" at the post trader's, for "The sutler kept an open account with the men, and their scanty pay was often hypothecated long before it was due." Most traders sold spirits until 1881, when Pres. James A. Garfield issued orders forbidding the sale of liquor or ardent spirits at army forts. This prohibition did not include beer, light wine, or ale.[48]

One officer, inspecting Texas in 1872, wrote of the post trader at Ringgold Barracks: "His stock of goods is small. I . . . saw little else than a billiard-table." The same officer found the post tradership at Fort Brown to be "Very insignificant, & useless because there are many good shops in the village." However, at Fort Duncan he wrote that post-trader John Carroll's "stock of goods is ample & his prices are reasonable."[49]

There is evidence that post traders, although not of the same social standing as antebellum sutlers, were not entirely shunned by the social elite at frontier garrisons. At Fort Concho in 1876, the officers and ladies of the Tenth Cavalry invited post-trader Loeb to join them at a masquerade party. His successor, James L. Millspaugh, was not so highly regarded at first. However, Millspaugh's personal stock soared in the summer of 1877 when the soldiers departed on an expedition and he took charge of a portion of the post's defense as security for the army families that were left behind. In the early 1880s at Fort Davis, George H. Abbott and his partner, Rep. John D. Davis of Ohio, built a comfortable compound with a store, bar, telegraph office, and residence—reportedly giving good service until Congress ended the post-trader system.[50]

The post-trader system disappeared in the spirit of army reform that echoed the liberal reforms of the early Progressive Movement in the 1890s. In 1889 the secretary of war authorized the establishment of Canteens at army posts, allowing the quartermaster general to purchase vacant post-trader buildings. The post Canteen was essentially a liquor-free, low-cost, small-goods store and recreation parlor, operated by the army for the convenience of the soldier. In 1890 Congress ended the post-trader system altogether in favor of the army Canteen, a move followed in 1892 by the Post Exchange system, which more or less remains in effect to this day.[51]

CHAPTER 7

Payday

Paymasters, Soldiers' Silver,
and Civilian Employment

During the Mexican War, when Capt. Mirabeau B. Lamar, a hero of San Jacinto and former president of the Republic of Texas, returned to the state with his company of Texas Rangers after a patrol to Monterrey, he stopped at Camargo to draw a little of the army pay that he had never collected. The paymaster, a self-important major, offered Lamar bureaucracy instead of coin, complaining that the captain's papers were not quite in order. To the delight of the local troops, the story flew around camp that Lamar quietly pocketed his papers and, before riding off with his Rangers, replied to the startled paymaster, "It is the first time that I ever asked for money and I reckon it will be the last, I bid you goodbye major."[1]

An officer stationed on the Rio Grande in 1847 complained, "When a man enters the pay office here he feels as if he were going before a board of bank directors to ask a favor instead of an officer of his government to demand his right."[2]

While these sentiments toward army paymasters were not necessarily universal, they do reflect the proprietary attitude most paymasters were required by circumstances to adopt toward the money they disbursed. Army paymasters had to face two harsh realities in the antebellum army: first, the financial panics of the 1830s created a government distrust of banks and, up to the Civil War, the medium of army payment was hard specie—either gold or silver coin—and, second, the paymaster was responsible for every cent. If an unwary officer accidentally handed out a single undeserved Liberty penny, it became a personal liability that the government did not treat lightly.

The fact that the government paid its debts in specie by law—the Independent Treasury Act of 1846—created a serious burden and risk for paymasters, quartermasters, subsistence officers, and other military personnel responsible for issuing payments from the public treasury. One Mexican War paymaster reported that to haul the $300,000 he needed to pay the army required eight wagonloads of coins. Typical of the problem was the experience of Capt. Samuel G. French. One of the first quartermasters to arrive in the state when the army deployed to Texas after the Mexican War, French rode a stagecoach from Galveston to Austin in December, 1848, without an armed escort while carrying $5,000 in gold in a box under his seat.[3]

An officer in 1849 noted for Congress the dangers and problems of dealing with bulk funds once they left the security of a Treasury vault: "Each officer is to take care of them in the best manner his caution or ingenuity suggests . . . reduced to the necessity of hazarding their funds within their own offices—offices which have only the ordinary strength of common houses. . . . The fact of such deposits in such insecure places would generally be known, and invite attempts at robbing by the strongest hopes of success. . . . It may also be remarked, that the labor of counting this amount . . . consume an extraordinary portion of time. In some instances I paid out, in the course of a day, from one to three hundred thousand dollars. . . . To count out two hundred thousand dollars in gold would be the ordinary work of a day—perhaps more." The officer went on to state that much of the problem of security could be solved "by allowing the use of approved banks. . . . It is true that banks have not always been sound: still such banks can be selected."[4]

The burden and danger of the specie pay system can be illustrated by events on the night of January 18, 1854, when three robbers broke into the office of San Antonio paymaster Maj. F. A. Cunningham. After knocking the major unconscious, the thieves took the keys to his safe and stole six bags of gold and silver containing $36,085. It took a special act of Congress in 1857 to relieve Cunningham of his direct liability for the missing specie.[5]

Captain William Blair brought his younger brother Lewis from Virginia to be his hired clerk and help run the commissary of subsistence at the San Antonio depot in 1851. The army paid Lewis $75 per month and he worked for his brother for more than four years. While this was certainly nepotism, it was also an imminently practical arrangement: Who better to trust than one's own kin when handling large sums of gold coin? Consider, too, the 1856 case of San Antonio quartermaster Capt. James Belger, whose trusted clerk absconded with $8,422, leaving Belger personally responsible to the government. Then there was Fort Davis subsistence clerk O. W. Dickerson, who in 1872 embezzled $2,000 in War Department funds. Finally, as previously mentioned, 2d Lt. Henry O. Flipper's being cashiered over the loss of $1,440 he had stored in a trunk is another case in point.[6]

In addition to security problems, the paymasters, quartermasters, and commissary officers who required coins had to compete for adequate amounts of specie—a relatively rare resource in Texas. Army payment was supposed to be in gold, but Mexican silver was often the medium of currency, particularly in the border regions. A great deal of Mexican silver was exported through and out of Texas, creating a shortage of surplus coinage for the Texas economy, a situation neatly summarized in an 1852 newspaper editorial as "Money is scarce." In January, 1856, the importation of silver from Chihuahua was slowed by a Mexican export tax of 3.5 percent, a tariff that increased to 6 percent in February, 1857. Frederick Law Olmsted, traveling in Texas in 1854, observed a scarcity of cash, reporting that the little hard money present came from new emigrants, casual travelers, and army contracts. Ten years later, a post–Civil War Ohio volunteer soldier at Indianola recorded: "We get Mexican silver for change. Citizens say fractional currency has never been used here, and that before the war . . . greenbacks were seldom seen. The currency of the neighborhood is silver."[7]

Operating in a coin or barter economy, borderland merchants and citizens distrusted paper of all forms. During the Mexican War, quartermasters discovered that Texans tended to discount U.S. Treasury notes by 5 percent when cashed or used as payment. After the Civil War, when paymasters began to disburse paper money, soldiers faced a similar discount when trying to spend it. A soldier on the Texas frontier in 1867 explained that "The circulating medium was entirely in silver dollars; when our greenbacks were presented, the merchant invariably discounted them, all prices being in coin." The discount was usually 30 percent because Texans "looked with much suspicion on our greenbacks, more particularly from their recent experience in Confederate money."[8]

During the antebellum era soldiers' pay unquestionably was a major source of coinage on the Texas frontier. In 1853 paymaster officers Jeremiah G. Dashiell and George C. Hutter at San Antonio, Henry Hill at Corpus Christi, and the legendary Albert Sidney Johnston at Austin, all kept large sums of specie on hand. By regulation, troops were supposed to be paid every two months, but in Texas every four months was the routine considering the distance the paymasters traveled. Dashiell traveled a 430-mile circuit each four months, paying $188,982 in 1853 to Forts Inge, Duncan, and Clark. Hutter rode 600 miles quarterly to pay $100,000 yearly to Forts Martin Scott, Mason, Chadbourne, McKavett, and Terrett. Hill covered a 600-mile circle to pay an annual $120,000 to the Rio Grande forts, as well as Forts Ewell and Merrill. Johnston rode 620 miles each pay trip, disbursing $112,000 per annum to the garrisons at Austin, Phantom Hill, Belknap, Worth, Graham, and Croghan. These paymasters obtained their specie by going to the paymaster's office in New Orleans or by trading paper drafts on New Orleans banks to San Antonio merchants for enough gold to meet a payment schedule. All in all, these four paymasters put $500,000 in gold and silver into circulation in the state in 1853.[9]

By 1856 there were still four Texas paymasters, but with slightly altered routes and stations. Two paymasters were stationed in San Antonio, one paying San Antonio installations and Forts Duncan and Clark, the other disbursing to Forts Mason, McKavett, Chadbourne, Belknap, and Cooper. The paymaster at Corpus Christi paid Forts Davis and Lancaster every four months. The Fort Brown paymaster paid the river forts of McIntosh and Ringgold Barracks.[10]

Traveling the 1856 pay circuit required a considerable amount of equipment and personnel. There were also a number of risks. On the Devil's River in mid-May, 1856, for example, Indians attacked Maj. Henry Hill, the Corpus Christi paymaster, while he was en route to pay Fort Davis. As a results of this type of danger, and the extended journeys required to make the circuit, each paymaster had a four-mule army ambulance and driver, plus a six-mule army wagon and driver to haul camp equipment and rations for the escort. The escort, depending on the route's conditions, varied from four to twenty soldiers. With all four paymasters continuously making their circuits, the department commander had to divert to paymaster duties the equivalent resources of a one-company frontier post: four officers and about a line company's worth of escorts, as well as eight wagons, eighty mules, and eight teamsters.[11]

In the post–Civil War era, as in the antebellum period, the troops were supposed to be paid monthly, but it was often six months between paydays due to the long distances in Texas. A typical post–Civil War pay trip is recorded in the diary of Maj. Peter P. G. Hall's civilian clerk, who accompanied Hall on the Fort Davis route. Hall departed San Antonio with his clerk, several wagons and teamsters, and an escort of eighteen soldiers, on May 6, 1871, traveling by way of Fredericksburg, Fort Mason, and Fort McKavett, and arriving at Fort Concho after eleven days. From there, Hall rode sixty miles to the Middle Concho River to Johnson's Station and to Camp Charlotte on Kiowa Creek. At Melbourne Station—also called Camp Melvin—on the Pecos River, the pay party arrived just after an attack by a mixed party of Indians and two white men, who had shot a soldier and driven off nineteen mules. After arriving at Fort Davis on May 24 and making disbursements there, Major Hall's party returned to San Antonio by way of old Fort Lancaster and Fort Clark, reaching the city after a five-week round-trip.[12]

The 1876 pay circuit is illustrative of the amounts of cash the paymasters were delivering to the Texas frontier after the Civil War. To pay Fort Elliott, Maj. Edmund H. Brooke made a seventeen-day, 1,192-mile circuit from Fort Leavenworth, Kansas, disbursing $392,769 in soldier pay. Major Thomas T. Thornburg, stationed at Fort Brown, traveling in alternating months, made a seventeen-day, 480-mile trip to pay Ringgold Barracks and Fort McIntosh, disbursing a total of $207,469. Three paymasters operated from San Antonio. Major Alfred E. Bates paid out $216,597 on his twenty-one-day, 1,192-mile circuits to Fort Griffin and Fort Richardson. Major Charles I. Wilson spent an average of twenty-four days traveling the 1,372-mile route to pay $216,597 to Forts McKavett, Concho, Stockton, Davis, Quitman and Bliss. Major Frank M. Coxe paid $214,658 to soldiers at Forts Clark and Duncan during his circuit of nine days and 343 miles. Altogether in 1876, these paymasters disbursed $1,239,229 to 3,106 soldiers in the state. However, pay circuits were sharply curtailed in 1877. Southern Democrats tagged amendments to the army appropriations bill to try and neutralize military involvement in Louisiana Reconstruction politics. Republicans refused to pass the bill and the army literally went without pay from July to November, 1877, when Pres. Rutherford B. Hayes called a special session of Congress. While enlisted soldiers could depend on issue rations and clothing, those five months were particularly harsh on officers, many of whom had to borrow money at usurious interest rates in order to survive.[13]

Texas pay officers were generally honest and efficient, and paymaster corruption was the exception rather than the rule. Nevertheless, in 1869 the civilian clerk assisting San Antonio paymaster Maj. Isaac S. Stewart recorded that on the previous pay circuit to Fort Concho, "The major being drunk the entire 47 days that we were absent, having several attacks of the tremens and was almost unbearable at times." Shortly after an 1870 trip to Galveston, the clerk reported the major had lost heavily at the gaming tables, paying his bad debts with government funds. When the department commander called for Stewart's court-martial for taking travel expenses on trips that were not made, the major resigned his commission. A Signal Service paymaster, Capt. Henry W. Howgate, was arrested in 1881 and indicted for embezzling $90,000. Howgate escaped jail, becoming a fugitive for twelve years until his capture and imprisonment in 1894. In 1883, Maj. James R. Wasson, who graduated first in the West Point class of 1871, lost $5,000 in government funds play-ing poker in Galveston and staged a phony robbery on a train to Fort Worth in an effort to cover it up. Wasson was caught, cashiered, and spent eighteen months at the military prison in Leavenworth.[14]

Enlisted pay in the nineteenth century was Spartan, but about on a par with the average farm worker receiving room and board. In 1850 an infantry-man earned $7 per month, and his cavalry and artillery brethren made $8. Congress raised enlisted pay by $4 in 1854, adding $2 per month for a second enlistment. The antebellum private could earn an additional 18¢ to 25¢ a day if he performed extra duty, but also lost a quarter per month to the Soldiers' Home plus whatever he owed for extra clothing, the laundress bill, sutler's credit, and debts to fellow soldiers. Privates earned $13 per month from the 1870s through the turn of the century, with an extra dollar a month for each year of service after the third year. To combat the high desertion rate during this era, the army withheld $3 from each private's monthly pay, to be paid out in a lump sum upon completion of his enlistment—a practice that le-gally ended in 1895.[15]

A Fifth Infantry captain at Ringgold Barracks wrote in March, 1855: "The paymaster has been here several days. . . . As usual after a payment we had much drunkenness and of consequences much trouble." This letter reflects that much of the money earned by enlisted men went quickly and directly into the hands of saloon owners and gamblers, as it did with many young Texas cowboys during the era. Post–Civil War Brackettville, a tiny, rough-and-tumble satellite village across Las Moras Creek from Fort Clark, had fifteen saloons and fifty professional gamblers. Fort Richardson's companion village of Jacksboro had a population of 650, with twenty-seven saloons, many of which grossed a thousand dollars on army payday. Payday, by law

TABLE II.

SOLDIERS' PAY IN TEXAS, 1849–1900

Category	Period				Total
	1849–1860	1869–1879	1880–1889	1890–1900	
Army pay in Texas	$7,700,000	$11,200,000	$10,200,000	$9,400,000	$38,500,000
Average annual army pay in Texas	$659,446	$1,019,445	$1,015,717	$854,580	$802,452

Source: Calculated from each year's "Report of the Paymaster General," in the annual *Report of the Secre-tary of War,* 1849–1900.

once a month but in practice every few months, was routinely boisterous. A Sixth Cavalry sergeant, recalling Fort Richardson in 1867, wrote, "A large percentage of the vast sums paid out annually . . . to officers, as well as men, vanished into thin air." In 1881 a Sixteenth Infantry corporal recorded that men in his company spent their pay in Eastland, Texas, and that "All the scum of humanity were represented in that place; gambling houses, dance halls, whiskey dens, and women joining hands to extract the hard-earned money. . . . Drunks and fights were the order of the day."[16]

While much of a soldier's pay was rapidly and wastefully transferred into the hands of local Texans, a soldier at Fort Richardson also observed, "Now and then some man saved his money and increased it by trading and loaning it." The record shows many positive examples of soldiers putting their pay to better use than card games, bottles of oh-be-joyful, and frolics with painted ladies.[17]

An antebellum inspector in Texas recognized in 1856 that a fundamental problem of the frontier army was the lack of a fiscal vehicle for soldiers to safeguard any surplus money they may have saved. Because Texas law prohibited state banks, in 1860 there was only one chartered bank in the state—at Galveston. By 1870 there were only four national banks, none of which were on the frontier. At any rate, soldiers in general distrusted financial institutions. The inspector general in 1856 suggested that soldiers be allowed to turn their money over to army quartermasters for safekeeping as the logisticians had a reasonable system for handling large amounts of specie. Such a depository would be an advantage to the soldier and "Would operate very much to prevent his spending his surplus money in rum and dissipation, under the impression he would either be robbed of it, or lose it, if he attempted to keep it."[18]

Such a soldier savings system eventually came amid the army reforms of the 1870s. Recognizing the problem, in 1873 the army created a system for depositing soldier pay in a federal savings program. Soldiers electing this option simply left their money in the treasury or on the pay books and drew a small amount of interest. Armywide in 1873, soldiers deposited $200,000 into the program, which grew to more than $400,000 in deposits by 1885. A commander on the Texas frontier in 1879 reported of his Tenth Cavalry company on payday, "A large portion . . . made deposits which pleased me very much, but . . . amazed the Paymaster." Still, this savings system represented only about 3 percent of the $11 million to $13 million worth of annual army pay in the nation. On February 27, 1893, Congress, acting to ease the cash burden on paymasters and to provide additional security for soldiers, authorized the army to pay soldiers by check or mail express order if desired. The Texas department commander reported in 1896 that "The new system of payments by check seems to work satisfactorily to all concerned." By 1900, the paymaster general reported that nearly all soldiers requested their pay by check or express currency.[19]

The army's pay system of course put officers in a higher fiscal class than enlisted men. Although the base pay of her officer husband was only $63, a wife at the frontier post of Fort Inge in 1854 recalled, "The pay per month for a first lieutenant of Mounted Rifles was ninety-three dollars!—vast wealth, it seemed to me. More would have been useless, for there was nothing to buy." Officers, already financially better off than their enlisted subordinates, received a post–Mexican War base-pay increase of $20 in 1857. Because of additional entitlements, officer base pay should not be taken at face value. In 1861, during his last year in Texas, Lt. Col. Robert E. Lee of the Second Cavalry had a basic pay rate of $100.40 per month or $1,305.20 per year. Lee also received $123.75 for rations, a $47.30 servants allowance, $25.77 for forage, $4.90 for fuel, $17.17 for quarters, and $19.05 for transporting baggage, bringing his total monthly pay to $338.34, or $4,060.08 per year—about twenty-six times that of a private, and eight times that of a frontier laborer. His nephew, 2d Lt. Fitzhugh Lee, was also in Texas, serving in the same regiment. "Fitz" Lee's basic pay was $700 per year, or $58.30 per month, but with added entitlements totaling $1,689 per year or $140.75 per month,— two and a half times his basic pay. By 1890, a lieutenant colonel had a base pay of $3,500 per year, with an additional annual allowance of $375 for twenty years of service. An infantry second lieutenant earned $1,400 in annual base pay, with an additional $128 tacked on for five years of service.[20]

Married soldiers also received cash in lieu of the ration, although food could be expensive on the frontier. Recognizing this disadvantage to soldiers serving at remote sites, in May, 1857, the secretary of war authorized a dozen frontier forts to be "double ration" posts, with soldiers paid twice the normal rate of twenty seven cents a day, or eight dollars a month. In Texas these posts were Fort Lancaster and Camps Cooper, Colorado, and Verde. By 1859, only six western posts were authorized double rations, including Forts Quitman and Camp Hudson in Texas.[21]

Another example of soldiers putting their money to good use and having an impact on local real estate markets, was the practice of investing in Texas land, mines, or businesses. Lieutenant Col. Thomas T. Fauntleroy, while serving in the Second Dragoons, purchased 182 acres on the east edge of Austin, then sold it for $3,000 in 1850. Eighth Infantryman Hugh Sheridan bought land adjoining Fort Gates in 1850 and settled on it at the end of his enlistment. In the mid-1850s, Capt. William W. Chapman invested in town lots in Corpus Christi and developed a large Nueces County ranch on Santa Gertrudis Creek, where his Scots partner, James Bryden, introduced large-scale Scottish sheep production to south Texas in 1856. In 1854 Capt. Newton C. Givens of the Second Dragons bought a 7,000-acre ranch on the Clear Fork of the Brazos near Camp Cooper. A Mounted Rifles officer, Lt. Dabney H. Maury, bought a nearby ranch while stationed in San Antonio in 1855, raising fifteen hundred head of cattle and selling out at double his investment when the Civil War began. In the 1870s Maj. Anson Mills of the Tenth Cavalry, who eventually became wealthy through his invention of a new canvas cartridge belt, invested in considerable business real estate holdings around El Paso and the upper Rio Grande, earning the right to collect lease money on Fort Quitman. In 1881 the famous army scout leader Lt. John L. Bullis, along with Col. William R. "Pecos Bill" Shafter, bought four sections of land in the Big Bend country. In the 1880s Col. Benjamin H. Grierson invested in 126 town lots in Valentine, 5,843 acres near Fort Concho, and more than 3,000 acres near Fort Davis, at times incurring criticism from local businessmen who were critical of an active officer's competing with them in the real estate market. In all, Grierson's claims included 45,000 acres in three Trans-Pecos counties, while his niece's husband, Lt. Mason M. Maxon, bought a ranch in Musquiz Canyon near Fort Davis. An enlisted soldier, George A. Brenner, the Tenth Cavalry's chief musician, had a small real estate business purchasing land and lots around Fort Davis, while the Fort Davis ordnance sergeant, Charles Mulhern invested and settled as a cattle rancher in the area in the 1880s. In the late 1880s a Third Cavalry trooper, Francis Rooney invested near Fort Stockton, leaving the army to become a successful farmer, forage contractor, and real estate developer.[22]

Several officers put money into developing businesses in the Trans-Pecos. In 1885 Col. Ben Grierson, bandmaster Brenner, Lt. Samuel Woodward, and several local citizens invested in the Fort Davis and Marfa Railway Company, designed to connect Fort Davis to the vital economic artery of the Southern Pacific. The project failed when the county seat moved from the town of Fort Davis to Marfa. To develop silver deposits on land they owned in the Chinati Mountains, Lts. John L. Bullis and Louis Wilhelmi, their commander at Fort Davis, Colonel Shafter, and a civilian partner, rancher and prospector John W. Spencer, formed a mining partnership in 1880. Leasing their land to a California mining group and creating the Presidio Mining Company in 1883, the mine in Presidio County made the partners wealthy men, a rarity among army officers—who usually lost their money in frontier investment schemes. Employing up to three hundred workers, the Presidio mine operated off and on until 1942, becoming the longest producing mine in Texas and yielding 32.6 million ounces of silver and eighty-four hundred ounces of gold. The mine yielded 72 percent of the gold and 92 percent of the silver produced in Texas, pumping $60,000 per month into the regional economy. The army officers' enterprising silver strike spawned fourteen nearby mines and was the genesis of the development of the regional Shafter Mining District, which produced modest quantities of lead, silver, gold, copper, and zinc.[23]

As illustrated in Table 11, soldier pay brought $38.5 million into the Texas economy, about $7.7 million in the antebellum era, and more than $30 million after the Civil War. In the economically immature period after the Mexican War, the average yearly input of more than $500,000 was a boon to the state as a whole. In the economic devastation following the inflation and Confederate currency collapse after the Civil War, the $1 million a year soldiers' pay brought into the state was a great catalyst in reviving the economic potential of the Texas frontier, providing a ready distribution of currency in a cash-poor barter economy. In some satellite towns, soldier pay was the sinew that bound together the commercial structure of the community. The mayor of Jacksboro, near Fort Richardson, wrote: "The merchant and the farmer did not in those happy days spend their time whittling goods boxes or discussing crop prospects and the chances of a drought—for wet or dry, crops or no crops, the paymaster came at pretty regular intervals, and as he disbursed perhaps from four to six thousand dollars to each company present for duty at the post, nearly all of which, as stated, was expended forthwith for goods at rattling profits."[24]

CITIZEN EMPLOYMENT

When the army arrived in Texas in the summer of 1845, the Quartermaster's Department faced a shortage of local labor. Much of the logistical chain required, by law, civilian employees such as wagon teamsters, carpenters, blacksmiths, herdsmen, clerks, and stevedores—few of whom were either willing or able in the relatively thin population base in the state's coastal region.

Taylor's organization at Corpus Christi depleted the labor supply available through New Orleans, forcing the Quartermaster's Department to search farther up the Mississippi and Ohio Valleys to provide for Brig. Gen. John E. Wool's Center Division organizing at San Antonio in the summer of 1846.

Captain Simon Drum hired two hundred teamsters in Cincinnati for service in San Antonio and sent the men there by sea. At Port Lavaca, the forward logistical port for Wool's division, Capt. James Irwin hired 380 employees at a cost of $9,900 a month. Seven blacksmiths received $50 per month each, and 257 teamsters received an average of $23 and a ration per day.[25]

By the summer of 1847, Taylor's chief quartermaster had standardized teamster pay in the army at $30 per month and a ration per day, and the monthly payroll paid out of the quartermaster depot at Brazos Santiago reached $25,000. A small army of civilian carpenters, forage masters, clerks, mule packers, teamsters, blacksmiths, herdsmen, and laborers toiled away at the huge forward depot upriver at Camargo. Carpenters for coffins and wagon repair received $40 per month, plus a ration and a half. Thirty-four Mexican laborers received $1.50 per day or $45 a month, but no ration. When the ration per day is included, these wages were 300 to 400 percent higher than the $10.85 per month average wage, with board, of a U.S. farm laborer during the period. In general, army officers on the Rio Grande complained about the lack of control over teamsters and laborers, who were often rowdy and undisciplined.[26]

Not all employees were imported; the army did hire some local Texans. Take, for example, the case of an industrious twenty-year-old from the Brazos River in Washington County, John James Dix. Young Dix "bid adieu to home and Father's family to seek fortune," carried dispatches for Taylor at Corpus Christi, and worked for a sutler at Brazos Santiago. The quartermaster eventually hired him for sixty dollars per month to go to the mouth of the Rio Grande to oversee cargo transfer operations and supervise the construction of a wharf by thirty Mexican laborers.[27]

The Quartermaster's Department was responsible for hiring and paying the majority of civilian employees on the Texas frontier. In some cases, such as teamsters, the army hired civilians because it could not spare enough soldiers from combat duties to fulfill the requirements. In other cases, such as clerks, blacksmiths, or post guides, the civilians brought to the job special skills that could not be easily duplicated in the ranks. By far the most extraordinary workers hired by the Quartermaster's Department in Texas were the camel drivers who took part in Secretary of War Jefferson Davis's experiment with dromedaries on the frontier. In January, 1856, the Quartermaster's Department contracted with three Egyptians to come to the United States for one year at $10 per month, a ration per day, and passage home. In February two Turks were awarded a two-year contract calling for $15 a month and a ration per day. Additional support for the camels, which eventually were

TABLE 12.

ARMY CIVILIAN EMPLOYEES IN TEXAS,

SAMPLE YEARS, 1849–1893

Year	Total Number Civilian Employees, Department of Texas	Total Monthly Wages	Average Wage Per Month	Total Annual Wages
1849	26	$1,889	$73	$22,668
1851	488	$12,935	$27	$155,220
1856	356	$10,085	$28	$121,020
1878	230	$9,357	$41	$112,284
1884	170	$8,249	$49	$98,988
1889	106	$6,246	$59	$74,952
1893	68	$4,073	$60	$48,876

Source: With the exception of 1856, the army civilian employee figures for Texas are taken from that year's "Report of the Quartermaster General of the Army," in the annual *Report of the Secretary of War.* For the year 1856, see Martin L. Crimmins, ed., "Colonel J. F. K. Mansfield's Report of the Inspection of the Department of Texas in 1856," *Southwestern Historical Quarterly* 42, no.2 (Oct. 1938): 135–139, 141, 147; no. 3 (Jan. 1939): 235, 243; no. 4 (April 1939): 326, 354, 359.

based at Camp Verde, included a clerk, interpreter, and two laborers. The nine camel employees cost the chief quartermaster $2,340 per year.[28]

Even during periods of civilian workforce reductions, the post guide remained an indispensable element on the Texas military frontier. A number of Texans, including William A. A. "Bigfoot" Wallace and Ed Westfall, gained renown at this calling. The position also represented an example of equal-opportunity employment and ethnic diversity in an important job. Many post guides were Mexican nationals or Tejano natives of Texas who served with distinction and earned solid reputations while serving the army. Juan Galván, earning a standard forty dollars per month, served as a guide in the early 1850s at Fort Inge, while José María Flores was the guide for Fort Duncan, and Pedro Espinosa served at Fort Lincoln. One of the most famous of the frontier guides was José Policarpo "Polly" Rodríquez, who served as a surveyor and guide for Lt. William Whiting's 1849 expedition to El Paso, as well as the personal guide for Department Commander Persifor Smith. The son of a land-owning, upper-class Mexican family, Rodríquez spent most of the 1850s scouting for various army posts and participating in many of the major Indian skirmishes during the decade—all for forty-five dollars per month. Indians also served the army as scouts and guides. Delaware Indian John

McLoughlin served as the Second Cavalry guide at Fort Mason. One officer said that "An expedition from that post was not complete without him." Perhaps the most respected and skilled of the Delaware guides was Black Beaver. Black Beaver led an Indian company in a Texas volunteer regiment on the state's frontier during the Mexican War and served as chief guide to the 1849 Red River explorations of Capt. Randolph B. Marcy.[29]

The hiring of civilian doctors was an additional area of importance to the development of the Texas frontier, particularly in the antebellum era. Due to the shortage of army doctors, the Surgeon General let eighty-nine contracts at cost of $46,000 for medical services at Texas forts between 1849 and 1860. The seven or eight doctors hired each year at salaries ranging from $80 to $130 per month for two to twelve months, brought much needed medical skill into the state. In 1856, for example, a native Virginian and Columbia College graduate, Dr. Powhatan Jordan, arrived on the Texas frontier as the contract doctor for Fort Inge. At the end of his term of service, Jordon remained in the state, helping to organize the San Antonio Board of Health and the Western Texas Medical Association. In the post–Civil War years, thanks to an increase in the number of commissioned surgeons, the practice of hiring contract doctors began to wane. It was discontinued altogether in the 1890s.[30]

From 1849 to 1860 the characteristic Texas frontier wage for semiskilled or unskilled labor was $40 per month, while the U.S. average was $31. The per capita income of the average agricultural worker in Texas was $50 in 1850, rising to $80 in 1860. Civilian employees hired by the army on the Texas frontier were paid according to the demands of the job and the required skill level. In 1856, for example, teamsters and laborers were at the lower end of the scale, earning $20 to $25 per month and a ration per day. Skilled laborers such as wheelwrights, blacksmiths, and frontier guides earned $45 to $50 per month. White-collar workers, such as quartermaster clerks and accountants, were at the top of the salary scale at $65 per month. Quartermaster General Jesup, ordered by Secretary of War Conrad in 1851 to reduce the high cost of civilian labor, reluctantly tried to replace civilians with soldiers having the same skills by offering troopers an additional 15¢ cents per day during the antebellum period and 35¢ per day after the Civil War. This use of soldier labor, representing up to 10 percent of the army at any given time, had a detrimental impact on the "foxhole strength" of combat companies, which were already weakened by desertions, illness, and numerous fatigue details. The cutback in citizen labor drew howls of protest from local civilians, including the editor of the *Texas State Gazette,* who ran an editorial describing the measure as "So very penurious and parsimonious . . . to dismiss all citizen laborers, and the soldiers are now made to perform a great deal of bodily labor of every description . . . —leaving little or no time for drill and other duties of soldiers."[31]

In the post–Civil War years, army wages paid to Texas civilian employees fell somewhat behind the national average. In 1870 the U.S. average for skilled labor was $78 per month, with $40 per month typical for unskilled labor. On the Texas frontier during this period, post guides and other skilled laborers earned $75 per month, teamsters $36, and quartermaster clerks averaged $80 to $100 per month. By 1878, the army in Texas had reduced the number of civilian employees to 230, but employed 206 extra-duty soldiers in place of the civilians it let go. These soldier workers represented five and a half infantry companies, or about 5 percent of the combat strength of the army in Texas.[32]

In the relatively less populated Department of New Mexico the U.S. Army was the largest single employer in the region. However, this was not true in Texas. Compared to the current impact of military employment, the army's hiring of Texas civilians in the nineteenth century was relatively insignificant to the general Texas economy, representing $3 million or about 10 percent of the army's logistical expenses. However, as with other areas of supply, the local impact could be important in the nine or ten Texas counties with large posts. The huge quartermaster's depot in San Antonio typically accounted for half of all the civilians hired by the army in the state. In 1856, for example, of 356 army employees in Texas, 150 worked in San Antonio, bringing $54,168 worth of wages to Bexar County that year. In 1878, 150 of the 230 army employees in the state worked in San Antonio, bringing $78,000 worth of wages to the local economy. These army dollars were three times the wages earned in Bexar County from manufacturing, according to the 1870 census.[33]

CHAPTER 8

Army Engineers
*Exploration and Mapping, Road Building,
and River and Harbor Improvement*

Army engineer activities added $13 million to the $70 million the nineteenth-century Texas economy gained from army logistical operations and pay. However, the engineers' most significant impact was in the form of more intangible contributions such as increasing practical geographic knowledge through exploration and developing the state's major lines of communication. Many of the original military routes determined by army engineers continue to dictate the primary highway pattern in the Trans-Pecos and in southwest Texas. Besides a viable network of overland transportation, army engineers provided Texas with its principal late-nineteenth-century commercial harbor by transforming Galveston into a port capable of docking ocean-going deep-draft vessels.

Two groups of army engineers were active in Texas during the nineteenth century. From 1802 to 1863, Corps of Engineers officers—with an average of forty-five officers serving in the army during the 1850s—supported the operational forces by military construction and by building field and coastal fortifications. The Corps of Topographical Engineers, an independent War Department bureau from 1831 to 1838 and a separate corps from 1838 to 1863, had the responsibility for exploration, survey and mapping, road building, river and harbor improvements, and all civil engineering projects designated by Congress. After 1863, the two groups merged under the Corps of Engineers, whose post–Civil War scope included all aspects of mapping and building. Of the military engineers serving in the state, members of the Corps of Topographical Engineers had the most significant influence on antebellum Texas. The thirty-six "Topog" officers, led by the able and energetic Col. John J. Abert, were responsible for the first detailed mapping of the West. They were, in essence, armed scientists who recorded the flora, fauna, and natural geology in the process of their army duties.[1]

EXPLORATION, MAPPING, AND ROAD BUILDING

The army showed interest in Texas long before the Mexican War. Major Gen. James Wilkinson, governor of the Louisiana Territory in 1805, gained the first detailed American military knowledge of Texas from the activities of his young protégé Philip Nolan, a mustanger and filibuster who set out on trading expeditions in Texas as early as 1791. President Thomas Jefferson, seeking knowledge of the new lands acquired through western expansion, sent an army-escorted expedition under Thomas Freeman and Peter Custis up the Red River to the edge of Texas in 1806. Lieutenant Zebulon Pike crossed Texas the following year while returning from his explorations to find the sources of the Arkansas and Red Rivers. After the 1819 Adams-Onís Treaty established the Sabine and Red Rivers as the border between New Spain and the United States, Maj. Stephen H. Long, a topographical engineer, spent 1820 on a scientific and mapping expedition exploring the Platte and Arkansas Rivers and searching for the source of the Red River. He may have crossed the northern Llano Estacado in Texas on his return, marking the first contact between the regular army and the Kiowa-Comanche.[2]

The alarms of the Texas Revolution in 1836 brought 341 soldiers from the First Dragoons and Seventh Infantry to Nacogdoches, which they occupied from July to December. Four years later, in 1840 and 1841, Maj. James Duncan Graham surveyed the Sabine River boundary line between Texas and the United States as part of a combined project with the Republic of Texas.[3]

The coming of the Mexican War set off an explosion of army exploration and mapping in Texas, an effort that would continue well into the 1870s. From August to October, 1845, topographical engineer Lt. James W. Abert, son of the Topog chief, and Lt. William G. Peck—both detached from Capt. John C. Frémont's California expedition—conducted a detailed reconnaissance and mapping exploration of a portion of the Texas Panhandle. Departing from Bent's Fort, Colorado, the party explored the Llano Estacado, the Canadian River (with the help of a Kiowa guide), and the North Fork of the Red River, finishing the expedition at Fort Gibson in the Indian Territory. Abert's map and report, published in June, 1846, consolidated earlier information from Frémont, William B. Franklin, and Santa Fe trader Joshia Gregg. Their report was not only the army's first specific information on the Panhandle, it also provided valuable information on the ethnography and loca-tions of Comanche and Kiowa Indians in the area.[4]

The arrival of Taylor's Army of Observation at Corpus Christi in the summer of 1845 launched a series of coastal and interior Texas survey and mapping efforts. In October, 1845, Taylor sent Lt. George G. Meade, a Topog who later commanded the Union's Army of the Potomac at Gettysburg, to conduct a reconnaissance of the Nueces River and then, in November, to survey an overland route from Corpus Christi to Point Isabel. At the same time, Lt. Jacob E. Blake mapped the coastal route down Padre Island, rec-ommending Brazos Santiago for Taylor's logistical center. In January, 1846, Meade and Taylor's chief engineer, Capt. Joseph F. K. Mansfield, conducted a coastal survey of Aransas and Matagorda Bay. Two months later, Blake did the route survey from Point Isabel to Matamoros. In October, a month after Taylor captured Monterrey, Lt. Bryant P. Tilden Jr., detailed from the Sec-ond Infantry, set out with the steamboat *Major Brown* to map the navigation potential of the Rio Grande north of Camargo. When the steamboat grounded at Laredo, Tilden continued upriver in a dugout for 110 miles before being turned back by a series of rapids—later called Kingsbury Falls—below present-day Eagle Pass.[5]

The organization of Brigadier General Wool's Division of the Center at San Antonio in August and September, 1846, produced a second wave of mapping and army exploration in interior south-central Texas. Wool's chief topographer, Capt. George W. Hughes, working with Lt. Lorenzo Sitgreaves, mapped the route from Wool's coastal supply point at Port Lavaca through Goliad to San Antonio, while Lieutenants William Franklin and Francis T. Bryan mapped an alternate route from Victoria through Seguin. In the end, Hughes recommended the shorter Goliad route, which subsequently became a main artery of logistics and commerce from the coast to San Antonio. In September, 1846, Hughes's Topogs formed the advance party for Wool's army, conducting a reconnaissance and mapping survey that backtracked along Mexican Brig. Gen. Adrian Woll's 1842 invasion route west to the Leona River, and then southwest to Presidio del Rio Grande. As Wool's army moved west toward Mexico in late September, Wool's chief engineer, Capt. Robert E. Lee, supervised the road improvement that would eventually form that portion of the military road to El Paso as far as the Leona River—along what is now U.S. Highway 90.[6]

After the Mexican War, while much of the army was still returning from Mexico City, a group of San Antonio merchants hired Col. John C. "Jack" Hays, commander of the First Regiment of Texas Mounted Volunteers, to explore a wagon route to El Paso to open up trade with the silver-rich region of Chihuahua, Mexico. Ironically, this was Brigadier General Wool's original destination, although his army never reached it. Hays's exploration of routes across the Pecos River in the Presidio del Norte–El Paso area from August to December, 1848, did not produce a wagon-road solution but they did spark great commercial interest. His expedition also served as the foundation for opening routes into west Texas, finally linking San Antonio and El Paso. Hays supplied the details of his explorations to Secretary of War William L. Marcy in December, 1848, making a significant contribution to the army's knowledge of the Trans-Pecos region.[7]

The army's subsequent search for a wagon route to El Paso, and the multitude of army route surveys conducted in the state during the years 1849 to 1855, is characteristic of the mutual interests bonding the military-commercial relationship that existed in nineteenth-century Texas. Spurred by the discovery of gold in California and the lure of new land in the expanded domain, the nation demanded emigrant trails to the West. The army's leaders needed adequate supply routes to link the military posts on the Texas frontier, businessmen needed reliable paths between markets in the state, and freighters needed good wagon roads on which to move commercial and military cargo. Texas newspaper editors clamored for roads, and in Congress, Jefferson Davis, the chairman of the Senate Committee on Military Affairs, called for a wagon-road survey in the state, while two Texans—Sen. Thomas Rusk and Rep. Volney Howard—secured appropriations. At the War Department, Quartermaster General Jesup made the development of supply roads in Texas one of his highest priorities, and the chief of the Topographical Corps sent to the department one of the most experienced engineer officers in the army, Bvt. Lt. Col. Joseph E. Johnston. Within five years the combined force of these efforts and requirements opened a network of routes penetrating portions of the state long denied to the Spanish, Mexicans, or Texans of the Republic.[8]

Post–Mexican War military surveys by topographical engineers in Texas began in January, 1849, when Lieutenants Nathaniel Michler and Francis Bryan explored Aransas Pass and Corpus Christi while mapping a road to San Antonio. The following month, the two lieutenants made a reconnaissance of the route from San Antonio westward to the Leona River and southwest to Presidio del Rio Grande, essentially following Woll's and Wool's earlier trails.[9]

Meanwhile, in 1849, Congress appropriated $50,000 to finance surveys to find the most practicable wagon or railway route from the Mississippi

Valley to the Pacific Ocean. One of the four initial searches for this road occurred in Texas. The secretary of war directed the Texas department commander to explore the region from San Antonio to Santa Fe. Brevet Maj. Gen. William J. Worth, commander of the Eighth Military Department, ordered a twenty-four-year-old engineer officer, Lt. William Henry Chase Whiting, to conduct the reconnaissance from the Gulf of Mexico through San Antonio to El Paso. Lieutenant William F. Smith, a Topog, was attached to Whiting's party along with nine enlisted soldiers and several Anglo, Tejano, and Indian guides. While Whiting was preparing his expedition at Corpus Christi, he ran into an old West Point classmate, Richard Austin Howard. Howard had not graduated and was working as a civilian surveyor. More importantly, though, he had been with Jack Hays on the previous year's attempt to pioneer a route to El Paso. Whiting persuaded Howard to join the expedition while Howard persuaded Whiting to take twenty-one-year-old José "Polly" Rodríquez as a guide. Whiting's expedition left San Antonio for Fredericksburg on February 12, 1849.[10]

Departing Fredericksburg on February 21, Whiting pushed west across the Llano and moved along the San Saba, going three days without water to the Pecos River. West of the Pecos, Whiting's party marched to Comanche Spring and on into the Davis Mountains, encountering a party of two hundred suspicious Apache, with whom the explorers managed to negotiate safe passage. Polly Rodríquez named a stream they traced the Limpia, and collectively they named a picturesque defile Wild Rose Pass. Leaving the mountains, the group angled southwest to Ben Leaton's fort on the Rio Grande. Heading north along the river, the party arrived at Ponce's Ranch opposite El Paso on April 12. Whiting added Henry Skillman to his party for the 645-mile return trip, altering course and creating what would become the "lower" El Paso road. From El Paso, Whiting moved down the Rio Grande and then southeast, more directly to Limpia Canyon and beyond to the Pecos. Marching down the Pecos eighteen miles from Live Oak Creek, they struck southeast to the Devil's River, often called the San Pedro. From there the route carried them to San Felipe Springs and east to Los Moras Creek, the Nueces River, Fort Inge on the Leona, and into San Antonio on May 24, 1849, after 104 days on the trail. Whiting promptly recommended the advantages of the lower route to the chief engineer.[11]

While Whiting marched west, a second expedition, sponsored by Austin businessmen, set off to find a practical route connecting Austin to El Paso. Led by a Texas Ranger, Maj. Robert S. Neighbors, with John S. Ford and a group of Indian guides, the party departed Waco in mid-March, 1849.

They traveled to the upper Colorado, up the Concho River and west to Horsehead Crossing on the Pecos. From there they marched due west to the Rio Grande and up to El Paso, arriving on May 2. The expedition returned by way of the Guadalupe Mountains and south to the Pecos. After reaching San Antonio on June 2, Neighbors reported the results of his explorations to the department commander.[12]

Major General Worth died of cholera at San Antonio and in May, 1849, the new department commander, Bvt. Brig. Gen. William S. Harney, ordered Lieutenant Colonel Johnston to organize confirmation surveys of the upper and lower routes to El Paso. Lieutenant Bryan followed the Neighbors-Ford Trail, while Lieutenant Colonel Johnston surveyed Whiting's route. Johnston—taking Lieutenant William Smith and Richard A. Howard, who both had been with Whiting, plus a company from the First Infantry to serve as escort—led six companies from the Third Infantry to El Paso. They improved the road along the way with twenty civilian workers hired specifically for the task. Departing San Antonio the first week in June, the expedition labored one hundred days on the 650 miles of rough road, arriving at El Paso on September 8, 1849. Lieutenant Smith spent the rest of September and October exploring the Sacramento Mountains, while Johnston and Howard marched to the Pecos in October, turning southward across the head of the Devil's and Nueces Rivers, returning to San Antonio on November 23, 1849.[13]

While Johnston was testing the feasibility of the lower road, Lieutenant Bryan followed the upper route. Bryan left San Antonio via Fredericksburg on June 14, 1849. His party followed the Concho, then the Pecos, traveled through the Guadalupe Mountains, and reached El Paso on July 29. Bryan found the path suitable for wagons, although he recommended a series of wells be dug along the upper Pecos. Brevet Capt. John Pope, a Topog, eventually tried to drill the wells, and after the Civil War the Neighbors-Ford-Bryan route became the general path of the Texas Pacific Railroad across the Trans-Pecos.[14]

Whiting's lower road linked El Paso with San Antonio and the Texas coast, but, more significantly, the dependable wagon route pioneered by Neighbors and Ford and mapped by Bryan tied the upper South to California. Together, these two routes connected the nation below the line of the Santa Fe and Oregon Trails.

Although the center of attention remained focused on the El Paso route, a series of reconnaissance, survey, and mapping efforts began to piece together the network of roads and trails on Texas' military frontier 1849 and 1850. From June to August, 1849, Capt. Randolph B. Marcy and Lt. James H.

Simpson, a Topog, escorted gold seekers to the west. Along the way, they mapped an 895-mile route extending from Fort Smith, Arkansas, along the south side of the Canadian River, and crossing the Panhandle to Santa Fe. In late August, Marcy returned to Fort Smith, exploring portions of the Llano Estacado, the Trans-Pecos, and the Cross-timbers region, pioneering a viable emigrant route from the Guadalupe Mountains to the Pecos and then northeast to Preston on the Red River. In May, 1849, Lieutenant Nathaniel Michler mapped a road from Port Lavaca to San Antonio, and in June and July searched 217 miles from Corpus Christi for a direct road up the Nueces to the Frio and Leona Rivers and on to Fort Inge. In late July, 1849, Michler mapped a route from San Antonio north to Dallas and thence to Fort Washita in the Indian Territory. Using information gathered by Marcy, Michler left Fort Washita in November, exploring 446 miles across the Red, Big Wichita, Brazos, and Pecos Rivers. He then turned east to the head of the Concho, the San Saba, and Fredericksburg, arriving in San Antonio on January 20, 1850.[15]

Meanwhile, Whiting, hardly recovered from his great trek to El Paso, was ordered on October 1, 1849, to conduct a reconnaissance along the developing frontier line from the mouth of the Rio Grande to the Red River. After spending five months in the saddle gathering information for his notes, Whiting wrote a detailed account that was forwarded to the Senate in response to a congressional demand for an updated report on Texas made the previous July.[16]

While Whiting rode the settlement line, frontiersman and adventurer Harry Love, working for the Quartermaster's Department, launched a party of flatboats from Ringgold Barracks on March 11, 1850, pushing up the Rio Grande over a hundred miles above the mouth of the Pecos. Returning on August 11, Love declared the river navigable to its junction with the Pecos River. The skeptical chief topographer followed up with several boat expeditions to investigate. As a part of the Mexican boundary survey, a Topog party under Lieutenants William Smith and Bryan, went by flatboat down the Rio Grande from El Paso to Presido del Norte in May, 1850. There they met a reconnaissance party detached from Lieutenant Colonel Johnston, who made the trek by wagon along a route that roughly paralleled the Rio Grande from the mouth of the Devil's River. Shortly afterward, a party led by Lt. Martin L. Smith left Ringgold Barracks August 25, 1850, using flatboats and poles to explore 470 miles upriver on the Rio Grande—to a point 80 miles above the mouth of the Pecos. Unlike Love, Smith found the river to be partially navigable only 120 miles above Ringgold Barracks.[17]

As part of his Mexican boundary-survey duties, from August to November 1850, Lieutenant Michler, with the help of Lt. Martin Smith, spent August to November, 1850, mapping a route from San Antonio south to the junction of the Nueces River, and then southwest to Ringgold Barracks on the Rio Grande. In April, 1851, Lieutenant Bryan surveyed and cut a road from Fort Mason to Austin, while Lieutenant Colonel Johnson made a general reconnaissance of the frontier line from the headwaters of the Nueces, across the Llano, San Saba, and Concho Rivers to Fort Belknap.[18]

Captain Randolph B. Marcy led an expedition to the Red River in the summer of 1852 in an effort to make a final determination as to its source. Accompanied by his future son-in-law, Lt. George B. McClellan, and guided by Black Beaver, the Delaware Indian scout, Marcy's seventy-man party explored the upper reaches of the Red River, including the Palo Duro and Tule Canyons, returning with valuable information on the Wichita Indians, mineral deposits, and thirty-five new species of mammals and reptiles.[19]

Congress passed the Pacific Railroad Survey Bill in 1853, appropriating $150,000 for a detailed reconnaissance of the best routes from the Mississippi Valley to the Pacific Ocean. Arguments over the course the railroad should take generated vociferous sectional political infighting as each geographic region naturally wanted the rails to originate in their area and thus gain the mammoth economic advantage the western railroad terminus would offer. To solve the political dilemma, Congress eventually laid the question before the Corps of Topographical Engineers, which was ordered to survey routes across the northern and southern plains and recommend the most practical route based on an unbiased analysis. Four routes were selected for examination: a northern route between the 47th and 49th parallels from St. Paul, Minnesota; a central route between the 38th and 39th parallels probably to originate at St. Louis; a southern route along the 35th parallel from Fort Smith, Arkansas, across the Texas Panhandle to California; and a fourth route in California that would connect the 35th parallel with the already much explored 32d parallel. Lieutenant Ameil W. Whipple, with a group of civilian naturalists and geologists, surveyed the 35th parallel route, departing Fort Smith on July 14, 1853. Whipple followed the Canadian River, crossed the northern Llano Estacado in Texas by following Abert's and Pecks's 1845 route, reached the Rio Grande Valley at Albuquerque, and proceeded west to Colorado and California. Whipple reported the route was practical but generally lacking in water and timber.[20]

As an adjunct to the railroad survey, in October, 1853, Secretary of War Jefferson Davis directed Bvt. Capt. John Pope to explore a section of a proposed southern route on the 32d parallel from Preston on the Red River to El

Paso. Pope left Doña Ana, New Mexico, with seventy-five men on February 12, 1854. He and his party ventured through the Guadalupe Mountains, crossed the Pecos at Delaware Creek, and marched to the headwaters of the Colorado and on to Fort Belknap, turning northwest to the Trinity and beyond to Preston.[21]

Although the railroad surveys produced remarkable volumes of scientific information, resulting in the first detailed map of the Trans-Mississippi West, the political climate could not produce a favored route. Each had its champions and detractors, and the surveys were tainted by claims that the War Department and senior Topographical Engineers were politically and economically biased in favor of the southern routes. The transcontinental railroad would remain a dream until the passions of sectional rivalries were settled by the Civil War.

Aside from the railroad surveys, additional route explorations continued in Texas for another year. In 1854 Lieutenant Abert nearly repeated his 1845 trek. Leaving Colorado in August, he crossed the Llano Estacado and once again explored along the Canadian River, arriving in Arkansas in October. Also in 1854, Capt. Marcy organized an expedition at Fort Washita that included Indian Agent Robert S. Neighbors and forty-five Seventh Infantry soldiers. Staging out of Fort Belknap, the party explored much of the upper Brazos and Big Wichita Rivers while surveying sites for Texas Indian reservations. Marcy returned two years later and surveyed the headwaters of the Brazos and the Big Wichita Rivers.[22]

Hoping to improve the water supply on the emigrant and military trails across the Llano Estacado and New Mexico's *Jornado del Muerto,* Congress appropriated funds for Captain Pope to spend the better part of three years attempting to dig the first in a series of artesian wells in the Trans-Pecos. In June, 1855, Pope, with forty-three civilians and a military escort, began drilling the first well fourteen miles east of the Pecos on the 32d parallel. Three and a half months and 641 feet of drilling produced water, but without enough pressure to bring it to the surface. After three years, several thousand feet of holes in the arid Pecos flats, and a dozen defeats at various Texas locations, the stubborn Pope declared the experiment to be a noble failure. He reported in August, 1858, that the project had been overcome by impenetrable nature and frail technology, citing "The difficulties, mechanical and physical, which have so long embarrassed the work, and which I fear it will be impossible to surmount at a place so remote from every convenience."[23]

The secretary of war ordered a detailed reconnaissance of the Trans-Pecos in 1859 to locate an additional fort on the Rio Grande and, in the process, to test camels to supply that fort. Under the command of Lt. William H. Echols, the camel expedition departed Camp Hudson on the Devil's River in June, working to improve the road between Fort Stockton and Fort Davis and spending a month exploring the Big Bend area south of Fort Davis. Unable to achieve success, Echols tried again the following year, departing Camp Hudson on June 24, 1860, with twenty camels and an infantry escort. Marching five days over 120 barren miles to the Rio Grande, with the camels carrying water, Echols reported the command "Suffered greatly from the want of water. Indeed the lives of all were in peril, and but for the camels the results might have proved disastrous." After failing to find a shorter route to Fort Davis the expedition moved to the Rio Grande, locating a few suitable fort sites along the river, and finishing by surveying a route from Presido del Norte northward to Fort Stockton.[24]

The reconnaissances of the antebellum era mapped a network of practical wagon routes across Texas, the majority of the work accomplished by topographical engineer officers between 1849 and 1854. That pattern changed in the post–Civil War decades when the exploration of Texas' hidden corners, primarily in the Panhandle and Trans-Pecos, was accomplished not by the engineers but by several key leaders in infantry and cavalry combat commands during military campaigns.

When the army returned to Texas after the Civil War it seemed as if its hard-earned antebellum understanding of frontier routes had all but vanished. Slowly, primarily from scouts and expeditions against Indians, commanders accumulated new information about the region north and west of San Antonio, reestablishing a network of military and mail roads. Typical of these efforts was that of Capt. Edward S. Meyer of the Thirty-fifth Infantry. Ordered to conduct a new survey and to record details of water sources and camping sites on the old San Antonio–El Paso military road, Meyer's party departed San Antonio on May 27, 1867. They spent sixty days on the trail, producing a table of distances and description of key points for the department commander.[25]

In the summer and fall of 1870, Col. William Shafter of the Twenty-fourth Infantry, along with troops from the Ninth Cavalry, undertook a series of expeditions that took them from the lower Pecos and Devil's River country to the uncharted areas of the Sand Hills northeast of Fort Davis. The following year, starting in October, Shafter focused on scouting the Big Bend area. In the process of waging three campaigns against the Comanches beginning in October, 1871, Col. Ranald Mackenzie of the Fourth Cavalry penetrated the Llano Estacado and expanded on the army's knowledge of the region, joining forces with Shafter in 1872. The Red River War brought five military columns to the Staked Plains in 1874 and 1875, giving the army a thorough understanding of the Llano Estacado and its canyons between the lower forks of the Red River and the Canadian River. Shafter returned in the summer of 1875 on a five-month mapping expedition that dispelled the long-held notion that the region was a desert. With the end of Comanche military power, the area was at last opened to cattlemen. In May, 1876, shortly after Shafter's expedition, Lt. Ernest H. Ruffner of the Corps of Engineers led a mapping party west across the Texas Panhandle from newly established Fort Elliott. Ruffner's party conducted a six-week-long line survey and resource inventory of Palo Duro Canyon and the region surrounding the headwaters of the Red River.[26]

While they did not command large columns of troops across the plains, two other combat officers made significant contributions to the post–Civil War exploration of the Trans-Pecos. Lieutenant John Bullis, the son of New York Quakers and leader of the Seminole Negro-Indian scouts from 1873 to 1881, scouted for both Mackenzie and Shafter, conducting dozens of patrols into the wilder reaches of Texas' and Mexico's Rio Grande borderlands. Colonel Benjamin H. Grierson, commander of the Military District of the Pecos from 1878 to 1881, determined that military control of the water sources in the Trans-Pecos was the key to defense against marauders. In 1878 Grierson and his detachments began to systematically explore and map the waterholes and Indian trails of the region, discovering several unnoted springs in the process. In 1879 and 1880 Grierson built subposts at many of the water sources and focused on improving existing roads by having his troops level and grade steeper sections. In addition, he began developing a series of new wagon routes across the Trans-Pecos, such as a road from Fort Davis southwest to Presidio.[27]

Army engineer officers were the group most responsible for exploration and detailed mapping of the Texas frontier during the antebellum period, accomplishing most of the basic work by 1854. In the post–Civil War years the responsibility for exploration in Texas fell on field commanders while the Corps of Engineers concentrated on trying to develop the state's waterways and coastal areas.

RIVER AND HARBOR IMPROVEMENT

The story of the Corps of Engineers's attempts to improve Texas' harbors and rivers in the nineteenth century is one of ambitious schemes frustrated by piecemeal appropriations, and of grand designs stymied by inadequate technology and the fierce power of nature. Until the spectacular success at Galveston at the turn of the century, many of the river and coastal engineer projects in nineteenth-century Texas resulted in very temporary victories or in outright failure, all with marginal gains at enormous expense to the public treasury.

In 1849 Quartermaster General Jesup began pressing the secretary of war to seek funds from Congress to better the state's rivers and harbors. He informed the secretary in 1850 that "The improvement of the harbors of Texas, with that of the navigation of the Rio Grande, the Guadalupe, Colorado, Trinity and upper Red River, with the construction of good roads be-

TABLE 13.

ARMY ENGINEER PROJECT EXPENDITURES

IN TEXAS, 1849–1900

Projects	1849–1860	1869–1879	Period 1880–1889	1890–1900	Total
Galveston Harbor	$50,000	$477,000	$1,506,694	$5,925,072	$7,958,766
Galveston channels & Red Fish Bar		$69,332	$396,050	$176,062	$641,444
Buffalo Bayou			$124,434	$68,504	$192,938
Cypress Bayou		$94,459	$19,500	$16,504	$130,463
Cedar Bayou				$32,150	$32,150
San Jacinto River		$25,000			$25,000
Sabine Pass		$87,472	$758,976	$1,691,364	$2,537,812
Sabine River		$36,281	$30,877	$187,925	$255,083
Neches River		$12,892	$15,782	$4,167	$32,841
Trinity River		$6,196	$26,672	$34,200	$67,068
Pass Cavallo Matagorda Bay		$2,868	$261,631	$81	$264,580
Aransas Pass		$7,694	$532,805	$10,805	$551,304
Brazos Santiago		$6,000	$152,655	$4,145	$162,800
Fort Brown Flood Control		$15,704	$2,065		$17,769
Misc. Surveys & Projects	$6,500		$126,787	$50,733	$184,020
Total	$56,500	$840,898	$3,954,928	$8,201,712	$13,054,038

Source: Calculated from each year's "Report of the Quartermaster General of the Army," and "Report of the Chief of Engineers," in the annual *Report of the Secretary of War,* 1849–1900.

tween frontier posts and those posts and accessible points on the coast and rivers, would be worth infinitely more, in the defense of the frontier, than any system of fortification."[28]

Antebellum federal activity to improve Texas' rivers was short-lived and underfinanced. Three important interior Texas rivers—the Brazos, Colorado, and Trinity—had steamboat potential. Although partially restricted by hazards, the Brazos and Trinity Rivers had been well traveled by boats since the mid-1840s. On the other hand, rafts and other obstructions blocked the Colorado. Governor George T. Wood and the citizens of Columbus petitioned President Taylor in 1849 for federal help with opening up the Colorado from Matagorda Bay to Austin. Taylor had Quartermaster General Jesup send the government snag boat *Lavaca,* which unfortunately sank while en route on the Mississippi. Organizing the Colorado Navigation Company, Texas citizens made numerous attempts to clear the river without long-term success. Providing additional expertise, a Corps of Engineers party surveyed the Colorado in February, 1850, estimating the river could be cleared for $56,000. The intrepid explorer of the Trans-Pecos, Lt. William H. C. Whiting, along with Lieutenant William Smith, conducted an additional survey of the Colorado River in 1852. They declared that La Grange was the natural head of navigation for the river and that the primary obstacle was a large log raft located twenty-five miles above the mouth. Whiting recommended the government not expend money to attempt to clear the channel upriver from La Grange to Austin, but advocated federal support for the Colorado Navigation Company, which was desperately short of funds for its effort to clear the lower river. Although Whiting supervised the cutting of a channel around the raft by a government snag boat in 1853 and 1854, nature continuously defeated every nineteenth-century attempt to open the river to anything but a very occasional shallow-draft steamer.[29]

On the Brazos River, navigation was possible from Velasco to Washington-on-the Brazos, and four steamers were in operation by 1850, with the privately funded West Galveston Bay channel linking Galveston to the mouth of the river. Lieutenant Whiting conducted a survey of the Brazos in 1853, reporting the sandbar at the mouth of the river near Velasco to be the primary obstruction. Whiting was opposed to a government attempt to cut the bar because all exertions would be of such a temporary nature that it would have no lasting results. Eventually, in the 1880s, a Corps of Engineers project improved the mouth of the river as a coastal engineering proposal rather than one of interior navigation. Whiting also surveyed the Trinity River in 1853, finding it navigable at high water for nearly six hundred miles to Magnolia, and at low water for about sixty miles to Liberty. Although the primary obstructions were simple snags and overhanging limbs, army engineers did not begin to include it in improvement appropriations until the 1870s, and then in relatively small amounts. Finally, in 1902, the federal government began a substantial project that required $2 million and twenty years to create a series of locks and dams on the river.[30]

In east Texas, the huge logjam on the Red River, known as the Great Raft, backed up the waters of Cypress Bayou, literally creating a port out of Jefferson, Texas. The port became a commercial hub, allowing cotton growers and loggers to export by water from northeast Texas. In 1871, for example, the wharves at Jefferson received 226 steamboats and loaded 76,328 bales of cotton. Although Cypress Bayou was navigable for shallow steamers, the Corps of Engineers, starting in December, 1872, undertook several projects to improve the route along the fifty miles of bayou to the Red River at Shreveport, Louisiana. By 1874, using a dredge owned by the city of Jefferson and a government snag boat, they were able to widen twenty miles of channel to a point below Smithland. Work continued off and on toward Shreveport, despite the sinking of the dredge in 1878. By 1882, when the Great Raft on the Red River was finally conquered by the engineers, more than $94,000 had been invested in the project, thus practically neutralizing the hard efforts and fiscal investment on Cypress Bayou. Although work to improve Cypress Bayou continued until 1893, the destruction of the Red River log raft lowered the water level in the bayou and, concurrent with the port being bypassed by the railroad, destroyed Jefferson as a commercial center.[31]

Engineering efforts to clear the Great Raft on the Red River in the 1850s would have meant an economic boost to north and northeast Texas, but by the time the project achieved success in 1882 the efficiency of the railroad network had all but nullified the river's transportation potential. In 1825 the Great Raft was actually a ninety-mile series of logjams, one of the longest on any North American river, extending above present-day Shreveport. Steamboat captain Henry V. Shreve first cleared a large portion of the raft in 1834, but the jam of driftwood and trees had reaccumulated by 1841. A Corps of Engineers project in 1844, and a second one in 1856 and 1857, failed to clear and maintain a channel through the raft. In 1860 the chief of engineers estimated that given five years and half a million dollars, army engineers could open the raft to navigation. The third attempt by army engineers began in 1872 under Lt. Eugene A. Woodruff, and succeeded after a year in opening the river to Fulton, Arkansas. However, it required an additional decade of clearing and maintenance of the river channel. Within ten years the reduction of the raft had significantly altered the drainage pattern of the Red River Valley, drying up marginal wetlands and opening thousands of alluvial acres to agriculture.[32]

The engineers attempted an erosion control project to try and keep the Rio Grande from carrying away portions of the Fort Brown military reservation. In 1877 Congress gave the engineers $7,197 to construct a breakwater along five hundred feet of bank in the northwest corner of the post. Although the post engineers spent an equal sum maintaining the breakwater, it failed to stop the river's erosion of the fort's soft alluvial edges. In 1882 the chief engineer reported that the results of the $16,000 spent were not commensurate with the gain, and that it would be cheaper to move the buildings than to fight the river. By 1895 the riverbank was within four feet of the post administration building, every previous attempt to control the river having failed. The following year, after the river carried away the administration building's porch, the engineers constructed a brush mattress revetment pinned to the bank by wire cables, another labor that proved futile over time.[33]

While government efforts to improve internal river navigation in Texas remained modest in scale, the attention it gave to coastal areas and harbors was more earnest. With the Rivers and Harbors Act of August 30, 1852, Congress appropriated money for harbor surveys at Sabine Pass, Galveston, Pass Cavallo, Velasco, Corpus Christi, and Brazos Santiago. The chief engineer responded by asking Congress for a hundred thousand dollars to begin improvements on the Texas coast. He received $6,500 to pay for the surveys, but little else was accomplished until after the Civil War. Lieutenant George B. McClellan, who later commanded the Union's Army of the Potomac, had a major share of this coastal survey. McClellan spent the summer of 1852 assisting Capt. Randolph Marcy with the Red River Expedition and in October of that year began his portion of the coastal survey. Purchasing a schooner and setting up his headquarters at Corpus Christi, McClellan proceeded to examine and map Pass Cavallo, Indianola, Corpus Christi, the mouth of the Rio Grande, and Brazos Santiago, completing his investigation in March, 1853. He found the sandbar at Brazos Santiago to be "the roughest on the coast of Texas." He concluded that simple dredging offered no solution as the shifting bars blocking the entrances to Texas harbors were so unstable that "It is difficult to imagine anything more changeable." The general result of the survey was discouraging. Although no material gain came from the 1852–1853 survey, it significantly improved civil and military knowledge of the Texas coast, setting the stage for the post–Civil War projects.[34]

The nineteenth-century Corps of Engineers made only minor improvements to Brazos Santiago, the irascible old supply base supporting Mexican War operations and early military efforts on the Texas frontier. The first modest operation involved the removal of the debris of the bark *René de Mers* in the 1870s. That was followed in the 1880s by an attempt to deepen the inner harbor with a jetty. Funds ran out, however, and the project remained insolvent until after the turn of the century. In 1904 and 1905 the Corps of Engineers scoured a ten-by-seventy-foot channel across Laguna Madre from the bar up to Point Isabel. When the St. Louis, Brownsville, and Mexico Railway bypassed Point Isabel, further attempts to improve the area were abandoned until 1934, when the government spent $5 million extending the jetties and deepening the channel.[35]

The topographical engineers began a detailed survey of Matagorda Bay in 1850, and subsequent knowledge of the bay was amended by Lieutenant McClellan's survey of Pass Cavallo and Powder Horn-Indianola in 1853. McClellan found Indianola sufficient as it was, although of limited draft, suggesting that no improvements were necessary. A second survey in 1874 produced similar engineer observations. In 1871 and 1872 Indianola cleared 149 steamers carrying 170,052 tons and 101 schooners hauling 15,399 tons, the freight being primarily cotton and hides. The chief engineer reported that any improvements obtained by dredging would be of such a temporary nature that the estimated $700,000 cost of the project would not be justified given the relatively meager exports sent from the port. Despite the destruction of most of Indianola by a hurricane in 1875, serious federal efforts to deepen Matagorda Bay began in 1879 with the start of a jetty project, and expanded in 1881 when work began on a twelve-foot channel across the bar at Pass Cavallo. It was evident by 1887 that the $264,000 project was a failure. Efforts to complete a channel finally bore fruit in 1910, and further improvements were made in 1939.[36]

Lieutenant McClellan found no practical way to improve the harbor at Corpus Christi or Aransas Pass in 1853. However, from 1879 to 1885 the Corps of Engineers undertook to construct a jetty from Mustang Island to protect the head of the island from erosion. That project, along with a private jetty built along the same lines, failed to withstand the power of the sea. Finally, in 1907, the government managed to build two major jetties at Aransas Pass.[37]

Although nineteenth-century army engineers undertook numerous works that improved the mouth of the Trinity, Sabine, and Neches Rivers and other links to the sea, the successful deepening of Galveston Harbor was the Corps of Engineers's superlative coastal achievement in Texas. The series of individual projects to improve the harbor took a half-century and more than $7 million to complete. The foundation for the great port was laid in 1834 when Michel B. Menard and a group of investors purchased a league and labor of land on Galveston Island and laid out a town. In 1839 merchants Samuel May Williams and Thomas F. McKinney and others built wharves to serve their businesses, resulting by the following year in nearly a million dollars' worth of commerce, primarily in cotton trade. Menard gathered the various wharf owners in 1854 and formed what became the Galveston Wharf Company, a commercial giant that after 1859 dominated the port for several decades. Galveston's potential as a port was considerably limited by outer and inner sandbars that fixed the harbor's depth at twelve to fifteen feet, forcing deep-draft vessels to lighter, thus adding as much as $2,500 per shipment.[38]

Schemes to deepen Galveston Harbor began to surface in the 1850s. As part of the Corps of Engineers's 1853 river and harbor survey, Lt. Walter H. Stevens recommended raising the depth over the twelve-foot outer bar by prolonging the head of Galveston Island with a jetty or breakwater extension. Although the engineers built a road and wharf on the island, the matter more or less rested there until 1867, when a new coast survey prompted Lt. William S. Stanton to recommend dredging an eighty-foot-wide channel across the sandbar. Congress appropriated $25,000 for the project in 1870, and a seven-foot-deep, fifteen-hundred-foot-long channel was completed on the inner bar in 1873. However, recognizing the temporary nature of dredging work on a wave-swept bar, the Corps of Engineers began to think in terms of breakwaters and jetties to raise the harbor's level. The city of Galveston financed the start of a mile-long jetty extension from Fort Point in 1873, but the project soon ran into financial difficulties.[39]

By 1876, the general political climate of Reconstruction had, perhaps by extension, fostered among legislators a renewed sense of federal responsibility for public works and the nation's infrastructure. Congress began to appropriate large sums for the improvement of the southern coast, some of which was earmarked for Galveston. Stymied by the scarcity of large stone blocks needed to continue the jetty project, Capt. Charles W. Howell of the Corps of Engineers devised an experimental method to extend a breakwater from the city toward Bolivar Point. Using six-foot-high, six-foot-diameter wicker baskets—called gabions—filled with sand, Howell tried sinking them on the bay floor and covering them with hydraulic cement. It worked, after a fashion, as did a second gabionaide that extended a thousand feet from Fort Point by June, 1877. The disappearance of renewed federal funding— and the appearance of a hurricane in September, 1877—served to wreck much of the $447,000 worth of work already accomplished.[40]

In 1880 Maj. Samuel M. Mansfield, son of Col. Joseph Mansfield, who supervised the original construction of Fort Brown, took over supervision of the Galveston harbor project. Mansfield began a renewed attack on the outer bar using a new Congressional appropriation and a fresh scheme that involved building a four-mile-long North Jetty with a brush-mattress base topped with ten-ton stone ballasts. Mansfield estimated it would cost $2 million to build the jetties needed to raise the harbor's level. Congress gave him $825,000 in 1880 and 1882. The lack of a congressional appropriation from 1883 to 1886 brought the work to a halt, prompting the Texas legislature to authorize Galveston to raise a public bond for the project and, remarkably, to turn the money over to the Corps of Engineers. This also prompted James B. Eads, the civil engineer who opened the South Pass of the Mississippi at New Orleans, to declare he would, and could, deepen Galveston Harbor from twelve to thirty feet for $7 million.[41]

After nearly three years of inertia and the destructive effects of weather and climate on a partially completed construction project, Congress appropriated $300,000 for Galveston Harbor in August, 1886. Major Oswald H. Ernst, who had taken over from Mansfield, continued the North Jetty project in July, 1887, receiving an additional $500,000 in 1889. Ernst also contracted with W. A. M. Shannon and Company to complete the nineteen-thousand-foot-long South Jetty extension originating at Avenue A and Ninth Street in the city. In early 1890, funds for the project, appropriated in piecemeal packages, again dried up and work ground to a halt.[42]

By 1890, major commercial and business interests from Fort Worth to Denver and from Topeka to Omaha began to demand a major port for the Southwest that was closer than New Orleans. After considerable engineering and political investigation, Galveston became the focus of the these efforts, primarily through the intense lobbying and organizational efforts of Galveston's Deep-Water Committee—led first by William L. Moody and then by Walter Gresham. More importantly, when Congress passed the appropriation for the September, 1890, Rivers and Harbors Act, it set aside $500,000 for resuming the Galveston Harbor Project, with an unwritten promise that the full $6 million needed to complete the project would follow when work began. This provision, called a continuous-contract system, overcame the greatest obstacle to any engineering or army construction project in the West. The system of partial and piecemeal appropriations had meant work stoppages, deterioration of unfinished work, and new costs incurred with each start-up.[43]

Major Charles J. Allen, taking over the project in 1889, supervised the

Galveston North Jetty construction, contracting in August, 1891, for the South Jetty to be completed by O'Conner, Laing, and Smoot. Major Alexander Macomb Miller took over the Galveston Engineer Office in 1893 and oversaw the completion of the Galveston harbor project. The fruition of the plans drawn up by mostly West Point–trained army engineer officers beginning in 1853, and in labors starting in 1869, resulted in the 35,603-foot South Jetty and the 25,907-foot North Jetty, both completed in 1897. It was, at the time, the longest jetty system in the nation. In 1898 the jetties, constructed with 2 million tons of material, raised the harbor level twenty-five and a half feet over the outer bar and twenty-six feet over the inner bar, giving Galveston and Texas their first deepwater port.[44]

Galveston's success at creating deeper water spurred Houston to seek a twenty-five-foot-deep, one-hundred-foot-wide channel up Buffalo Bayou. Four million dollars and prodigious construction from 1912 to 1914 resulted in the Houston Ship Channel, giving Texas two major ports in relative proximity.[45]

Army engineers struggled for more than fifty years in nineteenth-century Texas, bringing to the state a level of expertise and dedicated enterprise that had a positive significance far outweighing their scant numbers and the $13 million disbursed for various projects. Although the industrious army engineers were successful in creating the deepwater port of Galveston, their attempts to improve Texas rivers and harbors met with only modest and temporary gains, stifled by the forces of nature and meager appropriations. The foremost contribution made by the Corps of Topographical Engineers and the Corps of Engineers to the economy and people of Texas was their pedestrian, persistent, and systematic effort to measure the landscape and define it on paper so that others might carve pathways for commerce across the state's vast territory.

CHAPTER 9

Contributions to the Economic Network

Stagecoaches, Mail, the Military Telegraph System, and the Weather Service

The development of stagecoach lines in Texas was intertwined with federal contracts with the postmaster general to deliver the U.S. mail on a dependable schedule. Stage lines often relied on hauling mail for a cash base and improved their profit margin by carrying paying passengers and freight. In either case, carrying mail or passengers was never easy, and the U.S. Army played an important role in the development of mail routes and stage lines across the state—all part of the expanding lines of communication within nineteenth-century Texas.

STAGECOACHES

When Texas became a state at the beginning of the Mexican War it had only a few stage lines between major communities, all developed during the period of the Republic. Typical of the early short stages operating in eastern Texas were an 1837 line from Houston to Harrisburg and an 1839 line from Houston to Austin. In 1845 stage lines began to proliferate in the populated areas. By the end of the war in 1848, the Texas U.S. Mail Line offered biweekly service from Houston to San Antonio, the Western U.S. Mail Line ran from Port Lavaca to San Antonio, and a half dozen additional lines connected Houston, Victoria, Corpus Christi, and other coastal areas. One of the largest operators was the firm of Brown and Tarbox, which ran the biweekly Houston, Austin, and San Antonio mail stage for a fee of twenty dollars for the route. When the postwar department commander, Bvt. Maj. Gen. David E. Twiggs, tried to ride this latter stagecoach from Houston to his headquarters in Austin in December, 1848, the stage bogged down in a sea of mud twenty-five miles from Houston, prompting the general to abandon his journey and return to New Orleans. Ten years later, in December, 1859, an army officer's wife took the same stage in the opposite direction, reporting that when a Norther' blew, the women and children had to forsake the comfortable coach and crowd into a small "mud-wagon" and the men walked all night. She wrote that those in the cramped wagon "ran equal chances of freezing or smothering."[1]

In 1851 James L. Allen opened a semiweekly stage line connecting Indianola to San Antonio at $12.50 per passenger. That September, Henry Skillman received a contract to provide mail service to Santa Fe, effectively connecting the Texas coast with New Mexico through San Antonio. The San Antonio–El Paso Mail was born when Skillman's heavily armed stage made its first westward run in November, 1851, with William A. A. "Bigfoot" Wallace at the reins. The following month, Skillman began passenger runs with the mail. Skillman and George H. Giddings formed a partnership in 1854, and in July, 1857, Giddings—without Skillman—extended his partnership and contract to include a semimonthly San Antonio–San Diego mail and passenger service that covered 1,476 miles. This first transcontinental stage service departed San Antonio on July 9, 1857, and spent nearly seven weeks reaching the California coast. Eventually the trip averaged twenty-seven days at a cost of $200 per passenger to San Diego and $100 to El Paso. Although he continued to operate his passenger service, Giddings lost most of his mail business to competition from the Butterfield Overland Mail and a series of forty-five robberies and Indian raids that cost him $229,000 between 1854 and 1861.[2]

The San Antonio–El Paso–San Diego mail route used military facilities, such as those at Fort Inge on the Leona River, as convenient safe havens for stock changing and as stations. Additionally, the natural dangers of the Trans-Pecos route and the constant threat of Indian raids on the stage line prompted army leaders to run patrols along the road and at times furnish direct escort for the stage. A civilian at Fort Inge in 1859 recalled: "It was customary for two and three soldiers [to go] along on horseback well armed as defense for mail and passengers [bound] for El Paso and California. Then at Fort Clark they would return with [the] Eastbound stage and other soldiers [would] take on [the] task as out riders."[3]

A second stage route to the Pacific began operating in northern Texas in

September, 1858, as the Butterfield or Southern Overland Mail. A $600,000 annual mail contract approved by Congress in March, 1857, obligated John Butterfield's company to a 2,795-mile, twenty-five-day, semiweekly passenger and mail service operating from St. Louis and Memphis, Tennessee, to Fort Smith, Arkansas, across northern Texas to El Paso, and westward to Tucson, Arizona, Los Angeles, and San Francisco. The original 645-mile, eight-day route in Texas crossed the Red River at Colbert's Ferry near Preston, then ran 122 miles southwest to Fort Belknap, seventy-three miles to the site of abandoned Fort Phantom Hill, fifty-eight miles to Fort Chadbourne, across the Middle Concho 122 miles to Horsehead Crossing on the Pecos, 160 miles up the Pecos to Delaware Springs, and west 110 miles to the Guadalupe Mountains, Hueco Tanks, and Franklin or El Paso. To improve the water supply, the route was altered in August, 1859, running southwest from Horsehead Crossing to Comanche Spring—soon to become Camp Stockton—and then picking up the military road to El Paso through Fort Davis and Fort Quitman.[4]

The first run began in September, 1858, with veteran driver Henry Skillman at the reins from the Pecos River to El Paso. The 1859 route change meant thirty-four stations or animal exchange points in Texas, five of them adjacent to federal forts. The Butterfield Overland Mail charged $150 to $200 for the entire route with forty pounds of baggage, or 10¢ a mile for individual legs of the route. The line carried mail for 10¢ per half ounce. The Butterfield Overland used three-thousand-pound Concord Coaches for the main improved routes, and lighter 'celerity' wagons on the frontier. At Fort Belknap the stages changed from horses to four- or six-mule teams for the long pull across the Trans-Pecos. Unlike the San Antonio–San Diego Mail, the Butterfield Overland seldom experienced losses from raids or robbers, perhaps losing as few as two hundred animals to raiders along the entire route. In early 1861 the postmaster general decided to shift the Southern Overland Mail route to central Kansas, a decision prompted by the difficulties of terrain and water in the Trans-Pecos and New Mexico. This decision was confirmed when Texas seceded in 1861. Although Congress transferred the route north of the state, Texas Confederates ultimately captured most of the equipment and stations used by the stage line.[5]

Soldier's tended to disagree about the comfort of the stage, depending on the section of the line they traveled. A Second Cavalry captain, taking the Butterfield Overland east from Fort Belknap on a journey to St. Louis in 1859 found the ride, "Easy and agreeable," although he became a bit concerned when the mules were replaced "With wild, unbroken mustangs . . .

never having been harnessed before. It took eight men to do it." Lieutenant George Crook rode the Butterfield stage across Texas from El Paso to Sherman in the fall of 1860, calling it "The severest ordeal I have ever experienced of this kind."[6]

The pattern for Texas stages during the post–Civil War years was one of dozens of small stage contracts between towns, rather than a large-scale stage company with a monopoly on the majority of routes. One of the longer lines was Risher and Hall Stage Lines, an expansion of an 1858 company that, by 1871, operated a series of lines from Victoria through San Antonio to Dallas. Stage service between San Antonio and El Paso resumed in April, 1866, when Bethel Coopwood started a line that was taken over by Ben Ficklin the following year. C. Bain and Company, run by Charles Bain, began service between San Antonio and Fort Concho in 1876, as well as between San Antonio and Laredo. The heyday of the frontier stage ended as quickly as railroad tracks reached communities in the early 1880s, although short lines from rail terminals to rural towns lingered to the turn of the century.[7]

Army families sometimes received cut-rate prices or free passes from stage companies that recognized the importance of the military to their security and continued operations. An example of this is the note and ticket Col. Benjamin Grierson sent his wife from Fort Concho in October, 1876: "Enclosed therein a pass for yourself and party from Austin to Fort Concho, in stage kindly & voluntarily furnished by one Mr. Taylor, the Gen. Manager of that line."[8]

Stage travel in the post–Civil War years remained a comfortless and hazardous undertaking. One former soldier complained that the two-day stage trip from Sherman to Fort Richardson he made in 1871 took longer than expected because of "The driver having lost his way . . . owing to the darkness and a bottle of whiskey." In July, 1872, Indians attacked the Fort Concho stagecoach, shooting the citizen driver, injuring the soldier escort, stealing the mules, and destroying the mail. While traveling at night on a stage from San Antonio to Fort McKavett, in December, 1877, 2d Lt. Henry Kirby, only recently graduated from West Point, got his introduction to the Texas frontier after being startled awake "By a man yelling at the driver to turn out from the road or he would blow his d—d head off." The robbers relieved Kirby of five dollars, but the clever lieutenant managed to drop the bulk of his money roll on the ground where it was overlooked by the bandits in the dark. At the same time, Kirby's classmate Lt. Calvin Easterly and his new bride were traveling to Fort Concho from Fort Worth. "The stage broke down in a drenching rain," Easterly reported, "which mishap necessitated a ride of seventeen miles in an old lumber wagon." On July 13, 1877, the San Antonio–Fort Concho stage flipped over near Menardville, breaking the arm of the Fort Concho quartermaster, Capt. E. B. Atwood. In August, 1880, Apaches attacked the stage making the run from Fort Quitman to Fort Davis in Quitman Canyon, killing passenger James J. Byrne, a former volunteer army officer then working as the chief surveyor for the Texas and Pacific Railroad. The Apaches again attacked the stage in Quitman Canyon in January, 1881, killing the driver and a passenger. A Sixteenth Infantry corporal recorded that the Indians left nothing behind "but scattered letters, charred trunks, and dead mules."[9]

The latter attack prompted the department commander, Brig. Gen. Christopher C. Auger, to clarify his policy regarding the use of federal military resources in the development of stage lines. He issued orders for the Pecos District commander, Col. Ben Grierson, to "Protect the stage line through your district by every means possible," and sent a courtesy copy of the telegram to the state government to insure it knew his stance on the issue.[10]

The army used every means possible to protect the stage lines during the antebellum era, but delegated the majority of the work to the black regiments operating in the state after the Civil War. Typically, at the stationmaster's request, a detail of four or five soldiers was assigned by the local commander to protect a remote stage station or ride escort aboard the line. Despite the valuable service the soldiers performed, their efforts often went unappreciated, exposing them to abuse at the hands of the very business they attempted to protect. At the end of their duty in 1871, the El Paso Mail Lines stationmaster at Leon Hole refused to provide food or shelter to a detail of black soldiers. He then forced them to walk to Fort Stockton because he was unwilling to mix them with white passengers on an eastbound stage. The stationmaster received a harsh rebuke from Col. William Shafter, the soldiers' commander. The situation had eased somewhat by 1878, when a black sergeant from the Twenty-fifth Infantry arrested the stationmaster at El Muerto for similar abuse and had his decision officially seconded by the Fort Davis commander. Although the mission of guarding stage stations and providing escorts for the mail severely stretched the manpower limitations of frontier commanders, already burdened by understrength companies, the soldiers performed a valuable service while mostly enjoying the break from routine garrison duties.[11]

The following are a few examples of the actions, dangers, and successes soldiers experienced while performing commerce-protection duty. On October 1, 1867, a detachment from Company D, Ninth Cavalry, engaged in a skirmish at Howard's Spring in which two soldiers were killed in action. In September, 1870, Indians attacked the Fort Smith stage twenty-two miles north of Fort Concho, killing the soldier acting as escort. On Christmas Day, 1869, a sergeant leading a detachment from Company E, Ninth Cavalry, successfully defended Johnson's Mail Station on the Middle Concho River against an attack by Indians. On June 15, 1872, a detachment from Company H, Eleventh Infantry at Fort Concho successfully defended the same stage stop against an Indian raid. On July 28, 1872, a corporal and four privates from the Twenty-fifth Infantry at Fort Stockton successfully defended Centralia Station, located between the Concho and Pecos Rivers, from an Indian attack. Although the army did its best, the line remained vulnerable. Indians attacked the San Antonio–El Paso Mail sixty-one times between 1867 and 1881, and the stage was robbed five times.[12]

While the soldier's role in route and station protection was significant to the development of Texas stagecoach lines, the army's direct fiscal input to the stage business was relatively meager. The army spent only $48,975 on 2,391 stage passengers nationwide in 1872, with about $6,000 and 310 passengers affecting the Texas economy. In 1873 the army in Texas had about 500 passengers and five hundred pounds of stage freight, at a total cost of $7,700. A decade later, in 1886, army stage costs in Texas were $1,611 for 598 passengers, and in 1888 the amount spent in the state fell to $1,366. Most of the army's passengers were by then traveling long distances by train, using stages to make the short trip between the closest rail station and their assigned fort. In 1887 the quartermaster awarded an annual contract to August Adelle to carry soldiers from the railhead at Marfa to Fort Davis for 95¢ per head.[13]

Although free of the danger of Indian attacks by the late 1880s, the short-haul lines continued to be uncomfortable. Lieutenant Cecil Stewart, reporting to his Third Cavalry assignment at Fort Concho in September, 1886, took the stage from the railhead at Abilene. The intoxicated driver lost control in the dark and the stage nearly tipped into the Colorado River. At one point it hit a mesquite tree, and, recalled Stewart, "The rest of the night I spent in hanging on and being slung around. It was the roughest ride I ever took."[14]

MAIL

The Republic of Texas developed a mail system in 1835 and 1836 that sent U.S.–bound mail through New Orleans. The regular soldiers in Taylor's army during the Mexican War considered the rates expensive. It cost 6¢ for 20 miles, 12¢ for 100 miles, and 25¢ for 200 miles to send a stamp-less cover—a folded sheet of paper without an envelope. Mail leaving Texas by ship had a 6¼¢ tariff tacked on. In 1845 the tariff was reduced to 5¢. Although they used the Texas postal system when away from camp, most of Taylor's soldiers at Corpus Christi in the summer of 1845 waited for a contract steamer heading eastward. They would hastily gather letters to place aboard, to be franked in New Orleans at regular federal rates, which were considerably cheaper. It took about two weeks to get a letter to Washington, D.C., in this manner, and soldiers fretted in constant anxiety about misplaced mail, many advising their love ones to number their letters so it would be possible to tell if any were lost.[15]

Federal postal rates took effect in Texas on May 29, 1846, reducing the cost of a letter to 5¢ for less than three hundred miles, and 10¢ for greater distances. As the army moved inland, the federal post office established a forward collection point at Point Isabel in July, 1846, then shifted across the bay in March, 1847, using postmarks reading "Brazos," "Brasos," or "Brazos St. Jago," at a rate of 10¢ per letter payable by the addressee upon receipt. Official correspondence of course was free, but beginning on March 1, 1847, mail weighing less than an ounce sent from relatives and friends to soldiers in the war zone was carried at no charge if "belonging to the Army" was added after the addressee's name. Although generally efficient, a few soldiers complained in their records about the mail system, one volunteer officer at Camargo noting that he received no letters in three months and that he believed the mail was terribly mishandled.[16]

When the army deployed to the Texas frontier in late 1848 and early 1849, it found a general lack of communication networks north and west of San Antonio. Within two years the army had sufficiently developed dependable lines of communication to the point where a First Infantry officer recalled that at Fort Duncan in 1852: "The mail arrived at post every Thursday afternoon. The officers were generally at the post office waiting for it." As it was imperative to communicate between posts and between department headquarters and the various stations, the army quartermaster established a series of contracts to hire express riders, a sort of private army mail system that also carried light packets of regular mail. Typical of these was an 1853 contract at Fort Inge in which the horse-mounted mail rider, usually called the "express," earned $35 a month to haul the mail by pack mule once a week to Fort Duncan at Eagle Pass. By 1858, the weekly express rider from Fort Inge to Fort Clark earned $75 a month and was subject to a $30 fine for failure to perform his weekly duty. Express riding could be dangerous business, as evidenced by an 1855 incident in which Comanches caught two soldier mail riders from Fort Chadbourne, tied them to a tree, and burned them alive.[17]

Although important for personal and military communications, Texas' frontier mail system also proved to be a vital fiscal network for long-distance commercial transactions. In 1853, for example, Reading W. Black opened a store and a mill and dealt in real estate near Fort Inge. The Fort Inge mail station became crucial to his business dealings with San Antonio, his diary reflecting numerous instances of sending or receiving letters of credit, business orders, drafts, and commercial correspondence through the mails at the fort.[18]

In the early 1850s, Texas mail to and from the East Coast and the Mississippi Valley funneled through the postmaster at New Orleans by postal-department contracted steamer once a week from Indianola and Brazos Santiago. By 1853, the chief quartermaster, using government and contract steamers, had thoroughly connected military ports on the Texas coast with each other and with New Orleans. He hired a mail sloop to run from department headquarters, then at Corpus Christi, to the primary port of Indianola, which had a weekly steamer to New Orleans, while the supply depot at Brazos Santiago and Fort Brown had a semimonthly steamer to New Orleans. This same connection in 1853 also served to deliver mail by weekly steamer up the Rio Grande to Ringgold Barracks and by express on to Fort McIntosh at Laredo, averaging two weeks to receive a letter from New Orleans.[19]

From these water connections the chief quartermaster by 1853 had established a solid web of overland express riders. From the headquarters at Corpus Christi the weekly express rode overland to posts on the Rio Grande and to the San Antonio quartermaster's depot, which became a mail hub. An express rider from nearly every post in Texas rode to San Antonio once a week, with Austin and Waco serving as additional connections for faraway north Texas. Mail from Fort Brown to San Antonio, for example, took from eight to twelve days by horseback. Most of the forts additionally had a weekly express to their nearest neighboring post. Even remote and forlorn Fort Phantom Hill in 1853 had a weekly mail delivery from Fort Belknap by express rider, with the mail routed from Austin to the postmaster at Waco. In a few cases, such as that of Fort Belknap's semimonthly express to Fort Washita, Indian Territory, the mail rider was a soldier rather than a hired citizen. However, by 1856, with the cutback on civilian employment in the army, nearly all express riders between posts were extra duty soldiers, with the exception of the San Antonio depot, which paid a civilian $204 per month but required him to furnish his own transportation. Regardless of who carried the mail, by 1854 the system had become reliable enough for an officer at Fort Duncan to report in a letter to New York that mail arrived weekly on Wednesday, departed for the "States" on Thursdays, and "the letters come as regularly and safely to this post as to any place in the U.S."[20]

Mail to most Texas forts was addressed with a soldier's name and rank, his regiment, and "care of U.S. Quartermaster, San Antonio, Texas." Lieutenant George H. Steuart at Fort Chadbourne wrote his sister Mary in Baltimore on August 16, 1854, and she received it on September 12, twenty-eight days later. His letter, and her return reply, both had envelopes, something unusual even five years previous, and both took a three-cent stamp franked through New Orleans.[21]

Besides the express riders and regular U.S. mail service, it was routine for any officer traveling between posts to be pressed into carrying letters, such as the medical lieutenant who, when transferred from Fort Duncan to Fort Davis in 1855, reported: "I carried the mail myself when I came up. It is small and packed easily in my trunks." The establishment of Fort Davis in the far Trans-Pecos in the fall of 1854 presented additional difficulties for the military express, which took ten days to reach Fort Clark and several more to get to San Antonio. One thoughtful officer stationed at Fort Davis in April, 1855—reflecting upon the Valentine Card that took forty days to reach him from Hamburg, New York—wrote his sweetheart:

> You would regard the mail that will carry this letter some hundreds of miles on
> its way to you as a very singular establishment . . . imagine what an ambulance drawn
> by four mules looks like. At the middle and end of the month an ambulance is started
> from this post[;] before it ride six armed men, their rifles carried at their saddle bows[;]
> they drive with them extra mules . . . , then comes the vehicle itself: its driver is armed,
> and more men with more weapons are seated in it; here ride the precious mail bags—
> I have learned to look upon them as precious sometimes[;] behind spurs on a rear
> guard of several men. . . . Think how this letter has traveled to your hands with its
> guard of men who risk their lives if need be to defend it.[22]

In the immediate aftermath of the Civil War the federal postal service was nonexistent within the state, and even the army mail system was in disarray. A volunteer Ohio soldier in Texas observed: "There is something wrong with the mail. Every one complains. Letters received speak of other letters and newspapers forwarded, but which have not reached camp." The mail routes developed slowly—concurrently with the stage lines as discussed above—but many frontier areas experienced tenuous mail service for several years after the war. Although Frederick P. Sawyer obtained the San Antonio–

El Paso mail contract in July, 1866, hiring Ben Ficklin to manage the line, he encountered difficulty establishing post offices along the route. At Uvalde, for example, two years after the war ended, the Fort Inge post commander was still trying to gain approval from the postmaster general to establish a local post office on the San Antonio–El Paso mail line.[23]

As in the antebellum period, post–Civil War army commanders initially established a system of military couriers and provided escorts for the public mails. In 1867 Fort Davis dispatched Ninth Cavalry patrols to escort mail wagons twenty-eight miles eastward to Barrilla Springs and ninety miles westward to Eagle Spring. At Fort Richardson, a cavalry patrol carried weekly mail from Weatherford to the post, where it was further distributed to Buffalo Springs and Fort Belknap. A Sixth Cavalry soldier remembered the constant loss of letters, observing that "it was an accident" if a newspaper should reach them. By 1870 the Fort Richardson quartermaster had contracted with a citizen to make the weekly four-day trip to Waco to carry the mail, while at Fort Concho Fourth Cavalry troops escorted the weekly mail coach through their area to El Paso.[24]

In 1871 Fort Richardson received mail twice a week via mail coach on the Fort Smith–El Paso mail line, which stopped at Jacksboro. From there a small contracted wagon carried the mail to Forts Griffin and Concho. Fort Concho also received mail twice a week directly from the San Antonio–El Paso mail line, as did Forts Stockton and Davis, while Fort Bliss at El Paso received mail from San Antonio once per week, and by weekly coach from Santa Fe, New Mexico. Between 1871 and 1875, Fort Davis furnished twelve soldiers for station guards and four per week to escort the mail. In 1875, citing manpower shortages, the post commander withdrew his station guards on the portion of the route between Fort Davis and Fort Quitman but was promptly ordered to reestablish the guard force. Poor management and criminal and Indian threats had deteriorated the San Antonio–El Paso mail to the point where, in October, 1875, the department commander established an army mail service between Forts Bliss, Quitman, Davis, Stockton, and Concho. By that time Fort Bliss was receiving mail twice a week from San Antonio and retained the weekly coach from Santa Fe, but also dispatched daily horse-and-rider runs on the 330-mile trip to Santa Fe. By mid-1876, a dependable civilian contract service was again in operation in the Trans-Pecos. At Fort Concho that year the weekly mail departed on Saturdays, going via Fort Worth and San Antonio. The rail connection in east Texas meant letters between Fort Concho and Jacksonville, Illinois, averaged about ten days, while those to New York took only an additional day. The railroad extensions to west Texas cut delivery time between Illinois and Forts Concho and Davis to five days by 1882. Rail connections not only improved the supply of garrisons and the general prosperity of the frontier, but they also sped the time and rate of delivery of mail to remote sites. In 1879 Fort Griffin, for example, ran a mail coach to Weatherford three times a week, where it made a stage connection to the rail terminal at Fort Worth.[25]

Thanks in large measure to the army's support, the speed and reliability of the federal mail service on the frontier improved with each passing year. However, in the mid-1870s, the Texas frontier would join with the remainder of the nation in experiencing a practical revolution in communications with the beginning of the installation of the military telegraph system.

MILITARY TELEGRAPH

Although the military telegraph system did not develop in the state until after the Civil War, the first commercial telegraph in Texas was established in 1854—a decade after Samuel F. B. Morse's invention was used to send the first public telegram from Baltimore to Washington, D.C. The Texas and Red River Telegraph Company opened an office in Marshall in February, 1854, with a line to New Orleans. The line soon extended to Galveston and Houston. The Texas and New Orleans Telegraph Company began construction of a line in 1856 that would, after six years, link Austin with New Orleans. In 1866 the Western Union Telegraph Company began to absorb the smaller commercial lines, within a decade owning 85 percent of the 105 public stations in Texas. The great majority of this commercial activity was in the eastern half of the state, while military authorities on the post–Civil War frontier sponsored the development and maintenance of the telegraph system.[26]

Colonel Albert James Myer, who had served as an army medical officer at Forts Davis and Duncan from 1854 to 1857, developed the army Signal Corps during the Civil War, serving as the brilliant and innovative soldier-scientist at its head until his death in 1880. The army's use of the field telegraph came to full maturity during the conflict. After the war, commanders and military administrators on the frontier were quick to demand a telegraph system for use as an instrument of command and control and as an apparatus for the quick dissemination of information in the vast region. On July 24, 1866, Congress called for the construction of government telegraph lines to be used by military and postal authorities in the West. The mission naturally fell to the army. However, at this same time, the terms of service of the volunteer signal experts at the Galveston headquarters were expiring. As these volunteers were mustered out in the spring of 1866, the regular army was left with but two signal officers in the state. For several years the project remained underfunded and nearly static, prompting the Texas department commander in 1869 to ask for money with which to construct a military telegraph connecting his headquarters at San Antonio with the Rio Grande and frontier posts.[27]

There were only three military telegraph sets in Texas in 1869, compared to twenty in the Department of the Platte. By the following year Texas had thirty-two sets, but not enough line material to establish a frontier system. Two years later the department commander once again appealed for the wire and funds to install a telegraph to connect the frontier posts. In 1872 an officer from the inspector general's office reported, after traveling to Texas posts: "The existing modes of communication . . . are slow, and defective. I therefore, urgently recommend that lines of telegraph be constructed. A system of this kind would afford the means of increasing the usefulness and efficiency of the troops, virtually doubling their numbers in operations." Finally, in June, 1874, nearly five years after the department commander's original request, Congress approved the bill and authorized funds for the construction of a military telegraph system for the Texas frontier.[28]

After several months of reconnaissance and organization of working parties by signal officers, progress remained slow until April, 1875, when Chief Signal Officer Myer sent 1st Lt. Adolphus W. Greely to take over the project. Greely was a scientifically-minded Fifth Cavalry officer who later became the chief signal officer and gained fame for his Arctic expeditions and for helping to organize the National Geographic Society. Using simultaneous construction parties consisting of a dozen officers and labor details from the Twenty-fourth, Tenth, Eleventh and other infantry regiments, Greely completed the majority of the line in eleven months. The first line, from Denison to Fort Richardson, was finished on May 8, 1875, while a second party installed a line from Fort Richardson north to the Red River to meet a group working south from Fort Sill, Indian Territory. From May to July a Twenty-fourth Infantry company worked from Fort Richardson west to Fort Griffin, while another company installed wire from June to September from Fort Clark to San Antonio A third company worked from Fort Brown to Ringgold Barracks between June and August. Throughout the end of summer and into the fall, the lines began to connect Fort Griffin to Fort Concho, Fort McKavett to Fort Concho, Fort Clark to Fort Duncan, and so on.[29]

In all, Greely spent $100,000 on the telegraph line, the majority of the money going for contracts to cut and deliver telegraph poles, particularly for the barren stretches of the frontier. "I scoured the country for timber," Greely recalled. "We built a telegraph line on poles which had grown a thousand miles distant." Cedar, pine, juniper, walnut, hackberry, elm, post oak—every wood imaginable and available went into the twelve-hundred miles of military telegraph. At twenty-five poles to the mile, it took about thirty thousand twenty-foot-long poles. For the 157-mile stretch from Fort Concho to Fort Stockton, for example, Greely contracted for 2,290 poles, mostly pine and cedar, at an average price of $2.80. Greely used American-made Watts and Trenton and English-manufactured Johnson galvanized wire, all hanging from thousands of Kenosha glass insulators.[30]

The first of the twenty-five military telegraph stations built in Texas in 1875 and 1876 became operational at Denison on September 1, 1875. The final station in that series, at Boerne, sent its first signal on May 9, 1876. In March, 1876, after completing 1,218 miles of telegraph lines, Greely was relieved of his duties as Texas' chief signal officer. He was succeeded by Lt. George S. Grimes of the Second Artillery. Typical of the military telegraph stations, nearly all run by intelligent and educated enlisted men, was that of Uvalde which came on line on September 6, 1875, operated by Pvt. C. F. Olinger. The Texas frontier military telegraph system in 1876 stretched from Brownsville through the Rio Grande forts to Fort Duncan and across to Fort Clark. From there it turned east to connect to San Antonio. At San Antonio it ran north to Forts McKavett and Concho, where it split. The eastern leg went to Forts Griffin and Richardson, where it divided again, heading north to Fort Sill and east to the rail hub of Denison. The western leg at Fort Concho went as far as Fort Stockton in 1876, but reached Fort Davis in 1878, and El Paso in 1879. At El Paso it connected to New Mexico and then ran westward to San Diego.[31]

Although designed for military communication, the army's telegraph system was open to any citizen who wanted to send a message and was willing to pay. The collection of message fees from local citizens helped defray the cost of maintenance on the lines. In 1871 commercial rates averaged $28 for a hundred words, whereas the government rate was $7 for a message of the same length. At Fort Griffin, the local paper reported that the military telegraph carried more civilian than army messages. By 1877, the military telegraph in Texas carried $22,947 worth of citizen messages, and another $23,072 in 1878, thus recouping part of the expense of maintenance.[32]

The job of maintaining the telegraph system was left to regular soldiers from nearby by forts. One corporal who served in Texas with the Sixteenth

Infantry and spent a great deal of his time splicing lines and replacing poles destroyed by fire, recalled, "We were soon as well acquainted with handling a crowbar as we were in the manual of arms or any other military exercises." The army began testing iron poles in Texas in 1877, finding them less susceptible to prairie fires and wind damage. As repairs became necessary, wood poles were replaced with iron ones. It seemed that as soon as repairs were made, either nature or man conspired to ruin the work—often deliberately. In August, 1880, for example, Apaches tore up telegraph lines and poles between Fort Davis and Fort Quitman. After repairs were completed the Indians destroyed the line again in May, 1881.[33]

Because the telegraph formed a parallel circuit rather than a series type, cutting one portion of the line did not stop traffic. As the chief signal officer explained it:

> A telegraph line well worked forms one of the most efficient of barriers against the raids of Indian war parties. . . . The object in view, with Indian war parties, is to pass between the posts and settlements without disturbing any of them; and they very much dread to leave any danger in their rear, or to so alarm the country as to cause their retreat to be cut off in their return toward the region occupied by their tribe. The existence of the telegraph line enhances both these dangers. It is useless to break it as the parties pass toward the scene of their incursion, for this alarms both the posts or settlements on both sides of the break . . . ; nor does it stop communication between the posts, for the messages may be sent circuitously by other wires perhaps covering hundreds of miles distance around the point at which the line has been disabled.[34]

The chief signal officer also observed that "Aside from the benefits from the connection of military posts," the military telegraph was useful to the local frontier region in "Aiding its development and advancing the commercial interests."[35]

In 1882, at the zenith of its short existence, the military telegraph system in Texas had 1,565 miles of line connecting twenty-four stations run by twenty-five enlisted men and twenty-six civilians. In that year the line carried 196,999 telegrams at a rate of 537 per day, each station averaging twenty-three messages a day. Nearly 75 percent of the traffic on the military line was in the form of paid citizen messages, earning the Treasury $31,000.[36]

By 1883, the secretary of war was abandoning army telegraph lines when appropriate commercial lines were constructed to serve the same location, or auctioning off military lines to interested business enterprises. The army in Texas auctioned 925 miles of line in 1883 and 1884 and abandoned an additional 443 miles, leaving only 197 miles of military telegraph line remaining in 1885. The two remaining lines connected Fort Brown to Fort Ringgold and Fort Stockton to Fort Davis. However, the government had abandoned without replacement the telegraph line between Fort Ringgold at Rio Grande City and Fort Duncan at Eagle Pass, leaving several hundred miles of the Rio Grande frontier without telegraph service. After closing down the Fort Stockton military line in June, 1886, the only army lines remaining were a twenty-two-mile stretch from Fort Davis to the rail station at Marfa, a short line from the department headquarters to the Western Union office in San Antonio, and the line connecting Forts Brown and Ringgold. Following the lead of American commercial communications practices, and recognizing the potential wartime need to take advantage of a growing number of civilians trained in telegraph operations, the secretary of war directed in the summer of 1886 that the army standard for message traffic would change from English Morse or Continental code to American Morse code.[37]

The first local telephone exchange in Texas opened in Galveston in 1879, and by 1882 most of the larger towns had similar city switchboards. In 1883 the first long-distance line was constructed, allowing conversation between Galveston and Houston. Headquartered in Austin and financed by eastern money, Erie Telegraph and Telephone was the largest Texas phone company in 1883. The army in Texas did not officially adopt the telephone until May 31, 1888, when the chief quartermaster contracted with Erie for one telephone at Fort Bliss for six dollars a month, and for five phones at the department headquarters in San Antonio for four dollars each per month. The addition of an army telephone from Fort Davis to Marfa in 1890 allowed the army to close that military telegraph in 1891, reducing the lines maintained in Texas to 112 miles.[38]

Although the army maintained a few short lines connecting railheads to local posts, the last important military telegraph line in nineteenth-century Texas connected Fort Brown to Fort Ringgold at Rio Grande City. The line proved so crucial to rapid military communications during the Garza War border troubles in 1891 that the chief signal officer requested funds to construct an extension to Fort McIntosh at Laredo as well as a duplicate line along the Rio Grande because the original line was being subjected to twenty-five interruptions or stoppages in a year. While the officer noted that some of the line wrecking was deliberate sabotage, there were also river cowboys and local vaqueros who had "A tendency to injure the line by pistol practice on the insulators and lariat practice on the poles."[39]

Texas department commander Brig. Gen. Frank Wheaton reiterated to the secretary of war in December, 1892, the need for funds to extend the lower Rio Grande military telegraph and to develop a second line. Congress approved the funds for 1893. Meanwhile, to provide military authorities with adequate communications during a series of border problems that had four army columns in the field along the Rio Grande, the chief signal officer on January 8, 1893, rushed one of his Flying Telegraph trains from Fort Riley, Kansas. Developed for field use in 1892, each of the five army Flying Telegraphs moved on rail cars like a traveling circus with a mobile telegraph station and wire and pole wagons. Each train had the ability to install fifteen miles of line in a single day. Manned by a signal lieutenant and a dozen signal sergeants, the Flying Telegraph arrived at Fort McIntosh and began installing its first line on January 14, 1893—six days after leaving Fort Riley. In short order the assets of four additional Flying Telegraphs arrived on the border as the chief signal officer stripped equipment from other military departments. Eventually seventy-four miles of telegraph and several dozen field stations were in operation for eight months in 1893, the chief signal officer considering the entire operation an excellent test of the army Flying Telegraph under field conditions.[40]

The $17,000 contract for building a telegraph line from Fort Ringgold to Fort McIntosh at Laredo went to Sam P. Wreford of Laredo, who completed the line on November 15, 1893. The chief signal officer observed that the telegraph line connecting Brownsville to Laredo was not only a key means of rapidly sending military orders during the border troubles of the 1890s, it was also the "Only means of immediate communication with the outside world for 200 miles along the Mexican frontier." By 1900 the majority of the 17,990 messages sent along the Brownsville–Laredo military telegraph were the private or business communications of local citizens.[41]

THE WEATHER SERVICE

Because the army's leadership was convinced that climate influenced disease, army doctors were required by the regulations of 1843 to record daily observations of temperature, wind direction, rain, and hygrometric readings. Army doctors at Texas posts, such as Col. Albert J. Myer, faithfully kept climatic records from 1850 through the mid-1870s. Their observations had limited local use but lacked broad synthesis and consolidated regional analysis, and had little utility for use as weather warnings or as predictability models of short-term patterns.[42]

Later, as the army's chief signal officer, Myer was not only interested in military signaling, he was also absorbed with meteorology and the idea of weather prediction by using the military telegraph and its stations as a data-collection base. On February 9, 1870, a joint resolution of Congress called for the secretary of war to establish meteorological stations to warn the Great Lakes and U.S. coastal areas of approaching storms. Myer established twenty-five stations during the year, the closest to Texas being those in New Orleans and Santa Fe, New Mexico. By October, 1871, a national system for issuing comprehensive storm and weather warnings by telegraph was in place, with twenty of the stations sending daily reports directly to the chief signal officer in Washington, D.C. The signal office collated the reports and in turn telegraphed the information to appropriate major cities, ports, and several scientific institutions. The army established its first meteorological station in Texas at Galveston on April 19, 1871. Sergeant William von Hake, who had attended the army's three-month signal training course at Fort Whipple, Virginia, set up his station on the roof of 67 Strand in the city. It featured a complete set of instruments, including a thermometer, wind vane, anemometer, and rain gauge. Von Hake received weather warnings and reports from eighteen different stations, sending six bulletins a day by telegraph to the collection station at New Orleans, which then passed them to other stations and to Washington, D.C. In March, 1872, the army weather-reporting stations made an impressive display by successfully tracking a storm along the Gulf of Mexico to the Atlantic coast, giving accurate predictions of the storm's path. Public confidence in the system began to grow as a second army weather-observation station, also manned by a knowledgeable sergeant, opened at Indianola on May 1, 1872. The two Texas stations were part of a system of ninety-two army observation stations, seventy-eight of which were in the United States, eleven in Canada, and three in the West Indies.[43]

A signal sergeant established Texas' third weather-observation station, the first to be set up inland, at Molloy's Hotel in Corsicana on September 1, 1874. Meanwhile, the signal sergeant at Galveston reported that local weather warnings issued by his station had been universally praised: "The farmer, the sailor, the merchant, the cotton factor, the physician, the journalist, and the scientist, are all alike and favorably impressed with the importance and utility of the signal-service system." Requests for additional army weather stations came to the chief signal officer from the citizens of Waco, the mayor and merchants of San Antonio, and a consortium of 135 businessmen from Dallas.[44]

In 1876 Texas had three of the 171 continental U.S. observation stations. The chief signal officer reported that the Galveston station gave the city eleven hours' advance warning of the storm of April 12 to 14, which saved many boats whose captains decided to remain in the safety of the harbor. The Galveston signal sergeant recorded a flood of local seafaring visitors to his office, all inquiring as to weather conditions before sailing. The evidence indicates that about this point, checking with the army weather service became a matter of routine for Texas coastal captains. At Indianola, the army weather station gave advance notice of storms in January, March, and of the devastating hurricane that struck the port on September 15 and 16, 1876. All twenty-six of Texas' frontier telegraph stations were equipped with some degree of weather instruments that year, and began to report local weather conditions daily to the collection stations at Galveston or Indianola. That led the San Antonio *Herald* to trumpet "Now The Weather Is Foretold" in recognition of the chief signal officer's weather reports. In spite of many early successes in meteorological prediction, it was not until the 1890s that the government fully organized a truly reliable storm warning system.[45]

The army's weather warning system not only served the maritime trade, it also served farmers, freighters, and even travelers on the frontier. In 1883, during an unseasonably hot January, Capt. John G. Leefe of the Nineteenth Infantry halted overnight at Fort McIntosh while moving his family to Fort Ringgold. In the evening the post received an army weather-warning telegram advising that a Texas Norther' would roar down during the night. Mrs. Leefe immediately unpacked blankets and flannels from their wagon. The next morning, amid rare snow flurries on the lower Rio Grande, the family was comfortably on its way.[46]

When Myer died in 1880, his post went to Brig. Gen. William B. Hazen, who, like his predecessor, had previously served in Texas. In the antebellum era Hazen had been one of the outstanding junior officers in the state, serving with the Eighth Infantry at Forts Davis and Inge and receiving a sword from the citizens of San Antonio in appreciation of his frontier combat leadership. Hazen continued to improve the Weather Bureau, promoting research and publication and strengthening its ties to the scientific community by working in close cooperation with the National Academy of Sciences and the Smithsonian Institution. In the summer of 1881 Hazen's Signal Service sponsored Lieutenant Adolphus Greely's Arctic expedition, an attempt that ended in failure and bungled rescue attempts, the blame for which ultimately came back to Hazen's doorstep as the senior signal officer. Greely was the young officer most directly responsible for the installation of the military telegraph system in Texas, and when Hazen died in 1887 Greely inherited his position and served in it for twenty years.[47]

The sophistication of the army weather service continued to develop as

the commercial and scientific communities began to have increasing requirements for data and analysis. In November, 1887, the secretary of war observed, "The demands of the Weather Bureau have led the Signal Service
further and further away from military duties, to scientific and meteorological observations and labors, which grow and extend with each year."[48]

Recognizing the value of meteorological collection and reporting, state-
sponsored weather services began to proliferate in 1888 and 1889. The Galveston *News* and the Dallas *Morning News* organized a limited private weather
service in 1888, but the enterprise rapidly expanded when aided by the expertise of Sgt. Allen Buell, the army weather observer at Galveston. The Galveston
Cotton Exchange covered the expenses and published the weekly data, known
as "cotton-belt reports," with information collected from fifty-five stations,
many of them volunteer observers at Western Union or railroad telegraph
stations. Called the Texas Weather Service, the organization focused on agricultural, rather than maritime, forecasts and issued its first weekly crop bulletin on January 4, 1889. This trend heralded an end to the army's involvement
in state and national weather services. In October, 1890, Congress transferred the weather service from the Signal Corps to control of the secretary
of agriculture, a move that went into effect in 1891 with the establishment of
the U.S. Weather Bureau.[49]

CHAPTER 10

Conclusion
Swords, Cities, and Plowshares

Historian Robert Wooster has advanced the thesis that nineteenth-century army officers and Texas politicians sometimes worked as convenient allies in a common cause of military-political cooperation to secure mutual benefit. The powerful Texas caucus in Congress sustained pro-army legislation and appropriations, defending the service when attacked by critics and suspicious skeptics of a standing army. As an informal quid pro quo, many senior army officers supported the views of the Texas lobby that demanded aggressive military solutions to the stubborn security problems faced by the state, particularly in the arena of Indian affairs and border troubles with Mexico. Similarly, a general thesis of this work is that America's largest nineteenth-century corporate organization, the U.S. Army, and the nation's largest geopolitical structure, the state of Texas, had a special economic relationship. It would not be correct to characterize that relationship as a military-industrial complex. Historians tend to disagree about the origins of the military-industrial complex, its beginning date, or even a clear definition. Recent scholarship seems to favor the mid- to late-nineteenth-century building of the steel navy as the birth of mutually beneficial and politically powerful relations between large American industrial firms and military leaders. The army's economic relationship with Texas and Texans in the nineteenth century had little to do with big industry, for Texas had none.[1]

In the process of providing logistical support for the operational army in Texas, military quartermasters developed what might best be described as a military-commercial cooperative with Texas businessmen and agriculturists, the majority of whom were hardscrabble, small-scale operators rather than capitalist giants. The relationship was generally trustworthy, amiable, and mutually beneficial. Texas was the army's largest theater of war, receiving up to 30 percent of the operating budget, while the army was Texas' most dependable source of ready currency and the agency most responsible for commercial development of the frontier.

A close study of the economic relationship between the army and Texans might challenge the rugged individualism imbedded in Texas frontier mythology. William G. Robbins, in *Colony and Empire: The Capitalist Transformation of the American West,* finds a degree of irony in the cherished notions of the independent and individualistic self-made westerner, when in fact, federal dollars were decisive to the development and expansion of business and capitalism on the frontier. In a similar vein, Earle Young records in *Galveston and the Great West* that the alliance between the private sector, local boosters, the state and federal governments, and the army's Corps of Engineers turned Galveston into a deepwater port—a triumph that contradicts the historical portrait of a period of laissez-faire capitalism and the beginning of the adversarial relationship between big business and the government in the Progressive Era.[2]

A unique problem the army faced in Texas was the lack of federal land that could be integrated into War Department plans for such projects as forts and Indian reservations. A lack of vision on the part of the U.S. Congress—and shrewd foresight on the part of the government of the Republic of Texas—gave the state control of the public domain when Texas joined the Union in 1845. The results were a transitory antebellum Indian reservation system at the mercy of state politicians, post commanders who were temporary renters and sometimes trespassers, and quartermaster officers frustrated by increasing lease expenses and complicated real-estate purchases. Nevertheless, army logisticians overcame the majority of these peculiar challenges in the perplexing theater of operations called Texas, establishing a logistical system that largely met the needs of the army while increasing the state's prosperity.

Each of the four distinct phases of quartermaster logistical systems in Texas had unique characteristics and varying degrees of impact on fiscal activities and geography. During the Mexican War of 1846 to 1848, most of the military supply and transportation services were contracted outside of the state. Army economic input and influence was substantial in the coastal areas and that portion of the lower Rio Grande navigable by river steamer. From 1848 to 1854, the army relied primarily on soldier labor, small local purchases, and a transportation system based on government wagon trains. The days of the big army contracts and legendary Texas commercial operators occurred between 1855 and the end of the 1870s, when the War Department became convinced of the efficiency and convenience of local economies of scale. That period passed with the coming of the railroad in the 1880s, which provided inexpensive and reliable freight transportation to the frontier, firmly linking army logistics to a national economic network that superseded the efficiency of local Texas markets.

Army dollars were important to the state throughout the last half of the nineteenth century. However, they were especially crucial to the cash-poor economy in two periods: after the Mexican War, when the Republic and its failed economy were transitioning into statehood, and in the aftermath of the Civil War, when state and personal finances were wrecked by inflation and the war's disastrous impact. Army influence was also regionally focused, having a greater impact on the coastal and frontier portions of the state than on the more prosperous and settled eastern woodlands.

Army quartermaster operations in nineteenth-century Texas pumped $32 million into the state's economy, army pay brought in $38.5 million, and army engineers spent $13,054,000 in the state. As discussed in chapter one, the $70.7 million in pay and operational expenses was double the total valuation of real and personal property in the state when Texas joined the Union. Army dollars spent in the state during the period 1849 to 1860 represented about 4 percent of the state's value growth in that antebellum period, and was equal to 20 percent of the increase in valuation in the 1870s.

Nineteenth-century Texas was largely a rural agricultural state, but it did have a nascent industrial sector. In 1860, 10 percent—about eleven thousand workers—of the state's population was engaged in some form of manufacturing or building trade. Milling of various forms was the most important industry in the state, with two hundred sawmills employing twelve hundred workers who cut $1.7 million worth of lumber for a $1 million profit. The U.S. Army was a service, but it was also, in its own way, an industry that produced consumers, contracts and cash, roads and lines of communication, forts, towns, markets, and ports. The army compared equally to the lumber industry in 1860, employing 3,009 soldiers and three hundred civilians, with an input of $1,092,000 into the Texas economy—$315,000 in contracts and operational expenses, and $777,000 in pay.[3]

In 1870 industry and manufacturing in Bexar County and San Antonio produced only $132,000 worth of goods. The largest single factory in the state was a cotton mill with 136 employees producing $236,000 worth of material. The leading industry for gross income was the state's five hundred grain mills, which produced $2.5 million worth of flour and meal, followed by three hundred sawmills producing $2 million worth of lumber. The eight thousand manufacturing and industrial workers in the state earned total wages of $1.75 million. In comparison, the army in Texas spent $4,336,000 in 1870, nearly equal in value to all of the production of the grain and lumber mills in the state. The army employed 4,842 soldiers and two hundred civilians, and spent $954,000 on pay. The logisticians expended $3,382,000 in contracts and purchases supporting the army in Texas.[4]

While not capitalists as a class, most army officers supported the idea of economic progress, a concept welded to a traditional liberal view of history as a linear upward path, measurable in the West by the appearance of towns, roads, railroad tracks, and the settler's wagon pushing ever toward the sunset. However, many officers were also suspicious of local political-economic pressures, expressing the opinion that much of the regional demand for protection against the Indian threat was a hue and cry designed to gain the army dollar. In 1850, when Texas' government petitioned President Taylor to increase the number of army units in the state to a point sufficient to actually protect the frontier, Taylor's reply, no doubt misquoted in Texas newspapers, was supposedly, "Humbug—the people and legislature of Texas misrepresented and exaggerated for the purpose of getting troops and having money disbursed among them." The people of Texas did not exaggerate. Governor P. H. Bell sent G. K. Lewis to lobby in Washington. Lewis provided Taylor with affidavits proving that in 1849 the Indians had killed or wounded 204 Texas citizens and stolen more than five hundred head of cattle. Ironically, while en route to Washington, Lewis himself was attacked by twenty Indians near Laredo. Although there were nineteen clashes between the army and Indians in Texas in 1857 a Sixth Infantry officer wrote that most of the frontier settlements were "Incapable of self-defense, and with no market for their produce. The Indian sees this weakness and robs and murders. If they do not, a passing emigrant shoots an Indian to try his rifle, or the settler does to get up a war and consequently a market. . . . Then must troops go to protect these settlers and give them three prices for their produce, and the nation's treasury must be emptied to sustain individuals and small communities in a self-chosen exile from civilization." A decade later, in 1868, Maj. Gen. Phil Sheridan, no stranger to the state, offered the secretary of war his opinion on the Indian alarms on the Texas frontier when he wrote that they were "Exaggerated reports, gotten up, in some instances, by frontier people to get a market for their produce, and, in other instances, by army contractors to make money." The army fought forty-three engagements with Indians in Texas in the three years following the pronouncement of Sheridan's skeptical opinion.[5]

From the beginning of army activity on the frontier to the final days of the century, local political-economic pressure on soldier leaders was greatest when military necessity translated into garrison removal and abandoned forts. An attempt to move the garrison opposite El Paso in 1849 generated an onslaught of petitions from local businessmen to the department commander. When the post finally closed in 1851, citizens engaged in an equally successful two-year lobbying effort aimed at the president, the War Department, and Texas' governor that brought the post back to life in 1853. At the end of the Indian Wars the reduction of the size of the garrison at Fort Davis spurred 108 local citizens to petition the president. Rumors of Fort Davis's closing in 1890 brought citizen appeals to congressmen and to the secretary of war. An 1881 order to move a forty-man, seventy-four-horse light-artillery company that spent several months using the beach near Corpus Christi as a firing range for its Gatling guns, brought an emotional plea from the community's leading citizens. They claimed they had grown very fond of the soldiers and did not want them transferred. "Regretting that I am obliged to break up such pleasant relations between the company and the good citizens of Corpus Christi," the department commander explained that military and economic necessity required the unit be moved to Fort Ringgold.[6]

Similar to the political pressures that delay modern base closures, Lt. Gen. William T. Sherman noted the emotional political reaction of the local civilian leadership to any scheme to shut down a nearby military installation. "Every such city from Maine to Texas," he wrote, "has a local pride in its fort and garrison. . . . Any attempt to withdraw the garrison or remove the flag is met by local opposition, often impossible to overcome."[7]

No organization in nineteenth-century Texas could match the army in diversity and scope of economic activity, particularly in the development of the state west of the 97th meridian. There the army not only influenced every commodity market from corn to real estate, but it was instrumental in developing transportation networks. In the antebellum era the army contract and military market in Texas benefited the rising agrarian and merchant middle class rather than strengthened the affluent class. Of 263 Texans with a net worth of more than $100,000 on the 1860 census, only nine had contractual dealings with the army, and eight of those were fairly modest agreements of short duration for a few thousand dollars. Significantly, five of the nine resided in Bexar County. Samuel A Maverick, worth $190,000 at the time of the census, collected $50 a month on a few military site leases, while merchants James and William Vance, worth $320,000, earned $445 a month from the lease of a barracks and headquarters building. Nathaniel Lewis, a partner in Lewis and Groesbeeck, contracted a single freight run to

El Paso in 1850 and had a small beef contract for that post in 1851. Neither contract was consequential to his $160,000 net worth in 1860. In contrast was George T. Howard, worth $150,000 in 1860—thanks in large part to his extensive army freight contracts in the 1850s.[8]

The army proved to be a crucial source of capital for the developing long-haul commercial wagon-freight industry in the state. On the frontier, wagon masters led their trains along roads and pathways built by army engineers. Army logisticians developed the river-steamer business on the Rio Grande and had a significant hand in the growth of the ports of Indianola, Port Lavaca, and Corpus Christi. Army engineers virtually transformed Galveston into a deepwater port.

The army dollar was an important economic multiplier in many Texas agricultural commodity markets. The army spent more than $1 million on twelve thousand Texas horses and mules needed to mount the cavalry and to pull wagons. Texas quartermasters spent more than $9 million on the forage needed to feed those horses and mules, in the process purchasing 4,197,700 bushels of corn, 2,860,000 bushels of oats, and 200,000 tons of hay. Rather than going into the big pockets of large-scale operators, these forage dollars were generally dispersed among a multitude of small growers, many of them frontier subsistence farmers trading their limited surplus for ready cash at a nearby fort. Texas farmers and ranchers also sold the army beef, flour, and vegetables in many unrecorded local open-dollar purchases. To cook these items and to heat barracks and quarters, army quartermasters in Texas bought 362,000 cords of wood and 282,000 bushels of charcoal—amounting to about $1.5 million worth of fuel for forts. In developing fort sites, the army spent more than $5 million on leases, site purchases, and construction costs. To speed communication between forts, the army in Texas created the frontier telegraph system and played a vital role in expanding frontier lines of communication with stagecoaches and mail delivery.

Much of the army's contribution to the maturation of the Texas frontier was intangible, immeasurable in charts and statistics. The army was a good Texas citizen, contributing to the sense of community necessary for developing the raw land. This was not quantifiable civic action, such as disaster relief in the form of rations given to stranded Mexican soldiers in 1880, or the thirteen thousand rations distributed to El Paso flood victims in 1897, or the twenty thousand rations to victims of the Brazos River flood of 1899. The army also provided good citizens to the state. H. H. McConnell, the former Sixth Cavalry first sergeant who became the mayor of Jacksboro, explained, "Many of the soldiers had married, others had formed attachments and friendships more or less permanent; nearly all the men who had been discharged from time to time had settled in the country."[9]

Typical of this type was the Fourth Cavalry's Sgt. John B. Charlton, a Virginian and veteran of the Palo Duro Canyon fight, who eventually became a rancher on the Nueces River. Another was Claron A. "Gus" Windus, a Wisconsin-born Civil War drummer boy and Sixth Cavalry trooper who earned a Medal of Honor on the Little Wichita in 1870. After his discharge in 1871, Windus settled permanently in Texas, working in Kinney County as a deputy sheriff and later as a federal customs agent. Charles Mulhern, discharged at Fort Davis in 1885, became a local real-estate manager and rancher. Former Tenth Cavalry Buffalo Soldier Archie Smith settled at Fort Davis, building a prosperous ranch, while another former trooper, Elijah Earl, became a prominent leader of the black community in Shackelford County.[10]

These soldiers, while still in uniform, helped to create many of the Texas towns in which they settled. However, the building of a fort did not necessarily guarantee the birth of a town—Camp Hudson and Fort Lancaster being cases in point. Nor did a satellite village always reach the point of stability needed to become self-sustaining. The town of Fort Griffin in Shackelford County is an example of a booming town with the advantage and stability of four separate trade markets in the 1870s: soldiers, buffalo hunters, cattle drovers, and local ranchers and farmers. In 1877 and 1878, Fort Griffin merchants carried $75,000 worth of merchandise, with sales of $10,000 per month. Their customers included a Tenth Cavalry troop at the post, cowboys pushing more than a hundred thousand head of cattle up the trail to Kansas, a good portion of the five thousand buffalo hunters working the plains, and a growing population of ranchers. This bright future rapidly dimmed within three short years. The buffalo herds ceased to exist by 1879, the post closed in 1881, and the railroad not only led to the inexorable decline of cattle drives, it bypassed Fort Griffin for Albany, a few miles to the south.[11]

In spite of the example of Fort Griffin, many towns became viable and vibrant enough to survive the closing of a nearby post. Uvalde, Brackettville, San Angelo, Fort Stockton, Fort Davis, Brownsville, Rio Grande City, and Eagle Pass were all born of the fort–satellite village relationship characteristic of the Texas frontier. Army activities also gave an enormous financial lift to the growth of other Texas cities, including San Antonio, Laredo, Del Rio, Corpus Christi, Indianola, and Jacksboro. At El Paso, for example, it was not until the mid-1880s that commercial activities eclipsed the local economic significance of its two-company army post. El Paso in 1882 had a population of only 650, with annual tax revenues of $5,397, while the yearly pay of the ninety-six soldiers at nearby Fort Bliss was more than $21,000 per year. Six years later, with the development of the railroad and mineral smelting activities, El Paso's population had swelled to 10,601, with annual tax revenues of $58,000—representing twice the value of the pay of the 117 soldiers at Fort Bliss.[12]

In the shadow of Fort Richardson, Jacksboro's mayor recorded, "Society, business, and the agricultural interest of the people were dominated by the influence of the post." Texas quartermaster Capt. Samuel G. French best summed up the army's relationship to the development of the frontier when he observed, "The sword plants the banner, and a city is built around it."[13]

APPENDIX I

Wagon Freight Contractors
with the U.S. Army in Texas, 1849–1890

Contractor	Route	Notes (cwt. = per 100 lbs.)
1849		
Henry P. Howard	Port Lavaca–Austin	20,000 rations, $1.75 cwt.
George T. Howard	Port Lavaca–San Antonio	Eighth Inf.'s baggage, $2 cwt.
1850		
David Waldo	Ft. Leavenworth, Kans.–El Paso	$13.75 cwt. for 125,000 lbs.
Benjamin F. Coons	Indianola–El Paso	$13.50 cwt.
Lewis & Groesbeeck	San Antonio–El Paso	$12 cwt. for 865,000 lbs. for entire distance
L. G. Capers	San Antonio–Pecos River	Carts, $230 each
L. G. Capers	San Antonio–El Paso	Carts, $115 each
Biggs & St. Vrain	Santa Fe–El Paso	$7 cwt. for distance
1851		
L. G. Capers	Hardee Expedition at Ft. Merrill, Ft. Duncan, and San Antonio River	Paid $2,088
George T. Howard	"	Paid $198
A. Coleman	"	Paid $9.25
D. T. Wheeler	"	Paid $25
F. Espinosa	"	Paid $374
Joseph Clymer	Ft. Leavenworth, Kans.–El Paso	$12 cwt. for distance
Black & Butt	Preston, Tex.–Brazos River	$8 cwt. for distance
1852		
No Contracts		

1853

| T. G. Wright | Wright's Landing–Preston, Tex. | $2 cwt. for 256,000 lbs. |

1854

Abm. Allen	Ft. Smith, Ark.–Ft. Inge	$6.50 a day x 5 wagons, Cos. A and K, Mounted Rifles baggage
William T. Smith	San Antonio–El Paso	$16 cwt. for 200,000 lbs.
J. R. Tullis	San Antonio–El Paso	$11 cwt. for 300 lbs.
Edward Hall	San Antonio–Ft. Bliss	$11 cwt. for 10,000 lbs. quartermaster stores
W. S. McKnight	San Antonio–El Paso	$14 cwt. for distance

1855

Majors & Russell	Ft. Leavenworth, Kans.–El Paso	$1.80 cwt. x 100 miles
George H. Giddings & J. R. Jefferson	Indianola–San Antonio	$1.25 cwt. for distance
"	San Antonio–Fts. Inge, Duncan, and Clark	$1.10 cwt. x 100 miles
"	San Antonio–Ft. Davis	$1.70 cwt. x 100 miles
"	San Antonio–Ft. Bliss	$1.50 cwt. x 100 miles
George T. Howard	San Antonio–Austin	85¢ cwt. for distance
"	San Antonio–Ft. McKavett	$1.75 cwt. for distance
"	San Antonio–Ft. Chadbourne	$2.75 cwt. for distance
"	San Antonio–Ft. Belknap	$4.50 cwt. for distance
H. Huguenin	Corpus Christi–Ft. Fillmore, N.M.	One train subsistence stores, $1.70 cwt. x 100 miles
J. G. Davis	Corpus Christi–Ft. Bliss	One train subsistence stores, $1.70 cwt. x 100 miles
William McHenry	Corpus Christi–Ft. Davis	One train of stores $1.70 cwt. x 100 miles

1856

Majors & Russell	Continuation of 1855 contract
George H. Giddings & J.R. Jefferson	Continuation of 1855 contract
George T. Howard	Continuation of 1855 contract

George T. Howard	Ft. Clark–Ft. Bliss	Transport public property, $371 per wagon of 6,000 lbs.
John Willett	Corpus Christi–Ft. McIntosh	99¢ cwt. for distance

1857

George T. Howard	Indianola–San Antonio	$1.25 cwt.
"	San Antonio–Fts. Inge, Clark, and Duncan	$1.10 cwt. x 100 miles
"	San Antonio–Fts. Davis, Bliss, and Fillmore	$1.70 cwt. x 100 miles
"	San Antonio–Austin	85¢ cwt. for distance
"	San Antonio–Ft. McKavett	$1.75 cwt. for distance
"	San Antonio–Ft. Chadbourne	$2.75 cwt. for distance
"	San Antonio–Ft. Belknap	$4.50 cwt. for distance
"	San Antonio–new posts between Fts. Clark and Davis	$1.50 cwt. x 100 miles
John Willett	Corpus Christi–Ft. McIntosh	Continuation of 1856 contract
William Smith	Ft. Bliss–Ft. Fillmore, N.M., and Ft. Union, N.M.	Mounted Rifles's baggage, 6 wagons x $225

1858

George T. Howard	Renewal of 1857 contract	

1859

George T. Howard	Indianola–San Antonio	$1.25 cwt. for distance
"	San Antonio–Fts. Inge, Clark, and Duncan	$1.10 cwt. x 100 miles
"	San Antonio–Fts. Davis, Bliss, Quitman, and Fillmore	$1.70 cwt. x 100 miles
"	San Antonio–Austin	85¢ cwt. for distance
"	San Antonio–Cp. Hudson, Fts. Lancaster, and Stockton	$1.50 cwt. x 100 miles
"	San Antonio–Ft. McKavett	$1.75 cwt. for distance
"	San Antonio–Ft. Chadbourne	$2.75 cwt. for distance
"	San Antonio–Ft. Belknap	$4.50 cwt. for distance
"	Camp Verde and points not over 120 miles	$1.06 x 100 miles

1860

Majors, Russell & Waddell	Ft. Leavenworth, Kans.– Ft. Bliss	$1.60 cwt. x 100 miles
James Duff		To receive at New Orleans, to move to Texas, to perform duties of quartermaster agent, to keep on hand all forage and fuel to supply at market prices
"	New Orleans–Indianola	$0.87 per barrel
"	Indianola–San Antonio	75¢ cwt. x 100 miles
"	San Antonio–Fts. Inge, Clark, Wood, Duncan, Hudson, Lancaster, Stockton, Verde, Mason, Chadbourne, Cooper, and Colorado	92¢ cwt. x 100 miles
"	San Antonio–Ft. Davis	$1.10 cwt. x 100 miles
"	San Antonio–Fts. Quitman and Bliss	$1.22 cwt. x 100 miles
George T. Howard	Indianola–Arizona	One train, 180,000 lbs., $1.70 cwt. x 100 miles

1868

Harden B. Adams & Ed. de Lacy Wickes	Indianola–San Antonio	$1.27 cwt. x 100 miles
"	Indianola–Austin	$1.67 cwt. x 100 miles
"	San Antonio–all posts in Texas east of 105 degrees longitude	$1.52 cwt. x 100 miles
"	Austin–same posts	$2.35 cwt. x 100 miles
George Berg	New Mexico–posts in Texas west of 105 degrees longitude	$1.03 cwt. x 100 miles
Andrew Stewart		One train

1869

Adams & Wickes	Indianola–Austin	$1.37 cwt. x 100 miles
"	Austin–posts in north Texas	$1.77 cwt. x 100 miles
"	San Antonio–frontier posts	$1.52 cwt. x 100 miles
E. C. Dewey	Railroad at Brenham–Austin	$1.36 cwt. x 100 miles
"	San Antonio–frontier posts	$1.64 cwt. x 100 miles
Robert Eager	Indianola–San Antonio	$1.20 cwt. x 100 miles

"	Corpus Christi–Rio Grande posts	$1.50 cwt. x 100 miles
A. M. Burnham	Marshall, Tex.–northeastern posts	$3.43 cwt. x 100 miles
Ben A. Rischer	Austin–San Antonio	Stage passenger baggage

1870

Adams & Wickes	Brenham–Austin	$1.67 cwt. x 100 miles
"	Indianola–San Antonio	$1.29 cwt. x 100 miles
"	Columbus–San Antonio	$1.37 cwt. x 100 miles
"	Columbus or San Antonio– northern posts	$1.30 cwt. x 100 miles
E. C. Dewey	Calvert and Jefferson–Red River	$4.40 cwt.
"	Austin–to western posts	$1.75 cwt. x 100 miles
Ben A. Rischer	Various posts as required	Stage passenger baggage
P. Doddridge	Corpus Christi–Ringgold Barracks	$1.23 cwt. x 100 miles
"	Ringgold Barracks–Ft. McIntosh	$1.37 cwt. x 100 miles
W. H. Moore	New Mexico–Texas posts	$1.25 cwt. x 100 miles

1871

Adams & Wickes	Redmond to Fts. Richardson and Griffin	$2.83 cwt. x 100 miles
"	San Antonio–Fts. McIntosh, Duncan, McKavett, Concho, Davis, and Griffin	$1.53 cwt. x 100 miles
W. C. Krueger	Indianola–San Antonio	$1.59 cwt. x 100 miles
Kenedy & King	Ringgold Barracks–Ft. McIntosh	$1.18 cwt. x 100 miles
W. C. Graham	St. Louis–Ft. Richardson	$5.70 cwt. for distance
"	St. Louis–Ft. Griffin	$4.70 cwt. for distance

1872

Adams & Wickes	Redmond–Fts. Richardson and Griffin	$2.23 cwt. x 100 miles
"	San Antonio–Fts. McIntosh, Duncan, McKavett, Concho, Davis, Griffin, Richardson, and Stockton	$1.23 cwt. x 100 miles
"	Indianola–San Antonio	$1.23 cwt. x 100 miles
W. C. Graham	St. Louis–Ft. Richardson	$5 cwt. for distance
"	St. Louis–Ft. Griffin	$6.20 cwt. for distance

1873

H. B. Adams	San Antonio–all posts except Fts. Ringgold and McIntosh	$1.06 cwt. x 100 miles
"	Corsicana–Fts. Richardson, and Griffin	$1.86 cwt. x 100 miles
"	Victoria–San Antonio	$1.02 cwt. for distance
Kenedy & King	Ft. Ringgold–Ft. McIntosh	$1.30 cwt. for distance

1874

H. B. Adams	Victoria–San Antonio	$1.21 cwt. x 100 miles
"	Austin–San Antonio	$1.20 cwt. x 100 miles
"	San Antonio–Fts. Clark, Concho, Davis, Duncan, Stockton, Quitman, Bliss, Griffin, McIntosh, McKavett, and Richardson	$1.11 cwt. x 100 miles
W. C. Graham	Denison–Ft. Richardson	$1.32 cwt. x 100 miles
"	Denison–Fts. Griffin and Concho	$1.27 cwt. x 100 miles
A. S. Mair	Austin–San Antonio	$1.20 cwt. x 100 miles
"	Austin–Ft. McKavett	$2.30 cwt. for distance
H. Chamberlain	Ft. Ringgold–Ft. McIntosh	$1.19 cwt. x 100 miles

1875

W. C. Graham	From railroad points north of 22 degrees latitude and east of the Brazos River–Ft. Richardson	$1.28 cwt. x 100 miles
"	"–Ft. Griffin	$1.24 cwt. x 100 miles
Edward Froboese	San Antonio or Austin–Fts. Bliss, Concho, Clark, Davis, Duncan, McIntosh, McKavett, Quitman, and Stockton	$1.02 cwt. x 100 miles

1876

Edward Fenlon	From railroad north and west of 32 degrees latitude and east of the Brazos River–Fts. Richardson and Griffin	$1.13 cwt. x 100 miles
James Callaghan	From railroad at Austin or San Antonio–Fts. Bliss, Quitman,	87¢ cwt. x 100 miles

	Davis, Clark, Concho, McKavett, Stockton, Duncan, and McIntosh	
Theo. Thompson	Any point on Missouri, Kansas, & Texas Railroad to posts north of 34 degrees latitude in Texas	$1.04 cwt. x 100 miles
Trinidad Romero	Santa Fe–Ft. Clark	Eighth Inf.'s baggage, $8/day per wagon, and $4/day returning to Santa Fe

1877

H. B. Adams	Railroad at Houston, Austin, or San Antonio–Texas posts north of 28 degrees latitude or south of 32 degrees	83¢ cwt. x 100 miles
George W. Howard	Railroad at Dallas–Fts. Richardson, Griffin, McKavett, and Concho; or railroad at Denison–Fts. Richardson and Griffin	95¢ cwt. x 100 miles
Edward Fenlon	Ft. Dodge, Kans.–Ft. Elliott	$1.79 cwt. for distance

1878

H. B. Adams	Railroad at Galveston, Houston, Austin or San Antonio–Texas posts north of 27 degrees latitude and south of 32 degrees	69¢ cwt. x 100 miles
W. J. Carson	Railroad at Fort Worth–Texas posts north of 31 degrees latitude and Fts. Richardson and Griffin	$1.42 ½ cwt. x 100 miles
"	"–Fts. Concho and McKavett	$1.15 cwt. x 100 miles
W. M. D. Lee	Ft. Dodge, Kans.–Ft. Elliott	$2.40 cwt. for distance
Thomas Carson	Stagecoach from Brazos Santiago– Ft. Brown	$2/officer, $1.50/soldier, 24¢ cwt. freight
"	Brazos Santiago–Ringgold Barracks	$12/officer, $7.50/soldier, 50¢ cwt. freight
"	Brazos Santiago–Ft. McIntosh	$12/officer, $7.50/soldier, $1.50 cwt. freight

1879

Jackson E. Labatt	Railroad at San Antonio or Austin–Texas posts north of 27 degrees latitude and south of 32 degrees	84¼¢ cwt. x 100 miles
John E. Barlow	Railroad at Fort Worth–Fts. Richardson, Griffin, McKavett, and Concho	86¢ cwt. x 100 miles
Thomas Carson	Brazos Santiago–Fts. Brown, Ringgold, and McIntosh	Scheduled rates
Edward Fenlon	Las Vegas, N.M.–Ft. Bliss	$4.22 cwt. for distance

1880

John E. Barlow	Fort Worth–Fts. Davis, Stockton, Griffin, McKavett, and Concho	80¢ cwt. x 100 miles
James Callaghan	Austin–Fts. Clark, Concho, Davis, Duncan, McIntosh, McKavett, Stockton, Camp Peña Colorado, San Felipe Springs, Mayer's Springs, and mouth of the Pecos River	66½¢ cwt. x 100 miles
Thomas Carson	Posts on Rio Grande	Steamboat and wagon scheduled rates
Gates & Smith	Waco–Fts. Concho, Davis, McKavett, and Stockton	75¢ cwt. x 100 miles
Uriah Lott	Route 5	Scheduled rates

1881

W. M. D. Lee	Dodge City, Kans.–Ft. Elliott	$1.38 cwt. for distance
Edward Fenlon	Las Vegas, N.M.–Ft. Bliss	$5 cwt. for distance
John E. Barlow	Fort Worth–Fts. Davis, Stockton, Griffin, McKavett, and Concho	$1 cwt. x 100 miles
"	Waco–Fts. Concho, Davis, McKavett, and Stockton	"
James Millspaugh	Abilene, Tex.–Fts. Davis, Concho, Stockton, and Griffin	$1.02 cwt. x 100 miles
Robert Wulfing	Austin, San Antonio, or Cuero–Fts. Clark, Concho, Davis, Duncan, McIntosh, McKavett, Stockton, Camp	64½¢ cwt. x 100 miles

	Peña Colorado, San Diego, San Felipe Springs, Mayer's Springs, and the mouth of the Pecos River	
Uriah Lott	Corpus Christi–San Diego, Tex.	50¢ cwt. for distance
"	"–Ft. McIntosh	95¢ cwt. for distance or 64¢ cwt. x 100 miles
"	"–Ft. Duncan	$1.40 cwt. for distance or 70¢ cwt. x 100 miles
"	"–Ft. Ringgold	75¢ cwt. for distance or 70¢ cwt. x 100 miles
"	"–Galveston	35¢ cwt. for distance
Harden B. Adams & James Callaghan	San Antonio or Austin or the railroad at Cuero–Fts. Clark, Concho, Davis, Duncan, McIntosh, McKavett, Stockton, Mason, Camps Peña Colorado, San Felipe Springs, and San Diego, Tex.	69¢ cwt. x 100 miles

1882

W. M. D. Lee	Dodge City, Kans.–Ft. Elliott	$3.26 cwt. for distance
Jackson E. Labatt	Abilene, Tex.–Fts. Davis, Concho, Stockton, and McKavett	$1.03 cwt. x 100 miles

1883

Edward Fenlon	Gainesville, Tex.–Ft. Sill, I.T.	$1.20 cwt. for distance
Henry G. Robinson	Henrietta, Tex.–Ft. Sill, I.T.	87¾¢ cwt. x 100 miles
W. M. D. Lee	Dodge City, Kans.–Ft. Elliott	$2.19 cwt. for distance
Jackson E. Labatt	Abilene, Tex.–Ft. Concho	93¢ cwt. for distance

1884

Jackson E. Labatt	Abilene, Tex.–Ft. Concho	89¢ cwt. for distance
F. M. Davis & E. P. Warden	Wichita Falls, Tex.–Ft. Sill, I.T	75¢ cwt. for distance
J. W. Orr	In and around San Antonio	Paid $1,464
Edgar G. Gleim	Murphyville–Ft. Davis	25¢ cwt. for distance
Daniel Murphy & Sons	Murphyville–Ft. Davis	19¢ cwt. for distance

1885

August Santleben & Edward Froboese	In and around San Antonio	Paid $2,874
J. W. Orr	Harold, Tex.–Ft. Elliott	$1.60 cwt. for distance
"	Wichita Falls, Tex.–Ft. Sill, I.T.	73¢ for distance
W. M. D. Lee	Dodge City, Kans.–Ft. Elliott	$2.11 cwt. for distance

1886

Franklin Reaves	Kiowa, Kans.–Ft. Elliott	$1.09 cwt. x 100 miles
O. P. Wood	Harold, Tex.–Ft. Elliott	$1.08 cwt. x 100 miles
Edgar G. Gleim	Railroad at Marfa–Ft. Davis	17½¢ cwt. for distance
Edward Walker	Railroad at Marfa–Ft. Davis	23¢ cwt. for distance
Max M. Deats	Ft. Ringold–Ft. McIntosh	$1.47 cwt. for distance
Manuel Guerra	Ft. Ringold–Ft. McIntosh	$1 cwt. for distance
Howard E. Niccolas	Abilene, Tex.–Ft. Concho	71¢ cwt. for distance
August Santleben & Edward Froboese	In and around San Antonio	Paid $2,155

1887

Owen Duffy	Kiowa, Kans.–Ft. Elliott	$1.14 cwt. x 100 miles
D. L. Bogard	Spofford Junction, Tex.–Ft. Clark	78¢ cwt. for distance
August Adelle	Marfa–Ft. Davis	Stage passengers, 95¢ for distance
Edgar G. Gleim	Railroad at Marfa–Ft. Davis	21¢ cwt. for distance
"	Murphyville–Ft. Davis	$15^{9}/_{10}$¢ cwt. for distance
John E. Mix	Ft. Ringold–Ft. McIntosh	$1.40 cwt. for distance
Howard E. Niccolas	Ballinger, Tex.–Ft. Concho	27¢ cwt. for distance
William Kelly	In and around Ft. Brown	Paid $141
J. E. Mugge	In and around San Antonio	Paid $2,073

1888

W. W. Dickerson	Miami, Tex.–Ft. Elliott	18¾¢ cwt. for distance
Adolph Baum	Marfa–Ft. Davis	15½¢ cwt. for distance
John E. Mix	Peña Station–Ft. Ringgold	75¢ cwt. for distance
D. L. Bogard	Spofford Junction, Tex.–Ft. Clark	12½¢ cwt. for distance
William Kelly	In and around Ft. Brown	2½¢ cwt., paid $336
Louis Scheihagen	In and around San Antonio	Paid $1,493

1889

James Lister	Miami, Tex.–Ft. Elliott	16⅔¢ cwt. for distance
John Hannum	Ballinger, Tex.–Ft. Concho	22¢ cwt. for distance
Joseph Sender	Marfa–Ft. Davis	15¢ cwt. for distance
John E. Mix	Peña Station–Ft. Ringgold	$1 cwt. for distance
James Cornell	Spofford Junction, Tex.–Ft. Clark	9¢ cwt. for distance

1890

Joseph Sender	Marfa–Ft. Davis	15¢ cwt. for distance
John E. Mix	Peña Station–Ft. Ringgold	$1 cwt. for distance
Louis Scheihagen	In and around San Antonio	1½¢ cwt.
H. Sherwood	In and around Ft. Brown	3½¢ cwt., paid $26

Sources: (1849) "The contracts made . . . ," *Senate Exec. Docs.,* 31st Cong., 1st sess. no. 26, serial 554, 18; (1850) "Statements of contracts and purchases, &c.," *House Exec. Docs.,* 31st Cong., 2d sess. no. 23, serial 599, 11–23; (1851) "Report of the Quartermaster General, Nov. 22, 1851," *House Exec. Docs.,* 32d Cong., 1st sess. no. 2, serial 634, 255; "Contracts—War Department," *House Exec. Docs.,* 32d Cong., 1st sess. no. 23, serial 640, 23; (1852) "Contracts," *House Exec. Docs.,* 32d Cong., 2d sess. no. 21, serial 676, 23–25; (1853) "Contracts made under the authority of the War Department . . . ," *Senate Exec. Docs.,* 33d Cong., 1st sess. no. 37, serial 698, 24; (1854) "Contracts—War Department," *House Exec. Docs.,* 33d Cong., 2d sess., no. 68, serial 788, 2–23; (1855) "List of contracts . . . ," *Senate Exec. Docs.,* 34th Cong., 1st sess., no. 7, serial 815, 9–11, 24, 26; (1856) "Statements showing the contracts made . . . ," *Senate Exec. Docs.,* 34th Cong., 3d sess. no. 32, serial 880, 2–32; (1857) "A statement of contracts . . . ," *Senate Exec. Docs.,* 35th Cong., 1st sess., no. 31, serial 924, 8, 16–18; (1858) "Contracts—War Department," *House Exec. Docs.,* 35th Cong., 2d sess. no. 50, serial 1006, 3, 11, 26, 28; (1859) "War Department—Contracts," *House Exec. Docs.,* 36th Cong., 1st sess. no. 22, serial 1047, 7; (1860) "Contracts of the War Department . . . ," *House Exec. Docs.,* 36th Cong., 2d sess., no. 47, serial 1099, 10, 25, 46–47; (1868) "Report of the Quartermaster General, Oct. 20, 1868," *House Exec. Docs.,* 40th Cong., 3d sess., no. 1, serial 1367, 830; (1869) "Report of the Quartermaster General, Oct. 20, 1869," *House Exec. Docs.,* 41st Cong., 2d sess. no. 1, pt. 2, serial 1412, 214; (1870) "Report of the Quartermaster General, 11 Oct. 1870," *House Exec. Docs.,* 41st Cong., 3d sess. no. 1, pt. 2, serial 1446, 260–61; (1871) "Report of the Quartermaster General, Oct. 19, 1871," *House Exec. Docs.,* 42d Cong., 2d sess. no. 1, pt. 2, serial 1503, 128, 218; (1872); "Report of the Quartermaster General, Oct. 10, 1872," *House Exec. Docs.,* 42d Cong., 3d sess. no. 1, pt. 2, serial 1558, 144, 216; (1873) "Report of the Quartermaster General, Oct. 10, 1873," *House Exec. Docs.,* 43d Cong., 1st sess. no. 1, pt. 2, vol. 2, serial 1597, 192; (1874) "Report of the Quartermaster General, Oct. 10, 1874," *House Exec. Docs.,* 43d Cong., 2d sess. no. 1, pt. 2, vol. 2, serial 1635, 172–73, 198–99; (1875) "Report of the Quartermaster General, Oct. 9, 1875," *House Exec. Docs.,* 44th Cong., 1st sess. no. 1, pt. 2, serial 1674, 191, 194, 275–80; (1876) "Report of the Quartermaster General, Oct. 10, 1876," *House Exec. Docs.,* 44th Cong., 2d sess. no. 1, pt. 2, serial 1742, 275–76; (1877) "Report of the Quartermaster General, Oct. 10, 1877," *House Exec. Docs.,* 45th Cong., 2d sess. no. 1, pt. 2, serial 1794, 301, 304; (1878) "Report of the Quartermaster General, Oct. 9, 1878," *House Exec. Docs.,* 45th Cong., 3d sess. no. 1, pt. 2, serial 1843, 355, 360–61; (1879) "Report of the Quartermaster General, Oct. 10, 1879," *House Exec. Docs.,* 46th Cong., 2d sess. no. 1, pt. 2, vol. 2, serial 1903, 339–43; (1880) "Annual Report, Texas, 1880," microfilm no. M666, roll 589, Letters Received by the Office of the Adjutant General (Main Series), 1871–1880, Records of the U.S. Army Adjutant General's Office, 1780–1917, National Archives RG 94; (1881) "Report of the Quartermaster General, Oct. 1, 1881," *House Exec. Docs.,* 47th Cong., 1st sess. no. 1, pt. 2, vol. 2, serial 2010, 368–76; (1882) "Report of the Quartermaster General, Oct. 9, 1882," *House Exec. Docs.,* 47th Cong., 2d sess. no. 1, pt. 2, vol. 2, serial 2091, 358; (1883) "Report of the Quartermaster General, Oct. 6, 1883," *House Exec. Docs.,* 48th Cong., 1st sess. no. 1, pt. 2, vol. 2, serial 2182, 538–40; (1884) "Report of the Quartermaster General, Oct. 9, 1884," *House Exec. Docs.,* 48th Cong., 2d sess. no. 1, pt. 2, vol. 2, serial 2277, 574–75; (1885) "Report of the Quartermaster General, Oct. 9, 1885," *House Exec. Docs.,* 49th Cong., 1st sess. no. 1, pt. 2, vol. 2, serial 2369, 588–593; (1886) "Report of the Quartermaster General, Oct. 9, 1886," *House Exec. Docs.,* 49th Cong., 2d sess. no. 1, vol. 2, serial 2461, 480–85; (1887) "Report of the Quartermaster General, Oct. 6, 1887," *House Exec. Docs.,* 50th Cong., 1st sess. no. 1, vol. 2, serial 2533, 462–63, 484; (1888) "Report of the Quartermaster General, Oct. 5, 1888," *House Exec. Docs.,* 50th Cong., 2d sess. no. 1, pt. 2, vol. 2, serial 2628, 512; (1889) "Report of the Quartermaster General, Oct. 5, 1889," *House Exec. Docs.,* 51st Cong., 1st sess. no. 1, pt. 2, serial 2715, 456–57, 634, 637; (1890) "Report of the Quartermaster General, Oct. 9, 1890," *House Exec. Docs.,* 51st Cong., 2d sess. no. 1, pt. 2, vol. 2, serial 2831, 645,762.

APPENDIX 2

Steamship Contractors with the U.S. Army in Texas, 1850–1890

Contractor	Route	Notes (cwt. = per 100 lbs.)
1850		
Steamer *E. A. Ogden*	Galveston–Baton Rogue, La.	Ordnance stores, paid $5,000
1851		
M. Kenedy & Co.	Brazos Santiago–Ft. Brown	General transportation, 30¢ cwt., $3/soldier, $5/horse
"	Ft. Brown–Ringgold Barracks	General transportation, $1 cwt., $8/soldier, $12/horse
Steamer *Fanny*	New Orleans–Aransas Bay	$15/officer, $8/soldier
Steamer *Portland*	New Orleans–Indianola	$20/officer, $8/soldier
1852		
M. Kenedy & Co.	Contract continued	
1853		
No contracts		
1854		
M. Kenedy & Co.	Brazos Santiago–Ft. Brown	General transportation, 30¢ cwt., $3/soldier, $5/horse
"	Ft. Brown–Ringgold Barracks	General transportation, 75¢ cwt., $5/soldier, $7/horse

1855

| J. P. Armstrong | Brazos Santiago–Ft. Brown | General transportation, 25¢ cwt., $2.50/soldier, $4/horse |
| " | Ft. Brown–Ringgold Barracks | General transportation, 60¢ cwt., $4/soldier, $6/horse |

1856

J. P. Armstrong	Contracts continued	
M. Kenedy & Co.	Brazos Santiago–Ringgold Barracks	Transport Fifth Inf., paid $4,000
Richard King	Ft. Brown–Brazos Santiago	Transport Cos. K & M Fourth Arty., paid $1,200
"	Ft. Brown–Brazos Santiago–to *Julis G. Tyler,* outside sandbar	Transport 8 companies Fifth Inf., paid $2,000
"	To Brazos Santiago	Transport B Co. Fourth Arty., paid $1,200

1857

Richard King	Brazos Santiago–Ft. Brown	Transport Cos. L & M First Arty., band of Second Cav., paid $950
"	Ringgold Barracks–Brazos Santiago	Transport 3 officers and 71 soldiers on steamer *Ranchero,* paid $800
Harris, Morgan & Co.	New Orleans–Indianola	Transport 4 officers x $20/ea., and 409 soldiers x $6/ea. on steamer *Texas,* paid $2,534

1858

| Harris, Morgan & Co. | New Orleans–Indianola | Transport 7 officers x $20/ea., and 414 soldiers x $6/ea. on *Mexico,* paid $2,624 |
| " | New Orleans–Indianola | Transport 1 officer x $25/ea., and 43 soldiers x $10/ea. on steamer *General Rusk,* paid $455 |

1859

No contracts

1860

Steamer *Arizona*	New Orleans–Brazos Santiago	Transport 4 officers x $25/ea., 61 soldiers x $12.50/ea., and 86 horses x $17/ea., paid $2,587
"	New Orleans–Brazos Santiago	Transport Co. C, First Arty., paid $1,000
Steamer *Austin*	New Orleans–Brazos Santiago	Transport 1 officer, 14 soldiers, 26 horses x $17/ea., paid $695
M. Kenedy & Co.	Ft. Brown–Ringgold Barracks	Transport Co. L, First Arty., on *Ranchero* for $10/ officer, $5/soldier, and 25¢ cwt. for baggage

1869

C. A. Whitney & Co.	New Orleans–Brazos Santiago– Ft. Brown, Ringgold Barracks, and Laredo	Scheduled rates

1870

C. A. Whitney & Co.	New Orleans–Brazos Santiago	Scheduled rates

1871

King & Kenedy	Brazos Santiago–Ft. Brown– Ringgold Barracks	85¢ cwt., troops at scheduled rates
C. A. Whitney & Co. agent of Charles Morgan	New Orleans–Galveston–Brazos Santiago	Scheduled rates

1872

King & Kenedy	Brazos Santiago–Ft. Brown– Ringgold Barracks	50¢ cwt.
C. A. Whitney & Co. agent of Charles Morgan	New Orleans–Galveston– Indianola–Brazos Santiago	Scheduled rates

1873

Kenedy & King	Brazos Santiago–Ft. Brown– Ringgold Barracks	Scheduled rates

C. A. Whitney & Co. agent of Charles Morgan	New Orleans–Galveston–Indianola–Brazos Santiago	Scheduled rates

1874

C. A. Whitney & Co. agent of Charles Morgan	New Orleans–Galveston–Indianola–Brazos Santiago	Scheduled rates
H. E. Woodhouse	Brazos Santiago–Ft. Brown–Ringgold Barracks	Scheduled rates

1875

H. K. Hazlett	Brazos Santiago–Ft. Brown–Ringgold Barracks–Ft. McIntosh	Scheduled rates
Charles A. Whitney	Galveston–Indianola–Brazos Santiago	Scheduled rates

1876

Charles A. Whitney	Galveston–Indianola–Brazos Santiago	Scheduled rates
Charles Best	Brazos Santiago–Ft. Brown–Ringgold Barracks–Ft. McIntosh	Scheduled rates

1877

Charles A. Whitney	New Orleans–Galveston–Indianola–Brazos Santiago	Scheduled rates

1878

No contracts

1879

Charles A. Whitney	New Orleans–Galveston–Corpus Christi–Indianola–Brazos Santiago	Scheduled rates

1880

No contracts

1881

Charles A. Whitney	New Orleans–Galveston–Corpus Christi–Indianola–	Scheduled rates

| | Brazos Santiago | |
| William Kelly | Brazos Santiago–Ft. Brown–Ft. Ringgold | Scheduled rates |

1882

Charles A. Whitney	New Orleans–Galveston–Corpus Christi–Indianola–Brazos Santiago	Scheduled rates
William Kelly	Brazos Santiago–Ft. Brown–Ft. Ringgold	Scheduled rates
Steamer *Lulu D*	Upriver from Ft. Brown	Chartered Sept. 10 for $200/ day to evacuate the Nineteenth Inf. to escape a yellow fever outbreak, paid $8,200

1883

| Charles A. Whitney | New Orleans–Galveston–Corpus Christi–Indianola–Brazos Santiago | Scheduled rates |
| William Kelly | Brazos Santiago–Ft. Brown–Ft. Ringgold | Scheduled rates |

1884

| William Kelly | Ft. Brown–Ft. Ringgold | 49¢ cwt., $12/officer, $9/soldier, paid $4,640 |

1885

| William Kelly & Co. | Ft. Brown–Ft. Ringgold | Paid $2,894 |

1886

William Kelly & Co.	Route 4: Ft. Brown–Ft. Ringgold	60¢ cwt., $12/officer, $6/soldier, $12/horse, paid $3,863
A. C. Hutchinson, Morgan's Louisiana & Texas Railroad & Steamship Co.	New Orleans–Galveston	30¢ cwt., $10/officer, $5/soldier, $7.50/horse
"	New Orleans–Corpus Christi	60¢ cwt., $25/officer, $12/soldier, $15/ horse

"	New Orleans–Brazos Santiago	60¢ cwt., $30/officer, $12/ soldier, $15/ horse
"	Galveston–Corpus Christi	60¢ cwt., $15/officer, $7.50/ soldier, $12/horse
"	Galveston–Brazos Santiago	60¢ cwt., $22/officer, $12/ soldier, $15/horse Total paid to Morgan's Louisiana & Texas Railroad & Steamship Co. in 1886: $1,214

1887

William Kelly & Co.	Route 4: Ft. Brown–Ft. Ringgold	60¢ cwt., $12/officer, $8/ soldier, $12/horse, paid $4,864
Southern Pacific Co.	New Orleans–Galveston– Corpus Christi–Brazos Santiago	Scheduled rates

1888

William Kelly & Co.	Ft. Brown–Ft. Ringgold	Paid $999

1889

William Kelly & Co. & steamer *Bessie*	Ft. Brown–Ft. Ringgold	50¢ cwt., $10/officer, $8/ soldier, $12/animal, paid $1,235

1890

William Kelly & Co. & steamer *Bessie*	Ft. Brown–Ft. Ringgold	60¢ cwt., $10/officer, $8/ soldier, $12/animal, paid $416

Sources: (1850) "Statements of contracts and purchases, &c.," *House Exec. Docs.,* 31st Cong., 2d sess. no. 23, serial 599, 23; (1851) "Contracts—War Department," *House Exec. Docs.,* 32d Cong., 1st sess. no. 23, serial 640, 24; (1852) "Contracts," *House Exec. Docs.,* 32d Cong., 2d sess. no. 21, serial 676, 7–8; (1853) "Contracts made under the authority of the War Department . . . ," *Senate Exec. Docs.,* 33d Cong., 1st sess. no. 37, serial 698, 24–39; (1854) "Contracts—War Department," *House Exec. Docs.,* 33d Cong., 2d sess., no. 68, serial 788, 2–23;

(1855) "List of contracts . . . ," *Senate Exec. Docs.,* 34th Cong., 1st sess., no. 7, serial 815, 2–26; (1856) "Statements showing the contracts made . . . ," *Senate Exec. Docs.,* 34th Cong., 3d sess. no. 32, serial 880, 2–32; (1857) "A statement of contracts . . . ," *Senate Exec. Docs.,* 35th Cong., 1st sess., no. 31, serial 924, 1–33; (1858) "Contracts—War Department," *House Exec. Docs.,* 35th Cong., 2d sess. no. 50, serial 1006, 2–27; (1859) "War Department—Contracts," *House Exec. Docs.,* 36th Cong., 1st sess. no. 22, serial 1047, 7; (1860) "Contracts of the War Department . . . ," *House Exec. Docs.,* 36th Cong., 2d sess., no. 47, serial 1099, 2–47; (1868) "Report of the Quartermaster General, Oct. 20, 1868," *House Exec. Docs.,* 40th Cong., 3d sess., no. 1, serial 1367, 830; (1869) "Report of the Quartermaster General, Oct. 20, 1869," *House Exec. Docs.,* 41st Cong., 2d sess. no. 1, pt. 2, serial 1412, 211; (1870) "Report of the Quartermaster General, Oct. 11, 1870," *House Exec. Docs.,* 41st Cong., 3d sess. no. 1, pt. 2, serial 1446, 257; (1871) "Report of the Quartermaster General, Oct. 19, 1871," *House Exec. Docs.,* 42d Cong., 2d sess. no. 1, pt. 2, serial 1503, 221; (1872); "Report of the Quartermaster General, Oct. 10, 1872," *House Exec. Docs.,* 42d Cong., 3d sess. no. 1, pt. 2, serial 1558, 211; (1873) "Report of the Quartermaster General, Oct. 20, 1873," *House Exec. Docs.,* 43d Cong., 1st sess. no. 1, pt. 2, vol. 2, serial 1597, 195; (1874) "Report of the Quartermaster General, Oct. 10, 1874," *House Exec. Docs.,* 43d Cong., 2d sess. no. 1, pt. 2, vol. 2, serial 1635, 174; (1875) "Report of the Quartermaster General, Oct. 9, 1875," *House Exec. Docs.,* 44th Cong., 1st sess. no. 1, pt. 2, serial 1674, 280; (1876) "Report of the Quartermaster General, Oct. 10, 1876," *House Exec. Docs.,* 44th Cong., 2d sess. no. 1, pt. 2, serial 1742, 283; (1877) "Report of the Quartermaster General, Oct. 10, 1877," *House Exec. Docs.,* 45th Cong., 2d sess. no. 1, pt. 2, serial 1794, 310; (1879) "Report of the Quartermaster General, Oct. 10, 1879," *House Exec. Docs.,* 46th Cong., 2d sess. no. 1, pt. 2, vol. 2, serial 1903, 343; (1881) "Report of the Quartermaster General, Oct. 1, 1881," *House Exec. Docs.,* 47th Cong., 1st sess. no. 1, pt. 2, vol. 2, serial 2010, 376; (1882) "Report of Brigadier General C. C. Auger, Oct. 2, 1882," "Report of the Quartermaster General, Oct. 9, 1882," *House Exec. Docs.,* 47th Cong., 2d sess. no. 1, pt. 2, vol. 2, serial 2091, 105, 359; (1884) "Report of the Quartermaster General, Oct. 9, 1884," *House Exec. Docs.,* 48th Cong., 2d sess. no. 1, pt. 2, vol. 2, serial 2277, 460, 566; (1885) "Report of the Quartermaster General, Oct. 9, 1885," *House Exec. Docs.,* 49th Cong., 1st sess. no. 1, pt. 2, vol. 2, serial 2369, 587–93; (1886) "Report of the Quartermaster General, Oct. 9, 1886," *House Exec. Docs.,* 49th Cong., 2d sess. no. 1, vol. 2, serial 2461, 459, 484–85; (1887) "Report of the Quartermaster General, Oct. 6, 1887," *House Exec. Docs.,* 50th Cong., 1st sess. no. 1, vol. 2, serial 2533, 460, 489; (1888) "Report of the Quartermaster General, Oct. 5, 1888," *House Exec. Docs.,* 50th Cong., 2d sess. no. 1, pt. 2, vol. 2, serial 2628, 396–98, 516; (1889) "Report of the Quartermaster General, Oct. 5, 1889," *House Exec. Docs.,* 51st Cong., 1st sess. no. 1, pt. 2, serial 2715, 455, 637; (1890) "Report of the Quartermaster General, Oct. 9, 1890," *House Exec. Docs.,* 51st Cong., 2d sess. no. 1, pt. 2, vol. 2, serial 2831, 644, 762.

APPENDIX 3

Forage Contracts with the U.S. Army in Texas, 1850–1860

Contractor	Forage (bu. = bushel,/tn. = ton)
1850	
John Welch	Corn, $1/bu., for Cos. I and F, Second Dragoons
L. G. Capers	Corn, $1.05/bu. delivered, Ft. Inge; $1.35/bu. delivered, San Antonio
J. & W. B. Burdit	Corn, $1.35/bu. delivered, Ft. Croghan
T. L. Chenoweth	Hay, $3.19/tn. x 100 tns., Ft. Worth
1851	
A. J. Mackaye	Corn, $1.76/bu., Ft. Gates
H. Cheatham & C. R. Johns	Corn, 98½¢/bu. shelled x 21,000 bu., Austin
Evan Williams	Corn, $1.36/bu. x 6,000 bu., Ft. Croghan
Joshia Fisk	Hay, $7.25/tn. x 100 tns., Austin
Samuel Mankin	Hay, $9.50/tn. x 150 tns., Ft. Croghan
Lewis A. Ogle	Hay, $7.50/tn. x 200 tns., Ft. Gates
1852	
G. W. Hill	Corn, $1.75/bu. for 1,200 bu./month for 12 months, Ft. Graham
G. N. Butts & J. D. Black	Corn, $2.40/bu. x 4,000 bu.; Oats, $1.60/bu. x 6,000 bu., Ft. Belknap
M. T. Johnson	Corn, $1.50/bu. x 18,000 bu., Ft. Belknap
S. H. Luckie	Corn, 90¢/bu. x 1,000 bu, Ft. Inge
J. J. McClellan	Hay, $11.44/tn. x 400 tns., San Antonio
L. Vandeever	Hay, $9/tn. x 300 tns., Ft. Mason; $9/tn. x 150 tns., Ft. Croghan

H. Barnard	Hay, $7.50/tn. x 150 tns., Ft. Graham
H. Barnard Jr.	Hay, $7.50/tn. x 200 tns., Ft. Graham
F. Deitrich	Hay, $8/tn. x 75 tns, Austin
J. C. Lee	Hay, $8/tn. x 75 tns., Austin
J. C. Durst	Hay, $4.09/tn. x 75 tns., Ft. Martin Scott
G. Jones	Hay, $15/tn. x 150 tns., Ft. Duncan
E. Batridge	Hay, $3.40/tn. x 400 tns., Preston, Tx.

1853

Frederick Mumme	Corn, 62½¢/bu. x 500 bu., Ft. Inge
A. Leinweber	Corn, 62½¢/bu. x 500 bu., Ft. Inge
A. Brodburg	Corn, 62½¢/bu. x 800 bu., Ft. Inge
L. Essor	Corn, 60¢/bu. x 500 bu., Ft. Inge
J. Neidenheifer	Corn, 60¢/bu. x 500 bu., Ft. Inge
J. Hughes	Corn, $1.40/bu. x 1,500 bu., Ft. Belknap
M. T. Johnson	Corn, 90¢/bu. x 10,000 bu., Ft. Belknap
J. W. Smith	Corn, 90¢/bu. x 10,000 bu., Ft. Belknap
Jesse Stem	Corn, 89¢/bu. x 5,000 bu., Ft. Belknap
Pyren & Thomas	Hay, $7.89/tn. x 250 tns., San Antonio
M. August	Hay, $7.50/tn. x 100 tns., San Antonio
J. C. Durst	Hay, $4.90/tn. x 50 tns., Ft. Martin Scott
F. V. D. Stucken	Hay, $7.23/tn. x 300 tns., Ft. Mason
Stucken & Shuhara	Hay, $9.96/tn. x 200 tns., Ft. Chadbourne
Guy Stokes	Hay, $7.45/tn. x 300 tns., Ft. Graham
Williams & Lake	Hay, $12/tn. x 200 tns., Ft. Croghan
H. Benseman	Hay, $8.25/tn. x 170 tns., Ft. Inge

1854

J. C. Gooch	Corn, $1.26/bu. x 4,000 bu., Ft. Chadbourne
J. Leydendecker	Corn, $1.35/bu. x 14,000 bu., Ft. Chadbourne
W. T. Smith	Corn, $2/bu. x 600 bu., troops to El Paso
George Wilson	Hay, $8.90/tn. x 200 tns., Ft. Worth
Cecilio Valle	Hay, $14/tn. x 100 tns., Ringgold Barracks
W. M. Robinson	Hay, $19.95/tn. x 400 tns., Ringgold Barracks
E. J. Davis	Hay, $20/tn. x 300 tns., Ft. McIntosh
Julius Sanders	Hay, $11.50/tn. x 60 tns., Ft. Clark
Franz Schafer	Hay, $7.35/tn. x 125 tns., San Antonio
Charles Koenig	Hay, $8.45/tn. x 250 tns., Ft. Chadbourne

1855

Chas. J. Burgess	Corn, $1.25/bu. x 20,000 bu., Ft. McIntosh
E. J. Davis	Hay, $20/tn. x 500 tns., Ft. McIntosh
H. P. Bee	Hay, $13.40/tn. x 400 tns., Ft. McIntosh
M. Lidwell	Hay, $14.25/tn. x 400 tns., Ft. McIntosh
A. Schwartz	Hay, $15/tn. x 250 tns., Ft. Belknap
C. Lehman	Hay, $13.75/tn. x 125 tns., San Antonio
Louis Varé	Hay, $11.50/tn. x 400 tns., Ft. Clark

1856

Conrad Bloom	Corn, 94½¢/bu., Ft. Brown, Ringgold Barracks
F. V. D. Stucken & W. Wahrmund	Corn, $2.75/bu. x 5,000 bu., Ft. McKavett $2.15/bu. x 14,000 bu., Ft. Mason
S. Caruthers	Corn, $2.50/bu. x 14,000 bu., Camp Colorado
G. N. Butts	Corn, $1.70/bu. x 4,000 bu., Ft. Belknap
John C. Gooch	Corn, $2.84/bu. shelled & stacked x 4,000 bu., Ft. Chadbourne
H. Clay Davis	Hay, $13.50/tn. x 450 tns., Ringgold Barracks
F. Schafer	Hay, $7.75/tn. x 160 tns., $8.45/tn. x 150 tns., San Antonio
L. H. McLean & C. Pierce	Hay, $13.90/tn. x 85 tns., cavalry camp at Bandera Pass
P. Murphy	Hay, $13.45/tn. x 100 tns., Ft. Belknap
J. & A. Leinweber	Hay, $13.48/tn. x 200 tns., Ft. Clark
Theo. H. Valadieck	Hay, $14.25/tn., Ft. Bliss

1857

Juan Galván	Corn, 98¢/bu., Ft. Brown
John D. Burgess	Corn, $5.48/fanega (154 lbs.) x 4,000 fanegas, Ft. Davis
James Duff	Corn, $2.30/bu. x 12,500 bu., Camp Colorado; $2.70/bu. x 6,000 bu., Ft. Chadbourne
F. Fresenius	Corn, $2.25/bu. x 15,000 bu., Ft. Mason; $2.60/bu. x 3,500 bu., Ft. McKavett; $2.10/bu. x 9,800 bu., Camp Verde
E. C. Dewey	Corn, $1.49/bu. x 5,800 bu., Ft. Inge
M. T. Johnson	Corn, $2.50/bu. x 2,500 bu., Camp Cooper
H. Clay Davis	Hay, $11.90/tn. x 250 tns., Ringgold Barracks
J. B. McCluskey	Hay, $11.30/tn. x 240 tns.; $11.30/tn. x tns., Ringgold Barracks
J. C. Gooch	Hay, $13.90/tn. x 150 tns., Camp Colorado

J. T. Ward	Hay, $19.50/tn. x 120 tns, Camp Colorado
Julius Sanders	Hay, $7.96/tn. x 125 tns., Camp Sabinal
H. Anderson	Hay, $11.90/tn. x 100 tns., Ft. Belknap
S. W. McAllister	Hay, $22.95/tn. x 200 tns., San Antonio
L. Martin	Hay, $16.50/tn. x 300 tns., Ft. Mason
J. D. Thien	Hay, $26.80/tn. x 100 tns., Ft. Lancaster
R. Martin	Hay, $12/tn., Ft. McIntosh
W. W. Arnett	Hay, $11.95/tn. x 140 tns., Ft. Inge
James Magoffin	Hay, $13/tn., Ft. Bliss
A. Leinweber	Hay, $9.40/tn. x 180 tns., Camp Verde
R. Kennedy	Hay, $16.40/tn. x 250 tns., Ft. Clark

1858

B. J. Dewitt	Corn, $1.88/bu. x 6,000 bu., Camp Hudson
Duelos, Ryan & Co.	Corn, $1.60/bu. x 20,000 bu., Ft. Clark
R. F. Duff	Corn, $1.87/bu. x 16,000 bu., Camp Cooper
Edwin D. Lane	Corn, 78¢/bu. x 10,000 bu., Ft. Mason; 78¢/bu. x 3,000 bu., Ft. McKavett; $1.13/bu. x 7,000 bu., Camp Colorado; $1.28/bu. 13,000 bu., Ft. Chadbourne
Lewis L. White	Corn, 72¢/bu. x 1,500 bu., Camp Verde
Julius Steinbeck	Corn, 82½¢/bu. x 3,000 bu., Ft. Inge
J. F. Crosby	Corn, $2.90/fanega, Ft. Bliss
A. T. Wulff	Corn, $1.36/bu. x 11,142 bu., Ft. Davis
J. D. Thien	Hay, $16/tn. x 40 tns., Ft. Clark
C. Steigler	Hay, $8.50/tn. x 200 tns., Ft. Clark
G. H. Jones	Hay, $16.50/tn. x 160 tns., Ft. Duncan
A. Oswald	Hay, $7.90/tn. x 160 tns., Ft Duncan
Otto Ludwig	Hay, $7.40/tn. x 350 tns., San Antonio
George Lyles	Hay, $12.99/tn. x 300 tns., Ft. Bliss
A. Leinweber	Hay, $14.90/tn. x 80 tns., Camp Verde
G. W. Wall	Hay, $6.84/tn. x 160 tns., Ft. Inge
D. E. Tessier	Hay, $16.10/tn. x 125 tns., Ft. Lancaster
B. J. Dewitt	Hay, $19/tn. x 100 tns., Camp Hudson
Cameron & Stricken	Hay, $16.75/tn. x 120 tns., Ft. McKavett
M. T. Johnson	Hay, $20/tn. x 250 tns., Ft. Belknap
William Glass	Hay, $7.95/tn. x 250 tns., Ft. Mason
E. Hall	Hay, $29.40/tn. x 200 tns, Ft. Davis
John C. Gooch	Hay, $8.95/tn. x 160 tns., Camp Colorado

1859

James Duff	Corn, $1.70/bu. x 16,000 bu., Ft. Belknap
B. Steinbock	Corn, 94¢/bu., Camp Hudson
A. Duelos	Corn, 74¢/bu. x 10,000 bu., Ft. Clark
Gooch & MacKay	Corn, $1.62/bu. x 15,000 bu., Camp Cooper
J. M. Hunter	Corn, $1.70/bu. x 13,000 bu., Camp Verde
Stucken & Wahrmund	Corn, $1.07/bu. x 8,000 bu., Ft. Mason; $1.40/bu. x 2,500 bu. Ft. Chadbourne
James T. Ward	Corn, $1.35/bu. x 8,000 bu., Camp Colorado
A. Duelos	Corn, 79¢/bu. x 3,200 bu., Ft. Inge
Vincent & St. Vrain	Corn, 7,142 bu., Ft. Bliss
James Magoffin	Hay, $28/tn. x 300 tns., Ft. Bliss
E. Cenae	Hay, $8.90/tn. x 100 tns., Ringgold Barracks
F. V. D. Stucken	Hay, $19.90/tn. x 1,150 tns., Ft. Davis
F. M. Johnson	Hay, $19.94/tn. x 350 tns., Ft. Clark
L. Martin	Hay, $8.39/tn. x 500 tns., Camp Cooper
Gooch & MacKay	Hay, $14.90/tn. x 200 tns., Camp Colorado
G. A. Leigh	Hay, $19.25/tn. x 20 tns., Ft. Chadbourne
Myers & Johnson	Hay, $15.94/tn. x 150 tns., San Antonio
F. M. Johnson	Hay, $16.44/tn. x 125 tns., Ft. Lancaster
Charles de Montel	Hay, $12.89/tn. x 160 tns., Camp Verde

1860

A. Young	Corn, $3.47/fanega x 2,000 fanegas, Ft. Davis
N. L. Stratton	Corn, $2.74/bu. x 2,000 bu., $2.16/bu. x 7,000 bu., Camp Wood
A. Duelos	Corn, $1.45/bu. x 500 bu., Camp Stockton
F. V. D. Stucken	Corn, $2.45/bu. x 500 bu., Camp Colorado
John D. Burges	Corn, $1.98/bu. x 2,000 bu., Camp Stockton
Behr Steinbock	Corn, $1.89/bu., Camp Hudson
Jeremiah Galvan	Corn, $1.68/bu. x 8,212/bu., Ringgold Barracks; $1.24/bu., Ft. Brown
James Shaw	Corn, $1.93/bu. x 10,000 bu., Ft. Clark
L. Colquhoun	Corn, $1.83/bu., Ft. Duncan
J. D. Holliday	Hay, $15/tn. x 100 tns., Camp Stockton
David E. Tessier & C. Brackenbush	Hay, $17.75/tn. x 40 tns., Camp Stockton

B. Steinbock	Hay, $29.69/tn. x 50 tns., Camp Hudson
Robert Adams	Hay, $12.47/tn. x 350 tns., San Antonio
J. B. McCluskey	Hay, $20/tn. x 240 tns., Ringgold Barracks
John Leinweber	Hay, $8.84/tn. x 250 tns., Ft. Clark
G. K. Moore	Hay, $9.99/tn. x 380 tns., Camp Verde
Gooch & MacKay	Hay, $35/tn. x 200 tns., Camp Cooper; $12/tn. x 400 tns., Ft. Chadbourne
G. A. Leigh	Hay, $27/tn. x 65 tns., Ft. Chadbourne
M. Childress	Hay, $14.75/tn. x 200 tns., Camp Colorado
John Diedrick Thien	Hay, $11.76/tn. x 75 tns., Ft. Lancaster
John H. T. Richarz	Hay, $9/tn. x 200 tns., Ft. Inge
Ross Kennedy	Hay, $150/tn. x 150 tns., Camp Wood
George Lyles	Hay, $20/tn. x 75 tns., Ft. Quitman
R. King	Hay, $13.95/tn., Ft. Brown

Sources: Does not reflect open market purchases. (1850) "Statements of contracts and purchases, &c.," *House Exec. Docs.,* 31st Cong., 2d sess. no. 23, serial 599, 13; (1851) "Contracts—War Department," *House Exec. Docs.,* 32d Cong., 1st sess. no. 23, serial 640, 15–23; (1852) "Contracts," *House Exec. Docs.,* 32d Cong., 2d sess. no. 21, serial 676, 2–22; (1853) "Contracts made under the authority of the War Department . . . ," *Senate Exec. Docs.,* 33d Cong., 1st sess. no. 37, serial 698, 24–37; (1854) "Contracts—War Department," *House Exec. Docs.,* 33d Cong., 2d sess., no. 68, serial 788, 2–23; (1855) "List of contracts . . . ," *Senate Exec. Docs.,* 34th Cong., 1st sess., no. 7, serial 815, 2–23; (1856) "Statements showing the contracts made . . . ," *Senate Exec. Docs.,* 34th Cong., 3d sess. no. 32, serial 880, 2–32; (1857) "A statement of contracts . . . ," *Senate Exec. Docs.,* 35th Cong., 1st sess., no. 31, serial 924, 8, 1–35; (1858) "Contracts—War Department," *House Exec. Docs.,* 35th Cong., 2d sess. no. 50, serial 1006, 2–27; (1859) "War Department-Contracts," *House Exec. Docs.,* 36th Cong., 1st sess. no. 22, serial 1047, 1–22; (1860) "Contracts of the War Department . . . ," *House Exec. Docs.,* 36th Cong., 2d sess., no. 47, serial 1099, 2–47.

APPENDIX 4

Beef Contractors with the U.S. Army in Texas, 1849–1860

Contractor	*Delivered To*
1849	
William Cocburn	Richland Creek
Thomas Dunbar	Brazos Station
C. Howard	Fredericksburg
L. Hooste	Austin
L. P. Keller	Camp Chadbourne
James Campbell	Post on the Leona
Nicholas Chano	Ft. Polk
C. Shannon	"
L. Vankiel	Ft. Brown
Henry C. Davis	Ringgold Barracks
H. P. Bee	Laredo
I. W. Lillig	"
Thomas A. Droyer	Camp Crawford
1850	
Mercer Fain	Towash Village
F. Jordan	Ft. Worth
H. Childers	Ft. Gates
Hays & Sotith	Franklin (El Paso)
Capers & Howard	Third Inf., El Paso
H. L. Kinney	Ft. Merrill
Ross & Timon	"
Nicholas Chano	Ft. Brown
Louis Varé	"

| H. P. Bee | Ft. McIntosh |
| William L. Cazneau | Ft. Duncan |

1851

S. Gilmore	Ft. Worth
A. F. Lenord	Ft. Graham
John Ross	Ft. Merrill
Lewis & Groesbeeck	El Paso
B. Benavides	Ft. McIntosh
G. W. Pierce	"
William L. Cazneau	Ft. Duncan

1852

G. P. Farmer	Ft. Worth
C. Copenhaven	Ft. Phantom Hill
L. Vandeveer	San Saba River
J. S. McClellan	"
L. Vandeveer	Concho River
L. Vandeveer	Llano River Post
J. S. McClellan	"
C. T. Webb	Post Near "Racia"
N. Nei	Ft. Lincoln
Samuel Everett	Ft. Inge
Nicholas Chano	Ft. Brown
B. Garcia	Ft. McIntosh
William L. Cazneau	Ft. Duncan

1853

S. Eliot	Ft. Worth
James Haley	Ft. Graham
W. Gambel	Ft. Merrill
Nicholas Chano	Ft. Brown
W. F. Alexander	Ft. McIntosh
J. H. Taylor	Ft. Duncan

1854

J. M. Gibbons	Ft. Belknap
J. C. Gooch	Ft. Chadbourne
T. B. Edmondson	Ft. Ewell

Nicholas Chano	Ft. Brown
A. Monnett	"
E. J. Davis	Ft. McIntosh

1855

P. Harmonson	Ft. Belknap
William T. Smith	Recruits en route Ft. Bliss
W. Stone	Ft. Duncan
Nicholas Chano	Ft. Brown
E. J. Davis	Ft. McIntosh

1856

Louis Martin	Ft. Chadbourne
Louis Martin	Camp Colorado
Louis Martin	Ft. McKavett
Louis Martin	Ft. Mason
Louis Varé	Ft. Clark
J. C. Crawford	"
James Dawson	Ft. Davis
W. Zink	Camp Verde
David E. Tessier	Camp Lancaster
H. P. Bee	Ft. McIntosh
J. H. Taylor	Ft. Duncan

1857

Louis Martin	Camp Colorado
Louis Martin	Ft. McKavett
Louis Martin	Ft. Mason
F. T. Roberski	Camp Verde
H. B. George	Camp Cooper
James Dawson	Ft. Davis
W. C. Watson	Ft. Inge
Denis Meade	"
Nicholas Chano	Ft. Brown

1858

Louis Martin	Ft. McKavett
J. C. Ridley	Camp Verde
T. Lambshead	Camp Cooper

James Taylor	Ft. Davis
P. M. Thompson	Artisian Well Expedition
Solomon Miller	Ft. Belknap
Robert Zeseh	Ft. Mason
David E. Tessier	Ft. Lancaster
John Reinhard	Ft. Clark
Mayers & Greaves	Camp Colorado
Henry Skillman	Ft. Bliss
A. Oswald	Ft. Duncan
M. Lidwell	Ft. McIntosh
Nicholas Chano	Ft. Brown

1859

John Moore	Ft. Davis
Pyson & Cochran	Ft. Quitman
Pyson & Cochran	Ft. Bliss
James Duff	"
J. D. Holliday	Camp Stockton
H. M. Childress	Camp Colorado
John Dunlap	Ft. Lancaster
E. Obrorski	Camp Verde
S. H. Nunn	Ft. Inge
G. C. Patching	San Antonio
Adam Joseph	Ft. Brown

1860

J. C. Gooch	Ft. Cobb, I.T.
F. V. D. Stucken	Ft. Stockton
Cameron & Mogford	Ft. Davis
H. M. Childress	Camp Colorado
James Lindsay	Ft. Chadbourne
J. G. Irwin	Camp Cooper
Tessier & Brackenbush	Ft. Lancaster
H. Behrens	Ft. Mason
James Dawson	To Expedition
C. Montague	Camp Verde
J. D. Thien	Camp Hudson
G. C. Patching	San Antonio
G. T. Nimmo	Camp Wood

W. H. Pulliam	Ft. Inge
James Shaw	Ft. Clark
James Mallett	Ft. Brown
S. Cenae	Ringgold Barracks
Thomas Kennedy	Ft. Duncan

Sources: (1849) "The contracts made . . . ," *Senate Exec. Docs.,* 31st Cong., 1st sess. no. 26, serial 554, 38–40; (1850) "Statements of contracts and purchases, &c.," *House Exec. Docs.,* 31st Cong., 2d sess. no. 23, serial 599, 9–10; (1851) "Contracts—War Department," *House Exec. Docs.,* 32d Cong., 1st sess. no. 23, serial 640, 11–13; (1852) "Contracts," *House Exec. Docs.,* 32d Cong., 2d sess. no. 21, serial 676, 23–25; (1853) "Contracts made under the authority of the War Department . . . ," *Senate Exec. Docs.,* 33d Cong., 1st sess. no. 37, serial 698, 13–14; (1854) "Contracts—War Department," *House Exec. Docs.,* 33d Cong., 2d sess., no. 68, serial 788, 35; (1855) "List of contracts . . . ," *Senate Exec. Docs.,* 34th Cong., 1st sess., no. 7, serial 815, 41–42; (1856) "Statements showing the contracts made . . . ," *Senate Exec. Docs.,* 34th Cong., 3d sess. no. 32, serial 880, 37–38; (1857) "A statement of contracts . . . ," *Senate Exec. Docs.,* 35th Cong., 1st sess., no. 31, serial 924, 38–40; (1858) "Contracts—War Department," *House Exec. Docs.,* 35th Cong., 2d sess. no. 50, serial 1006, 28–30; (1859) "War Department-Contracts," *House Exec. Docs.,* 36th Cong., 1st sess. no. 22, serial 1047, 24–26; (1860) "Contracts of the War Department . . . ," *House Exec. Docs.,* 36th Cong., 2d sess., no. 47, serial 1099, 48–49.

Notes

CHAPTER I.
THE ARMY DOLLAR IN TEXAS

1. On Jacksboro see H. H. McConnell, *Five Years a Cavalryman, or, Sketches of Regular Army Life on the Texas Frontier, 1866–1871*, 161; Allen Lee Hamilton, *Sentinel of the Southern Plains: Fort Richardson and the Northwest Texas Frontier, 1866–1878*, 43. On San Antonio, see Mary Olivia Handy, *History of Fort Sam Houston*, 49.

2. Joe B. Frantz, "The Significance of Frontier Forts to Texas," *Southwestern Historical Quarterly* LXXIV (Oct., 1970): (quote) 204–205.

3. Francis Paul Prucha, *Broadax and Bayonet: The Role of the United States Army in the Development of the Northwest, 1815–1860;* Robert G. Athearn, *William Tecumseh Sherman and the Settlement of the West;* Michael L. Tate, "The Multi-Purpose Army on the Frontier: A Call for Further Research," in *The American West: Essays in Honor of W. Eugene Hollon,* ed. Ronald Lora, 171–208.

4. Robert W. Frazer, *Forts and Supplies: The Role of the Army in the Economy of the Southwest, 1848–1861;* Darlis A. Miller, *Soldiers and Settlers: Military Supply in the Southwest, 1861–1885.*

5. On the statistical comparison of Texas and New Mexico, see Census Office, *A Compendium of the Tenth Census, June 1, 1880,* 1:4, 662, 674, 678.

6. Leroy P. Graf, "The Economic History of the Lower Rio Grande Valley, 1820–1875," 4 vols. (Ph.D. diss., Harvard University, 1942).

7. Ibid., 1:3, 11, 154–55, 207, 4:31. In Larry Earl Adams, "Economic Development in Texas during Reconstruction, 1865–1875" (Ph.D. diss., North Texas State University, 1980), the author examines the details of the significance of railroads, agriculture, and cattle to Texas commerce but ignores the value of the military dollar to the economic recovery of Texas after the Civil War. For other studies that slight or undervalue the impact of the army dollar, see Charles M. Robinson III, *The Frontier World of Fort Griffin: The Life and Death of A Western Town;* Richard G. Lowe and Randolph B. Campbell, *Planters and Plain Folk: Agriculture in Antebellum;* Edmund Thorton Miller, *A Financial History of Texas;* Vera Lea Dugas, "Texas Industry, 1860–1880," *Southwestern Historical Quarterly* LIX (Oct., 1955): 151–83; Randolph B. Campbell and Richard G. Lowe, "Some Economic Aspects of Antebellum Texas Agriculture," *Southwestern Historical Quarterly* LXXXII (Apr., 1979): 351–78; S. S. McKay, "Economic Conditions in Texas in the 1870s," *West Texas Historical Association Year Book* 55 (1949): 84–

127; Earl F. Woodward, "Internal Improvements in Texas under Governor Peter Hansborough Bell's Administration, 1849–1853," *Southwestern Historical Quarterly* LXXVI (Oct., 1972): 161–82.

8. Frantz, "The Significance of Frontier Forts to Texas," 204–205; Robert Wooster, *Soldiers, Sutlers, and Settlers: Garrison Life on the Texas Frontier,* 103–22; Robert Wooster, *History of Fort Davis, Texas,* 137–40, 190–217, 256–57, 361–63; W. H. Timmons, "The Merchants and the Military, 1849–1854," *Password* 28 (Summer, 1982): 51–61; Roy Swift and Leavitt Corning Jr., *Three Roads to Chihuahua: The Great Wagon Roads that Opened the Southwest, 1823–1883;* Ben E. Pingenot, "The Great Wagon Train Expedition of 1850," *Southwestern Historical Quarterly* XCVIII (Oct., 1994): 182–225; Brownson Malsch, *Indianola: The Mother of Western Texas;* Richard V. Francaviglia, *From Sail to Steam: Four Centuries of Texas Maritime History, 1500–1900,* 155, 160; Earle B. Young, *Galveston and the Great West,* 68–69, 192–94; Thomas T. Smith, "Fort Inge and the Texas Frontier Economy," *Military History of the Southwest* 21 (Fall, 1991): 135–56. See also Bruce Dinges, "Colonel Grierson Invests on the West Texas Frontier," *Fort Concho Report* XVI (Fall, 1984), 6–11. For an excellent unpublished study of the economic, social, and political interrelationship between the army and El Paso, see Garna Loy Christian, "Sword and Plowshare: The Symbiotic Development of Fort Bliss and El Paso, Texas, 1848–1918," (Ph.D. diss., Texas Tech University, 1977). For a similar economic study of a Kansas fort, see William A. Dobak, "Fort Riley and Its Neighbors: The Federal Government and Economic Development in the Nineteenth-Century American West," (Ph.D. diss., University of Kansas, 1995). Dobak's focus is on the military-political interrelationships between area businessmen and the forts. Rather than an outline of contractual arrangements and details of dollars spent, this study traces the development of business networks and political influence in the area. In *A Texas Frontier: The Clear Fork Country and Fort Griffin, 1849–1887,* historian Ty Cashion makes the argument that the army's economic impact has been an exaggerated aspect of local history and that Fort Griffin was not a significant contributor to the regional economy. However, Cashion offers few details of the army's fiscal arrangements, and no comparative evidence or dollar figures that would lend adequate support to this thesis.

9. "Report of the Quartermaster General, Oct. 19, 1871," *House Exec. Docs.,* 42d Cong., 2d sess., no. 1, pt. 2, serial 1503, 122; Erna Risch, *Quartermaster Support: A History of the Corps, 1775–1939,* 2–3, 181–325; James A. Huston, *The Sinews of War: Army Logistics, 1775–1953,* 112–13.

10. On the Twiggs quote, see Richard W. Johnson, *A Soldier's Reminiscences in Peace and War,* 94. On additional officers and men assigned to the department, see "Report of the Quartermaster General, Nov. 22, 1853," *Senate Exec. Docs.,* 33d Cong., 1st sess., no. 1, serial 691, 133; Risch, *Quartermaster Support,* 330, 334–35, 508–509. On Grant, see

Lloyd Lewis, *Captain Sam Grant,* 168–69; Ulysses S. Grant, *Personal Memoirs of U. S. Grant: Selected Letters 1839–1865,* 1:72–73.

11. Johnson, *A Soldier's Reminiscences,* 92.

12. Trade deficit and public debt are from William M. Gouge, *The Fiscal History of Texas: Embracing an Account of Its Revenues, Debts, and Currency from the Commencement of the Revolution in 1834 to 1851–52,* 128, 275–78; Miller, *Financial History of Texas,* 82, 117. Texas valuation figures are from "Economic Statistics—Table 31: Total Valuation of Property Assessed in the State for Years 1846–1891," in Dudley G. Wooton, ed., *A Comprehensive History of Texas 1685 to 1897,* 2:831; Miller, *Financial History of Texas,* 106–107, 413.

13. Miller, *Financial History of Texas,* 88, 252–53, 396; Adams, "Economic Development," 62, 66–71.

CHAPTER 2.
THE ARMY LOGISTICAL SYSTEM IN TEXAS

1. On the political boundaries Department of Tejas in the Mexican federal period, see Andrés Tijerina, *Tejanos and Texas under the Mexican Flag, 1821–1836,* 105. The best survey histories of the Mexican War include K. Jack Bauer, *The Mexican War, 1846–1848;* John S. D. Eisenhower, *So Far From God: The U. S. War with Mexico, 1846–1848;* Otis A. Singletary, *The Mexican War;* George Winston Smith and Charles Judah, *Chronicles of the Gringos: The U. S. Army In the Mexican War, 1846–1848;* Justin H. Smith, *The War with Mexico;* John Edward Weems, *To Conquer A Peace: The War Between the United States and Mexico.*

2. Risch, *Quartermaster Support,* 237–40.

3. Risch, *Quartermaster Support,* 240–41; Huston, *Sinews of War,* 137–58; Chester L. Kieffer, *Maligned General: The Biography of Thomas Sidney Jesup,* 244; Bauer, *The Mexican War,* 256 n. 28; Franklin Smith, *The Mexican War Journal of Captain Franklin Smith,* ed. Joseph E. Chance, 8.

4. Coleman McCampbell, *Texas Seaport: The Story of the Growth of Corpus Christi and the Coastal Bend Area,* 24–29, 170; Ron Tyler, ed., *New Handbook of Texas,* 2:332, 3:1117.

5. "H. S. Foote" (Lt. Daniel H. Hill) "The Army in Texas," *Southern Quarterly Review* 9 (Apr. 1846): 434–57, (quote) 452.

6. On St. Joseph's Island see Capt. George H. Crosman to Brig. Gen. Zachary Taylor, Sept. 29, 1845, Entry 333, Maj. George H. Crosman, Records of Quartermasters, 1819–1905, Office of the Quartermaster General, National Archives Record Group (hereafter cited as RG) 92. On Taylor's logistical foresight see Kieffer, *Maligned General,* 249, 257, 259–60, (first quote) 270–71; Bauer, *The Mexican War,* 84. On Taylor's lack

of use of the engineers see Lt. George G. Meade to Mrs. George Meade, June 12, 1846, in George Meade, ed., *The Life and Letters of George Gordon Meade, Major General United States Army*, (second quote) 1:101.

7. Kieffer, *Maligned General*, (first quote) 265; Lt. R. S. Ewell to Ben, Feb. 12, 1847, in Percy Gatlin Hamlin, ed., *The Making of a Soldier: Letters of General R. S. Ewell*, (second quote) 62. For the argument that logistical problems were a product of poor execution rather than staff planning, see Roger G. Miller, "Winfield Scott and the Sinews of War: The Logistics of the Mexico City Campaign, October 1846–Sept., 1847," masters thesis, North Texas State University, Denton, Tex., May, 1976).

8. Ethan Allen Hitchcock, *Fifty Years in Camp and Field: Diary of Major-General Ethan Allen Hitchcock, U.S.A.*, ed. W. A. Croffut, 206; Bauer, *The Mexican War*, 35. The quote is from Lt. Robert Hazlitt to Mrs. Ingersoll, Mar. 20, 1846 in Robert Hazlitt Letters, 1844–1846, Special Collections, United States Military Academy Library, West Point, N.Y. (Hereafter cited as USMA Special Collections.)

9. Post Returns, Fort Polk, Tex., Mar. 1846–Jan. 1850, microfilm no. M617, roll 947, Returns from U.S. Military Posts 1800–1916, Records of the U.S. Army Adjutant General's Office, 1780–1917, RG 94, hereafter cited as Post Returns, Fort Polk; Lt. Napoleon J. T. Dana to Mrs. Dana, Apr. 8, 1846, in Robert H. Ferrell, ed., *Monterrey Is Ours! The Mexican War Letters of Lieutenant Dana, 1845–1847*, 39; Risch, *Quartermaster Support*, 245; Kieffer, *Maligned General*, 249; Eisenhower, *So Far from God*, 52; Tyler, ed., *New Handbook of Texas*, 5:279.

10. Lt. R. S. Ewell to Ben, 12 Feb. 1847 in Hamlin, ed., *Making of a Soldier*, 59, (quote) 60; Parmenas Taylor Turnley, *Reminiscences of Parmenas Taylor Turnley From the Cradle to Three-Score and Ten*, 67–68, 216–17; Smith, *Mexican War Journal*, 98; Dan R. Manning, "The Mexican War Journal of John James Dix: A Texian," *Military History of the West* 23 (Spring, 1993): 46–74; Kieffer, *Maligned General*, 255–56.

11. Maj. Thomas B. Eastland to Quartermaster General Thomas Jesup, Mar. 23, 1847 (quote), "Letters Sent," vol. 1, Entry 341; Eastland to M. E. Morrell, Apr. 6, 1847, "Letters Sent, Routine Matters," vol. 1, Entry 342, Maj. Thomas B. Eastland, Records of Quartermasters, 1819–1905, Office of the Quartermaster General, RG 92; Post Returns, Brazos Santiago, Tex., June, 1846–June, 1848, microfilm no. M617, roll 140, Returns from U.S. Military Posts 1800–1916, Records of the U.S. Army Adjutant General's Office, 1780–1917, RG 94. (Hereafter cited as Post Returns, Brazos Santiago.)

12. Maj. Thomas B. Eastland to Quartermaster General Thomas Jesup, Mar. 24, 1847, Eastland to General Taylor, Mar. 25, 1847, Eastland to Col. Henry Whiting, Mar. 25, 1847, Eastland to Capt. Arthur B. Lansing, Mar. 27, 1847, Eastland to Samuel McRee, Apr. 3, 1847, Entry 341, "Letters Sent," vol. 1; Eastland to M. E. Morrell, Apr. 6, 1847, "Letters Sent, Routine Matters," vol. 1, Entry 342, Maj. Thomas B. Eastland, Records of Quartermasters, 1819–1905, Office of the Quartermaster General, RG 92.

13. Maj. Thomas B. Eastland to Col. Henry Whiting, May 18, 1847, Entry 341, "Letters Sent," vol. 1; Eastland to the Hon. Milford P. Norton, Judge of the Fourth Judicial District of Texas, Aug. 28, 1847, (quotes) Entry 341, "Letters Sent," vol. 2, Maj. Thomas B. Eastland, Records of Quartermasters, 1819–1905, Office of the Quartermaster General, RG 92.

14. Risch, *Quartermaster Support,* 285–86.

15. Manning, "Mexican War Journal," 63–65; Memorandum of Capt. John G. Todd, Nov. 16, 1846, in Smith and Judah, *Chronicles of the Gringos,* 371.

16. Tyler, ed., *New Handbook of Texas,* 1:776–79.

17. Smith, *Mexican War Journal,* 189, 215 n. 10; Bauer, *The Mexican War,* 87–88.

18. Misc. Circulars and Letters, Entry 333, Maj. George H. Crosman, Records of Quartermasters, 1819–1905, Office of the Quartermaster General, RG 92; Smith, *Mexican War Journal,* 14, 77, 93; Lt. Napoleon J. T. Dana to Mrs. Dana, Aug. 20, 1846, in Ferrell, ed., *Monterrey Is Ours!,* 107.

19. Kieffer, *Maligned General,* 262–63; Risch, *Quartermaster Support,* 261, 268. Smith, *Mexican War Journal,* 28, 38, 119–22. In his journal in the period Aug., 1846, to Feb., 1847, Capt. Franklin Smith, First Mississippi Rifles, who was detailed to run the subsistence depot at Camargo, records the following number of Rio Grande runs by these steamers: *Rough & Ready*—six; *Colonel Cross, J. E. Roberts* and *Corvette*—five; *Brownsville* and *Whiteville*—four; *Aid*—three; *Enterprise*—two; and one each by the *Virginia, Major Brown, Warren, Hatchee Eagle, A. Monroe, Exchange* and *Mercer.* Smith, *Mexican War Journal,* 10–210.

20. Smith, *Mexican War Journal,* 35–36.

21. On the Comanche raids, see Lt. Napoleon J. T. Dana to Mrs. Dana, July 29, 1846, in Ferrell, ed., *Monterrey Is Ours!,* 103; Smith, *Mexican War Journal,* 87, 170. On Urrea see Bauer, *The Mexican War,* 218–20.

22. Teresa Griffin Vielé, *Following the Drum: A Glimpse of Frontier Life,* 144–46; J. Lee and Lillian J. Stembaugh, *The Lower Rio Grande Valley of Texas,* 89; Tyler, ed., *New Handbook of Texas,* 5:584–85.

23. Post Returns, San Antonio, Tex., Oct., 1845–Sept. 1872, microfilm no. M617, roll 1083, Returns from U.S. Military Posts 1800–1916, Records of the U.S. Army Adjutant General's Office, 1780–1917, RG 94 (hereafter cited as Post Returns, San Antonio); Regimental Returns, Second Cavalry (Second Dragoons), Apr., 1844–Dec., 1845, 1846–1848, microfilm no. M744, rolls 14 and 15, Returns from Regular Army Cavalry Regiments, 1833–1916, Records of the U.S. Army Adjutant General's Office, 1780–1917, RG 94 (hereafter cited as Regimental Returns, Second Dragoons); Risch, *Quartermaster Support,* 274.

24. "Report of Persons Hired at Port Lavaca and List of Quartermaster Stores Transferred, Sept.–Oct., 1846," Entry 361, Capt. James R. Irwin, 1843–1851, Records of Quarter-

masters, 1819–1905, Office of the Quartermaster General, RG 92; Risch, *Quartermaster Support,* 149, 274, 276; Kieffer, *Maligned General,* 269, 279; Bauer, *The Mexican War,* 149; Tyler, ed., *New Handbook of Texas,* 5:281–82, 421–22; Richard Eighme Ahlborn, *The San Antonio Missions: Edward Everett and the American Occupation, 1847,* 8, 20; Francis B. Heitman, *Historical Register and Dictionary of the United States Army,* 1:565; *The Register of Graduates and Former Cadets of the United States Military Academy,* 211.

25. Regimental Returns, Second Dragoons, Nov., 1845; May, 1846; General Orders no. 30, May 11, 1849, Adjutant General's Office, War Department, RG 94.

26. "Report of Brig. Gen. E. O. C. Ord, Headquarters, Department of Texas, Sept. 10, 1875," *House Exec. Docs.,* 44th Cong., 1st sess., no. 1, pt. 2, serial 1674, 104–108.

27. On the Mar. 20, 1848, request for troops by the Texas legislature, see Roy Eugene Graham, "Federal Fort Architecture in Texas during the Nineteenth Century," *Southwestern Historical Quarterly* LXXIV (Oct., 1970): 166. On the traditional view of settlement patterns, see Walter Prescott Webb, *The Great Plains.* For an overview of Texas settlement, see Terry G. Jordan, "Environment and Environmental Perceptions in Texas," in *Texas History,* ed. Walter L. Buenger. For a good historiography and the arguments for adding transportation routes, see Myron P. Gutmann and Christi G. Sample, "Land, Climate, and Settlement on the Texas Frontier," *Southwestern Historical Quarterly* XCIX (Oct., 1995): 137–72.

28. General Orders no. 49, Aug. 31, 1848, General Orders no. 58, Nov. 7, 1848, Adjutant General's Office, War Department, General and Special Orders, 1847–1860, Records of the U.S. Army Adjutant General's Office, 1780–1917, RG 94.

29. Regimental Returns, First Infantry, Jan., 1844–Dec., 1848, microfilm no. M665, roll 3; and Regimental Returns, Eighth Infantry, Jan., 1848–Dec., 1857, roll 91; Returns from Regular Army Infantry Regiments, June, 1821–Dec., 1916, Records of the U.S. Army Adjutant General's Office, 1780–1917, RG 94; Regimental Returns, Second Dragoons, Oct.–Dec., 1848; Post Returns, San Antonio, Tex., Feb.–Apr., 1849; Post Returns, Austin, Tex., Nov., 1848–Aug., 1875, microfilm no. M617, roll 59, Returns from U.S. Military Posts 1800–1916, Records of the U.S. Army Adjutant General's Office, 1780–1917, RG 94 (hereafter cited as Post Returns, Austin, Tex.).

30. Smith to Secretary of War Conrad, Oct. 6, 1851, and May 24, 1852; Smith to Division AAG Lt. Col. W. W. Bliss, Oct. 6 and 21, 1851 and Nov. 3, 1851, "Letter Book, Headquarters, Department of Texas, 1851–1854," Persifor F. Smith Papers; Robert Wooster, "Military Strategy In the Southwest, 1848–1860," *Military History of Texas and the Southwest* XV, no. 2 (1979): 5–15; Frank M. Temple, "Federal Military Defense of the Trans-Pecos Region, 1850–1880," *West Texas Historical Association Year Book 30* (Oct., 1954): 40–60; Graham, "Federal Fort Architecture," 166–67.

31. "Report of the Secretary of War, Nov. 30, 1850," *House Exec. Docs.,* 31st Cong., 2d sess., no. 1, serial 595, (first quote) 8; "Report of the Secretary of War, Dec. 2, 1851,"

House Exec. Docs., 32d Cong., 1st sess., no. 2, serial 634, 109–11; "Report of the Quartermaster General, Nov. 22, 1851," *House Exec. Docs.,* 32d Cong., 1st sess., no. 2, serial 634, 216–25, (second quote) 221.

32. General Orders no. 30, Apr. 3, 1849, Adjutant General's Office, War Department, RG 94; Post Returns, San Antonio, Tex., June, 1849, and Jan.–Dec. 1857; Martin L. Crimmins, ed., "W. G. Freeman's Report on the Eighth Military Department," *Southwestern Historical Quarterly* LI (Oct., 1947): 168; Martin L. Crimmins, ed., "Colonel J. F. K. Mansfield's Report of the Inspection of the Department of Texas in 1856," *Southwestern Historical Quarterly* XXXXII (Oct., 1938): 134–35.

33. Crimmins, ed., "W. G. Freeman's Report," LI: 58, 167–72.

34. "Report of the Quartermaster General, 1851," 276–77; "Statements of contracts and purchases, &c. (1850)" *House Exec. Docs.,* 31st Cong., 2d sess., no. 23, serial 599, 14; Turnley, *Reminiscences,* 205; Malsch, *Indianola,* 8–23; Tyler, ed., *New Handbook of Texas,* 3:830–31.

35. Bvt. Maj. Gen. Persifor F. Smith to Adjutant General Jones, Dec. 7, 1851, and Smith to Division Adjutant General Bliss, Feb. 26, 1852, "Letter Book, Headquarters, Department of Texas, 1851–1854," Persifor F. Smith Papers; Crimmins, ed., "W. G. Freeman's Report," LI: 56, LIV: 214; Crimmins, ed., "Colonel Mansfield's Report," (quote) 129, 144–46.

36. Graf, "Economic History," 4:57; *Texas State Gazette,* Sept. 15, 1849, 27; "Report of the Quartermaster General, 1851," 273–74; Crimmins, ed., "W. G. Freeman's Report," LI: 352–53, 356–57; Crimmins, ed., "Colonel Mansfield's Report," 129–30, 146–48.

37. Crimmins, ed., "W. G. Freeman's Report," LI: (first quote) 58, (second quote) 173.

38. Crimmins, ed., "Colonel Mansfield's Report," (first quote) 129, 138–39; *Texas State Gazette,* Oct. 13, 1855, (second quote) 2.

39. Post Returns, Austin, Tex., Nov., 1848–Sept., 1849; Regimental Returns, Eighth Infantry, May–Sept., 1849; "Report of the Quartermaster General, 1851," 273–74.

40. Crimmins, ed., "W. G. Freeman's Report," LIII: 467–68.

41. On the establishment of forts and the supply system, see "Report of the Quartermaster General, 1851," 270, 272, 275; Crimmins, ed., "W. G. Freeman's Report," LIII: 465; Robert W. Frazer, *Forts of the West,* 148, 150, 155, 164; Herbert M. Hart, *Tour Guide to Old Western Forts,* 158, 160, 163, 168; Robert B. Roberts, *Encyclopedia of Historic Forts: The Military, Pioneer, and Trading Posts of the United States,* 759, 763, 781; Walter Prescott Webb, ed., *Handbook of Texas,* 1:623, 625–26, 629, 633–34; Tyler, ed., *New Handbook of Texas,* 2:1096, 1101–1102, 1110, 1122–23. On the Preston supply depot concept, see Bvt. Maj. Gen. Persifor F. Smith to Adjutant General Jones, Dec. 7, 1851, and Smith to Division Adjutant General Bliss, Feb. 26, 1852, "Letter Book, Headquarters, Department of Texas, 1851–1854," Persifor F. Smith Papers; Crimmins, ed., "W. G. Freeman's Report," LIV: 214; Tyler, ed., *New Handbook of Texas,* 5:334–35.

42. "Report of the Quartermaster General, 1851," 277–79, 287–88; Crimmins, ed., "W. G. Freeman's Report," LI: 257, 352, LIII: 73–74; Frazer, *Forts of the West*, 146, 150, 152–53, 156; Hart, *Tour Guide*, 156, 159, 161, 163–64; Roberts, *Encyclopedia of Historic Forts*, 758, 762, 767, 770; Webb, ed., *Handbook of Texas*, 1:622, 625, 627–29; Tyler, ed., *New Handbook of Texas*, 2:1092–94, 1100, 1105–1106, 1108, 1111; National Park Service, *Soldier and Brave: Historic Places Associated with Indian Affairs and the Indian Wars in the Trans–Mississippi West*, the National Survey of Historic Sites and Buildings, vol. 12, ed. Robert G. Ferris, 319–20.

43. Crimmins, ed., "W. G. Freeman's Report," LIII: 203, 207, 313, 315, 447, 451; Frazer, *Forts of the West*, 142, 145, 147, 155–57, 163; Hart, *Tour Guide*, 154, 156–58, 163–64, 167; Roberts, *Encyclopedia of Historic Forts*, 751, 757–58, 769, 772, 779; Webb, ed., *Handbook of Texas*, 1:279, 620, 622, 628–29, 630; Tyler, ed., *New Handbook of Texas*, 1:932–33; 2:1091, 1110–11, 1113–14; National Park Service, *Soldier and Brave*, 315–19, 331–32, 335.

44. Timmons, "Merchants and Military," 53–60; Leon C. Metz, *Desert Army: Fort Bliss on the Texas Border*, 28, 36–38.

45. "Report of the Secretary of War, Dec. 1, 1856," *Senate Exec. Docs.*, 34th Cong., 3d sess., no. 5, serial 876, 22–23, 242–43; Crimmins, ed., "Colonel Mansfield's Report," 134–36, 236, 255, 354, 367, 373; Frazer, *Forts of the West*, 147–53, 157–63; Hart, *Tour Guide*, 159–68; Roberts, *Encyclopedia of Historic Forts*, 758, 760, 765–67, 773, 779, 781; Webb, ed., *Handbook of Texas*, 1:279, 622–24, 627, 630–31, 632; Tyler, ed., *New Handbook of Texas*, 1:932–33, 939, 948–49; 2:1096–97, 1106–1107, 1113–15, 1119; National Park Service, *Soldier and Brave*, 313, 322–32, 334–35; Charles R. Schrader, *U.S. Military Logistics, 1607–1991: A Research Guide*, 300; Lewis Burt Lesley, ed., *Uncle Sam's Camels: The Journal of Humphreys Stacy Supplemented by the Report of Edward Fitzgerald Beale (1857–1858)*, 1–17, 47; Frank B. Lammons, "Operation Camel," *Southwestern Historical Quarterly* LXI (July, 1957): 40–50.

46. "Report of the Quartermaster General, Nov. 20, 1850," *House Exec. Docs.*, 31st Cong., 2d sess., no. 1, serial 595, 324–29; "Report of the Quartermaster General, 1851," 279, 282, 284; Turnley, *Reminiscences*, 209, 213–17; Martin L. Crimmins, ed. "Two Thousand Miles by Boat in the Rio Grande in 1850," *West Texas Historical and Scientific Society Bulletin* 48 (Dec., 1933): 44–52; Crimmins, ed., "W. G. Freeman's Report," LII: 104; Crimmins, ed., "Colonel Mansfield's Report," 218–39; Johnson, *A Soldier's Reminiscences*, 61.

47. "Report of the Quartermaster General, 1851," 284; Crimmins, ed., "W. G. Freeman's Report," LII: 101, LIV: 203; Crimmins, ed., "Colonel Mansfield's Report," 129–30, 218–19. On the ship hotel, called the Greenwood Saloon and run by Robert S. Leman, see Vielé, *Following the Drum*, 93–94 and Coker, ed., *News from Brownsville*, 7.

48. "Report of the Quartermaster General, 1851," 284–85; Crimmins, ed., "Colonel

Mansfield's Report," 215–20; John C. Tidball, Class of 1848, Box 1, "First Experiences," (quote) 3, USMA Special Collections; General Orders no. 29, June 14, 1848, Adjutant General's Office, War Department, RG 94; Crimmins, ed., "W. G. Freeman's Report," LII: 106; Turnley, *Reminiscences,* 209.

49. On the exodus of the army from Texas, see the following sources: "Report of Bvt. Lt. Col. I. V. D. Reeve, Eighth U.S. Infantry, of the Surrender of His Command at San Lucas Spring, Tex.," in War Department, *The War of the Rebellion: A Compilation of the Official Records of the Union and Confederate Armies,* series I, vol. 1, 567–71; J. J. Bowden, *The Exodus of Federal Forces from Texas, 1861;* Jeanne T. Heidler, "'Embarrassing Situation': David E. Twiggs and the Surrender of U.S. Forces in Texas, 1861," *Military History of the Southwest* 21 (Fall, 1991): 156–72. On the Frontier Regiment, see David Paul Smith, *Frontier Defense in the Civil War: Texas' Rangers and Rebels,* 30, 48, 50, 54–55, 87, 102, 168. For operations in the Indian Territory, see Larry C. and Donald L. Rampp, "The Civil War in the Indian Territory," *Military History of Texas and the Southwest* 10, no. 1 (1972): 30, 38–39; no. 2 (1972): 96–97, 102; 11, no. 4 (1973): 272. On the Sibley Campaign in New Mexico, see Donald S. Frazier, *Blood and Treasure: Confederate Empire in the Southwest,* 184–85, 239, 259, 260, 265, 300.

50. For a general summary of federal operations on the Texas coast and the army's return to Texas, see the following sources: Miscellaneous unit reports, *The War of the Rebellion,* series I, vol. 46, pt. 3:1168, 1193, 1195, 1206; vol. 48, pt. 2:819, 917, 1050, 1061, 1088, 1081, 1085; vol. 48, pt. 3:1093; "Report of Major General P. H. Sheridan, Department of the Gulf, Nov. 14, 1866," *House Exec. Docs.,* 39th Cong., 2d sess., no. 1, serial 1285, 44–50; John Salmon Ford, *RIP Ford's Texas,* Stephen B. Oates, ed., 331–407; Ralph A. Wooster, *Texas and Texans in the Civil War;* Alwyn Barr, "Texas Coastal Defense, 1861–1865," *Southwestern Historical Quarterly* LXXV (July, 1961): 14–18; Frank H. Smyrl, "Texas in Gray: The Civil War Years, 1861–1865," in *Texas History,* ed. Walter L. Buenger, 317–66.

51. Thomas W. Cutrer, ed., "'An Experience in Soldier's Life': The Civil War Letters of Volney Ellis, Adjutant, Twelfth Texas Infantry, Walker's Texas Division, C.S.A.," *Military History of the Southwest* 22 (Fall, 1992): (quote) 143–44; Ford, *RIP Ford's Texas,* 329, 341–343, 349, 360, 369; Peyton O. Abbott, "Business Travel Out of Texas During the Civil War: The Travel Diary of S. B. Brush, Pioneer Austin Merchant," *Southwestern Historical Quarterly* XCVI (Oct., 1992): 259–71.

52. Robert W. Shook, "The Federal Military in Texas, 1865–1870," *Texas Military History* 6 (Spring, 1967): 3–54; William L. Richter, *Army in Texas during Reconstruction,* 13–20; B. W. Aston, "Federal Military Reoccupation of the Texas Southwestern Frontier, 1865–1871," *Texas Military History* 8, no. 3 (1970): 123–34.

53. Max S. Lale, "Military Occupation of Marshall, Texas, by the Eighth Illinois Volunteer Infantry, U.S.A, 1865," *Military History of Texas and the Southwest* 13 (1976): 39–

47; Thomas S. Cogley, *History of the Seventh Indiana Cavalry Volunteers,* (quote) 171; Charles T. Clark, *Opdycke Tigers: 125th O.V.I,* 402; "Report of Maj. Gen. Sheridan, 1866," 48–49; Shook, "Federal Military in Texas," 19–20, 30; Richter, *Army in Texas,* 69–75; Aston, "Federal Military Reoccupation," 125–26.

54. Frazer, *Forts of the West,* 142–55, 157–58, 162; Hart, *Tour Guide,* 154–67; Roberts, *Encyclopedia of Historic Forts,* 751–55, 757–58, 760–69, 773, 779; Webb, ed., *Handbook of Texas,* 1:621–29, 631–32; Tyler, ed., *New Handbook of Texas,* 1:939, 943–46; 2:1089, 1091–99, 1102, 1104, 1106–16, 1119; National Park Service, *Soldier and Brave,* 313, 315–29, 330–31, 334–35.

55. "Report of Maj. Gen. Sheridan, 1866," 48; Quartermaster General's Office, *Outline Description of U.S. Military Posts and Stations in the Year 1871* (Washington, D.C.: Government Printing Office, 1872), 37, 40, 48; William M. Notson, "Fort Concho, 1868–1872: The Medical Officers Observations," ed. Stephen Schmidt, *Military History of Texas and the Southwest* 12, no. 1 (1975): 139.

56. Quartermaster General's Office, *Outline Description . . . 1871,* 45, 48, 52–53; Lynn M. Alperin, *Custodians of the Coast: History of the United States Army Engineers at Galveston,* 39–40.

57. Quartermaster General's Office, *Outline Description . . . 1871,* 37, 45, 52-53, 56; Headquarters, U.S. Army, "Descriptive Book of the District of Texas, July 1st 1868," microfilm no. 253, folio 6, RG 108, Records of the Headquarters of the Army, Entry 51, vol. 220.

58. Quartermaster General's Office, *Outline Description . . . 1871,* 40, 48–49, 53; Headquarters, U.S. Army, "Descriptive Book of the District of Texas . . . 1868," folios 49, 51, 53, 55; Joseph C. Sides, *Fort Brown Historical: History of Fort Brown, Texas Border Post on the Rio Grande,* 139–40.

59. Post Returns, San Antonio, Tex., Sept., 1865–Dec., 1866; Quartermaster General's Office, *Outline Description . . . 1871,* 39, 41, 43–45, 48–56; Headquarters, U.S. Army, "Descriptive Book of the District of Texas . . . 1868," folios 12–44.

60. Walter C. Conway, ed., "Col. Edmund Schriver's Inspector General's Report on Military Posts in Texas Nov., 1872–Jan., 1873," *Southwestern Historical Quarterly* LXVII (Apr., 1964): (quotes) 569–70.

61. "Report of the Quartermaster General, Oct. 20, 1868," *House Exec. Docs.,* 40th Cong., 3d sess., no. 1, serial 1367, (first quote) 861; "Report of the Quartermaster General, Oct. 11, 1870," *House Exec. Docs.,* 41st Cong., 3d sess., no. 1, pt. 2, serial 1446, (second quote) 154, 861.

62. "Report of the Quartermaster General, 1870," 154; "Report of the Quartermaster General, Oct. 10, 1876," *House Exec. Docs.,* 44th Cong., 2d sess., no. 1, pt. 2, serial 1742, 123; "Report of the Quartermaster General, Oct. 10, 1877," *House Exec. Docs.,* 45th Cong., 2d sess., no. 1, pt. 2, serial 1794, 188–89; "Report of the Quartermaster General, Oct. 9, 1878," *House Exec. Docs.,* 45th Cong., 3d sess., no. 1, pt. 2, serial 1843,

260–61; Eldon Cagle Jr., *Quadrangle: The History of Fort Sam Houston,* 28–35; Tyler, ed., *New Handbook of Texas,* 2:1117.

63. "Report of the Quartermaster General, 1868," 961, 811, 830, 857–58; Notson, "Fort Concho," 132–33; Conway, ed., "Colonel Schriver's Inspector General's Report," (quote) 562.

64. For an outline on the limitations that logistics placed on army campaigns in the West, see Robert M. Utley, "A Chained Dog: The Indian-Fighting Army," *American West* X (July, 1973): 18–24, 61. For an analysis of Texas frontier campaigns, see Thomas T. Smith, "U.S. Army Combat Operations in the Indian Wars of Texas, 1849–1881," *Southwestern Historical Quarterly* XCIX (Apr., 1996): 501–31. On the Red River War, see Robert M. Utley, *Frontier Regulars: The United States Army and the Indian, 1866–1891,* 225–39; Ernest Wallace, *Ranald S. Mackenzie on the Texas Frontier,* 48, 65, 157; Hamilton, *Sentinel of the Southern Plains,* 100; James L. Haley, *The Buffalo War: The History of the Red River Indian Uprising of 1874,* 171–73; Tyler, ed., *New Handbook of Texas,* 2:1099.

65. "Report of the Secretary of War, Nov. 24, 1873," *House Exec. Docs.,* 43d Cong., 1st sess., no. 1, pt. 2, vol. 2, serial 1597, 62–63; Headquarters of the Military Division of the Missouri, *Outline Descriptions of the Posts in the Military Division of the Missouri, Commanded by Lieutenant General P. H. Sherdian,* 190, 193; Lowell H. Harrison, "Supplying Texas Military Posts in 1876," *Texas Military History* 4 (Spring, 1964): 23–24.

66. On Indianola, see "Annual Report of the Chief Signal Officer, Oct. 10, 1876," *House Exec. Docs.,* 44th Cong., 2d sess., no. 1, pt. 2, vol. 4, serial 1747, 378–82; Malsch, *Indianola,* 232–33. On Brazos Santiago, see "Report of the Quartermaster General, Oct. 9, 1875," *House Exec. Docs.,* 44th Cong., 1st sess., no. 1, pt. 2, serial 1674, 197. On Austin, see Division of the Missouri, *Outline Descriptions,* 182. On Fort Elliott, see "Report of the Quartermaster General, 1876," 276.

67. "Report of the Quartermaster General, Oct. 10, 1879," *House Exec. Docs.,* 46th Cong., 2d sess., no. 1, pt. 2, vol. 2, serial 1903, 351–53.

68. "Report of the Quartermaster General, 9 Oct. 1884," *House Exec. Docs.,* 48th Cong., 2d sess., no. 1, pt. 2, vol. 2, serial 2277, 574–75; "Report of the Quartermaster General, Oct. 9, 1885," *House Exec. Docs.,* 49th Cong., 1st sess., no. 1, pt. 2, vol. 2, serial 2369, 503; Frazer, *Forts of the West,* 157–59, 165–67; Hart, *Tour Guide,* 157–59, 165–67; Roberts, *Encyclopedia of Historic Forts,* 758, 761–62, 764, 772–73, 779; Webb, ed., *Handbook of Texas,* 1:625–26, 628, 631–32; Tyler, ed., *New Handbook of Texas,* 1:943–44, 2:1094–95, 1098–99, 1102, 1104, 1111, 1115, 1119; National Park Service, *Soldier and Brave,* 331, 334–35.

69. "Report of the Commissary General of Subsistence, Oct. 1, 1895," *House Exec. Docs.,* 54th Cong., 1st sess., no. 2, vol. 3, serial 3370, 380; "Report of the Quartermaster General, Oct. 5, 1889," *House Exec. Docs.,* 51st Cong., 1st sess., no. 1, pt. 2, serial 2715,

418; Frazer, *Forts of the West,* 148–51; Hart, *Tour Guide,* 158–60, 164; Roberts, *Encyclo-pedia of Historic Forts,* 760–62, 764, 772; Webb, ed., *Handbook of Texas,* 1:623–26; Tyler, ed., *New Handbook of Texas,* 1:943–46, 2:1096–97, 1099, 1104; National Park Service, *Soldier and Brave,* 322–29.

70. "Report of the Adjutant General of the Army, Oct. 20, 1900," and "Report of the Quartermaster General, Oct. 16, 1900," *House Exec. Docs.,* 56th Cong., 2d sess., no. 2, vol. 3, serial 4071, 10, 417; Office of the Judge Advocate General, *United States Military Reservations, National Cemeteries and Military Parks: Title, Jurisdiction, Etc.,* 370–83.

71. Texas logistical expenditures are calculated from each year's "Report of the Quarter-master General of the Army," in the annual *Report of the Secretary of War,* 1849–1900.

72. On the 1851 inspection, see Kieffer, *Maligned General,* 302. On Van Bokkelen, see General Orders no. 5, May 23, 1857, Adjutant General's Office, War Department, RG 94.

73. Theodore D. Harris, ed., *Negro Frontiersman: The Western Memoirs of Henry O. Flip-per, First Negro Graduate of West Point,* vii, 18–20; Paul H. Carlson, *"Pecos Bill": A Military Biography of William R. Shafter,* 122–26; Bruce J. Dinges, "The Court-Martial of Lieutenant Henry O. Flipper: An Example of Black-White Relationships in the Army, 1881," *The American West* 9 (Jan., 1972): 12–17, 19, 21; Donald R. McClung, "Second Lieutenant Henry O. Flipper: A Negro Officer on the West Texas Frontier," *West Texas Historical Year Book* 48 (1971): 20–31.

CHAPTER 3.
TRANSPORTATION: PRAIRIE SCHOONERS, STEAMERS, AND THE IRON HORSE

1. Smith, *Mexican War Journal,* 59, 142; Risch, *Quartermaster Support,* 242, 270, 274, 277; Bauer, *The Mexican War,* 35, 67, 89.

2. Swift and Corning, *Three Roads to Chihuahua,* 154–55; Frederick Law Olmsted, *A Journey through Texas; or, a Saddle-Trip on the Southwestern Frontier,* 152–53.

3. On Mexican carts and American wagons, see August Santleben, *Texas Pioneer: Early Staging and Overland Freighting Days on the Frontiers of Texas and Mexico,* ed. I. D. Affleck, 107–109; Smith, *Mexican War Journal,* 142. On government wagons, see Santleben, 111; Risch, *Quartermaster Support,* 420–21; Swift and Corning, *Three Roads to Chihuahua,* 249–53; Percival G. Lowe, *Five Years a Dragoon ('49 to '54) and Other Adventures on the Great Plains,* 287; Randy Steffen, *The Horse Soldier, 1776–1943,* 4 vols., 2:91-93.

4. Santleben, *Texas Pioneer,* 116–18, 141; Lowe, *Five Years a Dragoon,* 204, 210.

5. Details on the yearly contracts are found in each year's "Report of the Quartermaster

General of the Army," in the annual *Report of the Secretary of War,* and the yearly separate document usually labeled "Contracts with the War Department" in the *House of Representatives Executive Documents.*

6. On the 1849 contracts with the Howards, see "The contracts made . . . 1849," *Senate Exec. Docs.,* 31st Cong., 1st sess., no. 26, serial 554, 18. On the advantages of contracted freighting, see Bvt. Maj. Gen. Persifor F. Smith to Bvt. Lt. Col. William W. S. Bliss, 22 Mar. 1852 (quote), "Letter Book," Smith Papers; Crimmins, ed., "Colonel Mansfield's Report," 134; Kieffer, *Maligned General,* 304; Risch, *Quartermaster Support,* 308–309. On the cost of forage, see "Report of the Quartermaster General, 1851," 234.

7. Special Orders no. 21, May 9, 1850, Headquarters, Department of Texas, as published in *Texas State Gazette,* May 18, 1850, 295; "Report of the Quartermaster General, 1851," 254, 256, 267.

8. On the El Paso contracts, see "Statements of contracts and purchases (1850)," 15–17. For details on the great train of 1850 to El Paso, see Turnley, *Reminiscences,* 117–21; Pingenot, "The Great Wagon Train Expedition of 1850," 182–225; Ben E. Pingenot, ed., "Journal of a Wagon Train Expedition from Fort Inge to El Paso del Norte in 1850," *Military History of the West* 25 (Spring, 1995): 69–105; Swift, *Three Roads to Chihuahua,* 108–13; Frazer, *Forts and Supplies,* 41–24.

9. On the French train, see Samuel G. French, *Two Wars: An Autobiography of Gen. Samuel G. French,* 106–18; "Report of the Quartermaster General, 1851," 221, 227–35; Risch, *Quartermaster Support,* 311. On Texas freight contracts for 1853 and 1854, see "Contracts made under the authority of the War Department during the year 1853," *Senate Exec. Docs.,* 33d Cong., 1st sess., no. 37, serial 698, 24; "Report of the Quartermaster General, Nov. 14, 1854," *House Exec. Docs.,* 33d Cong., 2d sess., no. 1, pt. 2, serial 778, 73; "Contracts—War Department, 1854," *House Exec. Docs.,* 33d Cong., 2d sess., no. 68, serial 788, 2–23; Frazer, *Forts and Supplies,* 96.

10. Risch, *Quartermaster Support,* 312.

11. For a history of Russell, Majors, and Waddell, see Raymond W. and Mary Lund Settle, *Empire on Wheels.* For the 1855 contracts, see "List of contracts . . . during the year 1855," *Senate Exec. Docs.,* 34th Cong., 1st sess., no. 7, serial 815, 9, 11, 24, 26.

12. George Thomas Howard died in Washington, D.C., on Aug. 6, 1866. Howard Lackman, "George Thomas Howard, Texas Frontiersman," (Ph.D. diss., University of Texas at Austin, 1954), 32, 67, 228, 229, 253, 282–364; Webb, ed., *Handbook of Texas,* 1:853; Tyler, ed., *New Handbook of Texas,* 3:744.

13. On contracts of 1856–1860, see "Statements showing the contracts made . . . during the year 1856," *Senate Exec. Docs.,* 34th Cong., 3d sess., no. 32, serial 880, 19; "A statement of contracts . . . during the year 1857," *Senate Exec. Docs.,* 35th Cong., 1st sess., no. 31, serial 924, 8, 16–17; "Contracts—War Department (1858)," *House Exec. Docs.,* 35th Cong., 2d sess., no. 50, serial 1006, 3, 11, 26, 28; "War Department—Contracts

(1859)," *House Exec. Docs.,* 36th Cong., 1st sess., no. 22, serial 1047, 7; "Contracts of the War Department for 1860," *House Exec. Docs.,* 36th Cong., 2d sess., no. 47, serial 1099, 10, 25, 46–47. On Howard's freight business, see St. Clair Griffin Reed, *A History of the Texas Railroads and of Transportation Conditions in Texas under Spain and Mexico and the Republic and the State,* 43–44; Lackman, "George Thomas Howard," 284–85, 290; Ralph A. Wooster, "Wealthy Texans, 1860," *Southwestern Historical Quarterly* LXXI (Oct., 1967): 163–80.

14. On Duff as post sutler, see Crimmins, ed., "Colonel Mansfield's Report," 375. On Duff's corn, flour, hay, and beef contracts see "A statement of contracts . . . 1857," 1–35, 40; "Contracts (1858)," 28–29; "War Department-Contracts (1859)," 1–22, 24–26. On Duff's post–Civil War background, see David S. Stanley, *Personal Memoirs of Major-General D. S. Stanley, U.S.A.,* 234–35.

15. "Report of the Quartermaster General, 1868," 811, 830, 857–58, 961.

16. Swift, *Three Roads to Chihuahua,* 238–42; "Report of the Quartermaster General, 1868," (quote) 857.

17. "Report of the Quartermaster General, 1875," 275–80.

18. "Report of the Quartermaster General, Oct. 1, 1881," *House Exec. Docs.,* 47th Cong., 1st sess., no. 1, pt. 2, vol. 2, serial 2010, 368, 371–76.

19. "Report of the Quartermaster General, 1884," 574–75; "Report of the Quartermaster General, 1885," 503; "Report of the Quartermaster General, Oct. 9, 1886," *House Exec. Docs.,* 49th Cong., 2d sess., no. 1, vol. 2, serial 2461, 462, 484; "Report of the Quartermaster General, Oct. 9, 1890," *House Exec. Docs.,* 51st Cong., 2d sess., no. 1, pt. 2, vol. 2, serial 2831, 645, 762; Wooster, *History of Fort Davis,* 104, 137–38, 187, 202, 265, 305, 316, 318, 361–63; Tyler, ed., *New Handbook of Texas,* 1:129–30.

20. Inflation rates are from the Bureau of the Census, *Historical Statistics of the United States: Colonial Times to 1970,* pt. 1, 201, 512, 518.

21. "Report of the Quartermaster General, Nov. 10, 1849," *Senate Exec. Docs.,* 31st Cong., 1st sess., no. 1, serial 549, 18; "List of contracts (1855)," 11, 26; Crimmins, ed., "Colonel Mansfield's Report, 129; "War Department—Contracts (1859)," 7; "Report of the Quartermaster General, 1868," 830, 857–61; "Report of the Quartermaster General, Oct. 20, 1869," *House Exec. Docs.,* 41st Cong., 2d sess., no. 1, pt. 2, serial 1412, 214; "Report of the Quartermaster General, 1871," 218; "Report of the Quartermaster General, Oct. 10, 1873," *House Exec. Docs.,* 43d Cong., 1st sess., no. 1, pt. 2, vol. 2, serial 1597, 192; "Report of the Quartermaster General, 1875," 275–80; "Report of the Quartermaster General, 1878," 360–61; "Report of the Quartermaster General, 1881," 374–75; "Report of the Quartermaster General, 1884," 574–75; "Report of the Quartermaster General, Oct. 5, 1888," *House Exec. Docs.,* 50th Cong., 2d sess., no. 1, pt. 2, vol. 2, serial 2628, 512, 516.

22. "Report of the Quartermaster General, 1869," 214; "Report of the Quartermaster

General, Oct. 10, 1874," *House Exec. Docs.*, 43d Cong., 2d sess., no. 1, pt. 2, vol. 2, serial 1635, 198–99; "Report of the Quartermaster General, 1881," 368–76; "Report of the Quartermaster General, 1885," 588–93; "Report of the Quartermaster General, Oct. 6, 1887," *House Exec. Docs.*, 50th Cong., 1st sess., no. 1, vol. 2, serial 2533, 484; "Report of the Quartermaster General, 1888," 512, 516.

23. Santleben, *Texas Pioneer,* 279; "Report of the Quartermaster General, 1868," 857–61; "Report of the Quartermaster General, 1888," 387, 512, 516; David A. Clary and Joseph W. A. Whitehorne, *The Inspectors General of the United States Army, 1777–1903,* 356.

24. Numbers of contracts and individual contractors are totaled from a survey of each year's "Report of the Quartermaster General of the Army," in the annual *Report of the Secretary of War,* 1849–1900, and from RG 92, Records of the Office of the Quartermaster General, Entry 1245, "Register of Contracts, 1871–1912," and from the annual *Senate* and *House of Representatives Executive Documents,* "War Department Contracts."

25. "Report of the Quartermaster General, 1871," 128.

26. Wallace, *Ranald S. Mackenzie,* 40, 62–63; Paul Andrew Hutton, *Phil Sheridan and His Army,* 237; Utley, *Frontier Regulars,* 255; Swift, *Three Roads to Chihuahua,* 238–39.

27. Wallace, *Ranald S. Mackenzie,* 63–64; Hutton, *Phil Sheridan,* 237; Swift, *Three Roads to Chihuahua,* 239.

28. Huston, *Sinews of War,* 44; Risch, *Quartermaster Support,* 265.

29. For a general overview of maritime development on the Texas coast and rivers in the mid-nineteenth century, see Francaviglia, *From Sail To Steam,* 98–101, 128–34, 153, 147, 160. On Morgan, see James P. Baughman, *Charles Morgan and the Development of Southern Transportation,* 22–40; Webb, ed., *Handbook of Texas,* 2:235; Tyler, ed., *New Handbook of Texas,* 4:834. On Mexican efforts to use steamboats on the Rio Grande, see Pat Kelly, *River of Lost Dreams: Navigation on the Rio Grande,* 18. On Henry Austin, see William R. Hogan, "The Life of Henry Austin," *Southwestern Historical Quarterly* XXXVIII (Jan., 1934): 185–214; Graf, "Economic History," 1:63–64, 4:22–23. On the *Neva* and *White Wing,* see Capt. George H. Crosman to Brig. Gen. Zachary Taylor, Sept. 29, 1845, file 333, Maj. George H. Crosman, Records of Quartermasters, 1819-1905, Office of the Quartermaster General, RG 92.

30. Kieffer, *Maligned General,* 290; Smith and Judah, *Chronicles of the Gringos,* 358; Capt. John Sanders to Maj. Gen. Thomas S. Jesup, 2 July 1846, in "Mexican War Correspondence," *House Exec. Docs.*, 30th Cong., 1st sess., no. 60, vol. 1, serial 520, 734; Ford, *RIP Ford's Texas,* 458; Risch, *Quartermaster Support,* 261.

31. "Report of the Chief, Topographical Engineers, Nov. 22, 1847," *Senate Exec. Docs.*, 30th Cong., 1st sess., no. 1, vol. 1, serial 503, 672–75; Adrian George Trass, *From the Golden Gate to Mexico City: The U.S. Army Topographical Engineers in the Mexican War, 1846–1848,* 214–15; Risch, *Quartermaster Support,* 261.

32. Lt. George G. Meade to Mrs. Meade, Sept., 14, 1845 in Meade ed., *Life and Letters,* 1:25; Lt. Napoleon J. T. Dana to Mrs. Dana, Sept. 12, 1845, in Ferrell, ed., *Monterrey Is Ours!,* 9; Manning, "Mexican War Journal," 67; Paul Horgan, *Great River: The Rio Grande in North American History,* 2:712–13, 782; Graf, "Economic History," 1:192; Smith, *Mexican War Journal,* 29–30; "Report of the Quartermaster General, 1850," 325.

33. Smith, *Mexican War Journal,* 10–14, 216 n. 12.

34. The additional original Kenedy and King partners were Brownsville merchant Charles Stillman and river captain James O'Donnell. "Contracts, (1852)" *House Exec. Docs.,* 32d Cong., 2d sess., no. 21, serial 676, 7–8; Tom Lea, *The King Ranch,* 1:43–54, 56–58, 72–73; Ford, *RIP Ford's Texas,* 457–70; Webb, ed., *Handbook of Texas,* 1:946–47, 959; Tyler, ed., *New Handbook of Texas,* 3:1064, 1107–1108.

35. On the antebellum profits and postwar monopoly of Kenedy and King, see Graf, "Economic History," 4:59, 129, and Lea, *The King Ranch,* 1:75–76, 87–89, 247. Details on the yearly contracts are available in each year's "Report of the Quartermaster General of the Army," in the annual *Report of the Secretary of War,* and the yearly separate document usually labeled "Contracts with the War Department" in the *House of Representatives Executive Documents.*

36. "Report of the Quartermaster General, 1875," 280; "Report of the Quartermaster General, 1876," 283; Jimmy M. Skaggs, "Military Operations on the Cattle Trails," *Texas Military History* 6 (Summer, 1967): 137–48; Michael G. Webster, "Intrigue on the Rio Grande: The *Rio Bravo* Affair, 1875," *Southwestern Historical Quarterly* LXXIV (Oct., 1970): 149–64; Robert L. Robinson, "The U.S. Navy vs. Cattle Rustlers: The *U.S.S. Rio Bravo* on the Rio Grande, 1876–1879," *Military History of Texas and the Southwest* 15, no. 2 (1979): 43–52.

37. Kelly's contracts are from each year's "Report of the Quartermaster General of the Army," in the annual *Report of the Secretary of War* for 1881–1889. Kelly's 1886 contract and freight rates are found in "Report of the Quartermaster General, 1886," 484. On Kelly's background, see Kelly, *River of Lost Dreams,* 82–85, and Lea, *The King Ranch,* 1:251. The Bliss quote is from "Report of Brig. Gen. Z. R. Bliss, Aug. 22, 1895," *House Exec. Docs.,* 54th Cong., 1st sess., no. 2, vol. 3, serial 3370, (first quote) 484; Horgan, *Great River,* (second quote) 2:943.

38. "The Commerce of Brazos de St. Iago (1849)," *Senate Exec. Docs.,* 31st Cong., 1st sess., no. 69, serial 562, 3–10; "Contracts (1853)," 24–39.

39. Webb, ed., *Handbook of Texas,* 2:235; Tyler, ed., *New Handbook of Texas,* 4:834; "Contracts (1858)," 2–27; Woodward, "Internal Improvements," 161–82.

40. "Report of the Quartermaster General, 1886," 484–85; "Report of the Quartermaster General, 1887," 489; Baughman, *Charles Morgan,* 209, 233.

41. "Report of the Quartermaster General, 1851," 221. On transportation estimates and

the railroad, see "Report of the Quartermaster General, Nov. 13, 1858," *House Exec. Docs.,* 35th Cong., 2d sess., no. 2, pt. 2, serial 999, 798. The first and second quotes are from "Report of the Quartermaster General, Nov. 2, 1852," *House Exec. Docs.,* 32d Cong., 2d sess., no. 1, serial 674, 72.

42. Reed, *A History of the Texas Railroads,* 30–38, 53–65; Charles A. Potts, *Railroad Transportation in Texas,* Bulletin no. 119 (Austin: University of Texas, Mar. 1, 1909): 23–27; Thomas Lloyd Miller, *The Public Lands of Texas, 1519–1970,* 95–102; Swift, *Three Roads to Chihuahua,* 274; Webb, ed., *Handbook of Texas,* 3:771–73; Woodward, "Internal Improvements," 173–77; Lydia Spencer Lane, *I Married a Soldier: or, Old Days in the Army,* (quote) 79.

43. *Pacific Railroad Reports,* 13 vols., 9:79–80; "Reports of Explorations and Surveys to Ascertain the Most Practicable and Economic Route for a Railroad from the Mississippi River to the Pacific Ocean [1855]," *House Exec. Docs.,* 33d Cong., 2d sess., no. 91, serial 801, 64, 79–80; William H. Goetzmann, *Army Exploration in the American West, 1803–1863,* 291–95.

44. "Report On Transcontinental Railways, 1883, by Col. O. M. Poe," *House Exec. Docs.,* 48th Cong., 1st sess., no. 1, pt. 2, vol. 2, serial 2182, 253–311; Reed, *A History of the Texas Railroads,* 193–94, 197–98, 311–21; Potts, *Railroad Transportation in Texas,* 101; Neill C. Wilson and Frank Taylor, *Southern Pacific,* 77; Swift, *Three Roads to Chihuahua,* 273–307; Baughman, *Charles Morgan,* 187–88, 208; Webb, ed., *Handbook of Texas,* 1:665,2:216–17,3:771–73; Santleben, *Texas Pioneer,* 278–79; AAG Maj. J. C. Martin to Commanders, Fort Clark and Fort Davis, Apr. 20, 1881, Letters Sent by Headquarters Department of Texas, vol. 16–19, Jan. 1, 1881–Dec. 30, 1882, microfilm no. M1114, roll 6, Letters Sent by Headquarters Department of Texas, 1870–1894 and 1897–1898, RG 393, Records of U.S. Army Continental Commands, 1821–1920.

45. On railroad rates, see "Report On Transcontinental Railways, 1883, by Col. O. M. Poe," 253; Reed, *A History of the Texas Railroads,* 608, 619. On Forts Clark and Davis, see "Report of the Quartermaster General, 1875," 275–80; "Report of the Quartermaster General, 1878," 360–61; "Report of the Quartermaster General, 1884," 574–75; "Report of the Quartermaster General, 1888," 512, 516.

46. Miller, *Public Lands,* 95–105.

47. "Report of the Quartermaster General, Oct. 11, 1866," *House Exec. Docs.,* 39th Cong., 2d sess., no. 1, serial 1285, 111–12; "Report of the Quartermaster General, 1868," 831, 834–35; "Report of the Quartermaster General, 1869," 149, 244–45; "Report of the Quartermaster General, 1870," 149, 244–45; "Report of the Quartermaster General, 1871," 132; "Report of the Quartermaster General, 1873," 166, 189.

48. James Larson, "Memoirs," Arthur W. Arndt Collection, 2L158, Center for American History, University of Texas at Austin, (first quote) 218; McConnell, *Five Years a Cavalryman,* (second quote) 28–29; Brit Allan Storey, ed., "An Army Officer In Texas,

1866–1867," *Southwestern Historical Quarterly* LXXII (Oct., 1968): (third quote) 248; Frederick V. Abbot, *History of the Class of 'Seventy-Nine at the U.S. Military Academy*, 128; Douglas C. McChristian, ed., *Garrison Tangles in the Friendless Tenth: The Journal of First Lieutenant John Bigelow Jr., Fort Davis, Texas*, 5; Mrs. Orsemus B. Boyd, *Cavalry Life in Tent and Field*, 304.

49. "Report of the Quartermaster General, 6 Oct. 1883," *House Exec. Docs.*, 48th Cong., 1st sess., no. 1, pt. 2, vol. 2, serial 2182, 335, 549; "Report of the Quartermaster General, 1884," 55, 477; "Report of the Quartermaster General, 1885," 459; "Report of the Quartermaster General, 1889," 418.

50. Helen Fuller Davis, "An account of a 10th Cavalry March with Gen. B. H. Grierson from Ft. Davis to Ft. Grant," as printed in Shirley Anne Leckie, ed., *The Colonel's Lady on the Western Frontier: The Correspondence of Alice Kirk Grierson*, 158–60.

51. "Report of the General of the Army, Nov. 6, 1871," *House Exec. Docs.*, 42d Cong., 2d sess., no. 1, pt. 2, serial 1503, 21; "Report of the General of the Army, 1882," *House Exec. Docs.*, 47th Cong., 2d sess., no. 1, pt. 2, vol. 2, serial 2091, 10, 12.

CHAPTER 4.
FORAGE: CORN, HAY, AND OATS

1. On the forage allowance, see "Report of the Quartermaster General, 1851," 241; General Orders no. 22, May 27, 1852, General Orders no. 29, July 26, 1852, General Orders no. 20, Aug. 6, 1860, Adjutant General's Office, War Department, RG 94; Risch, *Quartermaster Support*, 316.

2. For forage weights, see "Report of the Quartermaster General, 1851," 249; "Contracts (1853)," 24, 27, 29, 35; "Report of the Quartermaster General, 1878," 379; Kieffer, *Maligned General*, 283. For the comparison of forage costs, see "Report of the General-in-Chief, Nov. 30, 1850," *House Exec. Docs.*, 31st Cong., 2d sess., no. 1, serial 595, 110.

3. On Mexican War imports of forage, see "The Commerce of Brazos de St. Iago (1849)," 16–23; Kieffer, *Maligned General*, 282–83. On importing oats, see Bvt. Maj. Gen. Persifor F. Smith to Secretary of War Conrad, Oct. 6, 1851, "Letter Book," Smith Papers. For 1851 forage purchases, see "Report of the Quartermaster General, 1851," 257; "Contracts—War Department (1851)," *House Exec. Docs.*, 32d Cong., 1st sess., no. 23, serial 640, 15–33. For an excellent general analysis of farming in the 1850s, see Lowe and Campbell, *Planters and Plain Folk*.

4. Inflation rates and average national corn prices are from the Bureau of the Census, "Series E 52–63, Wholesale Price Indexes (Warren and Pearson), by Major Product Groups: 1749–1890," and "Series K 502–16, Corn, Wheat, Oats, and Barley—Acreage, Production, Price, and Stocks: 1839 to 1970," and "Series K 550–63, Hay, Cotton,

Cottonseed, Shorn Wool, and Tobacco—Acreage, Production, and Price: 1790–1970," in *Historical Statistics of the United States,* 1:201, 512, 518.

5. In 1850 Texas produced 6.9 million bushels of corn and 8,354 tons of hay. The thirteen counties were Comal, Guadalupe, Bexar, Medina, San Patricio, Goliad, Travis, Hays, Calwell, Bastrop, Williamson, Milam, and Gonzales. James D. B. De Bow, *Statistical View of the United States: Being a Compendium of the Seventh Census,* 515–19; Census Office, *Abstract of the Eleventh Census: 1890,* 87, 100. On Fort Davis, see Crimmins, ed., "Colonel Mansfield's Report," 354–55. On the purchase of corn from Mexico, see "Report of the Quartermaster General, 1850," 322. On the Chihuahua embargo, see "Reports From the Department of Texas," June 2, 1854," *Senate Exec. Docs.,* 34th Cong., 1st sess., no. 1, serial 811, (quote) 54; Wooster, *History of Fort Davis,* 298.

6. Joseph C. G. Kennedy, *Agriculture of the United States In 1860: Complied from the Original Returns of the Eighth Census,* 2:148–50; Army purchases are in "Contracts . . . 1860," 2–47.

7. On 1858 contracts, see Lt. Herman Biggs, Fort Inge, Tex., to Quartermaster General Thomas S. Jesup, July 22, 1858, Quartermaster General's Office, "Letters Received," RG 92; "Contracts (1858)," 2–27. On the crop failure of 1860, see Maj. David H. Vinton to Quartermaster General Thomas S. Jesup, Apr. 10, 1860, Quartermaster General's Office, "Letters Received," RG 92. For numbers of contractors, see "Report of the Quartermaster General" in the annual *Report of the Secretary of War,* 1849–1860.

8. For 1870–1890 corn and hay production figures see *Abstract of the Eleventh Census: 1890,* 87, 100; Francis A. Walker, *A Compendium of the Ninth Census, June 1, 1870,* 781; Census Office, *A Compendium of the Tenth Census,* 1:841. Army purchase figures are from "Report of the Quartermaster General, 1870," 187; RG 92, Entry 1245 "Register of Contracts 1881–1883," vol. 1, 1, 2, 17, 23, 34, 50–56; "Report of the Quartermaster General, 1890," 548, 749.

9. For average annual Texan consumption ratios, see Lowe and Campbell, *Planters and Plain Folk,* 172; Campbell and Lowe, "Some Economic Aspects," 351–78. For Texas corn production and population figures 1850–1890, see Wooton, ed., *Comprehensive History of Texas,* 762, 764. Average army strength in Texas 1850–1900 is calculated from the annual "Report of the Secretary of War, 1850–1900" in the *House of Representatives Executive Documents.*

10. On Julius Sanders, see "Population Schedules of Uvalde County, Texas, 1860, Eighth Census of the United States," microfilm no. M653, roll 1307; "Contracts (1854)," 12; "A statement of contracts . . . 1857," 14; Thomas Tyree Smith, *Fort Inge: Sharps, Spurs, and Sabers on the Texas Frontier, 1849–1869,* 48–49.

11. On Juan Galvan, see RG 92, Entry 1242 "Register of Contracts 1871–1876," vol. 2, no. 1, 34–37. On Middleton Tate Johnson, see "Contracts (1852)," 2–22; "Contracts (1853)," 24–37; "A statement of contracts . . . 1857," 1–35; "Contracts (1858)," 2–27; Webb, ed.,

Handbook of Texas, 1:916–17; Tyler, ed., *New Handbook of Texas,* 3:959–60; Oliver Knight, *Fort Worth,* 11, 20, 32, 43–51; Mildred P. Mayhall, "Camp Cooper—First Federal Fort in Texas to Fall, 1861, and Events Preceding Its Fall," *Texana* 5 (Winter, 1967): 318–42.

12. The contractor was James L. Millspaugh, who was also the post trader and who was prominent in the development of San Angelo. John Neilson, "'I Long to Return to Fort Concho': Acting Assistant Surgeon Samuel Smith's Letters from the Texas Military Frontier, 1878–1879," *Military History of the West* 24 (Fall, 1994): 122–86, (quote) 164; J. Evetts Haley, *Fort Concho and the Texas Frontier,* 303–307, Martin L. Crimmins, "Camp Pena Colorado, Texas," *West Texas Historical and Scientific Society* Bulletin no. 6 (Dec., 1935): 8–22.

13. The failed contract went to George W. Crutcher of Dallas. "Report of the Office of the Chief Quartermaster, Department of Texas, Aug. 13, 1888," microfilm no. M689, roll 662, Letters Received, Adjutant General's Office, 1881–1889, Records of the U.S. Army Adjutant General's Office, 1780–1917, RG 94.

14. Crimmins, "Camp Pena Colorado," 15; Robert G. Carter, *The Old Sergeant's Story: Winning the West from the Indians and Bad Men in 1870 to 1876,* 126–27.

CHAPTER 5.
REAL ESTATE: FORT LEASING, PURCHASE, BUILDING, AND REPAIR

1. On the heritage of Spanish and Mexican real estate laws see Tijerina, *Tejanos and Texas,* 119–21; Judge Advocate General, *U.S. Military Reservations* 370–83; "Report of the Quartermaster General, 1888," 468–69; Miller, *Public Lands,* vii.

2. Crimmins, ed., "W. G. Freeman's Report," LI:168; Jack D. Eaton, *Excavations at the Alamo Shrine (Mission San Antonio de Valero),* Special Report no. 10, 10, 16; Ahlborn, *San Antonio Missions,* 31; McConnell, *Five Years a Cavalryman,* (quote) 36.

3. "Statements showing the contracts . . . 1856," 9; Tyler, ed., *New Handbook of Texas,* 2:1117, 6:698.

4. "Statements of contracts and purchases (1850)," 14; "Contracts—War Department (1851)," 22; "Contracts . . . 1860," 6.

5. On Smith, see Bvt. Maj. Gen. Persifor F. Smith to Division AAG Lt. Col. W. W. S. Bliss, Mar. 22, 1852, "Letter Book," Smith Papers. On Fort Clark, see "Contracts (1852), 15. For Fort Chadbourne, see "Statements showing the contracts . . . 1856," 25. On Fort Inge, see "Contracts (1853)," 24. For Fort Davis, see "A statement of contracts . . . 1857," 2; Wooster, *History of Fort Davis,* 139–40. On Camp Hudson, see "War Department—Contracts (1859)," 10. For Fort Duncan, see "Contracts . . . 1860," 17; Crimmins, ed., "W. G. Freeman's Report," LII:444–45 n. 68.

6. "Report of the Quartermaster General, 1888," 468–69; Clayton W. Williams, *Texas' Last Frontier: Fort Stockton and the Trans-Pecos, 1861-1895,* 173.

7. On Fort Quitman, see George Ruhlen, "Quitman's Owners: A Sidelight on Frontier Realty. " *Password* 5 (Apr., 1960): 54–63. On Ringgold Barracks, see "Contracts (1853)," 38; "Contracts (1854)," 22; "Affairs in the Department of Texas, Aug. 30, 1860," *Senate Exec. Docs.,* 36th Cong., 2d sess., no. 1, pt. 2, serial 1079, 27–30; Judge Advocate General, *U.S. Military Reservations,* 381.

8. Cashion, *Texas Frontier,* 133–36, 161–67; Eula Haskew, "Stribling and Kirkland of Fort Griffin," *West Texas Historical Association Year Book* 32 (Oct., 1956): 55–69.

9. "Contracts (1853)," 39; "Contracts . . . 1860," 31; "Report of the Quartermaster General, 1875," 196. "Report of the Quartermaster General, 1888," 468; James E. Ivey, Thomas Medlin and Jack D. Eaton, "An Initial Archaeological Assessment of Areas Proposed for Modification at Fort McIntosh, Webb County, Texas." Archaeological Survey Report no. 23, Center for Archaeological Research, the University of Texas at San Antonio, 1977, 2–3.

10. Timmons, "Merchants and Military," 58–59; Pingenot, "The Great Wagon Train Expedition of 1850," 186, 216.

11. "Report of the Quartermaster General, 1854," 73–74; "Report of the Chief Engineer, Nov. 24, 1857," *House Exec. Docs.,* 35th Cong., 1st sess., no. 2, serial 943, 186; "Report of the Quartermaster General, 1871," 140–41; "Report of the Quartermaster General, 1873," 116; "Report of the Quartermaster General, 1874," 118–19; "Report of the Quartermaster General, 1875," 196.

12. "Report of the Quartermaster General, 1876," 124; "Report of the Quartermaster General, 1877," 190–91; "Report of the Quartermaster General, 1878," 260–61; "Report of the Quartermaster General, Sept. 30, 1880," *House Exec. Docs.,* 46th Cong., 3d sess., no. 1, pt. 2, vol. 2, serial 1952, 239; "Report of the Quartermaster General, 1883," 409; "Report of the Quartermaster General, 1889," 735; "Report of the Quartermaster General, Sept. 26, 1894," *House Exec. Docs.,* 53d Cong., 3d sess., no. 1, pt. 2, serial 3295, 254, 318.

13. "Report of the Quartermaster General, 1875," 196; "Report of the Quartermaster General, 1876," 124; "Report of the Quartermaster General, 1877," 190–91; "Report of the Quartermaster General, 1878," 260–61; "Report of the Quartermaster General, 1881," 230–31; "Report of the Quartermaster General, Oct. 6, 1883," 409; "Report of the Quartermaster General, 1885," 459; "Report of the Quartermaster General, 1895," 277; Judge Advocate General, *U.S. Military Reservations,* 374–76; Sides, *Fort Brown Historical,* 119–24.

14. Judge Advocate General, *U.S. Military Reservations,* 382–84; "Report of the Quartermaster General, 1883," 409; "Annual Report of the Secretary of War, 5 Dec. 1887," *House Exec. Docs.,* 50th Cong., 1st sess., no. 1, pt. 2, vol. 2, serial 2533, 46.

15. Judge Advocate General, *U.S. Military Reservations,* 373–74; "Report of the Quartermaster General, 1879," 227; "Report of Brig. Gen. Stanley, Sept. 4, 1886" *House Exec. Docs.,* 49th Cong., 2d sess., no. 1, pt. 2, vol. 2, serial 2461, 127; "Report of the Quartermaster General, 1890," 678; "Report of the Quartermaster General, Oct. 1, 1896," *House Exec. Docs.,* 54th Cong., 2d sess., no. 2, vol. 2, serial 3478, 279; "Report of the Quartermaster General, 1900," 417; Christian, "Sword and Plowshare," 20, 36, 52, 55, 58–69; Metz, *Desert Army,* 60–70.

16. "Report of the Quartermaster General, 1888," 438; "Report of the Quartermaster General, 1894," 254, 318; "Report of the Quartermaster General, 1900," 417; Metz, *Desert Army,* 70.

17. "Report of the Quartermaster General, 1888," 468; Judge Advocate General, *U.S. Military Reservations,* 370–83.

18. Crimmins, ed., "W. G. Freeman's Report," LI:(first quote) 252, (third quote) 449; Dabney Herndon Maury, *Recollections of A Virginian in the Mexican, Indian, and Civil Wars,* (second quote) 81.

19. Bvt. Maj. Gen. Persifor F. Smith to Bvt. Lt. Col. William W. S. Bliss, May 3, 1852 (quote), "Letter Book," Smith Papers. For an excellent overview of the construction of Texas forts see Robert Wooster's chapter titled "Building a Frontier Fort," in Wooster, *Soldiers, Sutlers, and Settlers,* 26–44.

20. Turnley, *Reminiscences,* (first quote) 116, (second quote) 121. Johnson, *A Soldier's Reminiscences,* (third quote) 77.

21. Cornelia and Garland Crook, "Fort Lincoln, Texas," *Texas Military History* 4 (Fall, 1964): 151; Crimmins, ed., "W. G. Freeman's Report," LIII:204, 312, 314, 318; Crimmins, ed., "Colonel Mansfield's Report," 233, (quote) 237.

22. General Orders no. 13, Feb. 28, 1851 (first and second quotes), General Orders no. 7, Apr. 11, 1859, Adjutant General's Office, War Department, RG 94; Assistant Adjutant General Capt. George Deas to Bvt. Lt. Col. John J. Abercrombie, Fort Phantom Hill, Dec. 8, 1851, "Letter Book," Smith Papers; "Report of the Commissary General, Oct. 25, 1855," *Senate Exec. Docs.,* 34th Cong., 1st sess., no. 1, serial 811, 22; Risch, *Quartermaster Support,* 304; Kieffer, *Maligned General,* 303.

23. Thomas T. Smith, ed., *A Dose of Frontier Soldiering: The Memoirs of Corporal E. A. Bode, Frontier Regular Infantry, 1877–1882,* (first quote) 65; A Late Captain of Infantry (Robert E. Patterson), *Hints Bearing on the U.S. Army with an Aim at the Adaptation, Availability, Efficiency and Economy Thereof,* (second quote) 26; Crimmins, ed., "W. G. Freeman's Report," LI:(third quote) 256, LIII:(fourth quote) 73.

24. Johnson, *A Soldier's Reminiscences,* (quote) 78; Crimmins, ed., "Colonel Mansfield's Report," 234–35, 244; David A. Clary, ed., "'I Am Already Quite a Texan': Albert J. Myer's Letters from Texas, 1854–1856," *Southwestern Historical Quarterly* LXXXII (July,

1978): 34; (quote) Smith to Adjutant General Jones, Mar. 22, 1852, "Letter Book," Smith Papers.

25. Crimmins, ed., "W. G. Freeman's Report," LII:73, LIII:312, 316.

26. Crimmins, ed., "W. G. Freeman's Report," LII:(first quote) 446, (second quote, original spelling) LIII:76; Caleb Coker and Janet G. Humphrey, "The Texas Frontier in 1850: Dr. Ebenezer Swift and the View from Fort Martin Scott," *Southwestern Historical Quarterly* XCVI (Jan., 1993): (third quote, original emphasis), 402; Lane, *I Married a Soldier,* (fourth quote) 30.

27. Anne A. Fox, "Mission Builders: Traces of Texas Archaeology," in *The Spanish Missionary Heritage of the United States,* eds., Dr. Howard Benoist and Sr. María Carolina Flores, C.P., 119–21; Graham, "Federal Fort Architecture," 165–88; Daniel E. Fox, *Traces of Texas History: Archeological Evidence of the Past 450 Years,* 239–84.

28. Maury, *Recollections,* (first quote) 76; Lane, *I Married a Soldier,* (second quote) 37.

29. McConnell, *Five Years a Cavalryman,* (quote) 53. On the Spanish colonial origins of *jacal* construction and its traditional use in Texas frontier buildings, see Fox, "Mission Builders," 119–21; Graham, "Federal Fort Architecture," 165–88; Daniel E. Fox, *Traces of Texas History,* 188, 265, 273, 275, 334, 339; Terry G. Jordan, *Texas Log Buildings: A Folk Architecture,* 4, 27, 177, 184.

30. Crimmins, ed., "W. G. Freeman's Report," LIII:203–204.

31. "Report of the Quartermaster General, 1851," 260–61, 272; "Contracts—War Department (1851)," 29.

32. Crimmins, ed., "W. G. Freeman's Report," LIII:207, 316, 453.

33. "Report of the Quartermaster General, 1851," 270, 273–75, 278, 286–88; *Texas State Gazette,* Oct. 6, 1849, 55; Lt. George H. Steuart to Headquarters, 8th Department, Aug. 12, 1851, "Fort Inge" File, Quartermaster Records, Letters Received, Office of the Quartermaster General, RG 92; Crimmins, ed., "W. G. Freeman's Report," LIII:461.

34. "Report of the Quartermaster General, 1851," 280, 283–85, 287–88; *Texas State Gazette,* Dec. 22, 1849, 144.

35. Steuart to Headquarters, 8th Department, Aug. 12, 1851; "Report of the Quartermaster General, 1851," 271–72, 274, 279, 277, 287–88; Crimmins, ed., "W. G. Freeman's Report," LIII:447, 452, 458; John H. Hatcher, "Fort Phantom Hill," *Texas Military History* 3 (Fall, 1963): 155.

36. "Report of the Quartermaster General, 1851," 279, (quote) 280, 283–86.

37. Crimmins, ed., "Colonel Mansfield's Report," 122–48, 215–57, 351–87.

38. On Fort Inge, see Steuart to Headquarters, 8th Department, Aug. 12, 1851; "Report of the Quartermaster General, 1851," 279; Smith, "Fort Inge and the Texas Frontier Economy," 143. On other posts, see "Letter from the Secretary of War Showing Expenditures for Construction and Repairs of Buildings at Each Fort and Military Post

in Texas, Feb. 9, 1872," *House Exec. Docs.,* 42d Cong., 2d sess., no. 124, serial 1513, 1–3.

39. "Letter from the Secretary of War . . . Feb. 9, 1872," 2–3.

40. Turnley, *Reminiscences,* 127–29; Crimmins, ed., "Colonel Mansfield's Report," 250, 253, (quote) 254; Graham, "Federal Fort Architecture," 183, 188.

41. Texas expenditures are calculated from each year's "Report of the Quartermaster General of the Army," in the annual *Report of the Secretary of War,* 1849–1861.

42. McConnell, *Five Years a Cavalryman,* (quote) 104.

43. "Report of the Quartermaster General, 1868," 862–64; McConnell, *Five Years a Cavalryman,* (quote) 91, 96–100.

44. McConnell, *Five Years a Cavalryman,* (quote) 144.

45. "Report of the Quartermaster General, 1868," 871; McConnell, *Five Years a Cavalryman,* (quote) 159; Wooster, *Soldiers, Sutlers, and Settlers,* 29.

46. "Report of the Quartermaster General, 1868," 864, 865–66, 867; Wooster, *Soldiers, Sutlers, and Settlers,* 29; Williams, *Texas' Last Frontier,* 104.

47. "Report of the Quartermaster General, 1868," 814, 871; "Letter from the Secretary of War . . . Feb. 9, 1872," 2–3; Wooster, *History of Fort Davis,* 190, (quote) 191, 192.

48. "Report of the Quartermaster General, 1868," 864–65.

49. Notson, "Fort Concho," 128, 130, (quote) 141; Quartermaster General's Office, *Outline Description . . . 1871,* 41–42; Headquarters, U.S. Army, "Descriptive Book of the District of Texas . . . 1868," folio 26; Inspector General's Office, *Outline Descriptions of the Posts and Stations of Troops in the Geographic Divisions and Departments of the United States (1872),* 178.

50. Notson, "Fort Concho," (quote) 137. For the influence of post commanders on fort construction patterns, see Graham, "Federal Fort Architecture," 172.

51. "Report of the Quartermaster General, 1875," 195.

52. Boyd, *Cavalry Life,* (quote) 249–250.

53. "Report of the Quartermaster General, 1870," 154; "Report of the Quartermaster General, 1871," 207; "Report of the Quartermaster General, Oct. 10, 1872," *House Exec. Docs.,* 42d Cong., 3d sess., no. 1, pt. 2, serial 1558, 148; "Report of the Secretary of War, Nov. 1, 1872," *House Exec. Docs.,* 42d Cong., 3d sess., no. 1, pt. 2, serial 1558, 6; "Report of the General of the Army, Nov. 1, 1872," *House Exec. Docs.,* 42d Cong., 3d sess., no. 1, pt. 2, serial 1558, (quote) 36; Mary Olivia Handy, *History of Fort Sam Houston,* 27–40.

54. "Report of the Secretary of War, 1873," 10–11; "Report of the Quartermaster General, 1873," 115; "Report of the Quartermaster General, 1874," (quote) 117; "Report of the Quartermaster General, 1875," 186, 195-196; "Report of the Quartermaster General, 1876," 123; "Report of the Quartermaster General, 1877," 220–26; Handy, *History of Fort Sam Houston,* 38–40.

55. "Report of the Quartermaster General, 1877," 188–89, 222; "Report of the Quarter-

master General, 1878," 260–61; "Report of the Quartermaster General, 1879," 227; Cagle, *Quadrangle,* 28–35; Tyler, ed., *New Handbook of Texas,* 2:1117.

56. "Report of the Quartermaster General, 1871," 207; "Report of the Quartermaster General, 1873," 114; "Report of the Quartermaster General, 1874," 117.

57. "Annual Report, Texas, 1880," microfilm no. M666, roll 589, Letters Received by the Office of the Adjutant General (Main Series), 1871–1880, Records of the U.S. Army Adjutant General's Office, 1780–1917, RG 94. (Hereafter cited as Annual Report, Texas, 1880.)

58. "Report of the Quartermaster General, 1884," 418–19.

59. "Report of the Quartermaster General, 1884," 419, 423; "Report of the Quartermaster General, 1885," 456; "Report of the Quartermaster General, 1886," 324; "Report of Brig. Gen. Stanley, Aug. 27, 1887," *House Exec. Docs.,* 50th Cong., 1st sess., no. 1, vol. 2, serial 2533, 136; "Report of the Quartermaster General, 1887," 362–67.

60. "Report of Brig. Gen. Stanley, 1887," (quote) 135.

61. Andrea Gerstle, Thomas C. Kelly, and Cristi Assad, *The Fort Sam Houston Project: An Archaeological and Historical Assessment,* 319; "Report of Brig. Gen. Stanley, 1887," 136; "Report of the Quartermaster General, 1887," 362–67; "Report of the Quartermaster General, 1889," 342, 485, 582; "Report of the Quartermaster General, 1890," 672; "Annual Report, Texas, 1888," microfilm no. M689, roll 662, Letters Received by the Office of the Adjutant General, Records of the U.S. Army Adjutant General's Office, 1780–1917, RG 94 (hereafter cited as Annual Report, Texas, 1888); "Report of the Quartermaster General, Oct. 3, 1891," *House Exec. Docs.,* 52d Cong., 1st sess., no. 1, pt. 2, serial 2921, 340; Cagle, *Quadrangle,* 34.

62. "Report of the Quartermaster General, Oct. 3, 1891," *House Exec. Docs.,* 52d Cong., 1st sess., no. 1, pt. 2, serial 2921, 259; "Report of the Quartermaster General, Oct. 1, 1892," *House Exec. Docs.,* 52d Cong., 2d sess., no. 1, pt. 2, serial 3077, 271, 259; Christian, "Sword and Plowshare," 70–72.

63. "Report of the Quartermaster General, Oct. 3, 1891," *House Exec. Docs.,* 52d Cong., 1st sess., no. 1, pt. 2, serial 2921, 259; "Report of the Quartermaster General, Oct. 1, 1892," *House Exec. Docs.,* 52d Cong., 2d sess., no. 1, pt. 2, serial 3077, 271, 259; "Report of the Quartermaster General, Oct. 1, 1897," *House Exec. Docs.,* 55th Cong., 2d sess., no. 2, vol. 2, serial 3630, 335, 361.

64. Robert Wooster, *Nelson A. Miles and the Twilight of the Frontier Army,* 210–11; "Report of the Quartermaster General, Oct. 31, 1898," *House Exec. Docs.,* 55th Cong., 3d sess., no. 2, vol. 2, serial 3744, 396, 491; "Report of the Quartermaster General, Oct. 16, 1899," *House Exec. Docs.,* 56th Cong., 1st sess., no. 2, vol. 3, serial 3900, 166, 259; "Report of the Quartermaster General, 1900," 283, 335, 387–88; Alperin, *Custodians of the Coast,* 178–81.

65. "Report of the General of the Army, 1882," (first quote) 10–12, 13; "Report of the

General of the Army, Nov. 3, 1881," *House Exec. Docs.,* 47th Cong., 1st sess., no. 1, pt. 2, vol. 2, serial 2010, 35.

66. On troop strengths and stations, see "Report of the Major General Commanding the Army, Oct. 10, 1896," *House Exec. Docs.,* 54th Cong., 2d sess., no. 2, vol. 2, serial 3478, 84, 90–93.

CHAPTER 6.
ADDITIONAL EXPENSES: FUEL, RATIONS, BEEF, HORSES AND MULES, MILITARY CEMETERIES, AND SUTLERS AND POST TRADERS

1. Circular, Mar. 3, 1845, Brig. Gen. Zachary Taylor, Entry 333, Maj. George H. Crosman, Records of Quartermasters, 1819–1905, Office of the Quartermaster General, RG 92; "Contracts (1852)," 2–22.

2. For the standard of a cord, see "Contracts (1858)," 17. For the fuel allowance, see "Report of the Quartermaster General, Oct. 9, 1882," *House Exec. Docs.,* 47th Cong., 2d sess., no. 1, pt. 2, vol. 2, serial 2091, 386, 436–37.

3. Amounts are calculated from a survey of each year's "Report of the Quartermaster General of the Army" in the annual *Report of the Secretary of War,* 1849–1900, and from RG 92, Records of the Office of the Quartermaster General, Entry 1245, "Register of Contracts, 1871–1912," and from the annual *Senate* and *House of Representatives Executive Documents,* "War Department Contracts."

4. On Fort Inge and Fort Terrett, see Crimmins, ed. "W. G. Freeman's Report, LIII:74, 318. On 1871 contracts, see RG 92, Entry 1242 "Register of Contracts 1871–1876, vol. 2, no. 1," 34–37.

5. Charles Judson Crane, *The Experiences of a Colonel of Infantry* (New York: The Knickerbocker Press, 1923), 79, (quote) 109.

6. Quote is from "Report of Brig. Gen. Stanley, 1887," 136; "Report of the Inspector General of the Army, Nov. 4, 1896," *House Exec. Docs.,* 54th Cong., 2d sess., no. 2, serial 3478, 119; "Report of the Quartermaster General, 1885," 400; "Report of the Quartermaster General, 1890," 548.

7. On the cost of the ration, see "Report of the Commissary General, Nov. 18, 1856," *Senate Exec. Docs.,* 34th Cong., 3d sess., no. 5, serial 876, 258–59; "Report of the Commissary General of Subsistence, Oct. 20, 1868," *House Exec. Docs.,* 40th Cong., 3d sess., no. 1, serial 1367, 961; "Report of the Secretary of War (1874)," *House Exec. Docs.,* 43d Cong., 2d sess., no. 1, pt. 2, serial 1635, 223; "Report of the Commissary General of Subsistence, Oct. 7, 1882," *House Exec. Docs.,* 47th Cong., 2d sess., no. 1, pt. 2., vol. 2, serial 2091, 465. For details on the ration of the 1870s, see "Report of the Commissary General of Subsistence, 10 Oct. 1881," *House Exec. Doc.,* 47th Cong., 1st sess., no.

I, pt. 2, vol. 2, serial 2010, 484–85. On hunting and fishing, see Johnson, *A Soldier's Reminiscences*, 77, 82; Maury, *Recollections*, 93–94, 97–98; Lane, *I Married a Soldier*, 31; Smith, ed., *A Dose of Frontier Soldiering*, 175; Boyd, *Cavalry Life*, 263–64; Leckie, ed., *The Colonel's Lady*, 78–79, 82, 86. On ice cream from hail, see Johnson, *A Soldier's Reminiscences*, 87. For an example of the authorized whiskey ration, see General Orders no. 9, June 23, 1857, Adjutant General's Office, War Department, RG 94. For a detailed examination of a post commissary and ration operation, see Douglas C. McChristian, "The Commissary Sergeant: His Life at Fort Davis," *Military History of Texas and the Southwest* 14, no. 1, (1978): 21–32. For the most current and detailed study of the post–Civil War ration, see David L. Wheeler and William H. Landis, "'It is beef every day . . . ': The Army Ration and the Enlisted Man, 1865–1890," *Military History of the West* 26 (Fall, 1996): 129–57.

8. Col. Henry Whiting to Col. Henry Stanton, Nov. 5, 1846, "Mexican War Correspondence," *House Exec. Docs.*, 30th Cong., 1st sess., no. 60, vol. 1, serial 520, 683–84; Smith and Judah, *Chronicles of the Gringos*, 364, 376; Risch, *Quartermaster Support*, 247.

9. On Brazos Santiago in 1848, see "The Commerce of Brazos de St. Iago (1849)," 24–29. For 1856, see Crimmins, ed., "Colonel Mansfield's Report," 137.

10. "Contracts (1853)," 24–39; "Contracts (1854)," 2–23; "List of contracts (1855)," 2–26; "Statements showing the contracts made . . . 1856," 2–32.

11. "Report of the Commissary General, Nov. 2, 1849," *Senate Exec. Docs.*, 31st Cong., 1st sess., no. 1, serial 549, 204–205. "Report of the Commissary General, 1855," 169–70; *Texas State Gazette*, Sept. 1, 1849, 15.

12. "Report of the Commissary General, 1855," 169–70. "List of contracts (1855)," 44; "Statements showing the contracts made . . . 1856," 36; "A statement of contracts . . . 1857," 40; "Contracts (1858)," 28–29; "War Department—Contracts (1859)," 24–25; "Contracts . . . 1860," 49; Timmons, "Merchants and Military," 55. For Texas flour prices in 1856, see Crimmins, ed., "Colonel Mansfield's Report," 355, 375; French, *Two Wars*, (quote) 116–17.

13. General Orders no. 1, Jan. 8, 1851, General Orders no. 3, Feb. 9, 1854, General Orders no. 20, Aug. 6, 1860, Adjutant General's Office, War Department, RG 94; "Report of the General-in-Chief, Nov. 22, 1852," *House Exec. Docs.*, 32d Cong., 2d sess., no. 1, serial 674, 35; Robert M. Utley, *Frontiersmen In Blue: The United States Army and the Indian, 1848–1865*, 36–37; Frazer, *Forts and Supplies*, 57, 70; Edward M. Coffman, *The Old Army: A Portrait of the American Army in Peacetime, 1784–1898*, 168–71; Crimmins, ed., "W. G. Freeman's Report," LIV:210; Wooster, *History of Fort Davis*, 199, 289.

14. "Report of the Commissary General of Subsistence, Oct. 9, 1875," *House Exec. Docs.*, 44th Cong., 1st sess., no. 1, pt. 2, serial 1674, 309–10; "Report of the Commissary General of Subsistence (1876)," *House Exec. Docs.*, 44th Cong., 2d sess., no. 1, pt. 2,

serial 1742, 301–302; "Report of the Commissary General of Subsistence (1877)," *House Exec. Docs.*, 45th Cong., 2d sess., no. 1, pt. 2, serial 1794, 340; "Report of the Commissary General of Subsistence, Oct. 8, 1883," *House Exec. Docs.*, 48th Cong., 1st sess., no. 1, pt. 2, vol. 2, serial 2182, 586; Donald W. Whisenhunt, "Frontier Military Life at Fort Richardson, Texas," *West Texas Historical Association Year Book* 42 (Oct., 1966): 21; McChristian, "The Commissary Sergeant," 27; Wheeler and Landis, "'It is beef every day,'" 147, 156.

15. McConnell, *Five Years a Cavalryman*, (first quote) 141–42; Ike Moore, *The Life and Diary of Reading W. Black*, (diary quotes) 60, 79, 88; Santleben, *Texas Pioneer*, 148; "Report of the Inspector General, Nov. 7, 1887," *House Exec. Docs.*, 50th Cong., 1st sess., no. 1, vol. 2, serial 2533, 110.

16. Moore, *Reading W. Black*, 79.

17. Crook and Crook, "Fort Lincoln, Texas," 145–61.

18. "The contracts made . . . 1849," 38–40; "Statements of contracts and purchases (1850)," 9–10; "Contracts—War Department (1851)," 11–13; "Contracts (1852)," 23–25; "Contracts (1853)," 13–14; "Contracts (1854)," 35; "List of contracts (1855)," 41–42; "Statements showing the contracts made . . . 1856," 37–38; "A statement of contracts . . . 1857," 38–40; "Contracts (1858)," 28–30; "War Department-Contracts (1859)," 24–26; "Contracts . . . 1860," 48–49. On Louis Martin's background, see Fox, *Traces of Texas History*, 221–22; Tyler, ed., *New Handbook of Texas*, 4:528. On total Texas cattle for the census of 1860, see Census Office, *A Compendium of the Tenth Census*, 1:679.

19. On the purchase of stolen beef from Comanches, see Smith, *Frontier Defense in the Civil War*, 70. On cattle stolen in south Texas, see Jerry D. Thompson, *Mexican Texans in the Union Army*, 22. For Texas total cattle numbers, see Census Office, *A Compendium of the Tenth Census*, 1:679. Average fresh beef prices are from each years "Report of the Commissary General of Subsistence," 1866–1890 and Miller, *Soldiers and Settlers*, 208–10.

20. On the Frazer and Mahle contracts, see Miller, *Soldiers and Settlers*, 210–211. On Herrford's contract, see Crimmins, "Camp Pena Colorado," 6.

21. On Arizona and New Mexico, see Miller, *Soldiers and Settlers*, 210. On average Texas contract price, see "Report of the Commissary General of Subsistence, 1883," 586; "Report of the Commissary General of Subsistence, Oct. 15, 1884," *House Exec. Docs.*, 48th Cong., 2d sess., no. 1, pt. 2, vol. 2, serial 2277, 699; "Report of the Commissary General of Subsistence, Oct. 10, 1889," *House Exec. Docs.*, 51st Cong., 1st sess., no. 1, pt. 2, serial 2715, 752.

22. "Report of the Commissary General of Subsistence, 1895," 380.

23. For examples of soldiers stealing cattle to eat, see McConnell, *Five Years a Cavalryman*, 32–33; Smith, ed., *A Dose of Frontier Soldiering*, 150. On the two combats, see Kenneth F. Neighbours, "Tonkaway Scouts and Guides," *West Texas Historical Asso-*

ciation Year Book 49 (1973): 100; Lt. Col. William H. Carter, *From Yorktown to Santiago with the Sixth U.S. Cavalry,* 159. On the Goodnight-Loving Trail, see "Report of Major General Halleck, Military Division of the South, Oct. 24, 1870," *House Exec. Docs.,* 41st Cong., 3d sess., no. 1, pt. 2, serial 1446, 42; Jimmy M. Skaggs, "Military Operations on the Cattle Trails," *Texas Military History* 6 (Summer, 1967): 137–48; Wallace, *Ranald S. Mackenzie,* 65, 85. On smuggling, see "Report of Brig. Gen. E. O. C. Ord, Oct. 1, 1879," *House Exec. Docs.,* 46th Cong., 2d Sess., no. 1, pt. 2, serial 1903, 109. For a good outline of the development of the Texas cattle industry and military aid on cattle drives, see Carl Coke Rister, *The Southwestern Frontier, 1865–1881,* 267–83.

24. French, *Two Wars,* 35; Grant, *Personal Memoirs,* 1:59.

25. Luther Giddings, *Sketches of the Campaign in Mexico,* 100–101, as cited in Smith and Judah, *Chronicles of the Gringos,* 374–75.

26. On Jesup's view of Western ponies, see Kieffer, *Maligned General,* 274; Smith and Judah, *Chronicles of the Gringos,* 373. On Drum's purchase of horses, see Capt. S. H. Drum to Maj. Gen. Thomas S. Jesup, Aug. 21, Sept. 10, and Sept. 16, 1846, in "Mexican War Correspondence," *House Exec. Docs.,* 30th Cong., 1st sess., no. 60, vol. 1, serial 520, 735–37; Risch, *Quartermaster Support,* 275–76.

27. On Ringgold's artillery horses, see French, *Two Wars,* 31–34. On throwing the horses overboard, see Smith, *Mexican War Journal,* 8. On the system of stalls, see Maj. Thomas B. Eastland to Quartermaster General Thomas Jesup, Mar. 23, 1847, Eastland to Col. Thomas Hunt, Mar. 27, 1847, "Letters Sent," vol. 1, Entry 342—Maj. Thomas B. Eastland, Records of Quartermasters, 1819–1905, Office of the Quartermaster General, RG 92. On Ewell, see Lt. R. S. Ewell to Ben, Feb. 12, 1847 in Hamlin, ed., *Making of a Soldier,* 59–60.

28. On local purchase of horses, see Col. Trueman Cross to Capt. George H. Crosman, Feb. 24, 1846, Entry 333—Maj. George H. Crosman, Records of Quartermasters, 1819–1905, Office of the Quartermaster General, RG 92. On Kinney and local purchase of mules, see Smith, *Mexican War Journal,* 32, 40, 140; Bauer, *The Mexican War,* 89; Risch, *Quartermaster Support,* 270–71.

29. Manning, "Mexican War Journal," 63; Maj. Thomas B. Eastland to Capt. George H. Crosman, May 9, 1847, Entry 341, "Letters Sent," vol. 1; Maj. Thomas B. Eastland to Quartermaster General Thomas Jesup, Oct. 30, 1847, Entry 341, "Letters Sent," vol. 2—Maj. Thomas B. Eastland, Records of Quartermasters, 1819–1905, Office of the Quartermaster General, RG 92.

30. On the 1871 reduction, see "Report of the Quartermaster General, 1871," 124; Crimmins, ed., "W. G. Freeman's Report," LIV: (first quote) 210; "Report of the Inspector General, Oct. 10, 1888," *House Exec. Docs.,* 50th Cong., 2d sess., no. 1, pt. 2, vol. 2, serial 2628, (second quote) 113; "Report of the Inspector General, 1896," (third quote) 124.

31. For an account of the San Antonio board of 1871–1872 and for the postwar horse

standards, see Escal F. Duke, "O. M. Smith— Frontier Pay Clerk," *West Texas Historical Association Year Book* 45 (1969): 45–57. On the 1876 standards, see Steffen, *Horse Soldier,* 2:204–205.

32. The total numbers of Texas horses for the key years in the U.S. Census years are as follows: 1850—76,760; 1860—325,698; 1870—424,504; 1880—805,606; and 1890—1,026,002. The total numbers of Texas mules and asses were: 1850—12,463; 1860—63,334; 1870—61,322; 1880—132,447; and 1890—227,432. See Census Office, "Table XLIII, General Statistics of Agriculture," in *Compendium of the Tenth Census,* 1:674–75; Census Office, "Table 4, Livestock," in *Abstract of the Eleventh Census: 1890,* 73. On the British army buying Texas mules, see Donald R. Morris, *The Washing of the Spears: A History of the Rise of the Zulu Nation under Shaka Zulu and Its Fall in the Zulu War of 1879,* 354.

33. Risch, *Quartermaster Support,* 431, 464.

34. Risch, *Quartermaster Support,* 431, 464–67; "Report of the Quartermaster General, 1868," 818–19; "Report of the Quartermaster General, 1869," 367, 376.

35. "Report of the Quartermaster General, Sept. 30, 1867," *House Exec. Docs.,* 40th Cong., 2d sess., no. 1, serial 1324, 552, 560; "Report of the Quartermaster General, 1868," 918–19, 945–46.

36. "Report of the Quartermaster General, 1867," 552, 560; "Report of the Quartermaster General, 1868," 918–19, 925, 945; "Report of the Quartermaster General, 1871," 198; "Report of the Quartermaster General, 1882," 442; Judge Advocate General, *U.S. Military Reservations,* 382. On Fort Elliott, see James J. Fisher, "Tombstone Mysteries Unraveling," *Kansas City Star,* Friday, Nov. 18, 1994, C-1.

37. "Report of the Quartermaster General, 1867," 552, 560; "Report of the Quartermaster General, 1868," 918–19, 925, 945; "Report of the Quartermaster General, 1870," 221; "Report of the Quartermaster General, 1871," 198; Judge Advocate General, *U.S. Military Reservations,* 376–77; Conway, ed., "Colonel Schriver's Inspector General's Report," (quote) 578.

38. For a detailed general history of army sutlers, see David Michael Delo, *Peddlers and Post Traders: The Army Sutler on the Frontier.* On Fort Graham, see Sandra L. Myres, "Fort Graham: Listening Post on the Texas Frontier," *West Texas Historical Association Year Book* 59 (1983): 44.

39. Delo, *Peddlers and Post Traders,* 48, 53, 153.

40. Lt. Napoleon J. T. Dana to Mrs. Dana, May 24, 1846, in Ferrell, ed., *Monterrey Is Ours!,* 82.

41. War Department General Orders no. 47, Sept. 21, 1849, Records of the Adjutant General's Office, War Department, RG 94, (quote); Crimmins, ed., "Colonel Mansfield's Report," 237; War Department General Orders no. 7, Apr. 11, 1859.

42. War Department General Orders no. 7, Apr. 11, 1859, and no. 16, July 6, 1859, Adjutant General's Office, War Department, RG 94.

43. Knight, *Fort Worth,* 17; Charles P. Roland and Richard C. Robbins, eds., "The Diary of Eliza (Mrs. Albert Sidney) Johnston: The Second Cavalry Comes to Texas," *Southwestern Historical Quarterly* LX (Apr., 1957): 489.

44. Grace King, Sherwood Noël McGuigan, and Gem Meacham, *From Muskets to Mohair: The History of Fort Terrett,* 55; Johnson, *A Soldier's Reminiscences,* (quote) 65.

45. Crimmins, ed., "W. G. Freeman's Report," LI: (first quote) 256; Crimmins, ed., "Colonel Mansfield's Report," 251, 254, 357, 360, 368, 373–75; Wooster, *Fort Davis,* 23.

46. "Letter from the Secretary of War in Relation to Sales to Enlisted Men by Post Traders, Apr. 18, 1870," *House Exec. Docs.,* 41st Cong., 2d sess., no. 249, serial 1425, 1; Delo, *Peddlers and Post Traders,* 142, 148, 152, 155; Duke, "O. M. Smith," (quote) 51; Whisenhunt, "Frontier Military Life," 23; Wooster, *Fort Davis,* 23; Wooster, *History of Fort Davis,* 200–203, 256–57. At Fort Stockton, post trader Joseph Friedlander earned the contempt of the garrison for being openly friendly with Capt. Andrew Geddes after the charges and countercharges of adultery and incest between the married captain, Lt. Louis Orleman, and Orleman's teenage daughter, Lillie. Marcos E. Kinevan, *Frontier Cavalryman: Lieutenant John Bigelow and the Buffalo Soldiers in Texas,* 169, 171, 182, 190.

47. Delo, *Peddlers and Post Traders,* 152; McConnell, *Five Years a Cavalryman,* (quote) 208,

48. McConnell, *Five Years a Cavalryman,* 79, (quote) 157, 209; "Report of the General of the Army, 1881," 45; General Order no. 24, 1881, Adjutant General of the Army to Commanding General, Military Division of the Missouri, Mar. 13, 1881, Letters Sent by Headquarters Department of Texas, vols. 16–19, Jan. 1, 1881–Dec. 30, 1882.

49. Conway, ed., "Colonel Schriver's Inspector General's Report," (first quote) 575, (second quote) 577, (third quote) 582.

50. Alice K. Grierson to son, Robert, Feb. 29, 1876, and to Ben Grierson, Aug. 4, 1877, Leckie, ed., *The Colonel's Lady,* 85–86, 106–107; Wooster, *Fort Davis,* 23, Wooster, *History of Fort Davis,* 257.

51. General Orders no. 10, Feb. 1, 1889, "Report of the Quartermaster General, 1890," 684; Delo, *Peddlers and Post Traders,* 204–205.

CHAPTER 7.
PAYDAY: PAYMASTERS, SOLDIERS' SILVER, AND CIVILIAN EMPLOYMENT

1. The paymaster was Maj. Archibald W. Burns. Smith, *Mexican War Journal,* (quote) 92.

2. Ibid., 100.

3. On eight wagon loads of specie, see "Report of the Secretary of War, Dec. 2, 1847," *House Exec. Docs.,* 30th Cong., 1st sess., no. 8, pt. 2, serial 515, 11–12. On French, see French, *Two Wars,* 98. The army inspector of 1853 noted that all payments in Texas were made in gold or silver specie. Crimmins, ed., "W. G. Freeman's Report," LI:170.

4. "Report of the Quartermaster General, 1849," (quote) 196–197.

5. "Report of the Paymaster General, 20 Nov. 1855," *Senate Exec. Docs.,* 34th Cong., 1st sess., no. 1, serial 811, 171; "General Account of the receipts and expenditures of the United States for the fiscal year ending June 30, 1857," *House Exec. Docs.,* 35th Cong., 1st sess., no. 13, serial 947, 414.

6. On Blair, see Charles E. Wynes, ed., "Lewis Harvie Blair: Texas Travels, 1851–1855," *Southwestern Historical Quarterly* LXVI (Oct., 1962): 262–70. On Belger, see Crimmins, ed., "Colonel Mansfield's Report," 136. On Dickerson, see Wooster, *History of Fort Davis,* 253. On Flipper, see Harris, ed., *Negro Frontiersman: The Western Memoirs of Henry O. Flipper,* 18–20; Carlson, *"Pecos Bill,"* 122–26; Dinges, "The Court-Martial of Lt. Flipper," 12–17, 19, 21; McClung, "2d Lt. Henry O. Flipper," 20–31.

7. Frazer, *Forts and Supplies,* 112–13; *Texas State Gazette,* Feb. 28, 1852, (first quote) 82; Olmsted, *Journey through Texas,* 152–53; Clark, *Opdycke Tigers,* (second quote) 403.

8. Smith, *Mexican War Journal,* 98; McConnell, *Five Years a Cavalryman,* (first quote) 36, (second quote) 200.

9. Crimmins, ed., "W. G. Freeman's Report," LI:170–71, 357; LIII:468–69.

10. Crimmins, ed., "Colonel Mansfield's Report,"140.

11. Crimmins, ed., "Colonel Mansfield's Report," 140, 247.

12. McConnell, *Five Years a Cavalryman,* 156; Duke, "O. M. Smith," 52–53.

13. "Report of the Secretary of War, 20 Nov. 1876," *House Exec. Docs.,* 44th Cong., 2d sess., no. 1, pt. 2, serial 1742, 344-345.

14. On Stewart see Duke, "O. M. Smith," (quote) 48–49. On Howgate, see Donald R. Whitnah, *A History of the United States Weather Bureau,* 46. For the Wasson case, see Oliver Knight, *Life and Manners in the Frontier Army,* 26.

15. On enlisted soldiers' pay, see General Orders no. 12, Aug. 11, 1854, Adjutant General's Office, War Department, RG 94; Utley, *Frontiersmen in Blue,* 36; Utley, *Frontier Regulars,* 23; Coffman, *The Old Army,* 154–55, 346–47; Don Rickey Jr., *Forty Miles a Day on Beans and Hay: The Enlisted Soldier Fighting the Indian Wars,* 21; Adjutant General's Office, *Official Army Register for 1890,* 386–89; Adjutant General's Office, *Official Army Register for 1898,* 350–53; "Report of the Paymaster General, Sept. 21, 1895," *House Exec. Docs.,* 54th Cong., 1st sess., no. 2, vol. 3, serial 3370, 558.

16. (First quote) Capt. William Chapman to son, Henley, Mar. 15, 1855, Papers of William Chapman, USMA Special Collections. On Brackettville, see Florence Fenley, *Oldtimers: Frontier Days in Uvalde Section of South West Texas,* 185; Boyd, *Cavalry Life,* 256. On Jacksboro, see Hamilton, *Sentinel of the Southern Plains,* 27, 42. McConnell,

Five Years a Cavalryman, (second quote) 157, 161; Smith, ed., *A Dose of Frontier Soldiering,* (third quote) 169.

17. McConnell, *Five Years a Cavalryman,* (quote) 157.

18. Crimmins, ed., "Colonel Mansfield's Report," (quote) 377. On Texas banks, see Miller, *Financial History of Texas,* 158–59.

19. "Report of the Paymaster General, 1895," 558; "Report of the Secretary of War, Nov. 24, 1896," *House Exec. Docs.,* 54th Cong., 2d sess., no. 2, vol. 2, serial 3478, 5; Kinevan, *Frontier Cavalryman,* (first quote) 208; "Report of Brig. Gen. Z. R. Bliss, Sept. 8, 1896," *House Exec. Docs.,* 54th Cong., 2d sess., no. 2, vol. 2, serial 3478, (second quote) 169; "Report of the Paymaster General, Sept. 20, 1900," *House Exec. Docs.,* 56th Cong., 2d sess., no. 2, vol. 3, serial 4071, 928.

20. Lane, *I Married a Soldier,* (quote) 30. For the pay increase of 1857, see General Orders no. 2, Feb. 28, 1857, Adjutant General's Office, War Department, RG 94. On the pay of the Lees, see "Army Register, 1861," *House Exec. Docs.,* 37th Cong., 2d sess., no. 54, serial 1100, 24–25. For the pay of 1890, see *Army Register for 1890,* 386–89.

21. General Orders no. 6, May 29, 1857, Adjutant General's Office, War Department, RG 94; General Orders no. 11, May 11, 1859, Adjutant General's Office, War Department RG 94.

22. On Fauntleroy, see *Texas State Gazette,* Feb. 28, 1852, 223. On Sheridan, see Mildred Watkins Mears, "The Three Forts in Coryell County," *Southwestern Historical Quarterly* LXVII (July, 1963), 5. On Chapman, see Coker, ed., *News from Brownsville,* 326; Graf, "Economic History," 90, 95. On Givens, see Mayhall, "Camp Cooper," 322. On Maury, see Maury, *Recollections,* 103. On Mills, see Anson Mills, *My Story,* ed. C. H. Claudy, 54, 207, 318; Ruhlen, "Quitman's Owners," 61–62. On Bullis and Shafter, see Carlson, *"Pecos Bill,"* 119. On Grierson, Maxon, Brenner, Mulhern, and Rooney, see Wooster, *Fort Davis,* 42; Wooster, *History of Fort Davis,* 256, 341, 366; Robert K. Grierson to Alice K. Grierson, June 22, 1885, in Leckie, ed., *The Colonel's Lady,* 6, 154–55, 163; Bruce J. Dinges, "Col. Grierson Invests on the West Texas Frontier," *Fort Concho Report* 16 (Fall, 1984), 7–9.

23. On Grierson, see Wooster, *Fort Davis,* 42; Robert K. Grierson to Alice K. Grierson June 22, 1885, Leckie, ed., *The Colonel's Lady,* 163; Dinges, "Colonel Grierson," 9–10. On Bullis, Shafter, and the mines, see Carlson, *"Pecos Bill,"* 119; Tyler, ed., *New Handbook of Texas,* 1:823–24; 5:988–90. For a more typical example of officers losing money on frontier mining schemes, see the discussion on George Crook's and Phil Sheridan's losses on their investment in the Murchie Mine in Nevada in George Crook, *General George Crook: His Autobiography,* ed. Martin F. Schmitt, 237–40.

24. McConnell, *Five Years a Cavalryman,* (quote) 161.

25. On Cincinnati, see Capt. S. H. Drum to Maj. Gen. Thomas S. Jesup, Aug. 21, 1846, in "Mexican War Correspondence," *House Exec. Docs.,* 30th Cong., 1st sess., no. 60,

vol. 1, serial 520, 735. Manning, "Mexican War Journal," 56. On Port Lavaca, see "Report of Persons Hired at Port Lavaca . . . " Entry 361—Capt. James R. Irwin, Records of Quartermasters, 1819–1905, Office of the Quartermaster General, RG 92.

26. On standardized pay see Circular, July 14, 1847, Col. Henry Whiting, Entry 333— Maj. George H. Crosman, Records of Quartermasters, 1819–1905, Office of the Quartermaster General, RG 92. On wages at Brazos Santiago, see Maj. Thomas B. Eastland to Capt. George H. Crosman, May 9, 1847, Entry 341, "Letters Sent," vol. 1—Maj. Thomas B. Eastland, Records of Quartermasters, 1819–1905, Office of the Quartermaster General, RG 92. On Camargo, see Smith, *Mexican War Journal,* 36, 47, 90–91, 147. On the average U.S. wage, see Bureau of the Census, "Series D 705–14. Farm Laborers-Average Monthly Earnings with Board, by Geographic Divisions: 1818 to 1948," in *Historical Statistics of the United States,* 1:163.

27. Manning, "Mexican War Journal," 47, 63, 65.

28. "Statements showing the contracts made . . . 1856," 11–12; Crimmins, ed., "Colonel Mansfield's Report," 141.

29. Smith, *Fort Inge,* 63; Ben E. Pingenot, ed., *Paso Del Águila: A Chronicle of Frontier Days on the Texas Border as Recorded in the Memoirs of Jesse Sumpter,* comp. Harry Warren, 17; Crook and Crook, "Fort Lincoln, Texas," 155; Richard Irving Dodge, *Our Wild Indians: Thirty-three Years' Personal Experience among the Red Men of the Great West,* 555, 564–67; Wayne R. Austerman, "José Policarpo Rodriquez: Chicano Plainsman," *West Texas Historical Association Year Book* 59 (1983): 52–74; Tyler, ed., *New Handbook of Texas,* 3:744, 5:654; George Frederick Price, *Across the Continent with the Fifth Cavalry,* (quote) 91; Capt. Randolph B. Marcy, *The Prairie Traveler,* 188–96.

30. On contracted antebellum doctors, see the annual *Senate* and *House of Representatives Executive Documents,* "War Department Contracts" for each year 1849–1860. For 1868 contract pay, see "Report of the Secretary of War, Nov. 20, 1868," *House Exec. Docs.,* 40th Cong., 3d sess., no. 1, pt. 2, serial 1367, 976; for Dr. Powhatan Jordan, see Webb, ed., *Handbook of Texas,* 3:458. For a general history, see Percy M. Ashburn, *A History of the Medical Department of the U.S. Army,* 89, 150. For an excellent summation of the topic and a good bibliography of specific sources on army doctors, see Neilson, "'I Long to Return.'"

31. Frontier and army labor prices in the antebellum era from Lt. George H. Steuart to Department Headquarters, San Antonio, Aug. 12, 1851, Quartermaster Files, Fort Inge, Texas, Quartermaster's Department, Letters Received, RG 92; Post Returns, Fort Inge, Texas, Mar., 1849–Jan., 1869, microfilm no. M617, roll 517, Returns from U.S. Military Posts 1800–1916, Records of the U.S. Army Adjutant General's Office, 1780–1917, RG 94 (hereafter cited as Post Returns, Fort Inge); Crimmins, ed., "Colonel Mansfield's Report," 135; Moore, *Reading W. Black,* 52, 54; Campbell and Lowe, "Some Economic

Aspects," 378. U.S. labor prices are from Bureau of the Census, "Series D 728, Daily Wages of Five Skilled Occupations and of Laborers, in Manufacturing Establishments: 1860–1880" in *Historical Statistics of the United States: Colonial Times to 1970,* 1:165. On soldier labor, see General Orders no. 43, July 25, 1851, Adjutant General's Office, War Department, RG 94; Report of the Quartermaster General, 1853," 133–34; *Texas State Gazette,* Oct. 23, 1852, (quote) 74.

32. U.S. average labor prices are from Bureau of the Census, "Series D 728, Daily Wages of Five Skilled Occupations and of Laborers, in Manufacturing Establishments: 1860–1880" in *Historical Statistics of the United States: Colonial Times to 1970,* 1:165. Army wage prices and soldier labor data are from Post Returns, Fort Inge, Sept.–Dec., 1868, and Jan., 1869; "Report of the Quartermaster General, 1878," 307, 315–16.

33. On New Mexico, see Miller, *Soldiers and Settlers,* xiv, Frazer, *Forts and Supplies,* 188. On Bexar County, see Crimmins, ed., "Colonel Mansfield's Report," 135; "Report of the Quartermaster General, 1878," 315; Walker, *A Compendium of the Ninth Census, June 1, 1870,* 840.

CHAPTER 8.
ARMY ENGINEERS: EXPLORATION AND MAPPING, ROAD BUILDING, AND RIVER AND HARBOR IMPROVEMENT

1. "Letter from the Secretary of War Showing the Strength of the Army [1789–1878], Jan. 14, 1879," *House Exec. Docs.,* 45th Cong., 3d sess., no. 23, serial 1852, 8–11; Goetzmann, *Army Exploration,* 6–12, 36–38; Trass, *From the Golden Gate,* 11–18, 222–23; W. Turrentine Jackson, *Wagon Roads West: A Study of Federal Road Surveys and Construction in the Trans-Mississippi West, 1846–1869,* 2–3; Russell F. Weigley, *History of the United States Army,* 105–106.

2. Francis Paul Prucha, *The Sword of the Republic: The United States Army on the Frontier, 1783–1846,* 87–94; Tyler, ed., *New Handbook of Texas,* 2:924–928; 5:746–47; 6:973–74. A number of sources indicate Long entered Texas but, according to Goetzmann, Long traced the North Fork of the Canadian, not crossing the current state boundary. Goetzmann, *Army Exploration,* 35, 42–44; Donald E. Chipman, *Spanish Texas, 1519–1821,* 226, 239.

3. Goetzmann, *Army Exploration,* 12; Prucha, *Sword of the Republic,* 309–10; Thomas Maitland Marshall, *A History of the Western Boundary of the Louisiana Purchase, 1819–1841,* 2:142–43; Tyler, ed., *New Handbook of Texas,* 2:917–28; 4:275–76.

4. Trass, *From the Golden Gate,* 46–47; Goetzmann, *Army Exploration,* 123–27; Prucha, *Sword of the Republic,* 394; Tyler, ed., *New Handbook of Texas,* 2:917–28.

5. Lt. George G. Meade to Mrs. George Meade, Oct. 9, 1845, Dece. 1, 1845, Feb. 18, 1846 in Meade, ed., *Life and Letters,* 1:25, 36, 47; Trass, *From the Golden Gate,* 117–23; Francaviglia, *From Steam to Sail,* 158–59.

6. Capt. George W. Hughes, "Memoir Descriptive of the March of a Division of the U.S. Army, under the Command of Brig. Gen. John E. Wool from San Antonio de Bexar, in Texas, to Saltillo, in Mexico," *Senate Exec. Docs.,* 31st Cong., 1st sess., no. 32, serial 562, 5–19; Trass, *From the Golden Gate,* 149–50; Goetzmann, *Army Exploration,* 149–52.

7. John C. Hays to Hon. W. Marcy, Dec. 13, 1848, in Trass, *From the Golden Gate,* 299–301; Swift, *Three Roads to Chihuahua,* 66–81; Goetzmann, *Army Exploration,* 227; Jackson, *Wagon Roads West,* 36–37; Tyler, ed., *New Handbook of Texas,* 2:917–28.

8. Goetzmann, *Army Exploration,* 225–26, 228, 273; Jackson, *Wagon Roads West,* 36–37; Swift, *Three Roads to Chihuahua,* 47, 78–81, 109.

9. "Reports of Explorations and Surveys . . . for a Railroad [1855]," 61; Goetzmann, *Army Exploration,* 233–34.

10. "Report of Lt. W. H. C. Whiting, 10 June 1849," in "Report of the Chief Engineer," *Senate Exec. Docs.,* 31st Cong., 1st sess., no. 1, serial 549, 281; "Report of the Secretary of War, 30 Nov. 1849," *Senate Exec. Docs.,* 31st Cong., 1st sess., no. 1, serial 549, 154–155; "Reports of the Secretary of War with Reconnaissances of Routes from San Antonio to El Paso, 24 July 1850," *Senate Exec. Docs.,* 31st Cong., 1st sess., no. 64, serial 562, 4–7; "Report of the Colonel of the Corps of Topographical Engineers, 14 Nov. 1850," *House Exec. Docs.,* 31st Cong., 2d sess., no. 1, serial 595, 385; "Reports of Explorations and Surveys. . . for a Railroad [1855]," 60; Swift, *Three Roads to Chihuahua,* 82–85; Goetzmann, *Army Exploration,* 228–230; Jackson, *Wagon Roads West,* 39–41; Tyler, ed., *New Handbook of Texas,* 3:744.

11. "Report of Lt. W. H. C. Whiting, June 10, 1849," 281–93; "Report of the Secretary of War, 1849," 154–55; "Reports of the Secretary of War with Reconnaissances of Routes from San Antonio to El Paso, 1850," 4–7; Reports of Explorations and Surveys . . . for a Railroad [1855], 60; Swift, *Three Roads to Chihuahua,* 66–81; Goetzmann, *Army Exploration,* 228–30; Jackson, *Wagon Roads West,* 39–41.

12. Ford, *RIP Ford's Texas,* 113–29; Goetzmann, *Army Exploration,* 230–31; Jackson, *Wagon Roads West,* 37; Swift, *Three Roads to Chihuahua,* 103–104.

13. "Report of the Colonel of the Corps of Topographical Engineers, 1850," 386; "Reports of . . . Reconnaissances of Routes . . . 1850," 13–14, 26–29; "Reports of Explorations and Surveys . . . for a Railroad [1855]," 61; Goetzmann, *Army Exploration,* 232–33; Jackson, *Wagon Roads West,* 40–42.

14. "Report of the Colonel of the Corps of Topographical Engineers, 1850," 386; "Reports of Explorations and Surveys . . . for a Railroad [1855]," 60; Goetzmann, *Army Exploration,* 231, 233; Jackson, *Wagon Roads West,* 42–43.

15. "Report of the Colonel of the Corps of Topographical Engineers, 1850," 385–86; "Reports of . . . Reconnaissances of Routes . . . 1850," 7–13, 29–39; "Reports of Explorations and Surveys . . . for a Railroad [1855]," 59, 61, 62; Jackson, *Wagon Roads West,* 24–29, 43–45; Goetzmann, *Army Exploration,* 233–34; Tyler, ed., *New Handbook of Texas,* 2:917–28.

16. "Reports of . . . Reconnaissances of Routes . . . 1850," 235–50.

17. "Report of the Quartermaster General, 1850," 324–29; Reports of Explorations and Surveys . . . for a Railroad [1855], 61, 62; Goetzmann, *Army Exploration,* 237; Coker, ed., *News from Brownsville,* 377–89; Martin L. Crimmins, ed., "Two Thousand Miles by Boat in the Rio Grande in 1850," *West Texas Historical and Scientific Society* Bulletin 48 (Dec., 1933): 44–52. Uncharacteristic of Martin L. Crimmins's careful scholarship, in this article, a reprint of quartermaster Capt. W. W. Chapman's report, Crimmins confuses frontiersman "Capt." Harry Love with Capt. John Love of the First Dragoons. Crimmins states in the introduction that Love traveled up the Rio Grande above the Big Bend to present-day Presidio. However, Chapman's report initially indicates Love went 261 miles above the Pecos, and then later places his furthermost advance 120 miles above the mouth of the Pecos River.

18. "Reports of Explorations and Surveys . . . for a Railroad [1855]," 62; Goetzmann, *Army Exploration,* 234; Jackson, *Wagon Roads West,* 45.

19. "Reports of Explorations and Surveys . . . for a Railroad [1855]," 64–65; Stephen W. Sears, *George B. McClellan: The Young Napoleon,* 33–36; Tyler, ed., *New Handbook of Texas,* 2:917–28; 4:502.

20. "Report of the Secretary of War, Dec. 1, 1853," *Senate Exec. Docs.,* 33d Cong., 1st sess., no. 1, serial 691, 17–24, 58–60; Stanley, *Personal Memoirs,* 27–34; Goetzmann, *Army Exploration,* 262–304; Jackson, *Wagon Roads West,* 242–44; Tyler, ed., *New Handbook of Texas,* 2:917–28.

21. "Reports of Explorations and Surveys . . . for a Railroad [1855]," 79–80; Goetzmann, *Army Exploration,* 277, 291–92; Tyler, ed., *New Handbook of Texas,* 2:917–28.

22. "Reports of Explorations and Surveys . . . for a Railroad [1855]," 85; Alperin, *Custodians of the Coast,* 13; Tyler, ed., *New Handbook of Texas,* 2:917–28; 4:502.

23. "Artesian Well Experiment, Reports of Capt. John Pope," in "Report of the Secretary of War, 1858," *House Exec. Docs.,* 35th Cong., 2d sess., no. 2, pt. 2, vol. 2, serial 998, 591–608, (quote) 607; Goetzmann, *Army Exploration,* 365–68.

24. "Affairs in the Department of Texas, 1860," 33–51; Jackson, *Wagon Roads West,* 45–46.

25. Escal F. Duke, ed., "A Description of the Route from San Antonio to El Paso by Capt. Edward S. Meyer," *West Texas Historical Association Year Book* 49 (1973): 128–41.

26. On Shafter's explorations, see Carlson, *"Pecos Bill,"* 52–63, 71–87; Wallace, *Ranald S. Mackenzie,* 46–165; Hamilton, *Sentinel of the Southern Plains,* 108–118, 126; Martin L. Crimmins, ed., "Shafter's Explorations in Western Texas, 1875," *West Texas Historical*

Association Year Book 9 (1933): 82–96. For an account of the Ruffner survey, see T. Lindsay Baker, ed., *The Texas Red River Country: The Official Surveys of the Headwaters, 1876.*

27. Edward S. Wallace, "Gen. John Lapham Bullis: The Thunderbolt of the Texas Frontier," *Southwestern Historical Quarterly* LIV (Apr., 1951): 452–61; LV (July, 1951): 77–85; Kenneth Wiggins Porter, "The Seminole Negro-Indian Scouts, 1870–1881," *Southwestern Historical Quarterly* LV (Jan., 1952): 358–377; Frank M. Temple, "Col. B. H. Grierson's Administration of the District of the Pecos," *West Texas Historical Association Year Book* 38 (Oct., 1962): 85–96; Martin L. Crimmins, ed. "General B. H. Grierson in West Texas," *West Texas Historical and Scientific Society* Bulletin 18 (Dec., 1937): 30–44.

28. "Report of the Quartermaster General, 1849," 194; "Report of the Quartermaster General, 1850," (quote) 124.

29. "Report of the Colonel of the Corps of Topographical Engineers, 1850," 386; "Report of the Chief Engineer, Nov. 30, 1853," *Senate Exec. Docs.,* 33d Cong., 1st sess., no. 1, serial 691, 567–72; "Report of the Chief Engineer, Nov. 29, 1854," *House Exec. Docs.,* 33d Cong., 2d sess., no. 1, pt. 2, serial 778, 167; *Texas State Gazette,* Oct. 13, 1849, 27; Nov. 17, 1849, 98; Sept. 27, 1851, 43; Woodward, "Internal Improvements," 161–67; Goetzmann, *Army Exploration,* 335–236.

30. "Report of the Chief Engineer, 1853," 566–67, 573; Woodward, "Internal Improvements," 161–67; Tyler, ed., *New Handbook of Texas,* 6:570–71.

31. "Report of the Chief of Engineers, Oct. 20, 1873," *House Exec. Docs.,* 43d Cong., 1st sess., no. 1, pt. 2, vol. 2, serial 1597, 64, 620; "Report of the Chief Engineer, Oct. 20, 1874," *House Exec. Docs.,* 43d Cong., 2d sess., , no. 1, pt. 2, vol. 2, serial 1636, 73; "Report of the Chief of Engineers, Oct. 19, 1878," *House Exec. Docs.,* 45th Cong., 3d sess., no. 1, pt. 2, vol. 2, serial 1844, 87; "Report of the Chief of Engineers, 1880," 146–50; "Report of the Chief of Engineers, Oct. 19, 1882," *House Exec. Docs.,* 47th Cong., 2d sess., no. 1, pt. 2., vol. 3, serial 2092, 194–97; "Report of the Secretary of War, Nov. 27, 1893," *House Exec. Docs.,* 53d Cong., 2d sess., no. 1, pt. 1, serial 3198, 45; Alperin, *Custodians of the Coast,* 40.

32. "Report of the Topographical Bureau, Nov. 14, 1860," *Senate Exec. Docs.,* 36th Cong., 2d sess., no. 1, pt. 2, serial 1057, 294, 505; Alperin, *Custodians of the Coast,* 40; Grant Foreman, "River Navigation in the Early Southwest," *The Mississippi Valley Historical Review* XV (June, 1928):39, 47, 50, 51–53; Judy Watson, "The Red River Raft," *Texana* 5 (Spring, 1967): 68–76.

33. "Report of the Chief of Engineers, Oct. 10, 1877," *House Exec. Docs.,* 45th Cong., 2d sess., no. 1, pt. 2, vol. 2, serial 1795, 75–76; "Report of the Chief of Engineers, Oct. 19, 1881," *House Exec. Docs.,* 47th Cong., 1st sess., no. 1, pt. 1, vol. 2, serial 2011, 197–204;

"Report of the Chief of Engineers, 1882," 194–197; "Report of Brig. Gen. Z. R. Bliss, 1895," 160; "Report of Brig. Gen. Z. R. Bliss, 1896," 166.

34. "Report of the Chief Engineer, 1853," 552–73, (first quote) 562, (second quote) 561; Alperin, *Custodians of the Coast,* 18, 33; Sears, *George B. McClellan,* 33–36.

35. "Report of the Chief of Engineers, 1882," 194–97; Alperin, *Custodians of the Coast,* 137–43.

36. "Report of the Colonel of the Corps of Topographical Engineers, 1850," 386; "Report of the Chief Engineer, 1853," 564–65; "Report of the Chief Engineer, 1874," 760, 762–63; Alperin, *Custodians of the Coast,* 166–68.

37. "Report of the Chief Engineer, 1853," 563–64; "Report of the Chief of Engineers, Oct. 20, 1879," *House Exec. Docs.,* 46th Cong., 2d sess., no. 1, pt. 2, vol. 2, serial 1904, 111; "Report of the Chief of Engineers, 1880," 146–50; Alperin, *Custodians of the Coast,* 127.

38. Alperin, *Custodians of the Coast,* 2–4, 40; Capt. William J. Judson, "The Services of Graduates as Explorers, Builder of Railways, Canals, Bridges, Lighthouses, Harbors, and the Like," in *The Centennial of the United States Military Academy at West Point, New York, 1802–1902,* 1:866–67; Tyler, ed., *New Handbook of Texas,* 3:51, 70; Gary Cartwright, *Galveston: A History of the Island,* 71–75.

39. "Report of the Chief Engineer, 1853," 559–60; "Report of the Chief Engineer, 1857," 186; "Report of the Engineer Bureau, Nov. 14, 1860," *Senate Exec. Docs.,* 36th Cong., 2d sess., no. 1, pt. 2, serial 1057, 253, 269, 272; "Report of the Chief of Engineers, Oct. 25, 1870," *House Exec. Docs.,* 41st Cong., 3d sess., no. 1, pt. 2, serial 1446, 31, 61; "Report of the Chief of Engineers, 1873," 65; Alperin, *Custodians of the Coast,* 22–23.

40. "Report of the Chief of Engineers, Oct. 10, 1876," *House Exec. Docs.,* 44th Cong., 2d sess., no. 1, pt. 2, vol. 2, serial 1743, 25, 75; "Report of the Chief of Engineers, 1877," 73–74; "Report of the Chief of Engineers, 1878," 82–83; Alperin, *Custodians of the Coast,* 25–33; Cartwright, *Galveston,* 137–39.

41. Alperin, *Custodians of the Coast,* 25–33.

42. Ibid., 50–55; Judson, "The Services of Graduates," 1:866–68.

43. Alperin, *Custodians of the Coast,* 51; Judson, "The Services of Graduates," 1:867; Young, *Galveston and the Great West,* 43, 89, 122–29, 134, 141–43.

44. "Report of the Secretary of War, Nov. 26, 1895," *House Exec. Docs.,* 54th Cong., 1st sess., no. 2, vol. 3, serial 3370, 25; Alperin, *Custodians of the Coast,* 51–55; Judson, "The Services of Graduates," 1:867, 873.

45. Alperin, *Custodians of the Coast,* 99–100.

CHAPTER 9.
CONTRIBUTIONS TO THE ECONOMIC NETWORK: STAGECOACHES, MAIL, THE MILITARY TELEGRAPH SYSTEM, AND THE WEATHER SERVICE

1. On Twiggs, see French, *Two Wars*, 98. On 1859, see Lane, *I Married a Soldier*, (quote) 78. On early stage lines, see Tyler, ed., *New Handbook of Texas*, 6:52; "Report of the Quartermaster General, 1851," 274.

2. Malsch, *Indianola*, 70; Jack C. Scannell, "A Survey of the Stagecoach Mail in the Trans-Pecos, 1850–1861," *West Texas Historical Association Year Book* 47 (1971): 115–26; Emmie Giddings W. Mahon and Chester V. Kielman, "George H. Giddings and the San Antonio–San Diego Mail Line," *Southwestern Historical Quarterly* LXI (Oct., 1957): 220–39; Wayne R. Austerman, *Sharps Rifles and Spanish Mules: The San Antonio–El Paso Mail, 1851–1881*, 23–43; Tyler, ed., *New Handbook of Texas*, 3:153; 5:804, 1072; 6:52.

3. H. G. Horton to A. W. Evans, Apr. 14, 1912, in Florence Anthon, "Uvalde and Surrounding Territory," an unpublished collection of interviews and letters, Archives of the El Progreso Library, Uvalde, Tex.

4. A. C. Greene, *900 Miles on the Butterfield Trail*, 33–119; Roscoe and Margaret B. Conkling, *The Butterfield Overland Mail, 1857–1869*, 1:115, 121–49, 285–335, 2:13–56; Scannell, "Survey of the Stagecoach Mail," 122–25; Webb, ed., *Handbook of Texas*, 1:258–59; 3:129; Tyler, ed., *New Handbook of Texas*, 1:870.

5. Greene, *900 Miles*, 17, 21, 25–26, 52, 67, 266–67; Conkling and Conkling, *Butterfield Overland Mail*, 1:375; Rupert Norval Richardson, *The Frontier of Northwest Texas, 1846–1876*, 213; Scannell, "Survey of the Stagecoach Mail," 123–26; Tyler, ed., *New Handbook of Texas*, 6:52–53.

6. Johnson, *A Soldier's Reminiscences*, (first quote) 123; Crook, *Gen. George Crook*, (second quote) 78.

7. Austerman, *Sharps Rifles*, 195–206; Tyler, ed., *New Handbook of Texas*, 6:53; 5:593.

8. Benjamin H. Grierson to Alice K. Grierson, Oct. 27, 1876, Leckie, ed., *The Colonel's Lady*, (quote) 89, 228 n. 13.

9. McConnell, *Five Years a Cavalryman*, (first quote) 272; Notson, "Fort Concho," 139; R. C. Crane, "Letters From Texas," *West Texas Historical Association Year Book* 25 (Oct., 1949): 110–26, (second quote), 117, (third quote), 115–16. The letters are the Texas portions of Albert Todd, *The Class of 1877*. Susan Miles, "Fort Concho In 1877," *West Texas Historical Association Year Book* 35 (Oct., 1959): 33; Greene, *900 Miles*, 25, 247–49; Smith, ed., *A Dose of Frontier Soldiering*, (quote) 178.

10. Telegram, Capt. Thomas M. Vincent, AAG, Department of Texas to Colonel Grierson, Commanding Officer, Pecos District, Jan. 10, 1881, Letters Sent by Headquarters

Department of Texas, vol. 16–19, Jan. 1, 1881–Dec. 30, 1882, microfilm no. M1114, roll 6, RG 393.

11. Arlen L. Fowler, *Black Infantry in the West, 1869–1891,* 25–28, 128.

12. "Report of the General of the Army, 1872," 28, 33; Duke, "O. M. Smith," 51; Carlson, *"Pecos Bill,"* 57–60; Smith, ed., *A Dose of Frontier Soldiering,* 184; Heitman, *Historical Register,* 2:429, 434, 437; John H. Nankivell, *History of the Twenty-Fifth Regiment, United States Infantry, 1869–1926,* 23; Austerman, *Sharps Rifles,* 320–23.

13. "Report of the Quartermaster General, 1872," 6; "Report of the Quartermaster General, 1873," 108; "Report of the Quartermaster General, 1886," 491; "Report of the Quartermaster General, 1888," 387; "Report of the Quartermaster General, 1887," 462.

14. United States Military Academy, *First Class Annual of the Class of '86, United States Military Academy, West Point, N.Y., for the Year 1887,* (quote), 71.

15. Harry M. Konwiser, *Texas Republic Postal System,* 14–17; Alex L. ter Brake, *Texas: The Drama of Its Postal Past,* 207–19; Tyler, ed., *New Handbook of Texas,* 5:290–91; W. L. Newsom, "The Postal System of the Republic of Texas," *Southwestern Historical Quarterly* XX (Oct., 1916): 115; Lt. George G. Meade to Mrs. Meade, Oct. 11, Dec. 17, 1845, in Meade, ed., *Life and Letters,* 1:32, 40; Lt. Napoleon J. T. Dana to Mrs. Dana, Sept. 23, 1845, in Ferrell, ed., *Monterrey Is Ours!,* 15.

16. Konwiser, *Texas Republic,* 32; ter Brake, *Texas,* 207–19; Dale R. Pulver, "Handling the U.S. Military Mails during the War with Mexico: 1846–48," *Stamp Chronicle* 98 (May, 1978): 86–93 and *Stamp Chronicle* 99 (Aug., 1978): 172–175; Karl C. Gebert, "All Quiet on the Frontier," *The Texas Postal History Society Journal* 16 (Feb., 1991): 2–5; Karl C. Gebert, "Excuse This Hasty Scrawl, My Horse is Saddled and My Company Gone," *The Texas Postal History Society Journal* 16 (Sept., 1991): 2–7; Smith, *Mexican War Journal,* 36.

17. Johnson, *A Soldier's Reminiscences,* (quote) 88. On Fort Inge, see Crimmins, ed., "W. G. Freeman's Report," LIII:74; Olmsted, *Journey through Texas,* 288; Arrie Barrett, "Federal Military Outposts in Texas, 1845–1861," (masters thesis, University of Texas, 1927), 2. On the 1855 incident, see Stanley, *Personal Memoirs,* 36.

18. Moore, *Reading W. Black,* 53–54, 63, 88.

19. Konwiser, *Texas Republic,* 39; Crimmins, ed., "W. G. Freeman's Report," LI:352; LII:101, 229, 351; Wynes, ed., "Lewis Harvie Blair," 269; Vielé, *Following the Drum,* 129.

20. Crimmins, ed., "W. G. Freeman's Report," LI:350, 352; LII:101, 229, 351; LIII:71, 74, 202, 204, 309, 315, 443, 448, 453, 459, 462, 465; Turnley, *Reminiscences,* 211; Crimmins, ed., "Colonel Mansfield's Report," 135, 250, 351, 374; David A. Clary, ed., "'I Am Already Quite a Texan': Albert J. Myer's Letters from Texas, 1854–1856," *Southwestern Historical Quarterly* LXXXII (July, 1978): (quote) 32.

21. Clary, ed., "'Already Quite a Texan,'" 32; Lt. George H. Steuart to Miss Mary Steuart,

Aug. 16, 1854; Mary Steuart to George, Sept. 14, 1854. Lt. George H. Steuart Correspondence, 1853–1855, Eberstadt Collection, Box 3N182, Center for American History, University of Texas at Austin.

22. Clary, ed., "'Already Quite a Texan,'" 32, 48, (first quote) 51, (second quote) 51.

23. Clark, *Opdycke Tigers,* (quote), 405; "Postmaster General, Site Reports, Fort Inge, June, 1867," RG 28; Wooster, *History of Fort Davis,* 176, 185.

24. McConnell, *Five Years a Cavalryman,* 47, 68, (quote) 100, 173; Notson, "Fort Concho," 139; Wooster, *History of Fort Davis,* 185.

25. Quartermaster General's Office, *Outline Description . . . 1871,* 37–56; Headquarters of the Military Division of the Missouri, *Outline Descriptions of the Posts,* 207–208; Alice K. Grierson to Ben Grierson, July 6, 1875; Aug. 16, 1877; Aug. 28, 1877; Alice to son, Robert, Nov. 9, 1875; Alice to son, Charlie, Dec. 28, 1875; Feb. 4, 1876; Feb. 4, 1877; Dec. 7, 1882 in Leckie, ed., *The Colonel's Lady,* 74, 80, 84, 93, 110–11, 153; Wooster, *History of Fort Davis,* 216–17; Vernon Lynch, "1879 in the Echo: A Year at Fort Griffin on the Texas Frontier," *West Texas Historical Association Year Book* 41 (Oct., 1965), 57; Fowler, *Black Infantry in the West, 1869–1891,* 128–29.

26. Tyler, ed., *New Handbook of Texas,* 6:243–44.

27. "Report of the Secretary of War, Nov. 20, 1871," *House Exec. Docs.,* 42d Cong., 2d sess., no. 1, pt. 2, serial 1503, 13–14; "Report of the Signal Officer, Oct. 20, 1866," *House Exec. Docs.,* 39th Cong., 2d sess., no. 1, serial 1285, 182; "Report of the Secretary of War, Nov. 20, 1869," *House Exec. Docs.,* 41st Cong., 2d sess., no. 1, pt. 2, serial 1412, 18; Paul J. Scheips, "Albert James Myer, an Army Doctor in Texas, 1854–1857," *Southwestern Historical Quarterly* LXXXII (July, 1978): 22–24.

28. "Report of the Chief Signal Officer, Oct. 20, 1869," *House Exec. Docs.,* 41st Cong., 2d sess., no. 1, pt. 2, serial 1412, 197; "Report of the Chief Signal Officer, Oct. 20, 1870," *House Exec. Docs.,* 41st Cong., 3d sess., no. 1, pt. 2, serial 1446, 111; "Report of Col. J. J. Reynolds, Sept. 30, 1871," *House Exec. Docs.,* 42d Cong., 2d sess., no. 1, pt. 2, serial 1503, 65–66; Conway, ed., "Colonel Schriver's Inspector General's Report," (quote) 566; "Report of the Secretary of War, Nov. 22, 1875," *House Exec. Docs.,* 44th Cong., 1st sess., no. 1, pt. 2, serial 1674, 8.

29. "Report of the Chief Signal Officer, 1876," 86–93; Adolphus W. Greely, *Reminiscences of Adventure and Service: A Record of Sixty-Five Years,* 153–54; L. Tuffly Ellis, ed., "Lieutenant A. W. Greely's Report on the Installation of Military Telegraph Lines in Texas, 1875–1876," *Southwestern Historical Quarterly* LXIX (July, 1965): 66–87.

30. Greely, *Reminiscences,* (quote) 153–54; Ellis, ed., "Lieutenant Greely's Report," 84–85.

31. "Report of the Chief Signal Officer, 1876," 86–93; "Report of the Chief Signal Officer, Nov. 10, 1878," *House Exec. Docs.,* 45th Cong., 3d sess., no. 1, pt. 2, vol. 4, serial 1848, 180; Headquarters of the Military Division of the Missouri, *Outline Descriptions of the*

Posts . . . (1876), 182–208; Greely, *Reminiscences,* 153–54; Ellis, ed., "Lieutenant Greely's Report," 74–87.

32. "Report of the Chief Signal Officer, Nov. 1, 1871," *House Exec. Docs.,* 42d Cong., 2d sess., no. 1, pt. 2, serial 1503, 391; Lynch, "1879 in the Echo," 54; "Report of the Chief Signal Officer, Nov. 10, 1877," *House Exec. Docs.,* 45th Cong., 2d sess., no. 1, pt. 2, vol. 4, serial 1798, 147; "Report of the Chief Signal Officer, 1878," 182; Mary Sutton, "Glimpses of Fort Concho through the Military Telegraph," *West Texas Historical Association Year Book* 32 (Oct., 1956): 125.

33. Smith, ed., *A Dose of Frontier Soldiering,* (quote) 75, 182; "Report of the Chief Signal Officer, Nov. 10, 1877," *House Exec. Docs.,* 45th Cong., 2d sess., no. 1, pt. 2, vol. 4, serial 1798, 174; Greene, *900 Miles,* 250.

34. "Report of the Chief Signal Officer, Nov. 10, 1877," *House Exec. Docs.,* 45th Cong., 2d sess., no. 1, pt. 2, vol. 4, serial 1798, (quote) 143–44.

35. As quoted, ibid.

36. "Report of the Chief Signal Officer, Sept. 15, 1882," *House Exec. Docs.,* 47th Cong., 2d sess., no. 1, pt. 2., vol. 7, serial 2096, 41–42.

37. "Report of the Chief Signal Officer, Oct. 10, 1885," *House Exec. Docs.,* 49th Cong., 1st sess., no. 1, pt. 2, vol. 8, serial 2375, 10, 549; "Report of the Chief Signal Officer, Oct. 15, 1884," *House Exec. Docs.,* 48th Cong., 2d sess., no. 1, pt. 2, vol. 8, serial 2283, 23, 51; "Report of the Chief Signal Officer, Oct. 10, 1885," *House Exec. Docs.,* 49th Cong., 1st sess., no. 1, pt. 2, vol. 8, serial 2375, 3, 11, 547–48; "Report of the Chief Signal Officer, Oct. 9, 1886," *House Exec. Docs.,* 49th Cong., 2d sess., no. 1, vol. 6, serial 2465, 182; "Report of the Chief Signal Officer, Sept. 30, 1889," *House Exec. Docs.,* 51st Cong., 1st sess., no. 1, pt. 2, vol. 7, serial 2720, 52–53.

38. "Report of the Quartermaster General, 1889," 549; Tyler, ed., *New Handbook of Texas,* 6:245–46; "Report of the Chief Signal Officer, Oct. 1, 1890," *House Exec. Docs.,* 51st Cong., 2d sess., no. 1, pt. 2, vol. 8, serial 2837, 49, 52; "Report of the Chief Signal Officer, Oct. 10, 1891," *House Exec. Docs.,* 52d Cong., 1st sess., no. 1, pt. 2, serial 2929, 45.

39. "Report of the Chief Signal Officer, Oct. 10, 1892," *House Exec. Docs.,* 52d Cong., 2d sess., no. 1, pt. 2, serial 3077, 594–95; "Report of the Chief Signal Officer, Oct. 1, 1894," *House Exec. Docs.,* 53d Cong., 3d sess., no. 1, pt. 2, serial 3295, (quote) 484.

40. "Report of the Chief Signal Officer, Oct. 9, 1893," *House Exec. Docs.,* 53d Cong., 2d sess., no. 1, pt. 1, serial 3198, 645–47; "Report of the Chief Signal Officer, 1892," 595.

41. "Report of the Chief Signal Officer, 1894," 483–484, 502; "Report of the Chief Signal Officer, 30 Sept. 1896," *House Exec. Docs.,* 54th Cong., 2d sess., no. 2, Vol. 2, serial 3478, (quote) 596; "Report of the Chief Signal Officer, 5 Oct. 1900," *House Exec. Docs.,* 56th Cong., 2d sess., no. 2, Vol. 3, serial 4071, 1006; "Report of the Chief Signal

Officer, 1 Oct. 1895," *House Exec. Docs.,* 54th Cong., 1st sess., no. 2, Vol. 3, serial 3370, 574–575.

42. On the regulations of 1843, see Scheips, "Albert James Myer," 18. For examples of climate records at Texas posts, see Crimmins, ed., "W. G. Freeman's Report," LI:258; LII:233, 353, 447; LIII:74, 76, 208, 313, 319, 447, 453, 459, 466; Notson, "Fort Concho," 137, 138, 143. For an example of the surgeon general collecting meteorological registers at Texas posts in 1852, see "Report of the Surgeon General, Nov. 4, 1852," *House Exec. Docs.,* 32d Cong., 2d sess., no. 1, serial 674, 138.

43. "Report of the Chief Signal Officer, 1870," 111; "Report of the Secretary of War, 1871," 13–14; "Report of the Chief Signal Officer, 1871," 263, 283, 309–10; "Report of the Chief Signal Officer, Oct. 1, 1872," *House Exec. Docs.,* 42d Cong., 3d sess., no. 1, pt. 2, serial 1558, 526, 750–51; "Report of the Secretary of War, 1873," 19; Scheips, "Albert James Myer," 23–24; Whitnah, *History of the U.S. Weather Bureau,* 22–24.

44. "Report of the Chief Signal Officer, Nov. 1, 1874," *House Exec. Docs.,* 43d Cong., 2d sess., no. 1, pt. 2, vol. 2, serial 1635, 444, (quote) 451, 818–19.

45. "Report of the Chief Signal Officer, 1876," 33–34, 86, 378–82; San Antonio *Herald,* June 28, 1878, 4; Whitnah, *History of the U.S. Weather Bureau,* 31.

46. Mary Leefe Laurence, *Daughter of the Regiment: Memoirs of a Childhood in the Frontier Army, 1878–1898,* ed. Thomas T. Smith, 67.

47. "Report of the Secretary of War, 1887," 33; Marvin E. Kroeker, "William B. Hazen," in *Soldiers West: Biographies from the Military Frontier,* ed. Paul Andrew Hutton with an introduction by Robert M. Utley, 193–212; Whitnah, *History of the U.S. Weather Bureau,* 47–53.

48. "Report of the Secretary of War, 1887," (quote) 33.

49. "Report of the Chief Signal Officer, Sept. 30, 1889," *House Exec. Docs.,* 51st Cong., 1st sess., no. 1, pt. 2, vol. 7, serial 2720, 85–88, (quote) 86; Tyler, ed., *New Handbook of Texas,* 6:858; Whitnah, *History of the U.S. Weather Bureau,* 59–61.

CHAPTER 10.
CONCLUSION: SWORDS, CITIES, AND PLOWSHARES

1. For examples of military-political cooperation, see Robert Wooster, *The Military and United States Indian Policy, 1865–1903,* 73–87, 93–96, and Robert Wooster, "The Army and the Politics of Expansion: Texas and the Southwest Borderlands, 1870–1886," *Southwestern Historical Quarterly* XCIII (Oct., 1989): 151–67. For arguments that place the origins of the military-industrial complex in the mid- to late-nineteenth century forging of special nautical equipment and in the building of a steel navy, see Kurt Hackemer, "The U.S. Navy and the Late-Nineteenth-Century Steel Industry," *The Historian* 57 (Summer, 1995): 703–21; Benjamin Franklin Cooling, *Gray Steel and Blue*

Water Navy: The Formative Years of America's Military Industrial Complex; James L. Abrahamson, *America Arms for a New Century: The Making of a Great Military Power;* Bruce G. Bruton, "An Historical Perspective on the Future of the Military-Industrial Complex," *The Social Science Journal* 28, no. 1 (1991): 45–62. For arguments that the military-industrial complex grew out of the World War I industrial boards and the logistical demands of that conflict, see Gregory Michael Hooks, *Forging the Military-Industrial Complex: World War II's Battle of the Potomac;* Paul A. C. Koistine, "The Industrial Military Complex in Historical Perspective: World War I," *Business History Review* 41 (Winter, 1967): 378–403. For a view of a later World War II development of the military-industrial complex, see Terrence J. Gough, "Origins of the Army Industrial College: Military-Business Tensions after World War I," *Armed Forces and Society* 17 (Winter, 1991): 259–75; Robert D. Cuff, *The War Industries Board: Business-Government Relations during World War I.*

2. William G. Robbins, *Colony and Empire: The Capitalist Transformation of the American West,* 274, 280; Young, *Galveston and the Great West,* 192–94.

3. Dugas, "Texas Industry," 153–67; "Contracts of the War Department for 1860," 2–47, 52; "Report of the Engineer Bureau, 1860," 269, 272; Report of the Topographical Bureau, 1860," 294.

4. Dugas, "Texas Industry," 160–67; "Report of the Quartermaster General, 1870," 85, 151, 154, 180–81, 186–88, 192, 221, 257, 260–61; "Report of the Paymaster General, (1870)," *House Exec. Docs.,* 41st Cong., 3d sess., no. 1, pt. 2, serial 1446, 282; "Report of the Chief of Engineers, 1870," 31, 61.

5. *Texas State Gazette,* May 18, 1850, (first quote) 297; A Late Captain of Infantry (Robert E. Patterson), *Hints Bearing on the U.S. Army,* (second quote) 24; "Report of Maj. Gen. P. H. Sheridan, 1866," (third quote) 48. On G. K. Lewis, see *Texas State Gazette,* May 25, 1850, 305. On citizen deaths and stolen animals for 1849, see *Texas State Gazette,* Dec. 29, 1849, 145, and Jan. 26, 1850, 180. For numbers of army-Indian combats in Texas by year, see Smith, "U.S. Army Combat Operations in the Indian Wars of Texas, 1849–1881," 507.

6. Timmons, "Merchants and Military," 53–60; Metz, *Desert Army,* 28, 36–38; Wooster, *History of Fort Davis,* 378; (quote) Brig. Gen. C. C. Auger to M. Kenedy, S. M. Johnson, R. King, and the Citizens of Corpus Christi, Jan. 31, 1881, Letters Sent by Headquarters Department of Texas, vol. 16–19, Jan. 1, 1881–Dec. 30, 1882, microfilm no. M1114, roll 6.

7. "Report of the General of the Army, Nov. 3, 1881," (quote) 35.

8. For the 263 Texans with a wealth of $100,000 or more in 1860, see Wooster, "Wealthy Texans, 1860," 163–80. Of the 263 wealthy Texans, only nine had army contracts in the 1850s. Bexar County had seven wealthy Texans, five of which—Maverick, the Vance Brothers, Lewis, and Howard—had some type of army contract as discussed.

In El Paso, Simeon Hart, whose net worth was $350,000, supplied flour to the army in the 1850s worth about $10,000. Hamilton P. Bee, with a net worth of $104,000 in Goliad County, sold $5,360 worth of hay to Fort McIntosh in 1855, and had small beef contracts with that post in 1849, 1850, and 1856. Charles Stillman of Cameron County was worth $100,000 and was a partner in the Rio Grande steamship contracts of Kenedy and King. In Bowie County, G. H. Jones, worth $182,000, had been involved in two modest hay contracts at Fort Duncan—one in 1852 worth $2,250, and one in 1858 for $2,640. For the beef, forage, and freight contracts, see Appendixes I through IV.

9. "Report of the Quartermaster General, 1880," 474; "Report of the Commissary General of Subsistence, 1897," 396–97; "Report of the Commissary General of Subsistence, 1900," 458; McConnell, *Five Years a Cavalryman,* (quote) 231.

10. Carter, *Old Sergeant's Story,* 213–14; Charles M. Neal Jr., "Claron A. Windus, 1851–1927," *Branches and Acorns: Southwest Texas Genealogical Society* X (Mar., 1995): 8–13; Wooster, *Fort Davis,* 23; Cashion, *Texas Frontier,* 241–42, 258, 260.

11. Lynch, "1879 in the Echo," 51–79; Robinson, *Frontier World of Fort Griffin,* 39, 159–72; Cashion, *Texas Frontier,* 262–73.

12. Christian, "Sword and Plowshare," 70; El Paso *Times,* Sept. 29, 1997, 3b; "Report of the General of the Army, 1882," 32–33; "Report of the General of the Army, Oct. 10, 1888," *House Exec. Docs.,* 50th Cong., 2d sess., no. 1, pt. 2, vol. 2, serial 2628, 78–79.

13. McConnell, *Five Years a Cavalryman,* (first quote) 297; French, *Two Wars,* (second quote) 99.

Bibliography

ARCHIVES AND DOCUMENTS

National Archives and Records Service, Washington, D.C. (hereafter cited as NARS). Records of the U.S. Army Adjutant General's Office, 1780–1917. Record Group (hereafter cited as RG) 94.

General and Special Orders, 1847–1860.

Returns from Regular Army Infantry Regiments, June, 1821–Dec., 1916.

Regimental Returns, First Infantry, Jan., 1844–Dec., 1848; Jan., 1849–Dec., 1855. Microfilm no. M665, rolls 3, 4.

Regimental Returns, Eighth Infantry, Jan., 1848–Dec., 1857. Microfilm no. M665, roll 91.

Returns from Regular Army Cavalry Regiments, 1833–1916.

Regimental Returns, Second Cavalry (Second Dragoons), Apr., 1844–Dec., 1845; 1846–1848; 1849–1855. Microfilm no. M744, rolls 14, 15.

Returns from U.S. Military Posts, 1800–1916.

Post Returns, San Antonio, Tex., Oct., 1845–Sept., 1872. Microfilm no. M617, roll 1083.

Post Returns, Austin, Tex., Nov., 1848–Aug., 1875. Microfilm no. M617, roll 59.

Post Returns, Brazos Santiago, Tex., June, 1846–June, 1848. Microfilm no. M617, roll 140.

Post Returns, Fort Polk, Tex., Mar., 1846–Jan., 1850. Microfilm no. M617, roll 947.

Post Returns, Fort Inge, Tex., Mar., 1849–Jan., 1869. Microfilm no. M617, roll 517.

Letters Received by the Office of the Adjutant General (Main Series), 1871–1880.

Annual Report, Texas, 1880. Microfilm no. M666, roll 589.

Annual Report, Texas, 1888. Microfilm no. M689, roll 662.

NARS, Records of U.S. Army Continental Commands, 1821–1920. RG 393.

Letters Sent by Headquarters, Department of Texas. Vol. 16–19. Jan. 1, 1881–Dec. 30, 1882. Microfilm no. M1114, roll 6.

NARS, Records of the Headquarters of the Army. RG 108.

Headquarters, U.S. Army, "Descriptive Book of the District of Texas, July 1, 1868." Entry 51, Vol. 220. Microfilm no. M253.

NARS, Records of the Office of the Quartermaster General. RG 92.

"Register of Contracts, 1871–1876." Vol. 2, no. 1. Entry 1242.

"Register of Contracts, 1881–1883." Vol. 1. Entry 1245.

"Fort Inge" File, Quartermaster's Department, Letters Received (no entry number).

Records of Quartermasters, 1819–1905.

Maj. George H. Crosman. Misc. Circulars and Letters. Entry 333.

Capt. James R. Irwin. 1843–1851. Entry 341.

"Report of Persons Hired at Port Lavaca and List of Quartermaster Stores Transferred, Sept.–Oct. 1846." Entry 361.

Maj. Thomas B. Eastland. "Letters Sent." Vol. 2. Entry 342.

———. "Letters Sent, Routine Matters." Vol. 1. Entry 342.

NARS. Records of the Postmaster General. RG 28.

Postmaster General, Site Reports. "Fort Inge, June, 1867."

U.S. Bureau of the Census.

"Population Schedules of Uvalde County, Tex., 1860, Eighth Census of the United States." Microfilm 653, roll 1307.

Special Collections. United States Military Academy Library. West Point, N.Y.

Papers of William Chapman.

Robert Hazlitt Letters, 1844–1846.

John C. Tidball. Manuscript, "First Experiences."

The Historical Society of Pennsylvania, Philadelphia.

Persifor F. Smith Papers.

Center for American History, Univ. of Texas at Austin.

James Larson. "Memoirs." Arthur W. Arndt Collection. 2L158.

Lt. George H. Steuart. Correspondence, 1853–1855. Eberstadt Collection. Box 3N182.

U.S. Senate and Congressional Records.

30th Cong., 1st sess.

Senate Executive Documents. No. 1, vol. 1, serial 503. "Report of the Chief, Topographical Engineers, Nov. 22, 1847."

Senate Executive Documents. No. 8, pt.2, serial 515. "Report of the Secretary of War, Dec. 2, 1847."

House Executive Documents. No. 60, vol. 1, serial 520. "Mexican War Correspondence."

Senate Executive Documents. No. 1, serial 549.

"Report of the Secretary of War, Nov. 30, 1849."

"Report of the Quartermaster General, Nov. 10, 1849."

"Report of the Commissary General, Nov. 2, 1849."

"Report of the Chief Engineer (1849)."

"Report of the Colonel of Topographical Engineers, Nov. 20, 1849."

"Report of Lt. W. H. C. Whiting, June 10, 1849."

Senate Executive Documents. No. 26, serial 554. "The contracts made . . . 1849."

Senate Executive Documents. No. 32, serial 562. Capt. George W. Hughes, "Memoir Descriptive of the March of a Division of the U.S. Army, under the Command of Brig. Gen. John E. Wool from San Antonio de Bexar, in Texas, to Saltillo, in Mexico."

Senate Executive Documents. No. 64, serial 562. "Reports of the Secretary of War with Reconnaissances of Routes from San Antonio to El Paso, July 24, 1850."

Senate Executive Documents. No. 69, serial 562. "The Commerce of Brazos de St. Iago (1849)."

31st Cong., 2d sess.

House Executive Documents. No. 1, serial 595.

"Report of the Secretary of War, Nov. 30, 1850,"

"Report of the General-in-Chief, Nov. 30, 1850."

"Report of the Quartermaster General, Nov. 20, 1850."

"Report of the Colonel of the Corps of Topographical Engineers, Nov. 14, 1850."

House Executive Documents. No. 23, serial 599. "Statements of contracts and purchases, &c. (1850)."

32d Cong., 1st sess.

House Executive Documents. No. 1, serial 634.

"Report of the Secretary of War, Dec. 2, 1851."

"Report of the Quartermaster General, Nov. 22, 1851."

House Executive Documents. No. 23, serial 640. "Contracts—War Department (1851)."

32d Cong., 2d sess.

House Executive Documents. No. 1, serial 674.

"Report of the General-in-Chief, Nov. 22, 1852."

"Report of the Quartermaster General, Nov. 20, 1852."

"Report of the Surgeon General, Nov. 4, 1852."

House Executive Documents. No.21 , serial 676. "Contracts (1852)."

33d Cong., 1st sess.

Senate Executive Documents. No. 1, serial 691.

"Report of the Secretary of War, Dec. 1, 1853."

"Report of the Quartermaster General, Nov. 22, 1853."

"Report of the Chief Engineer, Nov. 30, 1853."

Senate Executive Documents. No. 37, serial 698. "Contracts made under the authority of the War Department during the year 1853."

33d Cong., 2d Sess.

House Executive Documents. No. 1, pt. 2, serial 778.

"Report of the Quartermaster General, Nov. 14, 1854."

"Report of the Chief Engineer, Nov. 29, 1854."

House Executive Documents. No. 68, serial 788. "Contracts—War Department, 1854."

House Executive Documents. No.91, serial 801. "Reports of Explorations and Surveys to Ascertain the Most Practicable and Economic Route for a Railroad from the Mississippi River to the Pacific Ocean [1855]."

34th Cong., 1st sess.

Senate Executive Documents. No. 1, serial 811.

"Reports from the Department of Texas, June 2, 1854."

"Report of the Commissary General, Oct. 25, 1855."

"Report of the Paymaster General, Nov. 20, 1855."

Senate Executive Documents. No. 7, serial 815. "List of contracts . . . during the year 1855."

34th Cong., 3d sess.

Senate Executive Documents. No. 5, serial 876.

"Report of the Secretary of War, Dec. 1, 1856."

"Report of the Commissary General, Nov. 18, 1856."

Senate Executive Documents. No. 32, serial 880. "Statements showing the contracts made . . . during the year 1856."

35th Cong., 1st sess.

Senate Executive Documents. No. 31, serial 924. "A statement of contracts . . . during the year 1857."

House Executive Documents. No. 2, serial 943. "Report of the Chief Engineer, Nov. 24, 1857."

House Executive Documents. No. 13, serial 947. "General Account of the receipts and expenditures of the United States for the fiscal year ending June 30, 1857."

35th Cong., 2d sess.

House Executive Documents. No. 2, pt. 2, vol. 2, serial 998. "Artesian Well Experiment, Reports of Capt. John Pope."

House Executive Documents. No. 2, pt. 2, serial 999. "Report of the Quartermaster General, Nov. 13, 1858."

House Executive Documents. No. 50, serial 1006. "Contracts—War Department (1858)."

36th Cong., 1st sess.

House Executive Documents. No. 22, serial 1047. "War Department—Contracts (1859)."

36th Cong., 2d sess.

Senate Executive Documents. No. 1, pt. 2, serial 1057.

"Report of the Engineer Bureau, Nov. 14, 1860"

"Report of the Topographical Bureau, Nov. 14, 1860."

Senate Executive Documents. No. 1, pt. 2, serial 1079. "Affairs in the Department of

Texas, Aug. 30, 1860."

House Executive Documents. No. 47, serial 1099. "Contracts of the War Department for 1860."

37th Cong., 2d sess.

House Executive Documents. No. 54, serial 1100. "Army Register, 1861."

39th Cong., 2d sess.

House Executive Documents. No. 1, serial 1285.

"Report of Major General P. H. Sheridan, Department of the Gulf, Nov. 14, 1866."

"Report of the Quartermaster General, Oct. 11, 1866."

"Report of the Signal Officer, Oct. 20, 1866."

40th Cong., 2d sess.

House Executive Documents. No. 1, serial 1324.

"Report of the Quartermaster General, Sept. 30, 1867."

40th Cong., 3d sess.

House Executive Documents. No. 1, serial 1367.

"Report of the Secretary of War, Nov. 20, 1868."

"Report of the Quartermaster General, Oct. 20, 1868."

"Report of the Commissary General of Subsistence, Oct. 20, 1868."

41st Cong., 2d sess.

House Executive Documents. No. 1, pt. 2, serial 1412.

"Report of the Secretary of War, Nov. 20, 1869."

"Report of the Quartermaster General, Oct. 20, 1869."

"Report of the Chief Signal Officer, Oct. 20, 1869."

House Executive Documents. No. 249, serial 1425. "Letter from the Secretary of War in Relation to Sales to Enlisted Men by Post Traders, Apr. 18, 1870."

41st Cong., 3d sess.

House Executive Documents. No. 1, pt. 2, serial 1446.

"Report of Major General Halleck, Military Division of the South, Oct. 24, 1870."

"Report of the Quartermaster General, Oct. 11, 1870."

"Report of the Paymaster General, (1870)."

"Report of the Chief of Engineers, Oct. 25, 1870."

"Report of the Chief Signal Officer, Oct. 20, 1870."

42d Cong., 2d sess.

House Executive Documents. No. 1, pt. 2, serial 1503.

"Report of the Secretary of War, Nov. 20, 1871."

"Report of the General of the Army, Nov. 6, 1871."

"Report of Colonel J. J. Reynolds, Sept. 30, 1871."

"Report of the Quartermaster General, Oct. 19, 1871."

"Report of the Chief Signal Officer, Nov. 1, 1871."

House Executive Documents. No. 124, serial 1513. "Letter from the Secretary of War Showing Expenditures for Construction and Repairs of Buildings at Each Fort and Military Post in Texas, Feb. 9, 1872."

42d Cong., 3d sess.

House Executive Documents. No. 1, pt. 2, serial 1558.

"Report of the Secretary of War, Nov. 1, 1872."

"Report of the General of the Army, Nov. 1, 1872."

"Report of the Quartermaster General, Oct. 10, 1872."

"Report of the Chief Signal Officer, Oct. 1, 1872."

43d Cong., 1st sess.

House Executive Documents. No. 1, pt. 2, vol. 2, serial 1597.

"Report of the Secretary of War, Nov. 24, 1873."

"Report of the Quartermaster General, Oct. 10, 1873."

"Report of the Chief of Engineers, Oct. 20, 1873."

43d Cong., 2d sess.

House Executive Documents. No. 1, pt. 2, vol. 2, serial 1635.

"Report of the Secretary of War (1874)."

"Report of the Quartermaster General, Oct. 10, 1874."

"Report of the Chief Signal Officer, Nov. 1, 1874."

House Executive Documents. No. 1, pt. 2, vol. 2, serial 1636. "Report of the Chief Engineer, Oct. 20, 1874."

44th Cong., 1st sess.

House Executive Documents. No. 1, pt. 2, serial 1674.

"Report of the Secretary of War, Nov. 22, 1875."

"Report of Brig. Gen. E. O. C. Ord, Headquarters, Department of Texas, Sept. 10, 1875."

"Report of the Quartermaster General, Oct. 9, 1875."

"Report of the Commissary General of Subsistence, Oct. 9, 1875."

44th Cong., 2d sess.

House Executive Documents. No. 1, pt. 2, serial 1742.

"Report of the Secretary of War, Nov. 20, 1876."

"Report of the Quartermaster General, Oct. 10, 1876."

"Report of the Commissary General of Subsistence (1876)."

House Executive Documents. No. 1, pt. 2, vol. 2, serial 1743. "Report of the Chief of Engineers, Oct. 10, 1876."

House Executive Documents. No. 1, pt. 2, vol. 4, serial 1747. "Annual Report of the

Chief Signal Officer, Oct. 10, 1876."

45th Cong., 2d sess.

House Executive Documents. No. 1, pt. 2, serial 1794.

"Report of the Quartermaster General, Oct. 10, 1877."

"Report of the Commissary General of Subsistence (1877)."

House Executive Documents. No. 1, pt. 2, vol. 2, serial 1795. "Report of the Chief of Engineers, Oct. 10, 1877."

House Executive Documents. No.1, pt. 2, vol. 4, serial 1798. "Report of the Chief Signal Officer, Nov. 10, 1877."

45th Cong., 3d sess.

House Executive Documents. No. 1, pt. 2, serial 1843. "Report of the Quartermaster General, Oct. 9, 1878."

House Executive Documents. No. 1, pt. 2, vol. 2, serial 1844. "Report of the Chief of Engineers, Oct. 19, 1878."

House Executive Documents. No. 1, pt. 2, vol. 4, serial 1848. "Report of the Chief Signal Officer, Nov. 10, 1878."

House Executive Documents. No. 23, serial 1852. "Letter from the Secretary of War Showing the Strength of the Army [1789–1878], Jan. 14, 1879."

46th Cong., 2d sess.

House Executive Documents. No. 1, pt. 2, vol. 2, serial 1903.

"Report of Brig. Gen. E. O. C. Ord, Oct. 1, 1879."

"Report of the Quartermaster General, Oct. 10, 1879."

House Executive Documents. No. 1, pt. 2, vol. 2, serial 1904. "Report of the Chief of Engineers, Oct. 20, 1879."

46th Cong., 3d sess.

House Executive Documents. No. 1, pt. 2, vol. 2, serial 1952. "Report of the Quarter-master General, Sept. 30, 1880."

House Executive Documents. No. 1, pt. 2, vol. 3, serial 1953. "Report of the Chief of Engineers, Oct. 19, 1880."

47th Cong., 1st sess.

House Executive Documents. No. 1, pt. 2, vol. 2, serial 2010.

"Report of the General of the Army, Nov. 3, 1881."

"Report of the Quartermaster General, Oct. 1, 1881."

"Report of the Commissary General of Subsistence, Oct. 10, 1881."

House Executive Documents. No. 1, pt. 1, vol. 2, serial 2011. "Report of the Chief of Engineers, Oct. 19, 1881."

47th Cong., 2d sess.

House Executive Documents. No. 1, pt. 2, vol. 2, serial 2091.

"Report of the General of the Army, Nov. 6, 1882."

"Report of the Quartermaster General, Oct. 9, 1882."

"Report of the Commissary General of Subsistence, Oct. 7, 1882."

House Executive Documents. No. 1, pt. 2, vol. 3, serial 2092. "Report of the Chief of Engineers, Oct. 19, 1882."

House Executive Documents. No. 1, pt. 2, vol. 7, serial 2096. "Report of the Chief Signal Officer, Sept. 15, 1882."

48th Cong., 1st sess.

House Executive Documents. No. 1, pt. 2, vol. 2, serial 2182.

"Report of the Quartermaster General, Oct. 6, 1883."

"Report on Transcontinental Railways, 1883, by Colonel O. M. Poe."

"Report of the Commissary General of Subsistence, Oct. 8, 1883."

48th Cong., 2d sess.

House Executive Documents. No. 1, pt. 2, vol. 2, serial 2277.

"Report of the Quartermaster General, Oct. 9, 1884."

"Report of the Commissary General of Subsistence, Oct. 15, 1884."

House Executive Documents. No. 1, pt. 2, vol. 8, serial 2283. "Report of the Chief Signal Officer, Oct. 15, 1884."

49th Cong., 1st sess.

House Executive Documents. No. 1, pt. 2, vol. 2, serial 2369. "Report of the Quartermaster General, Oct. 9, 1885."

House Executive Documents. No. 1, pt. 2, vol. 8, serial 2375. "Report of the Chief Signal Officer, Oct. 10, 1885."

49th Cong., 2d sess.

House Executive Documents. No. 1, vol. 2, serial 2461.

"Report of Brigadier General Stanley, Sept. 4, 1886."

"Report of the Quartermaster General, Oct. 9, 1886."

House Executive Documents. No. 1, vol. 6, serial 2465. "Report of the Chief Signal Officer, Oct. 9, 1886."

50th Cong., 1st sess.

House Executive Documents. No. 1, vol. 2, serial 2533.

"Annual Report of the Secretary of War, Dec. 5, 1887."

"Report of Brigadier General Stanley, Aug. 27, 1887."

"Report of the Inspector General, Nov. 7, 1887."

"Report of the Quartermaster General, Oct. 6, 1887."

50th Cong., 2d sess.

House Executive Documents. No. 1, pt. 2, vol. 2, serial 2628.

"Report of the Inspector General, Oct. 10, 1888."

"Report of the Quartermaster General, Oct. 5, 1888."

51st Cong., 1st sess.

    House Executive Documents. No. 1, pt. 2, serial 2715.

      "Report of the Quartermaster General, Oct. 5, 1889."

      "Report of the Commissary General of Subsistence, Oct. 10, 1889."

    House Executive Documents. No. 1, pt. 2, vol. 7, serial 2720. "Report of the Chief Signal Officer, Sept. 30, 1889."

51st Cong., 2d sess.

    House Executive Documents. No. 1, pt. 2, vol. 2, serial 2831. "Report of the Quartermaster General, Oct. 9, 1890."

    House Executive Documents. No. 1, pt. 2, vol. 8, serial 2837. "Report of the Chief Signal Officer, Oct. 1, 1890."

52d Cong., 1st sess.

    House Executive Documents. No. 1, pt. 2, serial 2921. "Report of the Quartermaster General, Oct. 3, 1891."

    House Executive Documents. No. 1, pt. 2, serial 2929. "Report of the Chief Signal Officer, Oct. 10, 1891."

52d Cong., 2d sess.

    House Executive Documents. No. 1, pt. 2, serial 3077.

      "Report of the Quartermaster General, Oct. 1, 1892."

      "Report of the Chief Signal Officer, Oct. 10, 1892."

53d Cong., 2d sess.

    House Executive Documents. No. 1, pt. 1, serial 3198.

      "Report of the Secretary of War, Nov. 27, 1893."

      "Report of the Chief Signal Officer, Oct. 9, 1893."

53d Cong., 3d sess.

    House Executive Documents. No. 1, pt. 2, serial 3295.

      "Report of the Quartermaster General, Sept. 26, 1894."

      "Report of the Chief Signal Officer, Oct. 1, 1894."

54th Cong., 1st sess.

    House Executive Documents. No. 2, vol. 3, serial 3370.

      "Report of the Secretary of War, Nov. 26, 1895."

      "Report of Brig. Gen. Z. R. Bliss, Aug. 22, 1895."

      "Report of the Quartermaster General, Sept. 27, 1895."

      "Report of the Commissary General of Subsistence, Oct. 1, 1895."

      "Report of the Paymaster General, Sept. 21, 1895."

      "Report of the Chief Signal Officer, Oct. 1, 1895."

54th Cong., 2d sess.

    House Executive Documents. No. 2, vol. 2, serial 3478.

      "Report of the Secretary of War, Nov. 24, 1896."

"Report of the Major-General Commanding the Army, Oct. 10, 1896."

"Report of Brig. Gen. Z. R. Bliss, Sept. 8, 1896."

"Report of the Inspector General of the Army, Nov. 4, 1896."

"Report of the Quartermaster General, Oct. 1, 1896."

"Report of the Chief Signal Officer, Sept. 30, 1896."

55th Cong., 2d sess.

House Executive Documents. No. 2, vol. 2, serial 3630.

"Report of the Quartermaster General, Oct. 1, 1897."

"Report of the Commissary General of Subsistence, Oct. 1, 1897."

"Report of the Chief Signal Officer, Sept. 30, 1897."

54th Cong., 3d sess.

House Executive Documents. No. 2, vol. 2, serial 3744. "Report of the Quartermaster General, Oct. 31, 1898."

56th Cong., 1st sess.

House Executive Documents. No. 2, vol. 3, serial 3900. "Report of the Quartermaster General, Oct. 16, 1899."

56th Cong., 2d sess.

House Executive Documents. No. 2, vol. 3, serial 4071.

"Report of the Adjutant General of the Army, Oct. 20, 1900."

"Report of the Quartermaster General, Oct. 16, 1900."

"Report of the Commissary General of Subsistence, Oct. 23. 1900."

"Report of the Paymaster General, Sept. 20, 1900."

"Report of the Chief Signal Officer, Oct. 5, 1900."

BOOKS

A Late Captain of Infantry (Robert E. Patterson). *Hints Bearing on the United States Army with an Aim at the Adaptation, Availability, Efficiency and Economy Thereof.* Philadelphia: Henry B. Ashmead, 1858.

Abbot, Frederick V. *History of the Class of 'Seventy-Nine at the U.S. Military Academy.* New York: G. P. Putnam's Sons, 1884.

Abrahamson, James L. *America Arms for a New Century: The Making of A Great Military Power.* New York: Free Press, 1981.

Adjutant General's Office. *Official Army Register for 1898.* Washington, D.C.: Government Printing Office, 1898.

———. *Official Army Register for 1890.* Washington, D.C.: Government Printing Office, 1890.

Ahlborn, Richard Eighme. *The San Antonio Missions: Edward Everett and the American Occupation, 1847.* Fort Worth: Amon Carter Museum, 1985.

Alprin, Lynn M. *Custodians of the Coast: History of the United States Army Engineers at Galveston.* Galveston, Tex: Galveston District, U.S. Army Corps of Engineers, 1977.

Athearn, Robert G. *William Tecumseh Sherman and the Settlement of the West.* Norman: Univ. of Oklahoma Press, 1956.

Austerman, Wayne R. *Sharps Rifles and Spanish Mules: The San Antonio–El Paso Mail, 1851–1881.* College Station: Texas A&M Univ. Press, 1985.

Baker, T. Lindsay, ed. *The Texas Red River Country: The Official Surveys of the Headwaters, 1876.* Foreword by Dan. L. Flores. College Station: Texas A&M Univ. Press, 1998.

Bauer, K. Jack. *The Mexican War, 1846–1848.* New York: Macmillan, 1974.

Baughman, James P. *Charles Morgan and the Development of Southern Transportation.* Nashville: Vanderbilt Univ. Press, 1968.

Bowden, J. J. *The Exodus of Federal Forces from Texas, 1861.* Austin: Eakin Press, 1985.

Boyd, Mrs. Orsemus B. *Cavalry Life in Tent and Field.* New York: J. S. Tait, 1894. Reprint, with an introduction by Darlis A. Miller, Lincoln: Univ. of Nebraska Press, 1982.

Cagle, Eldon, Jr. *Quadrangle: The History of Fort Sam Houston.* Austin: Eakin Press, 1985.

Carlson, Paul H. *"Pecos Bill": A Military Biography of William R. Shafter.* College Station: Texas A&M Univ. Press, 1989.

Carter, Robert G. *From Yorktown to Santiago with the Sixth United States Cavalry.* Baltimore: Lord Baltimore, 1900. Reprint, Austin Tex.: State House Press, 1989.

———. *The Old Sergeant's Story: Winning the West from the Indians and Bad Men in 1870 to 1876.* New York: Frederick H. Hitchcock, 1926.

Cartwright, Gary. *Galveston: A History of the Island.* New York: Atheneum, 1991.

Cashion, Ty. *A Texas Frontier: The Clear Fork Country and Fort Griffin, 1849–1887.* Norman: Univ. of Oklahoma Press, 1996.

Catlin, George. *North American Indians.* 2 vols. 2d ed. Philadelphia: Leary, Stuart, 1913.

Census Office. *A Compendium of the Tenth Census, June 1, 1880.* 2 vols. Washington, D.C.: Government Printing Office, 1883.

———. *Abstract of the Eleventh Census: 1890.* Washington, D.C.: Government Printing Office,1894.

———. *Historical Statistics of the United States: Colonial Times to 1970.* Part 1. Washington, D.C.: Government Printing Office, 1975.

Chipman, Donald E. *Spanish Texas, 1519–1821.* Austin: Univ. of Texas Press, 1992.

Clark, Charles T. *Opdycke Tigers: 125th O. V. I.* Columbus. Ohio: Spahr and Glenn, 1895.

Clary, David A., and Joseph W. A. Whitehorne. *The Inspectors General of the United States Army, 1777–1903.* Washington, D.C.: Office of the Inspector General and Center of Military History, U.S. Army, 1987.

Coffman, Edward M. *The Old Army: A Portrait of the American Army in Peacetime, 1784–1898.* New York: Oxford Univ. Press, 1986.

Cogley, Thomas S. *History of the Seventh Indiana Cavalry Volunteers.* Laporte, Ind.: Herald, 1976.

Coker, Caleb, ed. *The News from Brownsville: Helen Chapman's Letters from the Texas Military Frontier, 1848–1852.* Austin: Texas State Historical Association, 1992.

Conkling, Roscoe and Margaret B. Conkling. *The Butterfield Overland Mail, 1857–1869.* 3 vols. Glendale, Calif.: Arthur H. Clark, 1947.

Cooling, Benjamin Franklin. *Gray Steel and Blue Water Navy: The Formative Years of America's Military Industrial Complex.* Hamden, Conn.: Archon, 1981.

Crook, George. *General George Crook: His Autobiography.* Edited by Martin F. Schmitt. Norman: Univ. of Oklahoma Press, 1960.

Cuff, Robert D. *The War Industries Board: Business-Government Relations during World War I.* Baltimore: Johns Hopkins Univ. Press, 1973.

De Bow, James D.B. *Statistical View of the United States: Being a Compendium of the Seventh Census. . . .* Washington, D.C.: Government Printing Office, 1854.

Delo, David Michael. *Peddlers and Post Traders: The Army Sutler on the Frontier.* Salt Lake City: Univ. of Utah Press, 1992.

Dodge, Richard Irving. *Our Wild Indians: Thirty-three Years' Personal Experience among the Red Men of the Great West.* Hartford, Conn.: 1882. Reprint, New York: Archer House, 1959.

Eaton, Jack D. *Excavations at the Alamo Shrine (Mission San Antonio de Valero).* Special Report No. 10. San Antonio: Center for Archaeological Research, Univ. of Texas at San Antonio, 1980.

Eisenhower, John S. D. *So Far from God: The U.S. War with Mexico, 1846–1848.* New York: Random House, 1989.

Fenley, Florence. *Oldtimers: Frontier Days in Uvalde Section of South West Texas.* Uvalde, Tex.: Hornby Press, 1939. Reprint, Austin, Tex.: State House Press, 1991.

Ferrell, Robert H. Ferrell, ed. *Monterrey Is Ours! The Mexican War Letters of Lieutenant Dana, 1845–1847.* Lexington: Univ. Press of Kentucky, 1990.

Ford, John Salmon. *RIP Ford's Texas.* Edited by Stephen B. Oates. Austin: Univ. of Texas Press, 1963.

Fowler, Arlen L. *Black Infantry in the West, 1869–1891.* Westport, Conn.: Greenwood, 1971. Reprint, with a foreword by William H. Leckie. Norman: Univ. of Oklahoma Press, 1996.

Fox, Daniel E. *Traces of Texas History: Archeological Evidence of the Past 450 Years.* San Antonio: Corona, 1983.

Francaviglia, Richard V. *From Sail to Steam: Four Centuries of Texas Maritime History, 1500–1900.* Austin: Univ. of Texas Press, 1998.

Frazer, Robert W. *Forts of the West.* Norman: Univ. of Oklahoma Press, 1965.

———. *Forts and Supplies: The Role of the Army in the Economy of the Southwest, 1846–1861.* Albuquerque: Univ. of New Mexico Press, 1983.

Frazier, Donald S. *Blood and Treasure: Confederate Empire in the Southwest.* College Station: Texas A&M Univ. Press, 1995.

French, Samuel G. *Two Wars: An Autobiography of Gen. Samuel G. French.* Nashville: Confederate Veteran, 1901.

Gerstle, Andrea, Thomas C. Kelly, and Cristi Assad. *The Fort Sam Houston Project: An Archaeological and Historical Assessment.* San Antonio: Center for Archaeological Research, Univ. of Texas at San Antonio, Archaeological Survey Report, No. 40, 1978.

Goetzmann, William H. *Army Exploration in the American West, 1803–1863.* New Haven, Conn.: Yale Univ. Press, 1959. Reprint, Lincoln: Univ. of Nebraska Press, 1979.

Gouge, William M. *The Fiscal History of Texas: Embracing an Account of Its Revenues, Debts, and Currency from the Commencement of the Revolution in 1834 to 1851–52.* Philadelphia: Lippincott, Grambo, 1852.

Grant, Ulysses S. *Personal Memoirs of U.S. Grant: Selected Letters, 1839–1865.* New York: Charles L. Webster, 1885. 2 vols. Reprint, New York: Library of America, 1990.

Greely, Adolphus W. *Reminiscences of Adventure and Service: A Record of Sixty-five Years.* New York: Charles Scribner's Sons, 1927.

Greene, A.C. *900 Miles on the Butterfield Trail.* Denton: Univ. of North Texas Press, 1994.

Haley, J. Evetts *Fort Concho and the Texas Frontier.* San Angelo, Tex.: *San Angelo Standard Times,* 1952.

Haley, James L. *The Buffalo War: The History of the Red River Indian Uprising of 1874.* Garden City, N.Y.: Doubleday, 1976. Reprint, Norman: Univ. of Oklahoma Press, 1985.

Hamilton, Allen Lee. *Sentinel of the Southern Plains: Fort Richardson and the Northwest Texas Frontier, 1866–1878.* Fort Worth: Texas Christian Univ. Press, 1988.

Handy, Mary Olivia. *History of Fort Sam Houston.* San Antonio: Naylor, 1951.

Harris, Theodore D., ed. *Negro Frontiersman: The Western Memoirs of Henry O. Flipper, First Negro Graduate of West Point.* El Paso: Texas Western College Press, 1963.

Hart, Herbert M. *Tour Guide to Old Western Forts.* Fort Collins, Colo.: Old Army Press, 1980.

Headquarters of the Military Division of the Missouri. *Outline Descriptions of the Posts in the Military Division of the Missouri, Commanded by Lt. Gen. P. H. Sherdian.* Chicago: Headquarters, Military Division of the Missouri, 1876. Reprint, Bellevue, Nebr.: The Old Army Press, 1969.

Heitman, Francis B. *Historical Register and Dictionary of the United States Army.* 2 vols. Washington, D.C.: Government Printing Office, 1903.

Hitchcock, Ethan Allen. *Fifty Years in Camp and Field: Diary of Major-General Ethan Allen Hitchcock, U.S.A.* Edited by W.A. Croffut. New York: G. P. Putnam's Sons, 1909.

Hooks, Gregory Michael. *Forging the Military-Industrial Complex: World War II's Battle of the Potomac.* Urbana: Univ. of Illinois Press, 1991.

Huston, James A. *The Sinews of War: Army Logistics, 1775–1953.* Washington, D.C.: U.S. Army Center of Military History, 1988.

Hutton, Paul Andrew. *Phil Sheridan and His Army.* Lincoln: Univ. of Nebraska Press, 1985.

Inspector General's Office. *Outline Descriptions of the Posts and Stations of Troops in the Geo-*

graphic Divisions and Departments of the United States (1872). Washington, D.C.: Government Printing Office, 1872.

Ivey, James E., Thomas Medlin, and Jack D. Eaton. *An Initial Archaeological Assessment of Areas Proposed for Modification at Fort McIntosh, Webb County, Texas*. Archaeological Survey Report no. 23. San Antonio: Center for Archaeological Research, Univ. of Texas at San Antonio, 1977.

Jackson, W. Turrentine. *Wagon Roads West: A Study of Federal Road Surveys and Construction in the Trans-Mississippi West, 1846–1869*. New Haven, Conn.: Yale Univ. Press, 1964. Reprint, with a foreword by William H. Goetzmann, Lincoln: Univ. of Nebraska Press, 1979.

Johnson, Richard W. *A Soldier's Reminiscences in Peace and War*. Philadelphia: J. P. Lippincott, 1886.

Jordan, Terry G. *Texas Log Buildings: A Folk Architecture*. Austin: Univ. of Texas Press, 1978.

Kelly, Pat. *River of Lost Dreams: Navigation on the Rio Grande*. Lincoln: Univ. of Nebraska Press, 1986.

Kennedy, Joseph C. G. *Agriculture of the United States In 1860:Compiled from the Original Returns of the Eighth Census*. 2 vols. Washington, D.C.: Government Printing Office, 1864.

Kieffer, Chester L. *Maligned General: The Biography of Thomas Sidney Jesup*. San Rafael, Calif.: Presido Press, 1979.

Kinevan, Marcos E. *Frontier Cavalryman: Lieutenant John Bigelow and the Buffalo Soldiers in Texas*. El Paso: Texas Western Press, 1998.

King, Grace, Sherwood Noël McGuigan, and Gem Meacham. *From Muskets to Mohair: The History of Fort Terrett*. Waco, Tex.: Texian Press, 1992.

Knight, Oliver. *Fort Worth on the Trinity*. Norman: Univ. of Oklahoma Press, 1954.

———. *Life and Manners in the Frontier Army*. Norman: Univ. of Oklahoma Press, 1978.

Konwiser, Harry M. *Texas Republic Postal System*. New York: Harry Lindquist, 1933.

Lane, Lydia Spencer. *I Married A Soldier: or, Old Days in the Army*. Philadelphia: J. P. Lippincott, 1893. Reprint, with an introduction by Darlis A. Miller, Albuquerque: Univ. of New Mexico Press, 1987.

Laurence, Mary Leefe. *Daughter of the Regiment: Memoirs of a Childhood in the Frontier Army, 1878–1898*. Edited by Thomas T. Smith. Lincoln: Univ. of Nebraska Press, 1996.

Lea, Tom. *The King Ranch*. 2 vols. Boston: Little, Brown, 1957.

Leckie, Shirley Anne, ed. *The Colonel's Lady on the Western Frontier: The Correspondence of Alice Kirk Grierson*. Lincoln: Univ. of Nebraska Press, 1989.

Lesley, Lewis Burt, ed. *Uncle Sam's Camels: The Journal of May Humphreys Stacy Supplemented by the Report of Edward Fitzgerald Beale (1857–1858)*. Cambridge, Mass.: Harvard Univ. Press, 1929. Reprint, Glorieta, N.M.: Rio Grande, 1970.

Lewis, Lloyd. *Captain Sam Grant*. Boston: Little, Brown, 1950.

Lowe, Percival G. *Five Years a Dragoon ('49 to '54) and Other Adventures on the Great Plains*.

Kansas City, Mo.: Franklin Hudson, 1906. Reprint, with an introduction by Don Russell and foreword by Jerome A. Greene, Norman: Univ. of Oklahoma Press, 1965.

Lowe, Richard G., and Randolph B. Campbell. *Planters and Plain Folk: Agriculture in Antebellum Texas.* Dallas: Southern Methodist Univ. Press, 1987.

Malsch, Brownson. *Indianola: The Mother of Western Texas.* Austin: Shoal Creek, 1977.

Marcy, Capt. Randolph B. *The Prairie Traveler.* New York: Harper and Brothers, 1859.

Marshall, Thomas Maitland. *A History of the Western Boundary of the Louisiana Purchase, 1819–1841.* 2 vols. Berkeley: Univ. of California Press, 1914.

Maury, Dabney Herndon. *Recollections of a Virginian in the Mexican, Indian, and Civil Wars.* New York: Charles Scribner's Sons, 1894.

McChristian, Douglas C., ed. *Garrison Tangles in the Friendless Tenth: The Journal of First Lieutenant John Bigelow Jr., Fort Davis, Tex.* Bryan, Tex.: J. M. Carroll, 1985.

McConnell, H. H. *Five Years a Cavalryman, or, Sketches of Regular Army Life on the Texas Frontier, 1866–1871.* Jacksboro, Tex.: J. N. Rogers, 1889. Reprint, with a foreword by William H. Leckie, Norman: Univ. of Oklahoma Press, 1996.

Meade, George, ed. *The Life and Letters of George Gordon Meade, Major General, United States Army.* 2 vols. New York: Charles Scribner's Sons, 1913.

Metz, Leon C. *Desert Army: Fort Bliss on the Texas Border.* El Paso: Mangan, 1988.

Miller, Darlis A. *Soldiers and Settlers: Military Supply in the Southwest, 1861–1885.* Albuquerque: Univ. of New Mexico Press, 1989.

Miller, Edmund Thorton. *A Financial History of Texas.* Austin: Univ. of Texas Bulletin no. 37, 1916.

Miller, Thomas Lloyd. *The Public Lands of Texas, 1519–1970.* Norman: Univ. of Oklahoma Press, 1971.

Mills, Anson. *My Story.* Edited by C. H. Claudy. Washington, D.C.: Anson Mills, 1918.

Moore, Ike. *The Life and Diary of Reading W. Black.* Uvalde, Tex.: El Progreso Club, 1934.

Morris, Donald R. *The Washing of the Spears: A History of the Rise of the Zulu Nation under Shaka Zulu and Its Fall in the Zulu War of 1879.* New York: Simon and Schuster, 1965.

Nankivell, John H. *History of the Twenty-fifth Regiment, United States Infantry, 1869–1926.* Denver: Smith-Brooks, 1927. Reprint, Fort Collins, Colo.: Old Army Press, 1972.

National Park Service. *Soldier and Brave: Historic Places Associated with Indian Affairs and the Indian Wars in the Trans-Mississippi West.* National Survey of Historic Sites and Buildings. Vol. 12. Edited by Robert G. Ferris. Washington, D.C.: U.S. Department of the Interior, National Park Service, 1971.

Office of the Judge Advocate General, *United States Military Reservations, National Cemeteries and Military Parks: Title, Jurisdiction, Etc.* Washington, D.C.: Government Printing Office, 1910.

Olmsted, Frederick Law. *A Journey through Texas, or, a Saddle-Trip on the Southwestern Frontier.* New York: Dix, Edwards, 1857. Reprint, Austin: Univ. of Texas Press, 1978.

Pacific Railroad Reports. 13 vols. Washington, D.C.: A. O. P. Nicholson, 1855–60.

Pingenot, Ben E., ed. *Paso Del Águila: A Chronicle of Frontier Days on the Texas Border as Recorded in the Memoirs of Jesse Sumpter.* Compiled by Harry Warren. Austin: Encino, 1969.

Potts, Charles A. *Railroad Transportation in Texas.* Bulletin no. 119. Austin: Univ. of Texas, Mar. 1, 1909.

Price, George Frederick. *Across the Continent with the Fifth Cavalry.* New York: Van Nostrand, 1883.

Prucha, Francis Paul. *Broadax and Bayonet: The Role of the United States Army in the Development of the Northwest, 1815–1860.* Madison: State Historical Society of Wisconsin, 1953. Reprint, Lincoln: Univ. of Nebraska Press, 1995.

———. *The Sword of the Republic: The United States Army on the Frontier, 1783–1846.* New York: Macmillan, 1969. Reprint, Lincoln: Univ. of Nebraska Press, 1986.

Quartermaster General's Office. *Outline Description of United States Military Posts and Stations in the Year 1871.* Washington, D.C.: Government Printing Office, 1872.

Reed, St. Clair Griffin. *A History of the Texas Railroads and of Transportation Conditions in Texas under Spain and Mexico and the Republic and the State.* Houston: St. Clair, 1941.

Richardson, Rupert Norval. *The Frontier of Northwest Texas, 1846–1876.* Glendale, Calif.: Arthur H. Clark, 1963.

Richter, William L. *The Army in Texas during Reconstruction.* College Station: Texas A&M Univ. Press, 1987.

Rickey, Don Jr. *Forty Miles a Day on Beans and Hay: The Enlisted Soldier Fighting the Indian Wars.* Norman: Univ. of Oklahoma Press, 1963.

Risch, Erna. *Quartermaster Support of the Army: A History of the Corps, 1775–1939.* Washington, D.C.: U.S. Army Center of Military History, 1962. Reprint, 1989.

Rister, Carl Coke. *The Southwestern Frontier, 1865–1881.* Cleveland: Arthur H. Clark, 1928.

Robbins, William G. *Colony and Empire: The Capitalist Transformation of the American West.* Lawrence, Kans.: Univ. Press of Kansas, 1994.

Roberts, Robert B. *Encyclopedia of Historic Forts: The Military, Pioneer, and Trading Posts of the United States.* New York: Macmillan, 1988.

Robinson, Charles M. III. *The Frontier World of Fort Griffin: The Life and Death of a Western Town.* Spokane, Wash.: Arthur H. Clark, 1992.

Santleben, August. *A Texas Pioneer: Early Staging and Overland Freighting Days on the Frontiers of Texas and Mexico.* Edited by I. D. Affleck. New York: Neal, 1910. Reprint, Castroville, Tex.: Castro Colonies Heritage Association, 1994.

Schrader, Charles R. *U.S. Military Logistics, 1607–1991: A Research Guide.* Westport, Conn.: Greenwood, 1992.

Sears, Stephen W. *George B. McClellan: The Young Napoleon.* New York: Ticknor and Fields, 1988.

Settle, Raymond W., and Mary Lund Settle. *Empire on Wheels*. Stanford, Calif.: Stanford Univ. Press, 1940.

Sides, Joseph C. *Fort Brown Historical: History of Fort Brown, Texas Border Post on the Rio Grande*. San Antonio: Naylor, 1942.

Singletary, Otis A. *The Mexican War*. Chicago: Univ. of Chicago Press, 1960.

Smith, David Paul. *Frontier Defense in the Civil War: Texas' Rangers and Rebels*. College Station: Texas A&M Univ. Press, 1992.

Smith, Franklin. *The Mexican War Journal of Capt. Franklin Smith*. Edited by Joseph E. Chance. Jackson: Univ. Press of Mississippi, 1991.

Smith, George Winston, and Charles Judah. *Chronicles of the Gringos: The U.S. Army in the Mexican War, 1846–1848*. Albuquerque: Univ. of New Mexico Press, 1968.

Smith, Thomas T. *Fort Inge: Sharps, Spurs, and Sabers on the Texas Frontier, 1849–1869*. Austin: Eakin Press, 1991.

Smith, Thomas T., ed. *A Dose of Frontier Soldiering: The Memoirs of Corporal E. A. Bode, Frontier Regular Infantry, 1877–1882*. Lincoln: Univ. of Nebraska Press, 1994.

Stanley, David S. *Personal Memoirs of Major-General D. S. Stanley, U.S.A.* Cambridge, Mass.: Harvard Univ. Press, 1917.

Steffen, Randy. *The Horse Soldier, 1776–1943*. 4 vols. Norman: Univ. of Oklahoma Press, 1978.

Swift, Roy, and Leavitt Corning Jr. *Three Roads to Chihuahua: The Great Wagon Roads that Opened the Southwest, 1823–1883*. Austin: Eakin Press, 1988.

The Register of Graduates and Former Cadets of the United States Military Academy. West Point, N.Y.: West Point Alumni Foundation, 1964.

Thompson, Jerry D. *Mexican Texans in the Union Army*. El Paso: Texas Western Press, 1986.

Tijerina, Andrés. *Tejanos and Texas under the Mexican Flag, 1821–1836*. College Station: Texas A&M Univ. Press, 1994.

Todd, Albert. *The Class of 1877*. Cambridge, Mass.: Riverside, 1878.

Trass, Adrian George. *From the Golden Gate to Mexico City: The U.S. Army Topographical Engineers in the Mexican War, 1846–1848*. Washington, D.C.: Office of History, Corps of Engineers and Center of Military History, 1993.

Turnley, Parmenas Taylor. *Reminiscences of Parmenas Taylor Turnley from the Cradle to Three-Score and Ten*. Chicago: Donohue and Henneberry, 1892.

Tyler, Ron, ed. *The New Handbook of Texas*. 6 vols. Austin: Texas State Historical Association, 1996.

United States Military Academy. *First Class Annual of the Class of '86, United States Military Academy, West Point, N.Y. for the Year 1887*. Poughkeepsie, N.Y.: Haight and Dudley, 1887.

Utley, Robert M. *Frontiersmen in Blue: The United States Army and the Indian, 1848–1865*. New York: Macmillan, 1967. Reprint, Lincoln: Univ. of Nebraska Press, 1981.

———. *Frontier Regulars: The United States Army and the Indian, 1866–1891*. New York: Macmillan, 1973.

Vielé, Teresa Griffin. *Following the Drum: A Glimpse of Frontier Life*. New York: Rudd and
Carleton, 1858. Reprint, with a foreword by Sandra L. Myres. Lincoln: Univ. of Nebraska
Press, 1984.

Walker, Francis A. *A Compendium of the Ninth Census, June 1, 1870*. Washington, D.C.: Government Printing Office, 1872.

Wallace, Ernest. *Ranald S. Mackenzie on the Texas Frontier*. Lubbock: West Texas Museum
Association, 1964. Reprint, College Station: Texas A&M Univ. Press, 1993.

War Department. *The War of the Rebellion: A Compilation of the Official Records of the Union
and Confederate Armies*. 128 pts. in 70 vols. Washington, D.C.: Government Printing Office,
1880–1901.

Webb, Walter Prescott. *The Great Plains*. New York: Ginn, 1931. Reprint, Lincoln: Univ. of
Nebraska Press, 1981.

———, ed. *The Handbook of Texas*. 3 vols. Austin: Texas State Historical Association, 1952.

Weems, John Edward. *To Conquer a Peace: The War Between the United States and Mexico*.
Garden City, N.Y.: Doubleday, 1974.

Weigley, Russell F. *History of the United States Army*. 2d ed. Bloomington: Indiana Univ. Press,
1984.

Whitnah, Donald R. *A History of the United States Weather Bureau*. Urbana: Univ. of Illinois
Press, 1961.

Wilhite, Robert, and Clifford Mishler. *Standard Guide to U.S. Coin and Paper Money Valua-
tions*. 5th ed. Iola, Wis.: Krause, 1978.

Williams, Clayton W. *Texas' Last Frontier: Fort Stockton and the Trans-Pecos, 1861–1895*. College
Station: Texas A&M Univ. Press, 1982.

Wilson, Neill C., and Frank Taylor. *Southern Pacific*. New York: McGraw Hill, 1952.

Wooster, Robert. *Soldiers, Sutlers, and Settlers: Garrison Life on the Texas Frontier*. College
Station: Texas A&M Univ. Press, 1987.

———. *The Military and United States Indian Policy, 1865–1903*. New Haven: Yale Univ. Press,
1988.

———. *History of Fort Davis, Texas*. Southwest Cultural Resources Center, Professional Paper no. 34. Santa Fe: Southwest Region, National Park Service, Department of the Interior, 1990.

———. *Nelson A. Miles and the Twilight of the Frontier Army*. Lincoln: Univ. of Nebraska
Press, 1993.

———. *Fort Davis: Outpost on the Texas Frontier*. Austin: Texas State Historical Association,
1994.

Wooton, Dudley G., ed. *A Comprehensive History of Texas, 1685 to 1897*. 2 vols. Dallas: William
G. Scarff, 1898.

Young, Earle B. *Galveston and the Great West*. College Station: Texas A&M Univ. Press, 1997.

ARTICLES, THESES, AND MANUSCRIPTS

Abbott, Peyton O. "Business Travel Out of Texas during the Civil War: The Travel Diary of S. B. Brush, Pioneer Austin Merchant." *Southwestern Historical Quarterly* XCVI (Oct., 1992): 259–71.

Adams, Larry Earl, "Economic Development in Texas during Reconstruction, 1865–1875." Ph.D. diss., North Texas State Univ., 1980.

Anthon, Florence. "Uvalde and Surrounding Territory." An unpublished collection of interviews, Archives of the El Progreso Library, Uvalde, Texas.

Aston, B. W. "Federal Military Reoccupation of the Texas Southwestern Frontier, 1865–1871." *Texas Military History* 8, no. 3 (1970): 123–34.

Austerman, Wayne R. "José Policarpo Rodriquez: Chicano Plainsman." *West Texas Historical Association Year Book* 59 (1983): 52–74.

Barr, Alwyn. "Texas Coastal Defense, 1861–1865." *Southwestern Historical Quarterly* LXXV (July, 1961): 14–18.

Barrett, Arrie. "Federal Military Outposts in Texas, 1845–1861." Master's thesis, Univ. of Texas, 1927.

Bruton, Bruce G. "An Historical Perspective on the Future of the Military-Industrial Complex." *The Social Science Journal* 28, no.1 (1991): 45–62.

Campbell, Randolph B., and Richard G. Lowe. "Some Economic Aspects of Antebellum Texas Agriculture." *Southwestern Historical Quarterly* LXXXII (Apr., 1979): 351–78.

Christian, Garna Loy. "Sword and Plowshare: The Symbiotic Development of Fort Bliss and El Paso, Texas, 1848–1918." Ph.D. diss., Texas Tech Univ., Aug., 1977.

Clary, David A., ed. "'I Am Already Quite a Texan': Albert J. Myer's Letters from Texas, 1854–1856." *Southwestern Historical Quarterly* LXXXII (July, 1978): 25–76.

Coker, Caleb, and Janet G. Humphrey. "The Texas Frontier in 1850: Dr. Ebenezer Swift and the View from Fort Martin Scott." *Southwestern Historical Quarterly* XCVI (Jan., 1993): 392–413.

Conway, Walter C., ed. "Colonel Edmund Schriver's Inspector General's Report on Military Posts in Texas, Nov., 1872–Jan., 1873." *Southwestern Historical Quarterly* LXVII (Apr., 1964): 559–83.

Crane, R.C., "Letters From Texas." *West Texas Historical Association Year Book* 25 (Oct., 1949): 110–26.

Crimmins, Martin L. "Shafter's Explorations in Western Texas, 1875." *West Texas Historical Association Year Book* 9 (1933): 82–96.

———. "Camp Pena Colorado, Texas." *West Texas Historical and Scientific Society* Bulletin 6 (Dec., 1935): 8–22.

———. General B.H. Grierson in West Texas." *West Texas Historical and Scientific Society* Bulletin 18 (Dec., 1937): 30–44.

————, ed. "Two Thousand Miles by Boat in the Rio Grande in 1850." *West Texas Historical and Scientific Society* Bulletin 48 (Dec., 1933): 44–52.

————, ed. "Colonel J. F. K. Mansfield's Report of the Inspection of the Department of Texas in 1856." *Southwestern Historical Quarterly* XXXXII, no.2 (Oct., 1938): 122–48; no. 3 (Jan., 1939): 215–17; no. 4 (Apr., 1939): 351–87.

————, ed. "W. G. Freeman's Report on the Eighth Military Department." *Southwestern Historical Quarterly* LI (July, 1947): 54–58; (Oct., 1947): 167–74; (Jan., 1948): 252–58; (Apr., 1948): 350–57; LII (July, 1948): 100–108; (Oct., 1948): 227–33; (Jan., 1949): 349–53; (April 1949): 444-447; LIII (July, 1949): 71–77; (Oct., 1949): 202–208; (Jan., 1950): 308–19; (Apr., 1950): 443–73; LIV (Oct., 1950): 204–18.

Crook, Garland, and Cornelia Crook. "Fort Lincoln, Texas." *Texas Military History* 4 (Fall, 1964): 145–61.

Cutrer, Thomas W., ed. "'An Experience in Soldier's Life': The Civil War Letters of Volney Ellis, Adjutant, Twelfth Texas Infantry, Walker's Texas Division, C.S.A." *Military History of the Southwest* 22 (Fall, 1992): 109–72.

Dinges, Bruce J. "The Court-Martial of Lieutenant Henry O. Flipper: An Example of Black-White Relationships in the Army, 1881." *The American West* 9 (Jan., 1972): 12–17, 19, 21.

————. "Colonel Grierson Invests on the West Texas Frontier." *Fort Concho Report* 16 (Fall, 1984): 2–14.

Dobak, William A. "Fort Riley and Its Neighbors: The Federal Government and Economic Development in the Nineteenth-Century American West." Ph.D diss., Univ. of Kansas, 1995.

Dugas, Vera Lea. "Texas Industry, 1860–1880." *Southwestern Historical Quarterly* LIX (Oct., 1955): 151–83.

Duke, Escal F. "O. M. Smith—Frontier Pay Clerk." *West Texas Historical Association Year Book* 45 (1969): 45–57.

————, ed. "A Description of the Route from San Antonio to El Paso by Capt. Edward S. Meyer." *West Texas Historical Association Year Book* 49 (1973): 128–41.

Ellis, Tuffly L., ed. "Lieutenant A. W. Greely's Report on the Installation of Military Telegraph Lines in Texas, 1875–1876." *Southwestern Historical Quarterly* LXIX (July, 1965): 66–87.

Fisher, James J. "Tombstone Mysteries Unraveling." *Kansas City Star,* Friday, Nov. 18, 1994, C-1.

Foreman, Grant. "River Navigation in the Early Southwest." *The Mississippi Valley Historical Review* XV (June, 1928): 34–55.

Fox, Anne A. "Mission Builders: Traces of Texas Archaeology." In *The Spanish Missionary Heritage of the United States.* Edited by Dr. Howard Benoist and Sr. María Carolina Flores, C.P. San Antonio: U.S. Department of the Interior, National Park Service, and Los Compadres de San Antonio Missions National Historical Park, San Antonio, 1990.

Frantz, Joe B. "The Significance of Frontier Forts to Texas." *Southwestern Historical Quarterly* LXXIV (Oct., 1970): 204–205.

Gough, Terrence J. "Origins of the Army Industrial College: Military-Business Tensions after World War I." *Armed Forces and Society* 17 (Winter, 1991): 259–75.

Graf, Leroy P. "The Economic History of the Lower Rio Grande Valley, 1820–1875." 4 vols. Ph.D. diss., Harvard Univ., 1942.

Graham, Roy Eugene. "Federal Fort Architecture in Texas during the Nineteenth Century." *Southwestern Historical Quarterly* LXXIV (Oct., 1970): 165–88.

Gutmann, Myron P., and Christi G. Sample. "Land, Climate, and Settlement on the Texas Frontier." *Southwestern Historical Quarterly* XCIX (Oct., 1995): 137–72.

Hackemer, Kurt. "The U.S. Navy and the Late Nineteenth-Century Steel Industry." *The Historian* 57 (Summer 1995): 703–21.

Harrison, Lowell H. "Supplying Texas Military Posts in 1876." *Texas Military History* 4 (Spring, 1964): 23–24.

Haskew, Eula. "Stribling and Kirkland of Fort Griffin." *West Texas Historical Association Year Book* 32 (Oct., 1956): 55–69.

Hatcher, John H. "Fort Phantom Hill." *Texas Military History* 3 (Fall, 1963): 154–64.

Heidler, Jeanne T. "'Embarrassing Situation': David E. Twiggs and the Surrender of U.S. forces in Texas, 1861." *Military History of the Southwest* 21 (Fall, 1991): 156–72.

"History of Fort Bliss." El Paso *Times*. Sept. 29, 1997, 36.

Hogan, William R. "The Life of Henry Austin." *Southwestern Historical Quarterly* XXXVIII (Jan., 1934): 185–214.

Jordan, Terry G. "Environment and Environmental Perceptions in Texas." In *Texas History*. Edited by Walter L. Buenger. Boston: American, 1983.

Judson, Capt. William J. "The Services of Graduates as Explorers, Builders of Railways, Canals, Bridges, Lighthouses, Harbors, and the Like." *The Centennial of the United States Military Academy at West Point, New York, 1802–1902.* 2 vols. Washington, D.C.: Government Printing Office, 1904.

Koistine, Paul A.C. "The Industrial Military Complex in Historical Perspective: World War I." *Business History Review* 41 (Winter, 1967): 378–403.

Kroeker, Marvin E. "William B. Hazen." In *Soldiers West: Biographies from the Military Frontier.* Edited by Paul Andrew Hutton, with an introduction by Robert M. Utley. Lincoln: Univ. of Nebraska Press, 1987.

Lackman, Howard. "George Thomas Howard, Texas Frontiersman." Ph.D. diss., Univ. of Texas at Austin, June, 1954.

Lale, Max S. "Military Occupation of Marshall, Texas, by the Eighth Illinois Volunteer Infantry, U.S.A, 1865." *Military History of Texas and the Southwest* 13 (1976): 39–47.

Lammons, Frank B. "Operation Camel." *Southwestern Historical Quarterly* LXI (July, 1957): 40–50.

Lynch, Vernon. "1879 in the Echo: A Year at Fort Griffin on the Texas Frontier." *West Texas Historical Association Year Book* 41 (Oct., 1965): 51–79.

Mahon, Emmie Giddings W., and Chester V. Kielman. "George H. Giddings and the San Antonio–San Diego Mail Line." *Southwestern Historical Quarterly* LXI (Oct., 1957): 220–39.

Manning, Dan R. "The Mexican War Journal of John James Dix: A Texian," *Military History of the West* 23 (Spring, 1993): 46–74.

Mayhall, Mildred P. "Camp Cooper–First Federal Fort in Texas to Fall, 1861, and Events Preceding its Fall." *Texana* 5 (Winter, 1967): 318–42.

McChristian, Doug. "The Commissary Sergeant: His Life at Fort Davis." *Military History of Texas and the Southwest* 14, no.1 (1978): 21–32.

McClung, Donald R. "Second Lieutenant Henry O. Flipper: A Negro Officer on the West Texas Frontier." *West Texas Historical Year Book* 48 (1971): 20–31.

McKay, S. S. "Economic Conditions in Texas in the 1870s." *West Texas Historical Association Year Book* 55 (1949): 84–127.

Mears, Mildred Watkins. "The Three Forts in Coryell County." *Southwestern Historical Quarterly* LXVII (July, 1963): 1–14.

Miles, Susan. "Fort Concho in 1877." *West Texas Historical Association Year Book* 35 (Oct., 1959): 29–49.

Miller, Roger G. "Winfield Scott and the Sinews of War: The Logistics of the Mexico City Campaign, October 1846—September 1847." Master's thesis, North Texas State Univ., May, 1976.

Myres, Sandra L. "Fort Graham: Listening Post on the Texas Frontier." *West Texas Historical Association Year Book* 59 (1983): 33–51.

Neal, Charles M. Jr. "Claron A. Windus, 1851–1927." *Branches and Acorns: Southwest Texas Genealogical Society* X (March 1995): 8–13.

Neighbours, Kenneth F. "Tonkaway Scouts and Guides." *West Texas Historical Association Year Book* 49 (1973): 90–112.

Neilson, John. "'I Long to Return to Fort Concho': Acting Assistant Surgeon Samuel Smith's Letters from the Texas Military Frontier, 1878–1879." *Military History of the West* 24 (Fall, 1994): 122–86.

Newsom, W. L. "The Postal System of the Republic of Texas." *Southwestern Historical Quarterly* XX (Oct., 1916): 103–31.

Notson, William M. "Fort Concho, 1868–1872: The Medical Officers Observations." Edited by Stephen Schmidt. *Military History of Texas and the Southwest* 12, no. 1 (1975): 125–49.

"Now the Weather is Foretold." San Antonio *Herald*. June 28, 1878, 1.

Pingenot, Ben E. "The Great Wagon Train Expedition of 1850." *Southwestern Historical Quarterly* XCVIII (Oct., 1994): 182–225.

Pingenot, Ben E., ed. "Journal of a Wagon Train Expedition from Fort Inge to El Paso del Norte in 1850." *Military History of the West* 25 (Spring, 1995): 69–105.

Porter, Kenneth Wiggins. "The Seminole Negro-Indian Scouts, 1870–1881." *Southwestern Historical Quarterly* LV (Jan., 1952): 358–77.

Rampp, Larry C., and Donald L. Rampp. "The Civil War in the Indian Territory." *Military History of Texas and the Southwest* 10, no. 1 (1972): 29–41; no. 2 (1972): 93–114; no. 3 (1972): 187–96; 11, no. 4 (1973): 251–80.

Robinson, Robert L. "The U.S. Navy vs. Cattle Rustlers: The *U.S.S. Rio Bravo* on the Rio Grande, 1875–1879." *Military History of Texas and the Southwest* 15, no. 2 (1979): 43–52.

Roland, Charles P., and Richard C. Robbins, eds. "The Diary of Eliza (Mrs. Albert Sidney) Johnston: The Second Cavalry Comes to Texas." *Southwestern Historical Quarterly* LX (Apr., 1957): 463–500.

Ruhlen, George. "Quitman's Owners: A Sidelight on Frontier Realty." *Password* 5 (Apr., 1960): 54–63.

Scannell, Jack C. "A Survey of the Stagecoach Mail in the Trans-Pecos, 1850–1861." *West Texas Historical Association Year Book* 47 (1971): 115–26.

Scheips, Paul J. "Albert James Myer, an Army Doctor in Texas, 1854–1857." *Southwestern Historical Quarterly* LXXXII (July, 1978): 1–24.

Shook, Robert W. "The Federal Military in Texas, 1865–1870." *Texas Military History* 6 (Spring, 1967): 3–54.

Skaggs, Jimmy M. "Military Operations on the Cattle Trails." *Texas Military History* 6 (Summer, 1967): 137–48.

Smith, Thomas T. "Fort Inge and the Texas Frontier Economy." *Military History of the Southwest* 21 (Fall, 1991): 135–56.

———. "U.S. Army Combat Operations in the Indian Wars of Texas, 1849–1881." *Southwestern Historical Quarterly* XCIX (Apr., 1996): 501–31.

Smyrl, Frank H. "Texas in Gray: The Civil War Years, 1861–1865." In *Texas History.* Edited by Walter L. Buenger. Boston: American, 1983.

Storey, Brit Allan, ed. "An Army Officer in Texas, 1866–1867." *Southwestern Historical Quarterly* LXXII (Oct., 1968): 241–51.

Sutton, Mary. "Glimpses of Fort Concho through the Military Telegraph." *West Texas Historical Association Year Book* 32 (Oct., 1956): 122–34.

Tate, Michael L. "The Multi-Purpose Army on the Frontier: A Call for Further Research." In *The American West: Essays in Honor of W. Eugene Hollon.* Edited by Ronald Lora. Toledo Ohio: Univ. of Toledo, 1980: 171–208.

Temple, Frank M. "Federal Military Defense of the Trans-Pecos Region, 1850–1880." *West Texas Historical Association Year Book* 30 (Oct., 1954): 40–60.

———. "Colonel B. H. Grierson's Administration of the District of the Pecos." *West Texas Historical Association Year Book* 38 (Oct., 1962): 85–96.

Texas State Gazette, 1849–56. Misc. editorials, letters, notices, military news, and advertisements.

Timmons, W. H. "The Merchants and the Military, 1849–1854." *Password* 28 (Summer, 1982): 51–61.

Utley, Robert M. "A Chained Dog: The Indian-Fighting Army." *American West* X (July, 1973): 18–24, 61.

Wallace, Edward S. "General John Lapham Bullis: The Thunderbolt of the Texas Frontier." *Southwestern Historical Quarterly* LIV (Apr., 1951): 452–61; LV (July, 1951): 77–85.

Watson, Judy. "The Red River Raft." *Texana* 5 (Spring, 1967): 68–76.

Webster, Michael G. "Intrigue on the Rio Grande: The Rio Bravo Affair, 1875." *Southwestern Historical Quarterly* LXXIV (Oct., 1970): 149–64.

Wheeler, David L., and William H. Landis. "'It is beef every day . . .': The Army Ration and the Enlisted Man, 1865–1890." *Military History of the West* 26 (Fall, 1996): 129–57.

Whisenhunt, Donald W. "Frontier Military Life at Fort Richardson, Texas." *West Texas Historical Association Year Book* 42 (Oct., 1966): 15–27.

Woodward, Earl F. "Internal Improvements in Texas under Governor Peter Hansborough Bell's Administration, 1849–1853." *Southwestern Historical Quarterly* LXXVI (Oct., 1972): 161–82.

Wooster, Ralph A. "Wealthy Texans, 1860." *Southwestern Historical Quarterly* LXXI (Oct., 1967): 163–80.

Wooster, Robert. "Military Strategy in the Southwest, 1848–1860." *Military History of Texas and the Southwest* XV, no.2 (1979): 5–15.

———. "The Army and the Politics of Expansion: Texas and the Southwest Borderlands, 1870–1886." *Southwestern Historical Quarterly* XCIII (Oct., 1989): 151–67.

Wynes, Charles E., ed. "Lewis Harvie Blair: Texas Travels, 1851–1855." *Southwestern Historical Quarterly* LXVI (Oct., 1962): 262–70.

Index

57, 67–69, 74, 79, 84, 88, 92, 101, 119, 124–27, 156, 161, 163, 166–67, 184–86, 188–93, 204–208, 211–13; construction of, 87, 91, 94, 96

Fort Cobb, Indian Territory, 212

Fort Concho, Tex.: 40, 42, 45, 56, 58, 75–76, 80, 110, 119, 121, 125–26, 130, 158–60, 164–67, 187–93; construction of, 94–96

Fort Crockett, Tex., 45, 101

Fort Croghan, Tex., 33–35, 74, 90, 125, 203–204

Fort Davis, Tex.: 3, 36, 39, 40, 42, 45–46, 50, 53, 55–58, 67–69, 74, 79–80, 84, 107–10, 119–23, 125–26, 130, 145–46, 157, 159–60, 163–65, 167–69, 172, 178, 180, 184–93, 205–207, 211–12; construction of, 91, 94–95, 98–99

Fort Davis and Marfa Railway Company, 130

Fort Dodge, Kans., 44, 55, 58, 189

Fort Duncan, Tex., 29, 37, 40, 42, 45, 53, 62, 79–80, 82, 84–85, 101, 119, 121, 124–26, 133, 161, 163, 165, 167, 169, 183–91, 204–207, 210–13; construction of, 85, 87, 90–92, 94, 98

Fort Elliott, Tex., 40, 44–45, 55–56, 58, 80, 96, 101, 117, 126, 146, 189–93

Fort Ewell, Tex., 34, 36, 80, 85, 119, 125, 210

Fort Fillmore, N.M., 53, 184–85

Fort Gates, Tex., 33–35, 52, 80, 90, 130, 203, 209

Fort Gibson, Indian Territory, 137

Fort Graham, Tex., 33–35, 73, 89–90, 117, 125, 203–204, 210

Fort Griffin, Tex., 40–42, 44–45, 81, 111, 126, 164–67, 180, 187–90; construction of, 93–94

Fort Hancock, Tex., 45, 84, 99

Fort Inge, Tex., 7, 34, 40, 42, 53, 74–76, 79, 87–88, 90–91, 104, 109, 124, 129, 133–34,

140, 142, 156, 161–62, 164, 172, 184–86, 203–208, 210–13

Fort Lancaster, Tex., 36, 40, 92, 119, 125–26, 129, 180, 185–86, 206–208, 211–12

Fort Leavenworth, Kans., 37, 44, 52–54, 126–27, 183–84, 186

Fort Lincoln, Tex.: 34, 109, 133, 210; construction of, 86, 90

Fort Martin Scott, Tex., 34, 40, 80, 87–89, 124, 204

Fort Mason, Tex., 35, 40, 54, 75, 86, 89, 109–10, 119, 124–25, 134, 143 186, 191, 203–207, 211–12

Fort McIntosh, Tex.: 32, 37, 40–41, 43, 45, 55, 62, 81, 84, 101, 111, 118, 125–26, 162, 169–70, 172, 185, 197–92, 198, 204–206, 210–12; construction of, 86–87, 90–92, 94, 99

Fort McKavett, Tex.: 35, 40, 42, 45, 53, 59, 75, 109, 119, 124–26, 158, 166–67, 184–85, 187–91, 205–206, 211; construction of, 86–87, 89, 91, 94

Fort Merrill, Tex., 34, 36, 90, 125, 183, 209–10

Fort Phantom Hill, Tex., 33, 35–36, 85, 89–90, 125, 157, 162, 210

Fort Point. *See* Fort San Jacinto, Tex.

Fort Polk, Tex., 20, 209

Fort Quitman, Tex., 36, 39–40, 42, 45, 80–81, 91, 94, 110, 126, 129–30, 157, 159, 164, 168, 185–86, 188, 208, 212

Fort Richardson, Tex.: 3, 40–42, 44–45, 59, 108, 120–21, 126–28, 131, 158, 164, 166–67, 181, 187–90; construction of, 88, 93

Fort Riley, Kans., 170

Fort Ringgold, Tex., 26, 45, 55, 62–64, 76, 82, 84, 101, 104, 169–70, 172, 178, 188, 191–93, 199, 200. *See also* Ringgold Barracks, Tex.

George, H. B., 211

Gibbons, J. M., 210

Gibson, Commissary General George, 106

Giddings, George H., 53, 156, 184

Giles, Alfred, 99

Gillespie County, Tex., 109

Gilmore, S., 209

Givens, Capt. Newton C., 130

Glanagan, Senator James, 97

Glass, William, 206

Gleim, Edgar G., 191–92

Glorieta Pass, N.M., 38

Goliad, Tex., 138

Goliad County, Tex., 233*n* 5

Gonzales County, Tex., 233*n* 5

Gooch, John C., 204–206, 210, 212

Gooch and MacKay, 207–208

Goodnight-Loving Trail, 111

Gould, Jay, 67

Government Hill, San Antonio, Tex., 98

Graf, Leroy P., 6

Graham, Maj. James Duncan, 137

Graham, W. C., 55, 187, 188

Grampus (steamboat), 63

Grant, Gen. Ulysses S., 10, 111–12

Great Lakes, 171

Greely, Lt. Adolphus W., 166–67, 172

Green Lake, Tex., 116

Greenwood Saloon, Brazos Santiago, Tex., 222*n* 47

Gregg, Joshia, 137

Gresham, Walter, 153

Grierson, Col. Benjamin H., 45, 130, 146, 158–59

Grimes, Lt. George S., 167

Groesbeeck, John D., 52, 210

Guadalupe County, Tex., 233*n* 5

Guadalupe Mountains, 141–42, 144, 157

Guadalupe River, 147

Guerra, Manuel, 192

Guerrero, Mexico, 37

Gulf, Western Texas and Pacific Railroad, 57

Gulf of Mexico, 30, 38, 140, 171

Gunter Hotel, San Antonio, Tex., 79

Haley, James, 210

Hall, Edward, 184, 206

Hall, Maj. Peter P. G., 125–26

Hallettsville, Tex., 39

Hamburg, N.Y., 163

Hamilton Creek, 28, 34

Hammer and Caples, 100

Hannum, John, 193

Hardee, Capt. William J., 52, 183

Harmonson, P., 211

Harney, Bvt. Brig. Gen. William S., 26, 141

Harold, Tex., 58, 192

Harris, Morgan and Co., 65, 196

Harrisburg, Tex., 155

Hart, Simeon, 7, 35, 83, 107, 260*n* 10

Hart's Mill, 83, 107

Hatchee Eagle (steamboat), 219*n* 19

Havana, Cuba, 39

Hayes, Pres. Rutherford B., 126

Hays, Col. John C. "Jack," 138–40

Hays and Sotith, 209

Hays County, Tex., 233*n* 5

Hazen, Brig. Gen. William B., 172

Hazlett, H. K., 64, 198

Hedwig's Hill, 109–10

Henrietta, Tex., 191

Hermann (ship), 112

Herrford, E. M., 110

Hill, G. W., 203

Hill, Maj. Henry, 124–25

Holliday, J. D., 207, 212

Hooste, L., 209

Horsehead Crossing of the Pecos River, 50, 111, 141, 157

horses and mules. *See* U.S. Army: horses and mules

hospitals. *See* U.S. Army: hospitals

Houston, Tex., 34, 52, 66–67, 106, 154–55, 165, 169, 189

Houston and Great Northern Railroad Company, 80

Houston and Texas Central Railroad, 67

Houston Ship Channel, 154

Howard, C., 209

Howard, Congressman Volney, 139

Howard, George Thomas, 36, 51, 53–54, 179, 183–86

Howard, George W., 189

Howard, Henry P., 51, 183

Howard, Richard Austin, 140–41

Howard and Lane, sutlers, 119

Howard's Springs, 36, 160

Howell, Capt. Charles W., 152

Howgate, Capt. Henry W., 126

Hueco Tanks, 157

Hughes, Capt. George W., 138

Hughes, J., 204

Hughes, W. H., 107

Huguenin, H., 184

Hunt, Lt. Col. Thomas F., 16

Hunter, J. M., 207

Huntington, Collis P., 67

Hutchinson, A. C., 199

Hutter, George C., 124

Illinois, 26

Indian Frontier Line, 29. *See also* First Federal Line

Indianola, Tex., 7, 10, 31, 32–34, 39, 41–42, 44, 46, 53–54, 57, 65, 68, 79, 106, 124, 150–51, 156, 162, 171–72, 179–80, 183–87, 195–99

Indianola Railroad, 68

Indian Point, Tex., 31. *See also* Indianola, Tex.

Indian Territory, 34, 38, 89

industry, in Texas: grain mills, 107–108, 176–77; lumber mills, 89–90, 176–77; manufacturing, 135, 176–77

International-Great Northern Railroad, 67

Irwin, Capt. James R., 26, 132

Irwin, J. G., 212

J. E. Roberts (steamboat), 219*n* 19

J. San Roman (steamboat), 63

Jacksboro, Tex., 3, 40, 88, 93, 108–109, 127, 131, 164, 179–81

Jacksonville, Ill., 164

James, John, 79–80

Jefferson, J. R., 53, 184

Jefferson, Pres. Thomas, 137

Jefferson, Tex., 41, 149, 187

Jefferson Barracks, Mo., 28

Jesup, Quartermaster General Thomas S., 16, 18, 22, 26–27, 30, 46, 51, 66, 82, 112, 134, 139, 147–48

Johns, C. R., 203

Johnson, F. M., 207

Johnson, Middleton Tate, 76, 203–206

Johnson's Mail Station, Tex., 125, 160

Johnson's Station, Tex., 76

Johnston, Col. Albert S., 36, 119, 124–25

Johnston, Lt. Col. Joseph E., 66, 139, 141–43

Jones, G., 204

Jones, G. H., 206

Jordan, Dr. Powhatan, 134

Jordan, F., 209

Jornado del Muerto, N.M., 144

Joseph, Adam, 212
Julis G. Tyler (ship), 196

Kansas, 38, 67, 157, 180
Keller, L. P., 209
Kelly, William, 64, 192, 199, 200
Kenedy, Mifflin, 37, 55, 61–64
Kenedy and King, 55, 62–64, 187, 188. *See also* M. Kenedy and Co.; King, Kenedy and Co.
Kennedy, Ross, 206, 208
Kennedy, Thomas, 213
Kenosha Glass, 167
Kentucky, 22, 25–26
Kerr, Lt. John B., 111
King, Kenedy and Co., 63–64, 197. *See also* M. Kenedy and Co.; Kenedy and King
King, Richard, 37, 55, 61–64, 196, 208
Kingsbury Falls, 138
Kinney, Henry L., 16, 31, 103, 105–106, 113, 209
Kinney County, Tex., 180
Kiowa, Kansas, 192
Kiowa-Comanche Indians. *See* Comanche-Kiowa Indians
Kiowa Creek, 125
Kiowa Indians, 137–38
Kirby, Lt. Henry, 158
Koenig, Charles, 204
Krueger, W. C., 187

Labatt, Jackson E., 56, 190–91
La Grange, Tex., 148
Laguna Madre, 20–21, 151
Lake Superior, 30
Lamar, Mirabeau B., 122
Lambshead, T., 211
Lane, Edwin D., 75, 119, 206

Lane, Lydia, 88, 96
Lanham, Samuel W. T., 83
La Noria Mesa, 83
Laredo, Tex., 3, 6, 39, 62, 67, 81, 138, 158, 169–70, 177, 180, 197, 209
Las Moras Creek, 34, 79, 127, 140
Las Vegas, N.M., 55, 190
Lavaca, Tex. *See* Port Lavaca, Tex.
Lavaca (steam dredge), 61, 148
Lawton, Lt. Henry W., 43
Leaton, Ben, 140
Lee, Bvt. Lt. Col. James G. C., 42
Lee, J. C., 204
Lee, Lt. Col. Robert E., 80, 129, 138
Lee, Lt. Fitzhugh, 129
Lee, W. M. D., 189–92
Leefe, Capt. John G., 172
Lehman, C., 205
Leigh, G. A., 207–208
Leinweber, A., 204–206
Leinweber, John, 205, 208
Leman, Robert S., 222*n* 47
Lenord, A. F., 210
Leona River, 34, 139–40, 142, 156
Leon River, 34
Leon Water Hole, 159
Lepier and Dunlap, sutlers, 119
Lewis, G. K., 177
Lewis, Nathaniel C., 52, 178
Lewis and Groesbeeck, 178, 183, 210
Leydendecker. J., 204
Liberty, Tex., 149
Lidwell, M., 205, 212
Lillig, I. W., 209
Limpia Canyon, 140
Limpia Creek, 36, 79, 140
Lindsay, James, 212
Lister, James, 193

Surgeon General of the Army, 9, 99, 134

sutlers and post traders. *See* U.S. Army: sutlers and post traders

Swift, Roy, 7

Tamaulipas I and II (steamboats), 63

Tarrant County, Tex., 76

Tate, Michael, 5

Taylor, Brig. Gen. Zachary, 15–20, 23–27, 31, 38, 48, 60, 103, 105, 111–13, 118, 131–32, 138, 148, 160, 177

Taylor, J. H., 210–11

Taylor, James, 212

Tejas, Mexican Department of, 15

telegraph: commercial, 165, 168–69; Flying Telegraph Train, 170; military, 8, 165–70, 179

Telegraph (steamboat), 29

telephone, use of, 42, 169

Tennessee, 119

Tessier, David E., 206–207, 211–12

Tessier and Brackenbush, 207, 212

Texarkana, Tex., 67

Texas, constitution of, 78, 83

Texas, Republic of, 12, 53, 76, 122, 137, 155, 160, 175

Texas, State of, 12, 153, 159, 174

Texas and New Orleans Telegraph Company, 165

Texas and Pacific Railroad, 67, 141, 159

Texas and Red River Telegraph Company, 165

Texas Central Railroad, 41

Texas Revolution, 27, 137

Texas State Gazette, 134

Texas State provisional government, 38

Texas (steamboat), 196

Texas United States Mail Line, 155

Texas Weather Service, 174

Thielepape, W. C. A., 116

Thien, John Diedrick, 206, 208, 212

Thomas, Maj. Charles, 26

Thompson, P. M., 212

Thompson, Theodore, 189

Thornburg, Maj. Thomas T., 126

Throckmorton, Texas Governor James W., 40

Tilden, Lt. Bryant P., Jr., 138

Timmons, W. H., 6

Topeka, Kans., 100, 153

Torres, Cesario, 77, 80

Towash Village, Tex., 209

Toyah Valley, 56

Trainer, Jim, 120

transportation: 48–70, 183–201; army expenses of, 13, 29–30, 48–49, 56–59, 61, 63–65, 68–69, 160

———, railroads, 5–6, 14, 30–31, 41, 44–45, 51, 57–58, 66–70, 73, 101, 108, 110–11, 130, 149, 165, 170, 176

———, stagecoaches: 155–60; "celerity" wagons, 157; Concord Coaches, 157

———, wagon freighting, 9–10, 13, 31, 36, 43–45, 48–60, 106, 175–76, 183–94; army and commercial wagons, 21, 36, 43–45, 48–60, 75; *carreta,* 50; Prairie Schooners, 50

———, water transportation: ships, 64–65, 75, 112; steamboats, 9–10, 16–29, 60–64, 162, 175–76; water transportation and freighting, 9–10, 13, 16–31, 60–65, 162, 175–76, 195–201

Travis County, Tex., 74, 233*n* 5

Trevino, Don Thomas, 81

Trinity River: 29, 33, 40, 89, 119, 144, 147–49, 151; West Fork of the, 28

Troy (steamboat), 25

Tucson, Ariz., 157

Tule Canyon, 143

Tullis, J. R., 184

Turnley, Lt. Parmenas Taylor, 85, 92

Turnley's Cottage, 92, 98

Twiggs, Bvt. Maj. Gen. David E., 10, 156

Twohig, John, 79–80, 82

Tyler, Pres. John, 15

U.S. Army: dollar input into local communities, 3–6, 8–9, 11–13, 24, 27, 30–33, 36,
45–46, 48–49, 58–59, 71–73, 76–77, 85,
89–92, 95, 98–100, 103–104, 109, 114, 117,
124–27, 129–31, 133, 135–36, 153–54, 160,
174–76, 178–81; military-commercial relations, 4–5, 35–36, 56, 97–98, 107–108,
134–35, 139, 152, 174–75, 183–212; military-
industrial complex, 174; military-political relations, 174–78; mission in Texas, 4,
27, 29; operations in Texas, 27, 29, 33–34,
43–54, 111, 159–60; organization in Texas,
16–17, 28–29, 36, 39–40, 44–46, 101
———, battles. *See* Battle of
———, beef and cattle, 9, 45, 105, 109–11,
209–13
———, camels, 36–37, 132–33, 145
———, cemeteries, military. *See* Quartermaster's Department, U.S. Army
———, corruption and fraud: civilian employees, 108; forage contractors, 76;
freight contractors, 59–60; horse sellers,
112; paymasters, 126–27; post traders, 117,
120–21; quartermasters, 46–47; wood
contractors, 104–105
———, crime, 117
———, desertion, 86, 117
———, employment: builders, 26, 90–91,
93–96, 100, 102; civilian, 30–31, 45, 131–
35, 162; civilian labor, 27, 49, 90–91, 93–
95, 100, 102, 123, 132, 134; civilian wages,
31, 90–91, 93, 132–35, 161–62; doctors, 134;
express riders, 161–62; guides and scouts,
133–34, 140–41; teamsters, 30, 45, 52, 131–
32
———, engineers. *See* engineers, U.S. Army,
Corps of Engineers and Corps of Topographic Engineers
———, exploration and mapping. *See* engineers, U.S. Army, Corps of Engineers
and Corps of Topographic Engineers
———, farms and gardens, 80, 105, 107–
108
———, forage: 9, 15, 30–31, 37, 43, 51, 71–
77, 179, 202–208; army purchases of corn
and hay, 73–76, 179; army purchases of
oats, 71–72, 179; army standard ration of
corn, hay, and oats, 71; army standard
weights of corn, hay, and oats, 71; con-
version of Mexican *fanega,* 71; corn, hay
and oat prices, 72; corn and hay contracts,
202–208
———, forts and posts: army purchase of
military reservations, 46, 82–84, 175, 179;
building construction and repair, 84–102;
construction policy, 86–87, 93, 95–97, 99,
101–102; leases and rents, 9, 30–31, 42, 78–
82, 92, 101–102, 175, 179; soldier labor for
construction, 85–87, 89–91, 102, 134–35
———, freighting. *See* transportation
———, fuel, 9, 103–105, 179; coal, 105; fuel
standards and regulations, 103–104; wood
and charcoal contracts, 9, 103–105, 179
———, horses and mules, 26, 30, 45, 48–
49, 52, 111–15, 179; army purchase, 9, 13,
111–15, 179; army sales, 114–15; army standards, 114–15; pack mules, 25, 43, 48–49,
113, 161
———, hospitals, 87–88, 98, 100
———, mail. *See* mail, U.S.

Wood, O. P., 192

Woodhouse, H. E., 198

Woodruff, Lt. Eugene A., 149

Woodward, Lt. Samuel, 130

Wool, Brig. Gen. John E., 26–27, 48, 112, 131–32, 138–39

Wooster, Robert, 6, 174

Worth, Col. and Bvt. Maj. Gen. William Jenkins, 28, 76, 140–41

Wreford, Sam P., 170

Wright, T. G., 184

Wright's Landing, Tex., 184

Wulff, A. T., 206

Wulfing, Robert, 190

Young, A., 207

Young, Alexander, 119

Young, Earle B., 7, 175

Zeseh, Robert, 212

Zink, W., 211

Zulu Campaign, 115

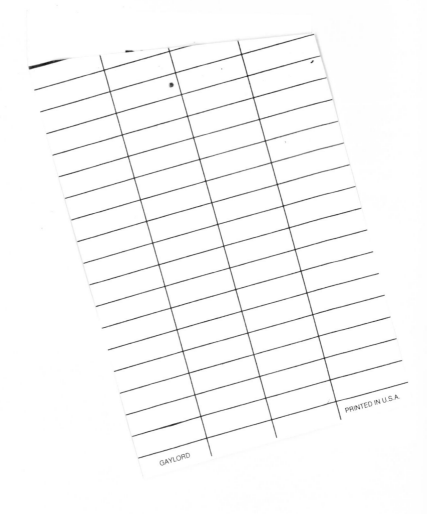

GAYLORD